for Manhood 2

❖

What Every Man Must Know

by

Kenneth W. Royce

Published by

JAVELIN PRESS

(Without any 4 USC §§ 105-110 "*Federal area*" or "*State*.")

www.javelinpress.com

Read the following disclaimer very carefully and thoroughly!

This book's information is presented *for academic study only* and should be approached with great caution. Some of the products or services (or combination thereof) discussed in this book may not currently (or in the future) be legal for use, possession, sale, or interstate transportation in certain jurisdictions. Therefore, You have the responsibility to consult with local law enforcement. We do not encourage or endorse You to break any laws or experiment with any activities of a criminal nature. You assume full responsibility for any application, direct or indirect, of the contents.

While reasonable efforts have been made to ensure that information and data provided herein is accurate, neither Javelin Press, nor the author, nor any personnel acting for or on behalf of the same accept any legal liability for the answers given or the information or data herein. In particular, but without limitation, no reliance should be placed on the answers, information, or data provided without recourse to independent verification. The answers, information, or data is for information only and is provided in good faith, to the best of our knowledge and belief, based on the sources of information available to us at the time of writing. Keep in mind the possibility of error and reflect independently in every instance. All liability for misrepresentation (other than fraudulent) and other torts (including negligence or breach of statutory duty) is hereby excluded to the fullest extent permitted by law.

Modules for Manhood 2 July 2016

Printed in the united states of America,
without any 4 USC §§ 105-110 "*Federal area*" or "*State*."

10 9 8 7 6 5 4 3 2 1 / 2021 2020 2019 2018 2017 2016

ISBN 1-888766-14-X

www.javelinpress.com

DEDICATION

I dedicate *Modules for Manhood 2* to every male struggling to become a Real Man. You're never too young nor too old to begin this lifelong journey!

ACKNOWLEDGMENTS

I thank all my readers who have so enthusiastically supported my fourteen other books (most written under the trademark pseudonym "Boston T. Party"). I have met many hundreds of you throughout the past 22 years, and I hope to have enriched your lives as much as you have enriched mine.

I especially thank my father and step-father for the good things they instilled in their son.

Titles by
Kenneth W. Royce
(a.k.a. Boston T. Party)

❖

Modules for Manhood 3
(2016 Volume 3 of 3)

Modules for Manhood 2
(2016 Volume 2 of 3)

Modules for Manhood
(2014 Volume 1 of 3)

Hologram of Liberty
(2012 second edition)

One Nation, Under Surveillance

You & The Police!
(2009 edition)

Safari Dreams

Molôn Labé!

Boston's Gun Bible
(2002 edition, revised 2003-2009)

Boston's Gun Bible
(2000 edition)

Boston on Surviving Y2K

Boston on Guns & Courage

Hologram of Liberty
(1997 first edition)

Bulletproof Privacy

You & The Police!
(1996 first edition)

Good-Bye April 15th!

TABLE OF CONTENTS

22 Fighting

23 Moving

"If —"

Rudyard Kipling

If you can keep your head when all about you
Are losing theirs and blaming it on you,
If you can trust yourself when all men doubt you
But make allowance for their doubting too,
If you can wait and not be tired by waiting,
Or being lied about, don't deal in lies,
Or being hated, don't give way to hating,
And yet don't look too good, nor talk too wise:

If you can dream — and not make dreams your master,
If you can think — and not make thoughts your aim;
If you can meet with Triumph and Disaster
And treat those two impostors just the same;
If you can bear to hear the truth you've spoken
Twisted by knaves to make a trap for fools,
Or watch the things you gave your life to, broken,
And stoop and build 'em up with worn-out tools:

If you can make one heap of all your winnings
And risk it all on one turn of pitch-and-toss,
And lose, and start again at your beginnings
And never breath a word about your loss;
If you can force your heart and nerve and sinew
To serve your turn long after they are gone,
And so hold on when there is nothing in you
Except the Will which says to them: "*Hold on!*"

If you can talk with crowds and keep your virtue,
Or walk with kings – nor lose the common touch,
If neither foes nor loving friends can hurt you;
If all men count with you, but none too much,
If you can fill the unforgiving minute
With sixty seconds' worth of distance run,
Yours is the Earth and everything that's in it,
And — which is more — you'll be a Man, my son!

INTRODUCTION

While 50% of people are male, a male is not necessarily a Man. The transformation of boy-to-man does not happen by accident, but rather through a proven process by fathers, brothers, uncles, grandfathers, and mentors. In the 21st century, most American males haven't access to such character-building role models, so they founder about as soft and incomplete males.

> *Among the other signs of times we discover that coping is unfashionable. As far as I can tell, today's young people are taught not to handle problems but rather to call for help. This is very bad conditioning.*
>
> ***The point is that a young man of 21 should be able to cope with the world around him in a general fashion.*** *. . . Before a young man leaves home, there are certain things he should know and certain skills at which he should be adept.*
>
> — Jeff Cooper, www.molonlabe.net/Commentaries/jeff13_10.html

We haven't fit men because today's males cannot *cope* with the world, and coping is what being a Real Man is all about. He handles things. Growing into an internally-ambitious, competent, self-sufficiently productive, self-governed, loving, and pleasant man of honor is a *serious* process. Very little about it is accidental. Good genetics and a quality up-bringing (both are forms of inheritance) help greatly, but they do not guarantee a successful life. (I know many losers with good genetics and good parents. Any inheritance can be squandered, and often is.) The "hardware" of people is all about the same — it's the "software" where the difference lies. Meaning, what you choose to learn and apply is what really matters.

Men's best is generally not very good, and most men cannot do their best but sporadically. *Modules For Manhood* will enhance your:

❶ ability to absorb what's happening
❷ ability to respond correctly (whether tragic or happy)
❸ reflection on what has gone before
❹ ability to share, and thus enlarge yourself

Life is a continual struggle against *something*, and usually several things at once. Childhood should be a rigorous boot-camp for Life. *Train hard — fight easy!* If parents are soft, their children they will find Life "too hard" and will become collectivists who whine for government to make it easier. Our country has become nearly ruined from sugared lives. A Man needs a taproot into Life to anchor himself in the soil for strength and nutrition. This taproot is grown only through intent and dedication.

some thoughts on reading this book

Before TV, a book like mine could have been easily read by the average high-school student. Back then, they didn't have minds of mush, and could actually read and think! So, I will not write "down" to the current level. My young readers must pull themselves up to what used to be the normal level. The concepts and ideas in *Modules for Manhood* are timeless, and some of them will take years to really get, much less apply and own.

Be patient, but I've included hundreds of quotations in the hope that a myriad of voices and perspectives will better awaken you (as they did me in my 20s). The right quote can change a life!

> *Of course everything has been said that needs to be said — but since no one was listening it has to be said again.*
> — author unknown

Yes, you *can* do it!

By the 12th grade, a boy has spent 8,000 hours in the classroom, and *12,000+* hours in front of videoscreens. Dump that 1,000+ hours/year of video crap, and start learning *real* things! You have but one Life here, and it's no dress rehearsal. Do not waste it! Acquire actual skills which can fulfill your purpose, make you money, help people, and thrill women.

Less than 6 hours/week in a year will achieve any one of these:

- ❒ speak an entirely new language credibly well
- ❒ own basic and reflexive skills in a solid martial art
- ❒ become a confident dancer (ballroom, Swing, etc.)
- ❒ learn to fly a small airplane and become a Private Pilot
- ❒ ride motorcycles (dirt and street)
- ❒ take up sailing and become proficient in a small boat
- ❒ get into public speaking and master this important art
- ❒ learn to write any kind of letter (business, personal, sales)
- ❒ become a credible cook, using ingredients from scratch
- ❒ play guitar or piano decently, with many songs in memory
- ❒ learn dozens of poems to recite from memory
- ❒ totally transform your body through vigorous exercise
- ❒ learn house construction, welding, or how to fix cars

Half of these skills can be learned with next to no money. *Any* of these are available if you'd spend only an hour/day for a year. Three hours/day for a year and you can own *three* of these skills. OK, want to impress the ladies? Get extremely fit, learn to fight and dance. Next year, learn the guitar, a foreign language, and to fly an airplane. **Talk about *studly*, and in just two years!** Everyone will think you've become James Bond. (Meanwhile, your old buddies were playing *Wii* and X-Box And what will they have to show for *that*? Zero.) So, if you commit yourself to a definite and worthy goal — and if you don't waste time with videoscreen entertainment and silly people — even teenagers can accomplish very impressive things. All a young man needs is a taste of real accomplishment, and he *will* succeed in Life.

what's covered in Volume 2

The general theme revolves around making a living, exercising and being subordinate to power, dealing with money, understanding the proper role of government, fighting off aggression and locomoting yourself about the planet. While Volume 1 a teenager could immediately put to use, most of this Volume 2 is more for young men >18 leaving the house and getting started in life on their own.

America will face some very tough times soon and there must be good Men for the future. I hope that you become one of them. You don't need money, good looks, big brains, a prominent family, or even luck. You need only clear thinking, solid goals, and the *will* to become a Man. Think of me as one of your guides.

As the saying goes, the best time to plant a tree is 20 years ago. The next best time is *today*. **Resolve to live with all your might, while you *do* live!** Stop wasting time, dump your excuses, get serious about your Life, and let's get started right now!

Kenneth W. Royce
June 2016

CHAPTER LIST

The entire series runs to nearly 1,400 pages, in three print volumes.

12

TEACHING

To acquire immunity to eloquence is of the utmost importance to the citizens of a democracy.
— Bertrand Russell

The teacher is like the candle which lights others in consuming self.
— Giovanni Ruffini

I hear and I forget.
I see and I remember.
I do and I understand.
I teach and I become.

A teacher is somebody who can help another learn something faster or better than he can on his own. As I've written elsewhere, Life is just too short to figure everything out for yourself. Do not "reinvent" any "wheel". Teachers are vital to save us all time.

a teacher must solidly know the subject

He must know what he knows, with such a great grasp of that knowledge that he also understands what he yet *doesn't* know.

the best way to know something, is to teach it

The reason why is that students will pull on your knowledge from directions different from how you learned the subject. As they do, you learn the final things about it as your mind makes the necessary connections between the bits. You won't realize the holes in your knowledge until you try to teach something you think you know.

if you can't teach a subject's basics to a 10 year old, . . .

. . . then you don't really know it yourself! You should be able to scale up and down the complexity level as your students need.

you mustn't know everything, just more than the student!

The historic Little Red Schoolhouse was an example of this. A one-room class had all ages of students, and the older ones helped in the teaching. A 10 year old may not know calculus, but he can help a 7 year old in basic math.

When I was in college, to supplement my pocket money I would tutor classes the semester after I'd completed them. I was no expert in any of these subjects, but I *did* know more than my students and could impart that effectively. Plus, my knowledge was quite fresh being only a semester old.

a teacher understands his student's mental blocks

If somebody is lost on the road, and calls you for help, you must quickly figure out where they are. A student, however, often cannot articulate "where they are" within their ignorance or snagged path. This is your task as a teacher to discern *how* the student isn't yet "getting it". You must get inside his head by asking the right questions, in a sort of "*Marco?—Polo!* " to feel your way around. The student usually won't be able to describe how/why they don't understand, because if they could, they'd understand and wouldn't need you!

you have a part in instilling manhood in boys

> *The difference between the old and the new education will be an important one. Where the old initiated, the new merely "conditions." The old dealt with its pupils as grown birds deal with the young birds when they teach them to fly; the new deals with them more as the poultry-keeper deals with young birds — making them thus or thus for purposes of which the birds know nothing. In a word, the old was a kind of propagation — men transmitting manhood to men; the new is merely propagana.*
>
> — C.S. Lewis, *The Abolition of Man* (1943)

create a desire for learning in your students; make it fun!

> *The art of teaching is not imparting truth but imparting a thirst for truth.*
>
> — Perry Tanksley

> *Tomorrow's illiterate will not be the man who can't read; he will be the man who has not learned how to learn.*
>
> — Alvin Toffler, *Future Shock* (1970)

Learning should be a joy, so don't treat the session as boot camp. You want students excited to learn, thus constant praise is vital. My tennis coach had a great line for a flubbed effort: "*I liked that try!*"

students must know how much you care, before they . . .

. . . care how much you know. Students must precede your ego!

A university is what a college becomes when the faculty loses interest in students.

— John Ciardi

convey knowledge before you convey your opinions

The true teacher defends his pupils against his own personal influence.

— Amos Alcott

If your opinions are correct, then a logical exposition will validate them. Let the student persuade himself through his own reasoning. At university I had a fantastic constitutional law professor who never once let on where he stood on any issue. His favorite initial rebuttal to an argument was "*Really?!*" Our class had fascinating discussions. To this day, I've no idea if we was a liberal or a conservative.

a teacher's ultimate goal is to become superfluous

The object of teaching a child is to enable him to get along without a teacher.

— Elbert Hubbard

As it is said, "*Give a man a fish, and you feed him for a day. Teach a man to fish, and you feed him for a lifetime.*"

you are worth a lot, so charge for it!

Good teachers cost much but poor teachers cost more.

— Perry Tanksley

Don't be too shy about your value in the marketplace. An appreciative student will understand your worth to him.

a teacher should have many tools and tricks

One of the best movies on this is the superb *The King's Speech*. A true story about King George VI who suffered a terrible stutter. He'd seen all the orthodox and respected speech therapists, to no avail. Finally, in desperation, he went to an unaccredited locutionist. This man, Lionel Logue, had helped veterans of WWI recover their speech from injury and trauma. Logue had quite a bag of tricks to help his royal student, and was brilliantly successful.

rote regurgitation is not long-term learning

Rote learning is only short-term, and usually a waste of everyone's time. What you want to impart as a teacher is a knowledge and understanding which your student *owns* as deeply as he owns important personal memories.

For example, after two weeks, your students will remember:

passive	10% of what they read (seeing words)
passive	20% of what they hear (hearing words)
passive	30% of what they see (seeing still pictures)
passive	50% of what they see and hear (watching video)
active	70% of what they say (giving a speech)
active	90% of what they say and do (real experience, simulation)
active	99% of what they teach (forces you to fill in the gaps)

Notice that only a max of 50% of knowledge comes from taking in the material, *i.e.*, being "impressed". For your students to know anything more deeply than merely 50%, you must require them to *express* from there, by speaking, doing, demonstrating, and teaching. What went in must come out through participation, and this creates new synapses.

analogy and metaphor are vital

Make a connection in your student's mind between what he already understands about anything and what you're trying to impart. Find any kind of example to make a connection.

always try to tell a story

Stories are inherently interesting, and thus memorable. A good story can pack in a lot of meaning within a small space.

pithy quotations are often powerful tools

Even more tightly packed meaning is found in a quotation. I'm a big fan of them, as is obvious from all my books. The right quotation can literally "turn on the light" of understanding. Have a few stories on every issue, to illuminate from different angles.

you are your most important student!

Teaching is a science, craft, and art. You can always improve, and you will learn nearly as much from your students as they do from you. Never become too haughty to learn from them. You will peak and then regress as a teacher once you cease learning. There is nothing more embarrassing than a teacher who obviously maxed out years hence and is still droning on with stale lessons.

how to get started

Don't worry if you haven't a degree or common accreditation. Start with free tutoring, and then begin to charge for lessons once you feel more solid. Remember, students care only about results.

Don't forget to volunteer teach somewhere. Find some homeschooling families who would benefit from your knowledge.

RECOMMENDED MOVIES

remaining true to yourself, living deliberately	*Dead Poets Society*
honor in the face of lies & betrayal	*Redbelt*
friendship, mentorship, learning, love, sacrifice	*The Man With No Face*
a teacher struggles with evil	*The Emperor's Club*

MENTAL MODES OF DEFENSE

We respond to life's anxieties with unconscious coping mechanisms or defenses, and these defenses tend to follow a recognizable pattern.

— summarizing the work of psychiatrist George Vaillant, in *A Question of Values*

About 95% of what we think and feel is habitual, if not automatic, determined by past experiences and reactions. There are three general types of unconscious defenses:

denial	("It never happened!")
escape	(avoid dealing with it)
externalization	(blaming others)

psychotic defenses (normal for children up to age 5)

delusional projection	paranoia, persecution complex
denial	*"I'm not in a mental hospital."*
distortion	*"I am Napoleon, or maybe God."*

immature defenses (ages 3-15 — adult character defects)

projection	attributing one's own feelings to others
schizoid fantasy	incapable of human intimacy, eccentric
hypochondria	imaginary illnesses (with real symptoms)
passive-aggression	manipulating others, stubborn and willful
acting out	always giving in to impulse (fighting, drugs)

neurotic defenses (exhausting internal conflicts)

disassociation	chronic desire to escape through change
reaction formation	overcompensation
repression	selective amnesia about unpleasant truths
intellectualization	hiding, need for control, rigidity
displacement	substituting (books for real life)

mature defenses

humor	provides detachment, perspective, release
altruism	helping others to forget your fears
sublimation	throwing yourself into useful work
anticipation	looking ahead, taking corrective steps now
suppression	toughness, Stoicism, acceptance of things as they are without deluding yourself

13

WISELY USING YOUR TIME

Time levels, and we are all in its path.
— Chinn Ho (Hawaii's "Chinese Rockefeller")

Things which matter most must never be at the mercy of things which matter least.
— Goethe

If you want to get the work done — ask any busy man. The other kind has no time.
— Elbert Hubbard

You cannot "make, save, or recover" time. You can only *spend* time. Each minute we have is the same minute everyone else has. Time is the only equal thing amongst humanity. (The movie *In Time* is built around this fact, and time is the only form of currency. Fascinating!)

The main mistake of youth is to squander their time, because they have no perspective of how limited it really is. You'll get about 80 trips around the sun, and that's *it*. If you had only $29,000 in net worth, would you consider yourself incredibly rich? Probably not. It's very easy to spend $29,000 these days. You'd probably spend it very wisely, knowing that it had to go a long way.

Well, are you spending your *time* as wisely? After all, you have only 29,200 days on this earth (assuming you live to about 80 years old). Or, 700,800 hours, and you're awake for only 467,200 of them.

Time is the fire in which we burn.
— *Star Trek*

your time is up to *you*, not to others

A task will swell in perceived importance and complexity in relation to the time allotted for its completion.

— Parkinson's Law

You will never "find" time for anything. If you want time you must make it.

— Charles Buston

Know the true value of time! Snatch, seize and enjoy every moment of it. No idleness, no laziness, no procrastination. Never put off till tomorrow what you can do today.

— Lord Chesterfield

Waste 15 minutes per day, and you waste 11 working days per year! Be busy and organized.

— Grant G. Gard, *Don't Just Talk About It — Do It!*

you must budget your time — create a daily schedule

An ounce of morning is worth a pound of afternoon.

— olde proverb

We don't wear a watch to know what time it is, we wear a watch to know what time it isn't.

— Larry Winget, *Shut Up, Stop Whining, Get A Life!*

Time will get filled up by random, trivial things unless you get a real handle on your Life. There is never enough time to do everything, but there is always enough time to do the most important things, so always start with them first.

increase your focus

Man who chases two rabbits loses both.

— Chinese proverb

Commit to completing just one . . . thing . . . at . . . a . . . time. Not "doing" one thing at a time, but *completing*. Your goal is to attack a project, and finish it so you can rid it from your mind.

start earlier — sleep less!

Each hour of sleep before midnight is worth two after midnight. This is not mere dogma, but proven fact. Early to bed and early to rise!

Also, *sleeping just a half hour less each day* will give you an extra 4½ working weeks every year! Every 11 years, you effectively get a free working year. Wow. So, sleep less and start earlier. (There are apps and devices which will wake you up on the top of your sleep cycle vs. during REM/delta sleep. This will make a huge difference in your morning energy.)

eliminate time-wasting people from your life!

> *Don't suffer fools or you'll become one. It is your job to train those around you to be effective and efficient.*
>
> – Timothy Ferriss, *4-Hour Work Week*

> *Arguing with anonymous strangers on the Internet is a sucker's game because they almost always turn out to be — or to be indistinguishable from — self-righteous sixteen-year-olds possessing infinite amounts of free time.*
>
> – Neil Stephenson, *Cryptonomicon*

Not everyone reckons time as you do. Many people waste their lives away, and they do it minute by minute, day in and day out. Do not be sucked in by these losers! If you do not enjoy their company enough to pay the opportunity cost elsewhere, cut them short or cut them off.

make *every* minute count – don't suffer a "near miss"!

> *Yesterday is past. Tomorrow does not exist. Today is important!*

If you study the history of inventions, you'll learn that many things were (and still are) developed independently in parallel with others without each other's knowledge. When the timing for an idea is right, be assured that more than one person is working on it. Do not waste a minute, else you'll get edged out. Some famous examples:

14 June 1907 – Leo Baekeland patents the first plastic ("Bakelite")
15 June 1907 – James Swinburne is *a day late* to have been first
(He wisely chose to go work for Leo Baekeland!)

14 February 1876 – Alexander Graham Bell patents the telephone
14 February 1876 – Elisha Gray is *a few hours* late to have been first
(He chose to act the bitter victim all his life.)

limit your amusement

> *When people say to me: "How do you do so many things?" I often answer them, without meaning to be cruel: "How do you do so little?"*
>
> *It seems to me that people have vast potential. Most people can do extraordinary things if they have confidence or take the*

risks. Yet most people don't. They sit in front of the telly and treat life as if it goes on forever.

— Phillip Adams

I once gave a talk on my book *You & The Police!* to a large college crowd. The Q&A session was fun, but also saddening to me in that half the questions were related to drug and alcohol issues. What a senseless waste of one's 20s! I've several friends in their 20s and 30s, and the time they fritter away with TV and X-Box just floors me. The average young person watches over 20 hours/week of TV — that's 43 days/year, eight years over a lifetime! You can become a *surgeon* in eight years. (Check out an organization called TV-Free America.)

The modern distractions available today are many times more tempting than what I had growing up (*i.e.*, only three channels of TV and young girls who looked like, well, young girls vs. college-age swimsuit models). Today's young men must develop *immense* strength of character to resist them.

To "muse" means to "think." To be "a-mused" means *not* to think. Amusement parks are *nonthinking* parks. Of course, Life should be fun as much as possible, but the trick is to combine fun with the essentials of learning and striving. Learning something new can always be fun if you have the right attitude. Make a contest of it. (Save actual amusement for times when learning is temporarily not fun.)

Young men under 35 should be maximizing their skill sets and creating surplus capital for savings and investment. If you understood what every hour on an X-Box truly means in opportunity costs, playing games would seem more expensive than they're worth. **Do not watch TV. It is a rectangular drain of your mind.** It is a time waste, especially when you are young. Ask yourself every hour:

Is what I'm doing right now advancing my goals?
Is what I'm doing right now increasing my skillset?

understand when to pay money to get it done

After your health, your most valuable asset is time, and the cheapest way to pay for anything is with money.

— John Ross, www.john-ross.net

The quicker you learn what is the highest use of your time, the earlier your success will come. If, for example, you command $20/hour, then it makes no sense to mow your own lawn when the kid next door will do so for a fraction of your wage. (Heart surgeons don't even crack open their patients' chests as such can be done by regular surgeons.)

Know what you are worth, and thus what is not worth your valuable time doing. Learn to pay for housecleaning, laundry, bookkeeping, and other tasks. ("Outsourcing" is discussed in *4-Hour Work Week*.) Besides, such will help others fulfill *their* purpose!

are you in *action*, or merely in motion?

Never confuse movement with action.
— Ernest Hemingway

Being busy is most often used as a guise for avoiding the few critically important but uncomfortable actions.

Effectiveness is doing the things that get you closer to your goals. Doing something unimportant well does not make it important. Slow down and remember this: Most things make no difference. Being busy is a form of laziness — lazy thinking and indiscriminate action. Lack of time is actually a lack of priorities.
— Timothy Ferriss, *4-Hour Work Week*

The great aim of education is not knowledge but action.
— Herbert Spencer

BE in control of what you are in control of!
— Robert M. DeGroff

Confusing movement for action and reading for immediately relevant knowledge is common. I do it, too. Always ask yourself:

Is this the highest and best use of my time right now?

Is this an A, or is it a B or C?

Touch it once.

Finish all today's business today.

is this the highest and best use of my time right now?

This is the foundation to all else. Be brutally honest with yourself on it, and don't stray into easy or comfortable territory.

Start with A, *not* with C

Your plan outline will show what is A, B, or C. Concentrate on "*the critical few versus the trivial many*".

touch it only *once*

I call it the Rule of FIDO: Fix/Forget It, Drive On. Life is just too short to revisit things that you should have resolved definitively by a *single* act. No halfway measures; complete what you start.

finish all today's business today

Tomorrow has enough for its own, and don't procrastinate on today's business (including doing the dishes!) by needlessly working on next month's. Follow those four rules, and you won't confuse movement with action, wasting time, and delaying your own project.

be efficient

> *The shortest way to do many things is to do only one thing at once.*
>
> — Samuel Smiles

> *If you prioritize properly, there is no need to multitask.*
>
> — Timothy Ferriss, *4-Hour Work Week*

> *Can you imagine anyone at the top of his profession who isn't organized?* (p. 321)
>
> — Robert G. Allen, *Multiple Streams of Income*

we are all given but 24 hours in a day

How effective and efficient we are with them is what varies between people. Effectiveness is "doing the right things" and efficiency is "doing things right." To be effective *and* efficient, you must be "doing the right things right."

learn to spot areas of inefficiency in your life

The easiest one to correct is no longer having to look for things that you "lost." I had a friend who spent a total of at least an hour every week looking for his car keys, a piece of mail, or his sunglasses. That's 52 hours a year of purely wasted time! Designate a constant "home" for your things, and make them "live there" at all times.

Another time waste is going back and forth to the same place (a room, or into town) for singular errands when you should combine them. I've lived in the country for over twenty years, usually 20-50 minutes from the nearest town. Going into town everyday would be a waste of valuable time. So, I go only 2 times/week. Each town day is well-planned out in advance so that I'm not needlessly driving north-south-north-south.

One method for efficiency is to devise combinations of tasks that complement each other. (In software, these are called "macros.")

managing paperwork

Work on one thing at a time Handle paper only once. Either delegate it, do it, file it, or throw it away. After it's done (and before filing) place it face-down so it cannot again get your attention. Simple.

excessive reading and studying is not *doing*

To know and not to do is not yet to know.
— Zen saying

Knowing is not enough; we must apply. Willing is not enough; we must do.
— Goethe

Verily, when the day of judgment comes, we shall not be asked what we have read, but what we have done.
— Thomas A. Kempis

You can read all the books on self-confidence, but it still takes successful experiences to build self-confidence.
— Grant G. Gard, *Don't Just Talk About It — Do It!*

Reading and studying are necessary, but only to a point. Once you've learned what you need to know, put down the books and begin to act.

categorizing tasks

If you will begin every day with your tasks in this order, you will always get the right things accomplished first and well.

❶ Important and Urgent	(health, relationships)
❷ Important but not Urgent	(education, medical)
❸ Urgent but not Important	(immediate favors)
❹ Unimportant and not Urgent	(busy work, organizing socks)
❺ Wasted Time	("*anything you feel bad after*")

Life tries to fill your days with 3s, 4s, and 5s — have you noticed?

A 1 cannot be blown off without painful consequences. So, people eventually take care of their 1s (though not early enough).

Most 1s are needlessly procrastinated 2s that became urgent over time. The moral here is to take care of your 2s, leaving no 1s that occur because of your own sloth. This is the highest use of your time management. (There will be plenty of unavoidable 1s to deal with throughout your Life. Take care of your 2s — especially regarding your health and relationships — allowing time and energy for the big 1s.) Stop postponing your 2s! *Action This Day* as Churchill used to say.

A similar hierarchy of tasks is the ABCDE method.

The ABCDE Method

A Task	important, and you must do
B Task	should do, but not an A
C Task	nice to do, but not radically life-changing
D Task	should be delegated
E Task	shouldn't be done at all, but eliminated

handle emails later, and infrequently

> *I answer emails only once or twice a day, but not first thing. If I do that, I find myself quickly sucked into issues and situations that (1) aren't that important, (2) can often be handled just as well by someone else, (3) don't advance my long-term goals, and (4) sap me of mental and emotional energy that could be put to better use elsewhere.*
>
> — Michael Masterson, *Automatic Wealth*

I learned this the hard way when I got online at a cafe and stupidly answered some unimportant (though interesting) emails. Then, the cafe's router went out before getting my important tasks done — leaving me offline for an hour. *Ouch!* And so avoidable! Now, I bear down on the necessary tasks first. Don't take your computer, the Internet, or your time for granted. First things first!

> *I know from experience that virtually everyone who puts off change fails to make it. When I hear someone say "I'm going to start after Christmas" or "next month" or "on Tuesday," I think, "Like hell you are."*
>
> *For when it comes to change, the sure sign of failure is procrastination.*
>
> — Michael Masterson, *Automatic Wealth*

Life's priorities

> *Unless something is well-defined and important, no one should do it. Eliminate before you delegate.*
>
> — Timothy Ferriss, *4-Hour Work Week*

> *A philosophy professor stood before his class and had some items in front of him. When class began, wordlessly he picked up a large empty mayonnaise jar and proceeded to fill it with rocks the size of golf balls. He then asked the students if the jar was full. They agreed that it was.*

> *So, the professor then picked up a box of pebbles and poured them into the jar. He shook the jar lightly, causing the pebbles to settle between the rocks. The students laughed. Is it full now? the professor asked. They agreed that it was.*
>
> *Finally, the professor poured into the jar a box of sand, which filled up all the remaining space. "Now," said the professor, "I want you to recognize that the jar is your life. The rocks are the important things – your family, your partner, your faith, your health, your children – anything so vital that its loss would nearly devastate you.*
>
> *"The pebbles are lesser things, but which still matter to you, like your job, your house, your car. The sand is everything else – the truly small stuff.*
>
> *"If you put the sand into the jar first, there is no room for the rocks or even the pebbles. The same is true for your life. If you spend all your energy and time on the small stuff, you will never have room for the truly important things. Pay attention to that which is critical to your joy. Play with your children. Take time to get medical checkups. Take your wife out dancing.*
>
> *"There will always be time to go to work, clean the house, give a dinner party, and fix the disposal.*
>
> *"Take care of the rocks first – the things that really matter. Set your priorities. The rest is just sand."*
>
> – author unknown

This parable is another way of saying "*start with A's, and not with C's.*"

> *Identify the few critical tasks that contribute most to income and schedule them with very short and clear deadlines. Learn to ask: "If this is the only thing I accomplish today, will I be satisfied with my day?" and "Am I inventing things to do to avoid the important?" and "Will I definitely use this information for something immediate and important?"*
>
> – Timothy Ferriss, *4-Hour Work Week*

> *So what time is it? Time to do the most important thing that needs to be done.*
>
> – Larry Winget, *Shut Up, Stop Whining, Get A Life!*

inaction can be the correct action

> *How beautiful it is to do nothing, and then rest afterward.*
>
> – Spanish proverb

Actions always have consequences. Inaction is a form of action. Sometimes, inaction is the right thing, especially if the situation is not requiring action then and more information is coming. This is not indecisiveness, it's knowing that a decision is not only not required, but better made later. When you feel powerfully inclined to wait, it's usually your subconscious trying to get your attention. Listen to it.

Always learn what the *true* deadline is for acting, and what is the *polite* deadline (for you don't want to make a habit of keeping others waiting until their last moment). The time difference between the two is your extra cushion, should you need it.

know which details are truly important

Many details are not important, or at least not immediately. Others are. I once needed to get online with my laptop at a coffee shop to get an afternoon's work done. One small detail: the electrical outlets of that old building were two-prong and I hadn't a 2-prong adapter. A half hour was lost until I could find a hardware store. (Now, the adapter goes with my laptop.) As the old poem goes:

For want of a nail, the shoe was lost.
For want of a shoe, the horse was lost.
For want of a horse, the rider was lost.
For want of the rider, the battle was lost.
For want of a battle, the war was lost.
For want of a war, the kingdom was lost.
And all for want of a nail.

decisions determine destiny!

We all do exactly what we decide to do; we are the sum of our decisions.

The best insurance for making the right decision is to know how to not make the wrong decision.

Every decision we make has consequences.
Every decision is at least a spiritual decision.
— Patrick Morley, *The Man In The Mirror*

Do not be flippant about your Life. Ponder deeply to choose wisely.

DAVID ALLEN'S *GTD* METHOD

Terence Gillespie of www.mcgillespie.com calls personal organization and time/space management "The One Skill That Can't Be Delegated". Great point! He recommends David Allen's *Getting Things Done* GTD method from www.davidco.com.

> *In traditional time management, priorities usually play a central role. In contrast, Allen's approach uses two key elements – control and perspective. He proposes a workflow process to gain control over all the tasks and commitments that one needs or wants to get done, and "6 different levels of focus" to provide them with useful perspective.*
>
> — www.en.wikipedia.org/wiki/Getting_Things_Done

Basically, Allen's goal for you is that you free your subconscious from all random "open loops" which tax out your mind's "RAM". His side remark, "*There is no reason ever to have the same thought twice, unless you like having that thought*" hit me right between the eyes. If your mind keeps coming back to some unresolved issue, it's because you have not placed that issue within a trusted (regularly emptied) system. By managing your actions, you manage your "stuff" to do. Allen's GTD method is all about creating such a system for your life. When your mind is clear of clutter, it is only then free to create:

> *Your ability to generate power is directly proportional to your ability to relax.*

When your mind wanders, it's because "open loops" have been begging for its attention, and the mind cannot help but dwell on them. The mind cannot distinguish a "do it later" from a "do it now" — the mind only knows the now, and "laters" get joined with the "nows". Anything which you cannot do right now becomes a "do it later" and absolutely must be collected somewhere outside of your mind. Allen's system is fantastic for convincing your mind that all is collected, and handled with progress, thus allowing your mind (*i.e.*, you!) to *r-e-l-a-x!*

14

SOLVING PROBLEMS

No man should be pitied because every day of his life he faces a hard, stubborn problem. It is the man who has no problems to solve, no hardships to face, who is to be pitied. He has nothing in life which will strengthen and form his character; nothing to call out his latent powers and deepen and widen his hold on life.
— Booker T. Washington

You can't let your problems be a problem.
— John C. Maxwell

The measure of success is not whether you have a tough problem to deal with, but whether it is the same problem you had last year.
— John Foster Dulles, former Secretary of State

The superior man makes the difficulty to be overcome his first interest; success comes only later.
— Confucius, c. 500 B.C.

HOW TO SOLVE ANY PROBLEM

Settle one difficulty and you keep hundreds away.
— Chinese Proverb

Certainly the world is full of trouble and problems, but the world is also full of the overcoming of trouble and the solving of problems. The chief duty of a human being is to endure life.
— Dr. Norman Vincent Peale, *Enthusiasm Makes the Difference*

Life is just a series of consecutive (and often concurrent) problems. The sooner you become unemotional about how you solve these problems, the fewer and shorter and less painful they will be. The main secret to solving problems is this:

> *Every problem contains within itself the seeds of its own solution.*
> — Stanley Arnold, *The Executive Breakthrough* (1967)

Learn how to disassemble a problem, reverse it, and invert it. See it from another's perspective. Problems contain their own solutions, and every problem has a soft spot.

there are just 3 kinds of problems

Credit goes to author Aubrey Andelin of *The Man of Steel and Velvet* for outlining these. The first can be avoided, the second you must continually weather through, and the third you must overcome.

problems due to your own weakness, foolishness, or sloth

These are the only generally avoidable problems, which include innocent mistakes and errors in judgment. They also embrace any integrity issue. Not being able to say *No* will result in many problems, and unnecessary ones:

> *I don't know the key to success, but the key to failure is to try to please everyone.*
> — Bill Cosby

problems that come just from living

Your environment can change, evil happens, and God may test or discipline you.

> *Circumstances are rulers of the weak, but they are weapons of the wise.*
> — Andy Andrews, *The Traveler's Gift*

problems that arise by setting high goals

> *A man can provide his own opposition, his own testing ground, by setting worthy and difficult goals for himself. As he engages in a worthy cause and assumes responsibilities which are great, he finds opposition, problems, tests and trials sufficient to prove his worth and refine his character. And the most important point is this: The problems will be of such a nature as to result in greater happiness rather than in sorrow and defeat.*

if you can't define it or act upon it — forget it

Before spending time on a stress-inducing question, big or otherwise, ensure that the answer is "yes" to the following two questions:

1. Have I decided on a single meaning for each term in this question?

2. Can an answer . . . be acted upon to improve things?

If you can't define it or act upon it, forget it.

– Timothy Ferriss, *4-Hour Work Week*

deal only with problems big enough to matter yet small enough to solve

Everything else must be ignored! This is the apex of maturity and will take years to master as small problems "want" to be treated as if they were big problems. Start practicing now!

decide trivial things quickly/immediately

Learn to distinguish between the trivial and the important. Develop your own standards in relation to money, time, and people. How much money is important? $20? $100? Draw a line somewhere so that you don't treat an unimportant $1 as an important $20. Regarding time, what difference will your decision make in one month? One year? Draw a line somewhere. With people, will your decision hurt anyone or sour a friendship?

Once you've classified a problem as trivial, deal with it at once and don't look back because it never really mattered too much how you solved it.

John C. Maxwell: how leaders solve problems

❶ they anticipate problems

❷ they accept the truth

In times like these it is good to remember that there have always been times like these.

– Paul Harvey

❸ they see the big picture

❹ they handle one thing at a time

Never try to solve all the problems at once – make them line up for you one-by-one.

– Richard Sloma

❺ they don't give up a major goal when they're down

Dr. N.V. Peale's 8 Sure-Fire Guidelines

don't panic

Stay calm, always, even if currently on fire. Stop. Drop. Roll.

don't be overwhelmed by your problem

It'll get solved. You and God can handle anything!

practice de-confusion

Break down the problem into its components. Divide and conquer it through making it clear and bite-sized.

skip the postmortems

Stop whining and crying and berating yourself — it's too late for that. Take your problem from where you are *now*.

find a solution for the next step

Don't try to solve the entire problem at once. The problem didn't happen all at once, but through incremental stages. That is how you will solve it, one step at a time.

> *Solve problems a piece at a time. Write down what you could do. Write down what you could read. Write down who you could ask. Every problem you've got can be solved.*
>
> — Jim Rohn, "Time Management" article for HerbaLife distributors

practice creative listening

This really means listening to yourself. Write down your thoughts, or go for a walk in the woods and tell your dog. Get your feelings and ideas out of your head so that you can hear yourself.

Also, solutions often have an elegant beauty about them:

> *When I am working on a problem, I never think about beauty. I think only of how to solve the problem. But when I have finished, if the solution is not beautiful, I know it is wrong.*
>
> — R. Buckminster Fuller

always ask yourself what is the *right* thing to do

If it's not the right thing, then it's the wrong thing. Nothing wrong ever turned out right. Do right to come out right.

keep praying, thinking, believing — keep enthusiastic

how to solve important problems

> *True genius resides in the capacity for evaluation of uncertain, hazardous, and conflicting information.*
>
> — Sir Winston Churchill

> *He that will not apply new remedies must expect new evils, for time is the greatest innovator.*
>
> — Francis Bacon

> *You can never solve a problem with the same kind of thinking that created the problem in the first place.*
>
> — Albert Einstein

There is a proven system to solving important problems. I got the below steps from William J. Reilly's fine little book *How to Get What You Want Out of Life.* (Just 25¢ at a thrift shop!)

Problem-solving is really all about making sound decisions. Most of your important problems — if you honestly look at them — are there because you originally made a poor decision or because you are procrastinating at making a sound (though difficult) decision.

> *I can usually tell if a decision is wrong or not before it hurts too much and, from this experience, I can have the wisdom to make the right one. If I don't make any decision, I get absolutely nowhere.* (said by a successful bank president in Colorado)
>
> — Grant G. Gard, *Don't Just Talk About It — Do It!*

> *One rule always holds good: you must give your problems to your subconscious mind in the form of definite assignments, after assembling all the essential facts, figures, and arguments. The cooking process must first be started by focusing our minds on this material long and intently enough to get it thoroughly heated with our best conscious thinking.* [Then] . . . *go fishing, golfing, or motoring, or if it's night, go peacefully to bed.*
>
> — Robert Updegraff

Once you've classified a problem as important, delay your response to it as long as possible while you think it through these steps:

Step 1: separate facts from opinions

Analyze from the standpoint of who, what, when, and where. Be specific, not general. Leave out your opinion so that you don't automatically begin discriminating between things.

Step 2: define the *real* problem and possible solutions

The *real* problem is the one which, if you solve it, will make the "problem" go away. (If it doesn't, then you've yet to define the *real* problem.) No matter how painful the analysis may be, you cannot fake or fuzz this step. What is *really* the problem? If this is still difficult, then write down everything that is *not* the problem — what's left should give you a pretty clear indication of the *real* problem.

Next, arrive at some "possible solutions." This doesn't mean *one* solution (there are always multiple solutions) or *impossible* solutions. Don't have an opinion yet about your preference of solutions; don't restrict your thinking to any single answer. Write down everything possible that could solve your problem, even if it sounds crazy or outlandish (such as moving away or changing jobs).

Step 3: secure evidence on those possible solutions

List what each of these possible solutions will take. Write down every penny and every minute of cost. What is good and bad about each? For example, let's say that you are unhappy with your present girlfriend. It is easy to make a list of all her faults, but don't forget that it will take you 6-24 months to learn what's wrong with your *next* girlfriend. You already know what's wrong with your current one, and that is an important advantage.

Step 4: weigh the pros and cons of each possible solution

Now that you know how to give proper weight to money, time, and people, draw up a "balance sheet" of the *realistic* pros and cons of each possible solution. If the best solution still isn't clear, go back and assign 1-10 values to each pro and con, and add them up. In the event of a tie, choose the one you *like* better. (As you can see, emotions are best left only as a tie-breaker.)

With human problems, there are no perfect answers. Once you've gone through these steps and made your decision, don't look back and second-guess yourself. Commit to that plan of action as long as it has not turned to disaster. You will gain in maturity with your capacity to live with imperfect solutions.

If you have to reverse your decision, you may not realize this for a long time, which tends to lock one into the "psychology of previous investment". Even still, sometimes a lengthy detour is necessary:

> *Sometimes a person has to go a very long distance out of his way to come back a short distance correctly.*
>
> — Edward Albee, *Zoo Story*

ASK FOR ADVICE OR HELP

He who asks is a fool for five minutes, but he who does not ask remains a fool forever.
– ancient Chinese proverb

I think sometimes just discussing the problem with a trusted friend or family member sometimes leads to a solution. At HBS we were advised to cultivate a "personal Board of Directors," comprising 3-7 people we trust and admire, who could be consulted for advice on major decisions. (Of course, unlike a real corporate board, you can always choose to ignore your personal board's advice, but it's probably helpful to get their thoughts anyway!)
– graduate of Harvard Business School

Unless you are uncommonly wise, introspective, and honest with yourself, you should often turn to the advice of others for a more objective opinion.

GETTING OUT OF A RUT

Those only are happy who have their minds fixed on some object other than their own happiness: on the happiness of others, on the improvement of mankind, even on some art or pursuit, followed not as a means, but as itself, an ideal end. Aiming, thus, at something else, they find happiness by the way.
– Earl Nightingale, *The Essence of Success*

You're human, and thus you'll get mired in the ruts of Life and of yourself. It happens, but how long you *stay* there is up to *you*.

stop digging – deal with negative emotions

when you are "bored"

If you're bored, just remember – it's your fault.
– Tim Ferris, *4 Hour Workweek*

Everybody gets bored sometimes, but it's wise not to make a habit of it. Why not use it to be productive? Here's an idea: keep a jar to draw slips of paper from. On those slips will be chores like:

polish your shoes	clean the toilet
iron your clothes	detail your car
fix a faucet	organize the garage

The trick is to do whatever that slip commands. Ironing clothes or cleaning your toilet aren't fun things, but need to be done. (That's what you get for being "bored," huh?)

Another idea is write a family member or old friend a letter (not an email, a real letter).

Often, the best thing to do is to work out. It's what your body needs, and usually clears out the mental cobwebs and stress. No TV!

when you are tired

You are in control of your body. Your body is not in control of you. When your body wants to shut down before it has a right to, do something *vigorous*. Shock it back into submission. Go for a jog or a tough hike. Exercise on your rebounder. Swim.

when you are depressed

> *Life is a grindstone. Whether it grinds you down or polishes you up depends upon what you are made of.*
>
> — author unknown

> *Don't audit life. No matter how you feel, get up, dress up, and show up. Show up and make the most of it now.*

Depression is a head activity. (Fear is, too.) So, get *outside* of your own head by doing something with body and soul instead. Get some fresh air outdoors. Hike. Walk the dog. Shovel snow. Work out.

M. Scott Peck observed that most depression stems from *anger*. Analyze what it is that you're angry about, and resolve the issue.

> *A person who is depressed is spending too much time thinking about the way things are now and not enough time thinking about how he wants things to be.*
>
> *Just as a clean breeze cleans smoke from the air, so a grateful spirit removes the cloud of despair. It is impossible for the seeds of depression to take root in a thankful heart.*
>
> — Andy Andrews, *The Traveler's Gift*

do something gratuitously kind for somebody

> *We should give as we would receive . . . cheerfully, quickly and without hesitation; for there is no grace in a benefit that sticks to our fingers.*
>
> — Seneca

> *It is one of the beautiful compensations of this life that no one can sincerely try to help another without helping himself.*
>
> — Charles Dudley Warner

Depression is a self-thing, so get out of yourself! Call up your grandmother for no reason other than you were thinking of her.

> *What do we live for, if not to make life less difficult for each other?*
>
> – George Eliot

> *You will find, as you look back upon your life, that the moments you have really lived are the moments when you have done things in the spirit of love.*
>
> – Henry Drummond

Find somebody else with a greater problem than your own, and help them. There are people who desperately need your help! A single favor, an hour of assistance, or a $20 bill could make all the difference. Look for hurts and needs out there, and you will quickly find them. As you uplift others, you will forget all about how "miserable" you were.

During the Vietnam war, an orphanage was hit by mortar and an eight year old boy was severely wounded. He desperately needed a transfusion, and so a call out was made to the orphans to donate blood. Hai, his friend, raised his hand and said, "*Me. I give.*" While on the stretcher in the hospital next to his friend, needle in his arm, Hai began to whimper, and then started crying. When asked if it hurt, Hai answered through his tears, "*How long will it take me to die?*" Having never heard of a blood transfusion, Hai thought that his friend would need *all* of his blood to live. What a Jesus-level of giving!

> *Do all the good you can,*
> *In all the ways you can,*
> *To all the souls you can,*
> *In every place you can,*
> *At all times you can,*
> *With all the zeal you can,*
> *As long as you can.*
>
> – John Wesley

> *It is well to remember that the entire population of the universe, with one trifling exception, is others.*
>
> – J.A. Holmes

crawling out of the rut

first, take responsibility for things

> *It is easy to dodge our responsibilities but we cannot dodge the consequences of dodging our responsibilities.*
>
> – Josiah Stamp

If you could kick the man responsible for most of your troubles, you wouldn't sit down for a week.
— Theodore Roosevelt

Neutralize any negative emotion by saying "*I am responsible!*"

if you're unhappy, what is it that you're not facing up to?

There is some root to your depression, and you're probably suppressing it. Get honest with yourself, and deal with your issues.

slow to a crawl if you must, but do not stop completely

Always keep moving forward (if only slowly), never being idle. Newton's Law of Energy Conservation applies equally to humans:

People at rest tend to remain at rest,
and people in motion tend to remain in motion.

Have you ever noticed a semi-truck driver creeping up to a stoplight? If possible, he will avoid coming to a complete stop because it takes so much energy to get started again. This technique saves an astonishing amount of fuel, and I practice it in my own cars.

Use this example with things in your own Life, such as working out or paying down debt. Always show up, if even for a short session. Crawl if you absolutely must, but *never stop*.

"*tomorrow ain't never now*"

There is nothing magical about the future. The future, when it comes, is just like the present.
— William J. Reilly, *How to Get What You Want Out of Life*

Latin Americans have a catch-all word for procrastination: *Mañana*. "Tomorrow." Our equivalent is "someday". Well, someday is no day. Don't fool yourself! Attach a due-date to a wish, and it's now a goal.

get yourself involved, even just a little bit, *today*

And no matter how much or how little of your time is involved in your first step, the most important fundamental for you to remember is to exercise the necessary patience to begin at the beginning and to lead an orderly, systematic, irresistible advance, one step at a time, toward your inevitable goal. (p. 110)
— William J. Reilly, *How to Get What You Want Out of Life*

Getting yourself involved today changes your state from rest to motion. You cannot *think* your way from rest to motion, you must act. Get off your brakes and step on the gas. Start slowly, but do *start*.

one step leads to the other — *when* we take the 1st step

> *The only way by which remedies can be provided is by looking disagreeable facts resolutely in the face and not by lying about them.*
>
> — Theodore Roosevelt

When I moved from Colorado to Wyoming, it took several stages because I had a lot of things. (That's changing!) My last haul was the one I really dreaded: cleaning out a full two-car garage and transferring the keepables into a large rental box truck for the two-day drive. Mice and wasps had gotten into everything, and I could hardly stand to even look at all the things I'd stuffed inside. It was a real mess.

Finally, I carved out the time needed, and drove down to Colorado to tackle my remaining "elephant". Waking up that first morning was hard because I had a clear and painful vision of what the task would require. I was tempted to feel overwhelmed, but I dove in and began. After a long first day, my progress didn't seem equal to the effort, but I kept at it the next day like a marathon — one foot in front of the other. At the end of Day 2, I knew that I had a handle on things. Day 3, I finished, and I treated myself to a small celebration. The next morning, I hit the road and unloaded it all in Wyoming two days later. Afterwards, a huge wave of relief crashed over me. By taking that first step, and continuing, I dissolved a very annoying and large task. That sense of accomplishment lasted for a very long time!

make and keep commitments to yourself

Devote just one hour a day to your goal. Schedule that hour and keep that appointment as you would with an important person. *You.*

do you want to be right, or do you want to be at peace?

Begin to practice letting some things *go*. Yes, I know the world is full of injustice. Do what you can to correct things, but let the rest *go*.

hold difficult matters in "*prayerful thinking*"

When you learn to "*let go and let God*" handle things for you through faith, those things get done.

just keep at it, and you'll break through!

> *Almost every one of the wealthy men* [that Napoleon Hill] *interviewed had achieved their great successes one step beyond what appeared to be their greatest failure. It was when every outward indication suggested that it was time to quit and to give up that they were the closest to breaking through to their goals.*
> — Brian Tracy

Protecting all new advances and great victories is a sort of "membrane" against the average and the mediocre. (Like bouncers at the door, demanding a cover charge.) This membrane will stretch against mere pedestrian effort, but only the exceptional will break through. A "breakthrough" in life is exactly that. In fact, you were conceived only because one particular spermatozoan broke through that ovum's wall. (After it did, the wall became impermeable against all others. Only the first wins!) When you've pushed against that membrane of a problem, and it seems to have absorbed all your energy and stopped you — ***that* is when it is on the verge of breaking!** That it has slowed you down to a stop is the best sign of your imminent victory. Just one . . . more . . . *push* . . .

> *Many of life's failures are men who did not realize how close they were to success when they gave up.*
> — Edison

> *Most people achieved their greatest successes one step beyond what looked like their greatest failure.*
> — Brian Tracy, *The Great Big Book of Wisdom*

> *You must know that in the game of life, nothing is less important than the score at halftime.* ***The tragedy of life is not that man loses, but that he almost wins.***
> *I do not fear failure, for in my life, failure is a myth.* ***Failure exists only for the person who quits.*** *I do not quit.*
> — Andy Andrews, *The Traveler's Gift*

> *Don't halfheartedly wound problems — kill them dead.*
> — Lockheed aircraft designer legend Kelly Johnson

Do not "almost win"! Never quit! *PUSH . . . THROUGH!*

RECOMMENDED MOVIES

solving a lethal emergency under pressure	*Apollo 13*
leadership, courage	*Das Boot*

15

POWER: USE & MISUSE

Being powerful is like being a lady. If you have to tell people you are, you aren't.
— Margaret Thatcher

Strength of character, hard work, and honesty are essential, but you will need more to achieve a successful life. You need to understand who or what has inordinate influence over your own will. That is "power". All of us, including presidents and billionaires, are under the power of others. What's at stake here is whether you can realize, isolate, and remove yourself from harmful power.

Conversely, all of us, even a homeless street person, has power over others. Can you project power over those people and things vital to your goals? And can you do so ethically?

If the world is like a giant scheming court and we are trapped inside it, there is no use in trying to opt out of the game. That will only render you powerless, and powerlessness will make you miserable. Instead of struggling against the inevitable, instead of arguing and whining and feeling guilty, it is far better to excel at power. In fact, the better you are at dealing with power, the better friend, lover, husband, wife and person you become.

If the game of power is inescapable, better to be an artist than a denier or a bungler.
— Robert Greene, *The 48 Laws of Power*

This book is a most valuable synopsis of power, and I will try to show you how to use it ethically and for good. We've all made mistakes of power on both ends. The trick is to learn from these mistakes, and thus never repeat them.

ETHICAL POWER STRATEGIES

Spiritual power is the power to influence others through one's own being – by example, by kindness, by humor, by wisdom and love.

Spiritual power is invariably civil.

Political power is achieved by ambition; spiritual power is not achieved at all; indeed, it often requires of its practitioner the renunciation of ambition. Political power has everything to do with control. Spiritual power has much to do with surrendering control.

– Dr. M. Scott Peck, *A World Waiting To Be Born*

It is not inherently unethical to seek power over certain people and situations, however you must always test your motives and your means against the results you want.

Law 1: Never outshine the master

Always make those above you feel comfortably superior.

Showing off your own greater brilliance or charm may feel good for the moment, but your boss will grow sullen, vowing to put you in your place. The more vain your boss, the riskier it is.

Reversal: only with falling stars, if they have become weak.

Law 2: Never put too much trust in friends, learn how to use enemies

Be wary of friends – they will betray you more quickly, for they are easily aroused to envy.

But hire a former enemy and he will be more loyal than a friend, because he has more to prove.

The more impressive you are as a person (looks, wealth, integrity, power, etc.) the more envious your friends will be. John Cleese of *Monty Python* described it well: he is pleased with his friends' success, as long as they don't create any masterpieces. (Law 46 also applies here, in not appearing too perfect to your friends.)

Excessive charity and kindness can have an embittering effect, leading to betrayal.

Men are more ready to repay an injury than a benefit, because gratitude is a burden and revenge a pleasure.

– Tacitus

When you see water flowing uphill, it means that someone is repaying a kindness.

– African folk saying

Keep some distance with your friends. Try never to employ them as friends and business rarely mix, and having a friend/business partner gives away too much power over you.

Enemies are valuable, because they are always pointing out your faults and weaknesses. (Friends rarely do this.)

> *Never let the presence of enemies upset or distress you — you are far better off with a declared opponent or two than not knowing where your real enemies lie. The man of power welcomes conflict, using enemies to enhance his reputation as a surefooted fighter who can be relied upon in times of uncertainty.*

Law 3: Conceal your intentions

> *Keep people off-balance and in the dark by never revealing the purpose behind your actions. If they have no clue what you are up to, they cannot prepare a defense.*

For the naturally frank and direct, this doesn't come easily. (I should know.) If people can predict you, they will feel superior to you. Don't always be an "open book":

> *By being unabashedly open you make yourself so predictable and familiar that it is almost impossible to respect or fear you, and power will not accrue to a person who cannot inspire such emotions.*

If you can do so ethically, use decoys to misdirect from your true object. Talk about a lesser thing while remaining silent about the real thing. Get your opponent to focus on the wrong pattern.

> *The paranoid and wary are often the easiest to deceive.*

> *Have you ever heard of a skillful general, who intends to surprise a citadel, announcing his plans to his enemy? Conceal your purpose and hide your progress; do not disclose the extent of your designs until they cannot be opposed, until the combat is over. Win the victory before you declare the war.*
>
> — Ninon de Lenclos

Law 4: Always say less than necessary

> *When you are trying to impress people with words, the more you say, the more common you appear, and the less in control. Even if you are saying something banal, it will seem original if you make it vague, open-ended, and sphinxlike. Powerful people impress and intimidate by saying less. The more you say, the more likely you are to say something foolish.*

The best movie example of this was *Being There* with Peter Sellers. An illiterate gardener who knew nothing but from the TV, he charmed and amazed the elite of Washington, D.C. with his seemingly profound statements and calm demeanor.

Those with power can more easily terrify with silence than with words. (A quietly seething parent is much more scary than a yelling one. Yelling means loss of control.) Silence activates the doomed imagination of others.

> *Never start moving your own lips and teeth before the subordinates do. The longer I keep quiet, the sooner others move their lips and teeth* [and] *I can thereby understand their real intentions. If the sovereign is not mysterious, the ministers will find opportunity to take and take.*
>
> — Han-fei-tzu, third century B.C. China

> *If you do not declare yourself immediately, you arouse expectation . . . . Mix a little mystery with everything, and the very mystery stirs up veneration. And when you explain, be not too explicit . . . . In this manner you imitate the Divine way when you cause men to wonder and watch.*
>
> — Baltasar Gracián

Law 5: Guard your reputation

> *Reputation is the cornerstone of power. Through reputation alone you can intimidate and win; once it slips, however, you are vulnerable, and will be attacked on all sides. Make your reputation unassailable.*
>
> *Make your reputation simple and base it on one sterling quality* [which] *becomes a kind of calling card that announces your presence and places others under a spell.*
>
> *Since we must live in society and must depend on the opinions of others, there is nothing to be gained by neglecting your reputation. By not caring how you are perceived, you let others decide this for you.*

How do you then defend a solid reputation? By always taking the highroad and never appearing too angry or defensive. A confident person would generally laugh off an attack with satire and ridicule. Going too far can seem vengeful.

Law 8: Make the other person come to you, with bait

> *The essence of power is the ability to keep the initiative, to get others to react to your moves, to keep your opponent and those around you on the defensive.*

This is a powerful sales technique; always make the potential buyer come to your table. Never take the goods over to his.

> *Good warriors make others come to them, and do not go to others. This is the principle of emptiness and fullness of others and self. When you induce opponents to come to you, then their force is always empty; as long as you do not go to them, your force is always full. Attacking emptiness with fullness is like throwing stones on eggs.*
>
> – Zhang Yu, 11th century China

If you can't make the other come to you, at least insist on a neutral location, with the "neutrality" shaded to your advantage, of course.

Law 9: Win through actions, never through argument

Any momentary triumph you think you have gained through argument is really a Pyrrhic victory: the resentment and ill will you stir up are stronger and last longer than any momentary change of opinion. It is much more powerful to get others to agree with you through your actions, without saying a word. Demonstrate, do not explicate.

Years ago, Bolivian President René Barrientos (also a pilot) was accused of profiteering on the purchase of inferior parachutes. He called for a press conference at an air force base. He had a reporter randomly pick out a chute from a pile, strapped it on, took off in a two-seater fighter, ejected himself, popped the chute, and landed on the tarmac in front of everyone. "*Now let's all get back to work*," he said.

Words are subject to rebuttal. Action ends the discussion.

> *Such is the double power of winning through actions rather than argument: No one is offended, and your point is proven.*

Be too clever to argue. *Show* it, don't tell it. An effective visceral demonstration will convince everyone.

> *The truth is generally seen, rarely heard.*
>
> – Baltasar Gracián

> *Never argue. In society nothing must be discussed; give only results.*
>
> – Benjamin Disraeli

Law 10: Avoid the unhappy and unlucky

The unfortunate sometimes draw misfortune on themselves; they will also draw it on you. Associate with the happy and fortunate instead.

I knew a guy who had the Midas touch in reverse: everything he was involved in got tainted. A perpetual whiner/victim whose plans were always going awry (through never any fault of his own, of course!). These people and their instabilities are infectious, and if you hang around with them, your reputation will suffer.

> *Recognize the fortunate so that you may choose their company, and the unfortunate so that you may avoid them. Misfortune is usually the crime of folly, and among those who suffer from it there is no malady more contagious: Never open your door to the lease of misfortunes, for, if you do, many others will follow in its train . . . . Do not die of another's misery.*
>
> — Baltasar Gracián

> *Shit begets shit.*
>
> — *Primary Colors*

> *Never associate with those who share your defects — they will reinforce everything that holds you back. Only create associations with positive affinities.*

One married couple I knew violated this maxim, as both were incredible slobs. They spent untold hours each week stepping over messes and piles, and searching for keys, etc. Their trailer looked like the practice home for a burglary school. Sadly, their children are continuing that legacy.

Law 13: Appeal to people's self-interest, never to their mercy or gratitude

While mercy or gratitude may occasionally coincide with somebody's self-interest, such cannot be relied upon. Learn what about your plan can benefit others, and the plan will nearly sell itself.

Law 15: Crush your enemy totally

> *All great leaders since Moses have known that a feared enemy must be crushed completely. (Sometimes they have learned this the hard way.) If one ember is left alight, no matter how dimly it smolders, a fire will eventually break out. More is lost through stopping halfway than through total annihilation: The enemy will recover, and will seek revenge. Crush him, not only in body but in spirit.*
>
> *The law governing fatal antagonisms reads: Reconciliation is out of the question. Only one side can win, and it must win totally.*

Christians may have a conflict here with the "*love your enemies*" admonition of Jesus. In a way, to love an enemy through *agape* (not *philos*) is to utterly crush his resistance, as hate cannot fight love.

Law 16: Use absence to increase respect and honor

If you are already established in a group, temporary withdrawal from it will make you more talked about, even more admired. You must learn when to leave. Create value through scarcity.

If you're on Facebook or MySpace, you've voluntarily cheapened your perceived value.

Familiarity breeds contempt.

Leave without notice, without explanation, without a forwarding address. Cease to be common public property — take back your Life and identity. Leave on your own terms, before people irrevocably grow tired of you.

Law 17: Cultivate an air of unpredictability

Humans are creatures of habit with an insatiable need to see familiarity in other people's actions. Your predictability gives them a sense of control. Turn the tables: Be deliberately unpredictable. Behavior that seems to have no consistency or purpose will keep them off-balance, and they will wear themselves out trying to explain your moves.

Only the terminally subordinate act in a predictable manner.

The classic example of this was in the 1972 World Championship of Chess as Bobby Fischer's unpredictability utterly unhinged the Soviet champion Boris Spassky — leaving him in tears of paranoia. (Soon after, Fischer applied Law 16 and pretty much disappeared. A movie was even made about it.)

> *The best calculation is the absence of calculation. Once you have attained a certain level of recognition, others generally figure that when you do something, it's for an intelligent reason. So it's really foolish to plot out your movements too carefully in advance. You're better off acting capriciously.*
>
> — Pablo Picasso

Law 18: Do not build fortresses — isolation is dangerous

Isolation exposes you to more dangers than it protects you from — it cuts you off from valuable information, it makes you conspicuous and an easy target. Better to circulate among people,

> *find allies, mingle. You are shielded from your enemies by the crowd.*
>
> *In moments of uncertainty and danger, you need to fight this desire to turn inward. Instead, make yourself more accessible, seek out old allies and make new ones, force yourself into more and more different circles. This has been the trick of powerful people for centuries.*
>
> *If you need time to think, then, choose isolation only as a last resort, and only in small doses. Be careful to keep your way back into society open.*

What you imagine to be dangerous is almost always less dangerous in person. Certainly, protect yourself, but within reason. Do not cut contact with the sources of your power.

Billionaire Howard Hughes became a paranoid hermit, whose isolation spurred the sociopath Clifford Irving to concoct a fake autobiography. Hughes had to break his treasured silence to disavow the book by telephone interview.

Law 19: Know who you are dealing with — do not offend the wrong person

Try to avoid these types: Mr. Arrogance, Mr. Hopelessly Insecure, Mr. Suspicion, and Mr. Serpent with a Long Memory. If they feel offended, their overreaction will be extreme.

> *Be convinced, that there are not persons so insignificant and inconsiderable, but may, some time or another, have it in their power to be of use to you; which they certainly will not, if you have once shown them contempt. Wrongs are often forgiven, but contempt never is. Our pride remembers it forever.*
>
> — Lord Chesterfield

Law 22: Know when to surrender

> *When you are weaker, never fight for honor's sake; choose surrender instead. Surrender gives you time to recover, time to torment and irritate your conqueror, time to wait for his power to wane.*
>
> *Measuring your power over time, never sacrifice long-term maneuverability for the short-lived glories of martyrdom.*

The oak tree that resists the wind, breaks. The willow tree bends with the wind, and is never broken. The hammer retreats in order to strike.

Law 23: Concentrate your forces

> *Intensity defeats extensity every time.*

Concentrate on a single goal, a single task, and beat it into submission.

A 110lb woman in high heels can crack a tile floor much easier than a 250lb man in sneakers. Concentration of force.

The World War II Allies invaded Europe on a beachfront less than 40 miles wide, and swarmed in like a leak in a dike. A half million men came through, and kept the door open. Germany surrendered 10 months later. Concentration of force.

Law 25: Re-create yourself

Do not accept the roles that society foists on you. Re-create yourself by forging a new identity, one that commands attention and never bores the audience.

This act of defiance is Promethean: It makes you responsible for your own creation.

In music, the archetype of self re-creation is Madonna. Every few years she comes up with a new image, and always just before the previous one wore out.

Law 26: Keep your hands clean

You must seem a paragon of civility and efficiency: Your hands are never soiled by mistakes and nasty deeds.

Law 28: Enter action with boldness

If you are unsure of a course of action, do not attempt it. Your doubts and hesitations will infect your execution. Timidity is dangerous: Better to enter with boldness. Any mistakes you commit through audacity are easily corrected with more audacity. Everyone admires the bold; no one honors the timid.

If boldness is not natural, neither is timidity. It is an acquired habit, picked up out of a desire to avoid conflict. If timidity has taken hold of you, then, root it out. Your fears of the consequences of a bold action are way out of proportion to reality, and in fact the consequences of timidity are worse. Your value is lowered and you create a self-fulfilling cycle of doubt and disaster.

If you merely touch the nettle, it will sting, but if you "grasp the nettle" tightly it cannot sting you.

I tell you on behalf of women; there is not one of us who does not prefer a little rough handling to too much consideration. Men lose

through blundering more hearts than virtue saves. Do not suppose us to be so very virtuous; forcing us to have too much of it.
— Ninon de Lenclos

I certainly think that it is better to be impetuous than cautious, for fortune is a woman, and it is necessary, if you wish to master her, to conquer her by force; and it can be seen that she lets herself be overcome by the bold rather than by those who proceed coldly.
— Machiavelli

Law 29: Plan all the way to the end

The ending is everything. Plan all the way to it, taking into account all the possible consequences, obstacles, and twists of fortune that might reverse your hard work and give the glory to others. By planning to the end you will not be overwhelmed by circumstances and you will know when to stop.

The most ordinary cause of people's mistakes is their being too much frightened at the present danger, and not enough so at that which is remote.
— Cardinal de Retz

Law 30: Make your accomplishments seem effortless

Your actions must seem natural and executed with ease. All the toil and practice that go into them, and also all the clever tricks, must be concealed. When you act, act effortlessly, as if you could do much more. Avoid the temptation of revealing how hard you work — it only raises questions. Teach no one your tricks or they will be used against you.

Keep your effort and your tricks to yourself and you seem to have the grace and ease of a god. One never sees the source of a god's power revealed; one only sees its effects.

What is not understandable is awe-inspiring.

People will have no idea of your limitations, and believe that you could do even more had you tried harder.

Law 31: Control the options — get others to play with the cards you deal

Give people options that come out in your favor whichever they choose.

There are many tactics for this: color the choices, force the resister, alter the playing field, shrink the options, brothers in crime through implication, horns of a dilemma, etc.

Law 32: Play to people's fantasies

The most detested person in the world is the one who always tells the truth, who never romances . . . .

— con artist Joseph Weil, "The Yellow Kid"

The truth is often avoided because it is ugly and unpleasant. Never appeal to truth and reality unless you are prepared for the anger that comes from disenchantment. Life is so harsh and distressing that people who can manufacture romance or conjure up fantasy are like oases in the desert: Everyone flocks to them. There is great power in tapping into the fantasies of the masses.

Law 33: Discover each man's thumbscrew

Look at the part of a person that is most visible — their greed, their lust, their intense fear. These are the emotions they cannot conceal, and over which they have the least control. And what people cannot control, you can control for them.

A man shows his character just in the way in which he deals with trifles – for then he is off his guard.

— Arthur Schopenhauer

All men are idolaters, some of fame, others of self-interest, most of pleasure. Skill consists in knowing these idols in order to bring them into play. Knowing any man's mainspring of motive you have as it were the key to his will.

— Baltasar Gracián

Law 34: Act like a king to be treated like one

The way you carry yourself will often determine how you are treated: In the long run, appearing vulgar or common will make people disrespect you.

It is up to you to set your own price. Ask for less and that is just what you will get.

Jimmy Carter (one of our worst presidents) never understood this. "Jimmy"? How presidential was that? *Walking* the inauguration route? He engendered no respect, and certainly no fear around the world — which had to spur on the Iranian hostage crisis.

Never lose your self-respect, nor be too familiar with yourself when you are alone. Come to hold yourself in awe . . .

— Baltasar Gracián

Men are swayed more by fear than by reverence.

— Aristotle

The secret of power is the knowledge that others are more cowardly than you are.
– Ludwig Boerne

Law 35: Master the art of timing

Never seem to be in a hurry – hurrying betrays a lack of control over yourself, and over time. Learn to stand back when the time is not yet ripe, and to strike fiercely when it has reached fruition.

Success depends not on ratiocination but on rhythm.
– Lieh Tzu

The ideal timing of something is something that is often out of your control, thus your only alternative is to learn to control yourself. Patience. When timing is right, strike. Boldness. With patience and boldness, you can accomplish anything.

Law 36: Disdain the things you cannot have – ignoring them is the best revenge

You choose to let things bother you. You can just as easily choose not to notice the irritating offender, to consider the matter trivial and unworthy of your interest. That is the powerful move. What you do not react to cannot drag you down in futile engagement.

What cannot be had or defeated is not worth your attention. What would be the point? The power to ignore is royal. The eagle does not swat at flies. You're rarely bigger than your enemies, and a puny opponent makes you look puny.

Law 37: Create compelling spectacles

The visual, on the other hand, short-circuits the labyrinth of words. It strikes with an emotional power and immediacy that leave no gaps for reflection and doubt. Like music, it leaps right over rational, reasonable thoughts.

Words put you on the defensive. If you have to explain yourself, your power is already in question. Words stir up arguments and divisions; images bring people together.

One of the most stunning openings Michael Jackson ever did was to explosively launch from beneath the stage into the air, land on two defiant feet, and just stand there. The crowd went *insane.*

Law 38: Think as you like, but behave like others

If you make a show of going against the times, flaunting your unconventional ideas and unorthodox ways, people will think that

> *you only want attention and that you look down upon them. They will find a way to punish you for making them feel inferior. It is far safer to blend in and nurture the common touch.*
>
> *Find a way to express your ideas subtly for those who understand you. Laying your pearls before swine will only bring you trouble.*

While there is truth and even wisdom in this, never take things too far in the common direction. Most of the world's way is sheer madness. The trick is to do your own thing, without rubbing it in too many faces.

> *The man who comes into the world with the notion that he is really going to instruct it in matters of the highest importance, may thank his stars if he escapes with a whole skin.*
>
> — Arthur Schopenhauer

If you can find a way to disguise your idea while insinuating them at the same time, your ideas will be more successful. Work within, as much as your conscience allows, the common protocol — if only so as not to needlessly offend. Sacrifice some trifles in order for the main goal to be swallowed.

Law 40: Despise the free lunch

What is offered for free is dangerous – it usually involves either a trick or a hidden obligation. What has worth is worth paying for. By paying your own way you stay clear of gratitude, guilt, and deceit. It is often wise to pay the full price – there is no cutting corners with excellence. Be lavish with your money and keep it circulating, for generosity is a sign and a magnet for power.

Law 41: Avoid stepping into a great man's shoes

What happens first always appears better and more original than what comes after. If you succeed a great man or have a famous parent, you will have to accomplish double their achievements to outshine them.

Unless you can outdo your father, don't go into his line of work. Just focus on outdoing yourself in your own game.

Law 43: Work on the hearts and minds of others

Emotions rule, not reason. When in despair, people crave relief.

Law 44: Disarm and infuriate with the mirror effect

When you mirror your enemies, doing exactly as they do, they cannot figure out your strategy. The Mirror Effect mocks and

> *humiliates them, making them overreact. By holding up a mirror to their psyches, you seduce them with the illusion that you share their values; by holding up a mirror to their actions, you teach them a lesson. Few can resist the power of the Mirror Effect.*

There are four main Mirror Effects: neutralizing, narcissus, moral, and hallucinatory. This law is easily misused and unethical, so always monitor your motives and actions.

Law 45: Preach the need for change, but never reform too much at once

> *Too much innovation is traumatic, and will lead to revolt. If you are new to a position of power, or an outsider trying to build a power base, make a show of respecting the old way of doing things. If change is necessary, make it feel like a gentle improvement on the past.*

> *It must be considered that there is nothing more difficult to carry out, nor more doubtful of success, nor more dangerous to handle, than to initiate a new order of things.*
>
> — Machiavelli

> *A new scientific truth does not triumph by convincing its opponents and making them see the light, but rather because its opponents eventually die, and a new generation grows up that is familiar with it.*
>
> — physicist Max Planck

Law 46: Never appear too perfect

> *Appearing better than others is always dangerous, but most dangerous of all is to appear to have no faults or weaknesses. Envy creates silent enemies. It is smart to occasionally display defects, and admit to harmless vices, in order to deflect envy and appear more human and approachable. Only gods and the dead can seem perfect with impunity.*
>
> *Once envy eats away at someone, everything you do only makes it grow, and day by day it festers inside him. Eventually he will attack.*

> *Success makes enemies. Be unsuccessful to have friends.*
>
> — *American Gangster*

> *Envy is the tax which all distinction must pay.*
>
> — Thoreau

> *Admiration is happy self-surrender; envy is unhappy self-assertion.*
>
> — Søren Kierkegaard

Of all the disorders of the soul, envy is the only one no one confesses to.
– Plutarch, 46-120 A.D.

One clever way to avoid envy of your power is to seem resistant in assuming that power. George Washington was a prime example.

Law 47: In victory, learn when to stop

If you quit while you're ahead, it's not quitting.
– American Gangster

Learn not to let success go to your head. I've read of countless downfalls by people having given in to the temptation of "just one more time". Don't be greedy. "*Fly it all the way to the chocks!*"

Also, be very wary just before you cross your finish line, as it is easy to relax too soon and stumble. The race is not won until it is *won*.

The greatest danger occurs at the moment of victory.
– Napoleon

Law 48: Assume formlessness

By taking shape, by having a visible plan, you open yourself to attack. Instead of taking a form for your enemy to grasp, keep yourself adaptable and on the move. Accept the fact that nothing is certain and no law is fixed. The best way to protect yourself is to be as fluid and formless as water; don't bet on stability or lasting order. Everything changes.

The first psychological requirement of formlessness is to train yourself to take nothing personally. Never show any defensiveness. When you act defensive, you show your emotions, revealing a clear form. Your opponents will realize they have hit a nerve, an Achilles' heel. And they will hit it again and again. So train yourself to take nothing personally. Never let anyone get your back up. Be like a slippery ball that cannot be held: Let no one know what gets to you, or where your weaknesses lie. Make your face a formless mask and you will infuriate and disorient your scheming colleagues and opponents.

The need for formlessness becomes greater the older we get, as we grow more likely to become set in our ways and assume too rigid a form. We become predictable, always the first sign of decrepitude.

When you want to fight us, we don't let you and you can't find us. But when we want to fight you, we make sure that you can't get away and we hit you squarely . . . and wipe you out . . . . The

enemy advances, we retreat; the enemy camps, we harass; the enemy tires, we attack; the enemy retreats, we pursue.
— Mao Tse-tung

UNETHICAL POWER STRATEGIES

Power will lead to increases in intensity and frequency of lying. (KWR note: Power rewards dishonesty with pleasure.)
— Columbia Professor Dana Carney, concluding an experiment on power and deception

Keep Hobbes in mind as you reflect, power is never where it seems to be.
— John Taylor Gatto, *Weapons of Mass Instruction*

Of Greene's 48 Laws of Power, about 20% seem to me much more appropriate for the corporate schemer, political hack, and sociopath. I review them to warn you of their use by others on you. Forewarned is forearmed.

. . . *so be ye wise as serpents and innocent as doves.*
— Jesus, in Matthew 10:16

Law 7: Get others to do the work for you, but always take the credit

The clever user of people will never do for themselves what others can do for them. Thus, they seem to have superhuman aura of efficiency and speed.

Law 11: Learn to keep people dependent on you

The more you depend on others, the less free you are. The users will try to create dependence, training you that you can't do without them. Nobody is irreplaceable or indispensable.

Law 12: Use selective honesty and generosity to disarm

If you already suspect or know somebody to be deceptive, never be taken in by some sudden honesty or kindness. This is a ruse to eliminate your suspicions. I had a sociopath "friend" who was paradoxically very tight with his things, yet astonishingly generous with new people. I later understood that it was merely a clever scheme to acquire a false impression as helpful. Distraction is the essence of deception, and a deceptive first impression lasts long. He first gave so that he could later take. It worked well on me the last time, when he lent me his truck to make an out-of-state trip so that he could leisurely go through my belongings and steal many valuables.

> *Everything turns gray when I don't have at least one mark on the horizon. Life then seems empty and depressing. I cannot understand honest men. They lead desperate lives, full of boredom.*
>
> — Count Victor Lustig, infamous con artist

A common sociopathic ploy is to offer up some painful admission (which is usually a lie, anyway) in the hopeful exchange for something juicy and useful from the victim. Don't fall for it.

Law 14: Pose as a friend, work as a spy

Be wary how much you reveal to friends, especially new ones. Become aware of conversational probing through indirect questions. Beware being tempted into acts of loyalty and honesty, as they may be a ruse to understand your "software".

Law 20: Do not commit to anyone

Those who champion their independence over all else can never be loyal to a friend or to a worthy cause. They are always looking out for *Numero Uno*.

Law 27: Play on people's need to believe to create a cultlike following

Beware of human focal points in new faiths, leaders who emphasize enthusiasm over rationality with vague promises. When you can discern rituals and sacrifices, the group takes on the smell of a cult. Quietly disengage.

Law 39: Stir up waters to catch fish

> *Petulance is not power, it is a sign of helplessness. People may temporarily be cowed by your tantrums, but in the end they lose respect for you. They also realize they can easily undermine a person with so little self-control.*
>
> *In the face of a hot-headed enemy, finally, an excellent response is no response. Follow the Talleyrand tactic: Nothing is as infuriating as a man who keeps his cool while others are losing theirs. If it will work to your advantage to unsettle people, affect the aristocratic, bored pose, neither mocking nor triumphant but simply indifferent. This will light their fuse.*

When you see somebody constantly needling folks, while remaining calm himself, you've found a troll. He is trying to foment tantrums in others, which creates doubts about their power.

> *Anger or hatred should never be shown otherwise than in what you do; and feelings will be all the more effective in action, in so far as you avoid the exhibition of them in any other way. It is only the cold-blooded animals whose bite is poisonous.*
>
> – Arthur Schopenhauer

On my Free State Wyoming forum I banished certain members who constantly stirred up dissension, before they became the eye of a whirlpool. Keep the weeds clipped short.

Law 42: Strike the shepherd and the sheep will scatter

People are followers, and always searching for a shepherd. Thus, their shepherd is the weak link.

I formed www.freestatewyoming.org (as a decentralized relocation catalyst) to not need a shepherd, as I want the FSW idea to continue on even without me if necessary.

In short, there will never be any type of shepherd in the FSW. I set that toboggan in motion, and people are free to hop aboard. There is no engine, and very little steering. Gravity and original direction alone will suffice. There is no real shepherd to strike.

RECOMMENDED MOVIES

the power of remaining true to conscience	*Man for All Seasons*
how to lose your soul, one gray moment at a time	*The Good Shepherd*
the awakening of conscience amongst great evil	*Schindler's List*
integrity in the face of authority figures	*Compliance*
behind the scenes of geo-political evil	*Manchurian Candidate*
hope, conviction, patience, planning, DIY justice	*Shawshank's Redemption*
a gray soul awakens to color, and begins to do right	*The Lives of Others*

16

LEADING

Discernment is the ability to find the root of the matter, and it relies on intuition as well as rational thought.
— John C. Maxwell, The 21 Indispensable Qualities of a Leader

A leader is a dealer in hope.
— Napoleon

The most simple definition I've heard is that a leader is somebody who has followers. Nearly everybody is a leader to some follower, and nearly everyone follows some leader. Even if you are still young, you probably have some followers (friends, younger siblings, your dog). Learn early how to well lead!

leaders know themselves

No man is fit to command another that cannot command himself.
— Emerson

Leaders fully comprehend their own strengths and limitations. They do not follow their weaknesses.

a boss is not necessarily a leader

The boss drives his men; the leader coaches them.
The boss depends upon authority; the leader on good will.
The boss inspires fear; the leader inspires enthusiasm.
The boss says "I"; the leader "we".
The boss fixes the blame; the leader fixes the breakdown.
The boss says "go"; the leader says "let's go!"
— H. Gordon Selfridge, merchant

A true leader hardly ever must command. He opines. He suggests. A raised eyebrow is as powerful as a shout. He will:

delegate clearly, with defined expectations and objectives
welcome opinions and feedback
trust others to work out their problems; don't micro-manage
build confidence through sincere praise and enthusiasm (catch them doing something right)

a leader steps up when needed

Leadership is action, not position.
— Donald H. McGannon

You could find yourself unexpectedly in a situation requiring instant leadership, such as a traffic accident, lethal emergency, family crisis, or natural disaster. If people seem to be milling around in confusion or despair, and you can help through your leadership, step right up! Do not deprive others of your gift, as only you may be the right Man at the right time at the right place.

leaders are self-confident people

A man who wants to lead the orchestra must turn his back on the crowd.
— James Crook

A leader trusts his own judgment over that of the masses, and he is not afraid to strike out on his own. Public opinion means little to him when he knows that he is right.

Balthasar Gracian on leadership

Let your Behaviour be Fine and Noble.
A great man ought not to be little in his behaviour. He ought never to pry too minutely into things, least of all in unpleasant matters. For though it is important to know all, it is not necessary to know all about all. One ought to act in such cases with the generosity of a gentleman, conduct worthy of a gallant man. To overlook forms a large part of the work of ruling. Most things must be left unnoticed among relatives and friends, and even among enemies. All superfluity is annoying, especially in things that annoy. To keep hovering around the object of your annoyance is a kind of mania.

The highest should have the door open for friendship; it may prove the gate of help. A friend must be free to advise, and even to upbraid, without feeling embarrassed.

A bad manner spoils everything, even reason and justice; a good one supplies everything, gilds a No, sweetens truth, and adds a touch of beauty to old age itself. The how plays a large part in affairs, a good manner steals into the affections. Fine behaviour is a joy in life, and a pleasant expression helps out of a difficulty in a remarkable way.

Common in Nothing.

First, not in taste. O great and wise, to be ill at ease when your deeds please the mob! The excesses of popular applause never satisfy the sensible. Some there are such chameleons of popularity that they find enjoyment not in the sweet savours of Apollo but in the breath of the mob. Secondly, not in intelligence. Take no pleasure in the wonder of the mob, for ignorance never gets beyond wonder. While vulgar folly wonders wisdom watches for the trick.

Distinction in Speech and Action.

By this you gain a position in many places and carry esteem beforehand. It shows itself in everything, in talk, in look, even in gait. It is a great victory to conquer men's hearts: it does not arise from any foolish presumption or pompous talk, but in a becoming tone of authority born of superior talent combined with true merit.

Prize Intensity more than Extent.

Excellence resides in quality not in quantity. The best is always few and rare: much lowers value. Even among men giants are commonly the real dwarfs.

One ought not to give way in everything nor to everybody.

To know how to refuse is therefore as important as to know how to consent. This is especially the case with men of position. All depends on the how. Some men's No is thought more of than the Yes of others: for a gilded No is more satisfactory than a dry Yes. There are some who always have No on their lips, whereby they make everything distasteful. No always comes first with them, and when sometimes they give way after all, it does them no good on account of the unpleasing herald. Your refusal need not be point-blank: let the disappointment come by degrees. Nor let the refusal be final; that would be to destroy dependence; let some spice of hope remain to soften the rejection.

Get used to the Failings of your Familiars,

as you do to ugly faces. It is indispensable if they depend on us, or we on them. There are wretched characters with whom one cannot live, nor yet without them. Therefore clever folk get used to them, as to ugly faces, so that they are not obliged to do so suddenly under the pressure of necessity. At first they arouse disgust, but gradually they lose this influence, and reflection provides for disgust or puts up with it.

Never be put out.

'Tis a great aim of prudence never to be embarrassed. It is the sign of a real man, of a noble heart, for magnanimity is not easily put out. The passions are the humours of the soul, and every excess in them weakens prudence; if they overflow through the mouth, the reputation will be in danger. Let a man therefore be so much and so great a master over himself that neither in the most fortunate nor in the most adverse circumstances can anything cause his reputation injury by disturbing his selfpossession, but rather enhance it by showing his superiority.

Do not parade your Position.

To outshine in dignity is more offensive than in personal attractions. To pose as a personage is to be hated: envy is surely enough. The more you seek esteem the less you obtain it, for it depends on the opinion of others. You cannot take it, but must earn and receive it from others.

Adapt Yourself to your Company.

There is no need to show your ability before every one. Employ no more force than is necessary. Let there be no unnecessary expenditure either of knowledge or of power.

Don't be a Bore.

The man of one business or of one topic is apt to be heavy. Brevity flatters and does better business; it gains by courtesy what it loses by curtness. Good things, when short, are twice as good. The quintessence of the matter is more effective than a whole farrago of details.

Allow Yourself some venial Fault.

Some such carelessness is often the greatest recommendation of talent. For envy exercises ostracism, most envenomed when most polite, It counts it to perfection as a failing that it has no faults; for being perfect in all it condemns it in all. It becomes an Argus, all eyes for imperfection: 'tis its only consolation. Blame is like the lightning; it hits the highest. Let Homer nod now and then and affect some negligence in valour or in intellect—not in prudence—so as to disarm malevolence, or at least to prevent its bursting with its own venom. You thus leave your cloak on the horns of Envy in order to save your immortal parts.

The Art of letting Things alone.

The more so the wilder the waves of public or of private life. There are hurricanes in human affairs, tempests of passion, when it is wise to retire to a harbour and ride at anchor. Remedies often make diseases worse: in such cases one has to leave them to their natural course and the moral suasion of time. It takes a wise doctor to know when not to prescribe, and at times the greater skill consists in not applying remedies. The proper way to still the storms of the vulgar is to hold your hand and let them calm down of themselves. To give way now is to conquer by and by. A fountain gets muddy with but little stirring up, and does not get clear by our meddling with it but by our leaving it alone. The best remedy for disturbances is to let them run their course, for so they quiet down.

Do and be seen Doing.

Things do not pass for what they are but for what they seem. To be of use and to know how to show yourself of use, is to be twice as useful. What is not seen is as if it was not. Even the Right does not receive proper consideration if it does not seem right.

The more pains you take with a thing, the more should you conceal them, so that it may appear to arise spontaneously from your own natural character.

Create a Feeling of Dependence.

When dependence disappears, good behaviour goes with it as well as respect. Let it be one of the chief lessons of experience to keep hope alive without entirely satisfying it,

Keep Matters for a Time in Suspense.

Admiration at their novelty heightens the value of your achievements, It is both useless and insipid to play with the cards on the table. If you do not declare yourself immediately, you arouse expectation, especially when the importance of your position makes you the object of general attention. Mix a little mystery with everything, and the very mystery arouses veneration. And when you explain, be not too explicit, just as you do not expose your inmost thoughts in ordinary intercourse. Cautious silence is the holy of holies of worldly wisdom. A resolution declared is never highly thought of; it only leaves room for criticism. And if it happens to fail, you are doubly unfortunate. Besides you imitate the Divine way when you cause men to wonder and watch.

Renew your Brilliance.

'Tis the privilege of the Phoenix. Ability is wont to grow old, and with it fame. The staleness of custom weakens admiration, and a mediocrity that's new often eclipses the highest excellence grown old. Try therefore to be born again in valour, in genius, in fortune, in all. Display startling novelties, rise afresh like the sun every day. Change too the scene on which you shine, so that your

loss may be felt in the old scenes of your triumph, while the novelty of your powers wins you applause in the new.

Do not wait till you are a Sinking Sun.
'Tis a maxim of the wise to leave things before things leave them. One should be able to snatch a triumph at the end, just as the sun even at its brightest often retires behind a cloud so as not to be seen sinking, and to leave in doubt whether he has sunk or no. Wisely withdraw from the chance of mishaps, lest you have to do so from the reality. Do not wait till they turn you the cold shoulder and carry you to the grave, alive in feeling but dead in esteem. Wise trainers put racers to grass before they arouse derision by falling on the course. A beauty should break her mirror early, lest she do so later with open eyes.

knowing when to dump problem people

Keeping a bad employee destroys your credibility with your other employees. Bad behavior then spreads like a cancer because there are no visible consequences.

— Larry Winget, *Shut Up, Stop Whining, Get A Life!*

Do not make Mistakes about Character.
That is the worst and yet easiest error. Better be cheated in the price than in the quality of goods. In dealing with men, more than with other things, it is necessary to look within. To know men is different from knowing things. It is profound philosophy to sound the depths of feeling and distinguish traits of character. Men must be studied as deeply as books.

— Balthasar Gracian

Men are basically smart or dumb and lazy or ambitious:
The dumb and ambitious ones are dangerous and I get rid of them.
The dumb and lazy ones I give mundane duties.
The smart ambitious ones I put on my staff.
The smart and lazy ones I make my commanders.

— Generalfeldmarschal Erwin Rommel

leaders are wise in handling people

In all Things keep Something in Reserve.
'Tis a sure means of keeping up your importance. A man should not employ all his capacity and power at once and on every occasion. Even in knowledge there should be a rearguard, so that your resources are doubled.

— Balthasar Gracian

Throw Straws in the Air,

to find how things will be received, especially those whose reception or success is doubtful. One can thus be assured of its turning out well, and an opportunity is afforded for going on in earnest or withdrawing entirely. By trying men's intentions in this way, the wise man knows on what ground he stands. This is the great rule of foresight in asking, in desiring, and in ruling.

— Balthasar Gracian

Double your Resources.
You thereby double your life. One must not depend on one thing or trust to only one resource, however pre-eminent. Everything should be kept double, especially the causes of success, of favour, or of esteem. The moon's mutability transcends everything and gives a limit to all existence, especially of things dependent on human will, the most brittle of all things. To guard against this inconstancy should be the sage's care, and for this the chief rule of life is to keep a double store of good and useful qualities. Thus as Nature gives us in duplicate the most important of our limbs and those most exposed to risk, so Art should deal with the qualities on which we depend for success.

— Balthasar Gracian

Wage War Honourably.
You may be obliged to wage war, but not to use poisoned arrows. Every one must needs act as he is, not as others would make him to be. Gallantry in the battle of life wins all men's praise: one should fight so as to conquer, not alone by force but by the way it is used. A mean victory brings no glory, but rather disgrace. Honour always has the upper hand. An honourable man never uses forbidden weapons, such as using a friendship that's ended for the purposes of a hatred just begun: a confidence must never be used for a vengeance. The slightest taint of treason tarnishes the good name. In men of honour the smallest trace of meanness repels: the noble and the ignoble should be miles apart. Be able to boast that if gallantry, generosity, and fidelity were lost in the world men would be able to find them again in your own breast.

— Balthasar Gracian

Nothing motivates a man more than to see his boss putting in an honest day's work.

— Wain

LEADERSHIP TECHNIQUES

In Joel Skousen's *The Secure Home* he writes about lifestyle changes under self-sufficiency, including how to match the correct leadership technique with your people's receptiveness and the situation. He wisely urges leaders to "*make sure peace and good judgment are always present*" and to "*remember to be perceptive of what kind of innate spirit each person has.*"

permissive leadership

noncritical situations; just nice to have it done your way
you lack authority over that person
no consequences for their refusal

leadership by active example

a high form of leadership, which takes much time and effort

persuasive leadership

when change is very important, but freedom to fail is also
can include increasing pressure to achieve compliance

authoritarian leadership

when time is of the essence, with no room for persuasion
when rebellion or malice requires threat of physical force

A FINE EXAMPLE

On the back cover of this book is a 1945 color photo of a WWII fighter squadron commander, Major Robin Olds. He was 22 at the time, and already a leader of men in aerial combat — the quintessential example of how far a quality young man can go (vs. Obama's PajamaBoy). The more I learn of Gen. Olds, the more correct my choice seems to be.

At Oshkosh 2014 I had a chance to meet his daughter Christina, who'd helped her ailing dad finish his memoirs *Fighter Pilot*. I gave her a copy of Volume 1 *Modules for Manhood*, and she wrote, "*Wow — you have done Robin proud! Many thanks for your good work.*"

The below passage is from when he took over the 8th Tactical Fighter Wing during the Vietnam War. Here was his opening speech as commanding officer:

> *My name is Olds and I'm your new boss. I've been around the air force a little while and I'm really glad to be here. You guys know a lot I don't know and I'm here to learn from you. I'll be flying as your wingman for a couple of weeks. You are going to teach me, but you'd better teach me good and you'd better teach me fast because I'm going to fly* [as a subordinate until I think I am qualified to command as] *Lead. When you get me ready, I'll be Mission Commander, and we'll get it done together. Now, you just stay ahead of me because as long as you know more than I do, we are going to get along just fine. I will listen to you and learn from you, but soon I'm gonna be better than all of you, and when I know more about your job than you do, look out.*

Now *that* is the way to lead new men! Even though was already a double fighter ace with 12 kills in WWII, he nonetheless required himself to earn their respect on their own turf. He obeyed lieutenants before he led them as their colonel.

> *They taught me well, both on the ground and in the air. I was out front in less than two weeks.*
>
> *This method of taking over a new command was deeply ingrained in me. My father had shown me how to be a leader by his own example. It was reinforced by other great commanders who had earned my respect, leaders like Hub Zemke, Tooey Spaatz, Jimmy Doolittle, and many more. They all connected with their troops on a personal level and learned everything they could about every part of their organization.*
>
> *Here's what I'd learned over the years. Know the mission, what is expected of you and your people. Get to know those people, their attitudes and expectations. Visit all the shops and sections. Ask questions. Don't be shy. Learn what each does, how the parts fit into the whole. Find out what supplies and equipment are lacking, what the workers need. To whom does each shop chief report? Does that officer really know the people under him, is he aware of their needs, their training? Does that NCO supervise or just make out reports without checking facts? Remember, those reports eventually come back to you. Don't try to bullshit the troops, but make sure they know the buck stops with you, and you'll shoulder the blame when things go wrong. Correct without revenge or anger. Recognize accomplishment. Reward accordingly. Foster spirit through self-pride, not slogans, and never at the expense of another unit. It won't take long, but only your genuine interest and concern, plus follow-up on your promises, will earn you respect. Out of that you gain loyalty and obedience. Your outfit will be a standout. But for God's sake, don't ever try to be popular! That weakens your position, makes you vulnerable. Don't have favorites. That breeds resentment.*

Respect the talents of your people. Have the courage to delegate responsibility and give the authority to go with it. Again, make clear to your troops you are the one who'll take the heat.

— Robin Olds, *Fighter Pilot*

RECOMMENDED MOVIES

leadership, friendship, determination, war at sea, duty	*Master and Commander*
grit, determination, hard work, thick skin	*The Iron Lady*
the late awakening of a man/husband/father	*Courageous*
leadership, courage	*Das Boot*
spontaneous, combustible leadership	*Spartacus*
defending family and country	*The Patriot*
sheer heroism	*Braveheart*
earning what others have sacrificed for you	*Saving Private Ryan*
dark and gritty story about awakened manhood	*Fight Club*

17

WORKING & SUCCESS

I never knew an early rising, hard working, prudent man, careful of his earning and strictly honest, who complained of bad luck. A good character, good habits and iron industry are impregnable to the assaults of all luck that fools ever dreamed of.
— Joseph Addison

We work to become, not to acquire.
— Elbert Hubbard

Work keeps us from three great evils: boredom, vice, and need.
— Voltaire

HOW TO BECOME POOR

The easiest thing in the world to become, is poor. Most people on this planet, and very many even here in America, are born poor. It is the human default, and the process is enthusiastically replicated.

The poor keep getting poorer because they keep doing whatever it was that made them poor in the first place. Ditto for the rich.

There is nothing at all unexpected or unforeseen about the behavior that's responsible for most of the poverty in this country. If you ignore your education, fail to develop a work ethic, do drugs, get pregnant before you're out of high school or before you can afford to raise a child, become a petty criminal, join a gang, hang with what you obviously know to be a wrong crowd, become a drinker, or generally comport yourself like a self-loathing slob, guess what? You're probably not going to make one hell of a lot of money! You're going to end up poor, with nothing to do but work at that occasional minimum-wage job you may find while spending the rest of your time complaining that the government isn't doing enough for you.

Your situation has nothing to do with luck or fortune. You did this to yourself. You're suffering the obvious and easily predictable result of your own failures and laziness. And things aren't going to get any better until you stop clinging to that idea that you're "less fortunate" and start looking in the mirror for the source of your problems.

There's just one little bitty problem with the phrase "income redistribution," though. Income, you see, isn't distributed in the first place. It's earned.

Barring some sort of mental or physical disaster, the people living in what we describe as poverty in this country are there because of the sum total of the decisions and choices they made during their lives up to this point. Poverty isn't a condition; it's a behavioral disorder at best, and a mental disease at worst.

— Neal Boortz, *Somebody's Gotta Say It*

If you are a grown adult in America without some drastic physical or mental handicap, yet you are poor: it is your own damned fault.

Few people will turn to themselves to take responsibility for their results until they have exhausted all opportunities to blame someone else.

Stop expecting the world to rescue you. The Lone Ranger isn't coming. Your life is your fault. You created it. Life does not just happen to you; you happen to life. So you got dealt a crummy hand. It happens. Pick up the cards, shuffle them, and deal yourself a new hand. If your life sucks it's because you suck. It's not because conditions suck. It's you.

Three main reasons people are not successful:

1. *You're stupid.*
2. *You're lazy.*
3. *You don't give a damn.*

Reasons are real. Excuses are not real. Yes, they exist, but they are not real in the sense that they are keeping you from doing well. They are only excuses that give you a way to keep from accepting responsibility.

How can you look your family in the eye and admit to them you are able to provide a better life for them but won't because you don't love them enough to read a book, take a class, get up a little earlier, turn off the TV a little quicker, or work a little harder or longer? If you are mentally and physically able to be better than you are, and to do better than you do, and you don't do it — . . . you don't care enough about yourself and your family to do so.

You have created everything that has happened in your life, both the good and the bad. You created your situation. It was easy. All you did was think, speak, and do. You never really have a money problem, a relationship problem, a business problem, or a health problem. You only have a problem with your thinking, your words, and your actions. And when you straighten out your thoughts, words, and actions, everything will begin to turn around for you.

The life you want comes at a price. Everything comes at a price. Nothing is free. No matter what it is in life you choose, there will be a price tag attached.

Want to be fit, trim, and healthy? The price tag is decreased calories and increased exercise. In other words, you don't get fit, trim, and healthy. You give up the things that are making you fat.

Want to be rich? You either have to work harder, longer, or smarter – probably all three. You don't just get rich. You have to _give up_ the things that are keeping you broke.

Stop doing the things you don't enjoy doing.

Your results are your own fault.

Being healthy is a choice.

Happiness comes only when you rise above the approval of others.

Everything in life gets better when you get better, and nothing gets better until you get better.

Fun should be a way of life, not something you have from time to time.

Everything in life is a lesson. Refusing to learn the lesson means that it will be repeated until the lesson is learned.

– Larry Winget, *Shut Up, Stop Whining, Get A Life!*

Learning to fly an airplane is the perfect example of sequential lessons. You cannot go to D unless you have learned ABC. Then, if D stumps you, it must be retaught until you finally get it, and then can move on to E. There are no shortcuts, and you cannot skip any of the core modules of pilot training. You may be brilliant at everything except for one thing (for most students, it's crosswind landings), but until you sufficiently master that one thing they will not pass you as a Private Pilot. A university degree is another example of something requiring sequential and total completion of tasks. Just one missing class will prevent graduation.

Now, Life is exactly the same way, but not so obviously because it is more of a constant journey of learning and self-improvement without the "I did it!" milestones inherent to passing a course or becoming a licensed Private Pilot. Meaning, too many people accomplish ABCDE, stop at F, and thus stall out in Life as some $8/hour unskilled worker. Their unpassed lesson F returns to them over and over, but they see it as "unfair" pain and suffering.

On average, people spend about 100 hours per year reading, but nearly 2,000 hours per year watching TV. (By the way 2,000 hours/year is 40 hours/week, and thus equal to a second full-time job! So, I call B.S. on TV-watchers who whine that they haven't time to earn more money or learn a new skill.)

> *The crucial truths of the current age may be these: First, people will watch any television rather than no television. Second, sooner or later they will begin to imitate what they see on the screen. Third, while you can't fool all of the people all of the time, you can fool enough of them enough of the time, especially if you are a lot smarter than they are, and do it patiently, calculatedly, over time, like water eroding stone. And that is all it takes. Finally, television is scalable: Swathing the earth in Baywatch is not much harder than covering a state.*
>
> — Fred Reed,

Larry Winget recommends not associating with people who don't read, and are on the path to stupidity — and I agree!

> *There are no secrets* [to success]. *None. There is no new information. What it took to be successful a thousand years ago is exactly what it takes to be successful today.*
>
> — Larry Winget, *Shut Up, Stop Whining, Get A Life!*

Now, if you change what you do, you can change what you have. I will show you how, right now, in this chapter.

> *As the mother of Ben* [Carson, M.D., a world reknowned pediatric brain surgeon] *and his brother, Curtis* [a successful engineer], *I had a lot of challenges. Being one of twenty-four children, getting married at age thirteen, and later having to get a divorce after finding out my husband was a bigamist were just a few of them. But God helped me every step of the way, even when I didn't notice.*
>
> *Fortunately, I could see what happens to people on welfare and decided I would try my best to make sure it would not happen to my boys.*
>
> *Remember this as you go through life. The person who has the most to do with what happens to you is you! You make the choices; you decide whether you're going to give up or ante up when the going gets tough. Ultimately, it's you who decides whether you will be a success or not . . .*
>
> — Sonya Carson, from *Gifted Hands*

Sonya Carson, a black housekeeper in wealthy white homes, studied her employers and learned vital lessons for success. What to think and how to behave. How to set goals and remain determined. She limited her sons to only three TV programs a week, and required them to read two books a week. Her son Ben read himself out of the bottom of the class, to the top in just two years. He took "lowly" jobs but did them so well that he always got a better one. During the economic recession of the early 1970s, when nobody else that he knew was getting hired, he went to a former employer who told him, "*Ben, for a guy like you, there's always a job.*" That is the mark of a winner. As Ben described it, "*If you're good, you'll be recognized.*"

ONLY 4 WAYS TO GET ANYTHING

1. make it yourself
2. buy or trade for it
3. accept it as a gift
4. steal it (directly, or indirectly in a political kleptocracy)

If you're going to buy or trade for what you want, you must have something *they* want. This brings us to the next crucial point:

WHY *ANYONE* PAYS YOU *ANYTHING*

Here comes a key lesson of my book. Ready? Here it is:

People act only from one motivation:

perceived self-interest

The key here is their *perception* of self-interest. It doesn't matter what *you* perceive, but what *they* do. Whether they are young or old, rich or poor, brilliant or stupid — you must be able to perceive another's self-interest as they do, not as you do. Find out what makes each person "tick". If you fully understand that people operate only on their *own* perceived self-interests, then you can do well in Life.

According to David Friedman's *The Machinery of Freedom*, perceived self-interest (or psychological "utility") has three components:

Fear/Force
Love/Affection
Trade (*quid pro quo* — this for that)

You pay outrageous taxes because of Fear.
Your Mom makes you dinner because of Love.
Your car was manufactured by strangers because of Trade.

Love and Trade are often intertwined. For example, while I don't often give away my books to friends (because gift books are often unread), I do sell to them at a steep discount. Love and Fear can be mixed, say, in the case of a child obeying his parents. (Trade and Fear do not mix.)

why you must "make money"

> *You can have anything you want in this life if you'll just help enough other people get what they want.*
> — Zig Ziglar

> *I love humans — you pay all my bills!*
> — comic Rick Overton, www.rickoverton.net

Most goals in Life are achieved not through Love or Fear, but through Trade. Yes, you can barter goods directly, but this is inefficient. In order to trade efficiently, you will need to acquire a medium of exchange. *Money.* **Money comes from other people**, who trade it to you only in exchange for perceived value (goods and services). Nobody ever got rich by helping themselves. Wealth comes from helping others achieve their goals (if they can compensate you, of course).

You must become a perceived high value to others. Without this, even through hard work you will have only menial jobs. If you want to earn more than you get, you must first become worth more than you are paid. Period. You must contribute high value to others before you receive great wealth in exchange. I believe that nearly everyone is capable of enriching others in some way. Author John T. Reed outlines the process:

First, identify your distinctive competence,
and match it with a market opportunity.

Then, go where your strengths are valued and rare,
and where your weaknesses are unimportant.

Finally, live beneath your means when younger,
and then only up to your means in middle-age.

All three steps are key, and you cannot skip or do poorly on any of them. I'd estimate that fewer than 10% of people apply these to their lives. In Larry Winget's book *Shut Up, Stop Whining, Get A Life!* he described a guy who in the summer goes door-to-door repainting curbside house numbers for $5. He makes enought to pay his tuition, room and board for the year at the University of Oklahoma.

work is *mandatory* — all must work

> *The only place where success comes before work is in the dictionary.*
>
> — Donald Kendall

Understand this from the outset: human beings were *designed* to work. While you may choose to work differently, or less often, or easier — you cannot ever *stop* working. Even if you still have money to survive, the cessation of work will kill you. I've learned this from a family member. He worked hard for over 40 years, with the goal of "*doing nothing*" in retirement. We all thought he was rather joking, but after a decade of literally doing *nothing*, we believe him now. He eats, reads, watches TV, and sleeps — period. Naturally, his body is shutting down from nonuse. He came down with adult-onset diabetes. (He is now too decrepit to even play golf, if that says anything.) His entire purpose in Life was evidently to "retire", which is just a glacial form of death.

The wise wealthy continue to work long after they stop needing additional income, because working remains vital to their mental, physical, and spiritual health. The wise retiree at least takes on a part-time job or charity service.

> *The highest reward for a man's toil is not what he gets for it but what he becomes by it.*
>
> — John Rushkin

> *The more we have to do, the more we are rested — the less we have to do, the more tired we are. Nothing rests a man so much as plenty to do.*
>
> — Bishop Quayle

> *Men need a forum in which to find their significance and make their contribution. That forum is work.*
>
> — Patrick Morley, *The Man In The Mirror*

> *We don't consider manual work as a curse, or a bitter necessity, not even as a means of making a living. We consider it as a high human function, as a basis of human life, the most dignified thing*

in the life of the human being, and which ought to be free, creative. Men ought to be proud of it.
— David Ben-Gurion

The sort of life which I had previous to this popular success was one that required endurance, a life of clawing and scratching, but it was a good life because it was the sort of life for which the human organism is created. I was not aware of how much vital energy had gone into this struggle until the struggle was removed. This was security at last. I sat down and looked about me and was suddenly very depressed.
— playwright Tennessee Williams, after he wrote *The Glass Menagerie* but before he wrote *A Streetcar Named Desire*

Show me a thoroughly satisfied man, and I will show you a failure.
— Thomas Edison

Work or die. You really have no other choice.

know yourself, and what work you will *love* doing

If you don't love your job, you will lose it to someone who does. You must not merely tolerate your job, else you'll lose it to somebody who loves it. Never stay in a job you hate, for life is just too short.
— John T. Reed

Since it is becoming easier for more and more people to actually make money doing what they love to do, your competition will get tougher and tougher. Passion shines through one's work product, and if you hate what you do it will be obvious. (Some 45% of Americans would change careers if they could!) So, what would you *love* to do?

Do your homework. Learn everything about your business <40.
Develop your own style. Learn what's comfortable for you <40.
Put your emotional life in order. Get rid of entanglements.
Know your weaknesses, dislikes, inabilities.
Focus on strengths.
Know your strengths, likes, abilities.
Plan for your retirement, and start saving now.
Forget about Social Security.
Establish a network.
Learn to delegate, pick the right people and trust them.
Learn when to shut up, keep quiet/look wise, and don't gossip.
Be loyal. Develop an unshakable reputation.
Keep your sense of humor. Nothing on Earth lasts forever.
— from Dec. 1987 *Reader's Digest*

it's soon a Winner-Take-All world in most professions

If you are in a profession that is about to go winner-take-all, you'd better be the winner, find a niche the winner can't serve, or find a whole new profession.

The Internet permits everybody with anything of value to offer, however narrowly focused it is by historic standards, to market their information worldwide inexpensively.

In the 21st Century, you will have to compete with the best people nationwide and worldwide in your field.

Millions of people who [in the 20th Century] *formerly competed with locals and made decent money will find they cannot compete with the world's best, especially when those competitors sell their products or services at cut rates* [through the Internet], *and will see a drop in income. They will be forced to shift to work that they love for two reasons:*

– *to be as competitive as possible*

– *to substitute, in part, satisfaction for income lost*

– John T. Reed

thinking is not always working

It is how you act, not what you think, that will determine your success. It is how you think, not what you do, that will determine your happiness.

– Michael Masterson, *Automatic Wealth*

I'm not knocking thinking as an occupation; it's what I do. But after some point, you have to translate thoughts and ideas into action and things. You cannot read your way to success, you must work your way to success. You cannot plow a field by turning it over in your mind.

Knowing is not enough, we must apply.
Willing is not enough, we must do.

– Goethe

"working" means *working*

The secret of success is to be like a duck – smooth and unruffled on top, but paddling furiously underneath.

– William H. Danforth

Effort is only effort when it begins to hurt.

– Ortega y Gasset

While there are smart ways of working, in the beginning there is no real shortcut to hard work. Later on, after you've achieved some success you won't have to work *as* hard, but please do understand now that the day you stop producing is the day you start dying.

Success isn't about passion. Success is about the combination of hard work and excellence. Yes, the combination of the two. Excellence isn't enough. I see people who are excellent at what they do but don't work hard enough to ever become successful. Hard work isn't enough either. There are people who work very hard but simply aren't any good at what they do.

Passion might qualify me to stand on the street corner and preach my message, but it wouldn't allow me to make a living. ***Excellence gets me paid. And years of hard work, study, and practice made me excellent.***

— Larry Winget, *Shut Up, Stop Whining, Get A Life!*

All successful people have the habit of doing the things failures don't like to do. They don't like doing them either necessarily. But their disliking is subordinated to the strength of their purpose.

— Albert E. Gray

Failures want pleasing methods, successes want pleasing results.

— Earl Nightingale

It takes twenty years to make an overnight success.

— Eddie Cantor

Nothing is particularly hard if you divide it into small jobs.

— Henry Ford

I know the price of success — dedication, hard work and an unremitting devotion to the things you want to see happen.

— Frank Lloyd Wright

work means *creating value*

My university degree was in International Finance. Basically, I was trained to manipulate money and manage investments. I did not choose this field, mainly because I came to realize that it produces little value. The repetitive sale of stocks and bonds merely trades value already created by others. Sure, stock traders expend much effort in their career, but if no *value* is created then can stock trading truly be called "work"? (Not all effort is actual work.) Now, funding a new business during start-up is one thing, but pure speculation and arbitrage do little to produce products or services of value.

Choose loss rather than shameful gains.

— Greek. Chilon Fr. 10. Diels

Those who earn $8/hour provide $8 worth of service (perceived value to others) over the span of one hour. Those who earn $80/hour provide $80 of service in the same hour. Both are working an hour, but one provides 10x the service, thus he receives 10x the reward. As Larry Winget commented:

> *Hard work makes you tired but it does not necessarily make you rich. Work that provides the most service to others makes you rich. Make a list of all the ways you can add value to the lives of others: your customers, your boss, your family, your friends, even strangers. Begin now to think of your job in terms of service instead of just putting in the hours. Start focusing on the service and how you can continually add more value to everyone you work with. Do this and you will be amazed at how much better you feel about yourself, your job, and the people you serve. Plus, more money will show up. Do more than you are paid to do. Soon you will be paid more for what you do.*

work means serving other people

> *You only get to keep and enjoy what you share and give away.*
>
> — Charlie "Tremendous" Jones

Even if you "work for yourself" in your own business, you cannot *pay* yourself. You cannot earn a living by meeting your *own* needs, but by meeting the needs of *others*. Ironically, your selfishness is served by serving others (who then take care of your needs).

> *The man is no fool who gives up what he can't keep to gain what he can't lose.*
>
> — Jim Elliot

working is honorable, and there is no shame in sweat

> *Nobody ever drowned in his own sweat.*
>
> — Ann Landers

> *Sweat is the cologne of accomplishment.*
>
> — Heywood Hale Broun

> *There has never yet been a man in our history who led a life of ease whose name is worth remembering.*
>
> *Far and away the best prize that life offers is the chance to work hard at work worth doing.*
>
> — Theodore Roosevelt

> *There's always work available for people willing to perform dirty, difficult or dangerous jobs. Since these terms are subjective only*

you can decide what they mean. Ideally, something others consider difficult is not difficult for you. Same goes for dirty or dangerous.
— www.mcgillespie.com, Terence Gillespie

Respect the burden, Madame, always respect the man with a burden.
— Napoleon, to a society lady who ordered workmen out of her way

don't ignore the details

Sometimes when I consider what tremendous consequence come from little things . . . I am tempted to think . . . there are no little things.
— Bruce Barton

For want of a nail the shoe was lost.
For want of a shoe the horse was lost.
For want of a horse the knight was lost.
For want of a knight the battle was lost.
For want of a battle the kingdom was lost.
And all for the want of a horseshoe nail.

For want of a nail the shoe was lost,
for want of a shoe the horse was lost,
for want of a horse the knight was lost,
for want of a knight the battle was lost.
So it was a kingdom was lost — all for want of a nail.

be grateful for what you *do* have!

The first step toward discarding a scarcity mentality involves giving thanks for everything that you are and everything that you have.
— Dr. Wayne Dyer

When we hear somebody complaining that he has not enough, we may know that he has not expressed enough appreciation for what he already has.
— Lowell Fillmore

Don't hate the rich. No poor man ever gave you a job.

always do *quality* work — surprise them with a bit extra

There is nothing so fatal to character as half-finished tasks.
— David Lloyd George

The reward of a thing well done is to have done it.
— Emerson

It takes less time to do a thing right than it does to explain why you did it wrong.

– Perry Tanksley

Opportunity is missed by most people because it is dressed in overalls, and looks like work.

– Thomas Edison

Responsible people never protest, "That's not my job." They're willing to do whatever it takes to complete the work needed by the organization. If you want to succeed, be willing to put the organization ahead of your agenda.

– John C. Maxwell, *The 21 Indispensible Qualities of a Leader*

Mediocrity – You can't promote it – You can't fire it – And you can't win with it.

– Grant G. Gard, *Don't Just Talk About It – Do It!*

According to a brilliant jazz musician, the secret to virtuosity is "*never practicing a mistake*". Be a virtuoso at whatever you do.

How many times can you remember being surprised by receiving *more* than what you expected? Pretty rare, isn't it? One time still sticks in mind, when I ordered a replica leather holster for my WWI Colt .45 revolver. (An authentic period holster in fine condition was $200+, and I didn't want to spend that.) The replica holster was only $40, and from the ad I surmised that it was made overseas, so I didn't hope for too much. When it arrived, I was shocked at its superb quality. The leather was thick, the color just right, the stamping perfect, the stitching excellent. A bargain at twice the price!

In whatever your job or business, you've lots of competition. Go the extra mile, because so few others do. Give your customer a real spit and polish, and throw in a bit extra. They'll never forget it.

take bigger and bigger jobs

You can pretty accurately judge a man by whether he would ask for a light burden or a strong back if he were given the choice.

– Perry Tanksley

If what you did yesterday still looks big to you, you haven't done much today.

– John C. Maxwell, *The 21 Indispensable Qualities of a Leader*

A man who had been bypassed for promotion went to the president and complained, saying that he had fifteen years of experience with the firm. The president answered him, "*Not so. You have had one year of experience — fifteen times.*"

Don't take a lesser career or position because you lack self-esteem to go after what you really want and are best suited for. Increase yourself to match your dreams — don't reduce your dreams to equal your current human volume.

your work is up to *you*

Nothing is really work unless you would rather be doing something else.
— Sir James M. Barrie

Don't do what you sincerely don't want to do.
— Ernest Hemingway

You have much more choice in your work than you imagine. Average intelligence coupled with a strong work ethic means that you can acquire the skills for 95% of all jobs out there. If you don't like your current work, I'll show you how to change it.

The world has never been in such a whirlwind of change as it is now. You must constantly perceive correctly the reality around you, and adapt yourself to it. You should probably seriously question going to college to learn a single life-long profession.

Author John C. Maxwell's theory of focus:

focus 70% on Strengths
focus 25% on New Things
focus 5% on Weakness

❶ shift to strengths
(list 3-4 things you do well, and dedicate 70% of time)
❷ staff your weaknesses (forget about "doing it all")
❸ create an edge (keep honing your strengths)

don't forget to play . . . afterwards

When you play, play hard; when you work, don't play at all.
— Theodore Roosevelt

Never get so busy making a living that you forget to make a life.
— author unknown

Making money early on should not be your highest goal. Get to know yourself, improve yourself, grow, travel to expand your experience/horizons/language skills, and increase your skillset. If you don't do it early, you may not have time for it later. If you start out as a workaholic, you may never reach a balanced life.

8 Habits of Highly Successful Wealth Builders

From Michael Masterson of *Automatic Wealth*:

They work hard.
They are good at what they do.
They have multiple streams of income.
They live in (relatively) inexpensive homes.
They are moderate in their spending.
They are extraordinary in their saving.
They pay themselves first.
They count their money.

8 Habits of Highly *NON*successful Wealth Builders

See if you recognize in yourself the converses:

They don't work hard.
They are poor or mediocre at what they do.
They have only one stream of income.
They live in a house more expensive than they deserve.
They are extravagant in their spending.
They don't save.
They pay themselves last.
They never count their money.

Look, these things have been written before, many times by many people. **None of this wisdom is any secret.**

Allen's *Multiple Streams of Income*, Masterson's Automatic Wealth, Covey's *7 Habits*, etc. — all of them I found at my local thrift store for 50 cents each. Even at the used book store for half of cover price, the wisdom contained is a bargain. My point? **The answers are (A) out there, and they are (B) affordable by anyone.** For less than $5, a street bum could acquire a basic book collection to help get him on his feet. Is $5 too much? Then there's always the public library for free. (I highlight and notate in all my books, so I don't use the library — but that's just me.) My other point? Ignorance is no excuse because the necessary knowledge costs nothing but the time to read it and the commitment to use it.

Larry Winget: *"Get your attitude right about money."*

What is your attitude about money? You have a "money attitude" whether you are aware of it or not.

A prosperity consciousness is based on your belief that there is more than enough for you and everyone else to be secure in all areas of life. All you have to do is be willing to do whatever it takes in order to make it happen. On the other hand, a poverty consciousness is based on a belief system of lack and limitation. It's buried in the fear that in order for someone else to win, someone must lose. It believes that all abundance, including money, is limited. It also believes that no matter what you do, you will never have enough.

. . . your belief in abundance or lack is deeply rooted and has determined how much money you have.

— Larry Winget, *Shut Up, Stop Whining, Get A Life!*

People — Information — Things

As explained in the fabulous book *What Color Is Your Parachute?* all of what we do is embraced by one or more of these three categories:

People	sales, counseling, nursing
Information	accounting, web development, science
Things	mechanic, manufacturing

ultimately we are *all* in the "people business"

Even if you're in the Information and Things business, you're still actually in the People business. Everything we do — all of us — ultimately serves people, their wants, needs, and problems. The most important of People, Information, and Things is, of course, People. If you are good with people, then you will have access to whatever information and things you need. You must be respectable, trustable, likeable, believable, and admirable. Your opinion of yourself will mostly form others' opinion of you.

You must have a pleasant manner and be able to make a favorable impression within 30 seconds.

— Arthur C. Fuller

Our success is dependent upon the types of people we can attract and influence.

— Grant G. Gard, *Don't Just Talk About It — Do It!*

Before you are employable as a worker, you must first become *hireable* as a person. Those who bounce from job to job are often unhireable as human beings, regardless of their skillsets. They are foul, or lazy, or dishonest, or incessantly abrasive. Nobody wants them no matter *what* they know or can do! They are unhireable.

Regardless of your company or career, to be successful you must be able to effectively work with others as you relate your knowledge to them. Become hireable, and then become employable. Your success and happiness come mostly from other people. A Carnegie study of 10,000 people concluded that only 15% of success is due to training/brains/skill – and 85% of success stems from having a personality to deal smoothly with other people. Regardless of your occupation, you are always in the People business. And people only want to know what it is you can *do for them.*

> *We are always in danger of telling others much more about ourselves than they are interested in knowing. People are not interested in processes. People are interested only in results. People will never know what you've been through. People don't care. That's the secret cross you'll have to bear alone. People don't give a hoot how difficult it was for you to arrive at something worthwhile. They only want to know what it will do for them.*
>
> – William J. Reilly, Ph.D.

> *People won't care about you until they first know how much you care about them. The right motives are even more important than the right moves.*
>
> – Grant G. Gard, *Don't Just Talk About It – Do It!*

"It's not what you know, but who you know."

A college course had this test: you're given a barometer and tasked to ascertain the height of a brownstone apartment building. Various answers were: measure the barometric pressure difference between the street and the roof, lower the barometer from the roof and measure the string, and drop the barometer off the roof and measure time to impact. A people person, however, offered the most interesting solution: knock on the superintendent's door and say, "*If you tell me how high your building is, I'll give you this nice barometer!*"

A people person doesn't have to know anything but who the right person is to answer the question, and what will motivate him to answer it! That is why it's often said that "*the world is run by C students.*" People persons are not usually scholars, but they know how to effectively use scholars.

Although a person with skills/personality solely within the realm of Information or Things can certainly make a living in this world, his life will be needlessly bland and snaggy. He will often encounter difficult situations that could be easily solved if he were more of a "people person."

increasing your value to others

He who does not teach his son a trade teaches him to steal.
– Jewish proverb

To facilitate your goals, learn to increase your perceived value to others. This is done by widening and deepening your "skill set." For example, a computer wonk (Information) should not only deepen (learning Linux after mastering Windows), but diversify:

Widening into People: massage therapy
Deepening: learning Accupressure

Widening into Things: carpentry
Deepening: learning marine carpentry

Think about who you know. Are they narrow and deep, or wide and shallow? There is greater stability in width, because width is more generally useful in life than depth. Width, being more difficult to attain, is more rare in these days of speciality.

Always be adding new colors to your crayonbox and tools to your toolbox! Colors increase your vibrancy; tools increase your skillset. Have two years of experience in a trade (*e.g.*, carpenter, electrician, welder, auto mechanic, plumber), and also be able to sell. Also, have skills which are marketable to high and low, rich and poor, in good times and in bad. (Another form of diversification.) If you have marketable skills in at least two areas, and if you aren't lazy, you *will* succeed in Life — *period.*

choose your career by defining your ideal day

If you don't like the days, you'll hate the weeks and years. (However, keep in mind that there's a shovel of shit in every job.)
– Terence Gillespie, www.mcgillespie.com

Draw up your "blue sky" kind of work day. Early morning rising, or night shift? Inside or outside? In a cubicle left alone, or with people? Repetitive tasks, or something new every day?

The really successful man is the fellow who gets paid for doing the thing he likes to do.
– Dr. Thurman B. Rice, Professor of Public Health, Indiana Univ.

The person in the wrong job who fails works ever so much harder than the man in the right job who succeeds. (p. 43)
— William J. Reilly, *How to Get What You Want Out of Life*

Author John T. Reed offers some good sample self-questions:

what kind of work do you like?
intense bursts of activity vs. plodding along?
all hours? long hours? 40 hours? night-shift?
project oriented vs. repetitive tasks?
nomadic vs. stationary?
geographical location?
in or outside the U.S.?
indoors vs. outdoors?
creative vs. routine?
front men vs. guys in back? (determined by genes, not desires)

Check out some potential career paths through "reconnaissance and rehearsal". Recon a particular job by hanging around for a few days, rehearsing in your mind how you would fit in and if it'd be fulfilling.

HOW MUCH MONEY IS "ENOUGH"?

How much money, then, does a man need?
As much as will keep him and his loved ones in what he considers solid comfort, along with enough luxury so that he may feel he has tasted the treats of life.
— Napoleon Hill, *Grow Rich with Peace of Mind*

"The love of money is the root of all evil." (I Timothy 6:10). That's why Jesus issues more warning about materialism and wealth than any other sin. Obviously, it takes a steady hand to hold a full cup.
— Dr. James Dobson, *Life on the Edge*, p. 230

Just a little more.
— billionaire John D. Rockefeller, Sr., answering "How much money does it take to satisfy a man?"

Nothing is enough for the man to whom enough is too little.
— Epicurus

Even if you sleep in a 1,000 mat room, you can only sleep on one mat.
— Japanese proverb

Net worth is not self-worth. I once dated a very successful corporate climber who had a very impressive track record with university and career. However, such were her *only* areas of success. She was emotionally, socially, and romantically a basket case — like a confused teenager, really. She had put *so* much emphasis on education and career that everything else suffered greatly. Now in her early 30s, she will find it very difficult (if not impossible) to catch up and become healthy there because her career absorbs 60-80 hours/week, leaving her no remaining time or energy to work on her psychic deficits.

So, how much in dollars is "enough"? Here is a helpful guide (subject, of course, to increasing price inflation):

> *There are four basic income levels:*
>
> *1. If you have a family income of less than $50,000, it's tough to make ends meet.*
>
> *2. If you earn between $50,000 and $150,000, you are getting by. Your bills are paid and you can afford some small luxuries, but you have to be careful.*
>
> *3. Exceeding $150,000 you are living well and want for nothing (unless you have 10 children).*
>
> *4. Exceeding $1,000,000 you can spend money without much thinking. You don't need a budget. You can be extravagant.*
>
> — Michael Masterson, *Automatic Wealth*

> *Median household income in the U.S. declined from $51,726 in 2008 to $50,221 in 2009. That was the second yearly decline in a row.*
>
> —http://theeconomiccollapseblog.com/archives/the-proof-is-in-the-numbers-america-is-getting-poorer

Less than $50,000/year is a tough way for a family to live, as many of you know. A few make between $50,000 and $150,000, and most basic worries are solved at this level. Very few exceed $150,000, or $1,000,000. Most millionaires did not inherit their wealth; they earned it through wise, hard work. So can you.

don't try to earn more money than you need!

Earnings cost, and sometimes more than the earnings are themselves worth. For most people, their job is primarily a means to an end (and not the end goal itself). There is no point to excess wealth if it costs you more than it is worth, and you haven't the time to use it anyway.

There's a great story on this very point. A businessman on holiday in Mexico strikes up a conversation with a local who is closing his taco stand at 2P.M. "*Why are you closing at two o'clock?*" The Mexican answers, "*So I can go to my casa, sit on my porch, and sip Sangria with my wife.*" The businessman then launches into a lecture about what great tacos he makes, and how he should create a national franchise. "*After about 10 years, you'd be a multimillionaire!*" The Mexican asks, "*So, what would I do then, with all that money?*" The American replies, "*Why, you could be at your casa at midday, sit on your porch, and sip Sangria with your wife!*"

The Mexican shrugs and says, "*I already can do that. I guess I have enough.*"

> *Then He said to them, "Watch out and guard yourself from all types of greed, because one's life does not consist in the abundance of his possessions."*
> – Jesus, in Luke 12:15

THE DIFFERENT COSTS OF MONEY

> *Everything you do involves a choice between what is important and what is less important. Choose well.*
> – Brian Tracy, The Great Big Book of Wisdom

> *Jesus said no to good things so he could say yes to the right thing.*
> – Max Lucado, *Cure for the Common Life*

Not all $/year of earnings cost the same. You must first understand *all* the costs, and then pick the best "deal" for you. Don't settle for a "bird in the hand" if it's not the optimal bird for you.

opportunity costs

What else would you be able to do if not for this? Is it your highest goal to be doing what you're now doing to earn money?

financial costs

Yes, it takes money to earn money, but some jobs and businesses are more of a bargain than others. Do you need to pay for additional wardrobe, training, or lifestyle?

time costs

How much per hour does your job or business require of you? Think of your commute, and your time during evenings and weekends. How much vacation time have you?

social costs

Must you be with people otherwise avoided? (This is one of the primary benefits of working from home!) Must you live in a city or neighborhood not otherwise of your own choosing?

family costs

This is the big one: will your spouse, children, and relatives suffer inordinately because of how you make money? It's especially important regarding small children: who will raise them if you're at the office 60 hours/week and haven't enough energy for them on weekends? Does your business preclude sufficient quality time with your own children? Why rob tomorrow's memories with today's excessive ambition?

> *If you bungle raising your children, nothing else that you do well will matter very much.*
> — Jacqueline Kennedy Onnasis

integrity costs

As self-published author John T. Reed says, no employee can be more honest than his boss. "*Bad company corrupts good morals*" as was so wisely observed in 1 Corinthians 15:33. Moral surrenders are rarely clear, big, or dramatic — rather, they come in small, grey portions. Over a long time, they are cumulative in their detriment.

health costs

Does your job or business negatively affect your diet, your sleep habits, or exercise routine? Is the work environment toxic? Is the stress so intense that you're constantly sick?

> *Success is being all you can be in each area of your life without sacrificing your ability to be all you can be in each and every* <u>*other*</u> *area of your life.*
>
> [Between play and work] *balance is the key. Think of your life in terms of a wheel with spokes. Each spoke represents the various areas of your life: physical, intellectual, spiritual, social, financial, career, family, fun and play, alone time, friends, and civic responsibility. With each of these areas as the spoke of a wheel, considering your own life, how smooth is the ride? Do all of your spokes hit the ground on a regular basis? Or do you have some flat spots?*
> — Larry Winget, *Shut Up, Stop Whining, Get A Life!*

TWO MODELS OF TRADING LABOR

Now that you understand the three motivations of others to relinquish to you their valuable goods and services, and what category these good and services come in, let's talk about Trade. There are only two models of trading your labor: the *employee* model, and the *entrepreneur* model. It's all about whether you will sell yourself wholesale or retail.

the employee model

Your job is not your security — your ability to *produce* is your security. With that, you can always get another job. Remember, the top-10 jobs in 2010 did not even exist in 2004! Become adaptable.

> *The only real security I know of is a store of resourcefulness acquired by meeting trouble head on and looking it squarely in the eye.*
> — Danny Thomas

Besides, it's not "your" job, anyway; it's your employer's job to offer and retract at his will. Erase any soul-stunting union mentality from your mind about this. Your job is not a property right.

> *People are always blaming their circumstances for what they are. I don't believe in circumstances. The people who get on in this world are the people who look for the circumstances they want, and if they can't find them, make them.*
> — George Bernard Shaw

> *There are some jobs in which it is impossible for a man to be virtuous.*
> — Aristotle

To succeed as a member of a group or team, you must be neither significantly worse nor significantly better than the rest of the team, and you must not be "bureaucratically challenged". According to John T. Reed, a promoter of entrepreneurship, a career requires:

sucking up
attending meetings
stifling your opinions that others might not like
complying with zillions of rules and regulations
violating rules and regulations to get things done

CYA (covering your ass)
forming alliances with the right people
avoiding persons not liked by bosses
going out drinking after work with the boss if he wants
looking the part according to the group norm where you work
defeating enemies in your organization

The employee model is where several decades of corporate or government labor was rewarded by good salaries, benefits, and retirement. **That model is no longer *valid*.** (In fact, it was valid for only a century, from about 1875 to 1975.) Government has killed the (private-sector) employee model. (How it did so is a long story of destruction: money, contracts, and family.)

> [The book *Fat and Mean* by Johns Hopkins University Press] *reported that while the American economy had grown massively through the 1960s, real spendable working class wages hadn't grown at all for 30 years* [because of much higher income taxes]. *During the booms of the 1980s and 1990s, purchasing power had risen steeply for 20% of the population, but it actually declined for all the rest by 13%.* ***After inflation was factored in, purchasing power of a working couple in 1995 was only 8% greater than for a single working man in 1905.***
>
> — John Taylor Gatto *Weapons of Mass Instruction*, pp. 66-67

As I've explained elsewhere, the wife's take-home pay doesn't go to the family; it pays for modern high taxes. All she does is keep government (somewhat) off her husband's back. **You're going to have to learn to fend for yourself as an entrepreneur in a dynamic marketplace.** Wake up, fellas! It's a sucker's game out there.

> *We live in an age of corporate dominion just as we once lived in an age of domination by royal families, kings, and warlords. From inside the hologram there is no history, no memory, no way to equate the tribute rendered to the credit card companies, the insurance companies, the IRS, the power cartels, and the home mortgage banks with the kind of debt bondage they actually represent. Yet we must pay such tribute to be allowed to survive in our society, even if that tribute is a trailer payment at usury rates or allowing a credit card company access to our medical insurance payment history. We must trade liberty and privacy in increments for comfort and perceived security. That has been the Devil's bargain from the beginning. If middle-class Americans do not feel threatened by the slow encroachment of the police state or the Patriot Act, it is because they live comfortably enough and exercise their liberties very lightly, never testing the boundaries.*

You never know you are in prison unless you try the door. *America's much-ballyhooed liberty is largely fictional.*

. . . Every human experience in America is mediated for profit by a middleman or by a sparkling new pleasure technology. The process was accelerated half a century ago when television began to seize the political and intellectual world away from ordinary Americans. Now the pseudo-experience of television has shifted into cyberspace. But is the cyberworld's infinite and abstract universe expanding or contracting? Are we being freed or crushed? We cannot know until it is too late.

"The people" like cheap gas. They like post-Thanksgiving Day Christmas sales. And if fascism comes, they will like that too if the cost of gas isn't too high and Comcast comes through with a 24-hour NFL channel.

That is the American hologram. *That is the peculiar illusion we live within, the illusion that holds us together, makes us alike, yet tells each of us that we are unique. And it will remain in force until the whole shiteree comes down around our heads. . . . Meanwhile, for the people, it is football and NASCAR and a republic free from married queers and trigger locks on guns. That's what they voted for — an armed and moral republic. And that's what we get when we stand by and watch the humanity get hammered out of our fellow citizens, letting them be worked cheap and farmed like a human crop for profit.*

— Joe Bageant, *Deer Hunting with Jesus*

the Government mandated "minimum wage"

If you're an adult between the ages of 18 and 65 who has been in the workplace longer than six months, and you still can't manage to earn more than the minimum wage . . . YOU'RE A PATHETIC LOSER!

What's a better word for someone born into the most spectacular nation on earth, who somehow manages to completely ignore the educational and developmental opportunities it has to offer for years on end — and thus becomes yet another adult American without the skills necessary to earn a wage above the government-established minimum?

— Neal Boortz, *Somebody's Gotta Say It* (2007)

I bargained with Life for a penny,
And Life would pay no more,
However, I begged at evening when
I count my scanty store.
For Life is just employer,
He gives you what you ask,
But once you have set the wages,
Why, you must bear the task.
I worked for a menial's hire,

Only to learn, dismayed,
That any wage I had asked of Life,
Life would have willingly paid.
— author unknown

Always the gods give small things to the small.
— Callimachus

Because of increasing Government, salaries do not keep up with inflation and taxes, benefits are becoming skimpy, and retirement funds are locked up (by government decree) in deflating paper assets. Being a mere wage-earner is now a *losing* strategy.

> *The problem with salary or wage employment is that there are only a limited selection of "holes": clerk, middle manager, driver, and so forth. So your chances of getting a perfect match — and thereby achieving happiness — as an employee are slim.*
>
> *But when you are self-employed, you can tailor your "hole" to exactly fit your personal characteristics. Result: happiness and success. That's why self-employment is by far the best way to live — if you are one of the few who is capable of it.*
>
> *Many have analyzed entrepreneurs as if they were an odd species. Before this century, virtually everyone had to be an entrepreneur whether they had the "entrepreneurial" personality or not. It wasn't called entrepreneurship then. It was called living.*
>
> *Each of us needs to think of ourselves as an independent business-person — even the organization employees among us. An employee's employer is really his customer for his management services. Having only one "customer" is dangerous for the employee.*
>
> *Skills that used to provide a lifetime of earnings now often become obsolete within decades. One now needs more broadly defined skills and they must be production- or sales-oriented — not ivory-tower stuff.*
>
> *Get lean. Depend on yourself. Diversify. Abandon what stops working. Keep reinventing yourself.*
>
> — John T. Reed

As economist F.A. Hayek proved in his classic book, we are on *The Road To Serfdom*. And it will be the youthful generation now who will be forced to pay for it later:

> *If you're reading this and under 30, let me be absolutely clear about one indubitable point: your government is going to sacrifice your future in order to pay for its own mistakes from the past.*

> *. . . If you're angry that your government is saddling you with the responsibility to pay off generations of bad decisions, then get out of dodge. Stop playing by the same rules of the game that used to work in the past- the old playbook of "go to school, get a good job, work your way up the ladder" simply doesn't apply anymore.*
>
> *Don't stick around a society that has completely forsaken you and is waiting with knife and fork in hand to carve up your earnings once you finally enter the labor market . . . get out of dodge now, while it's easy to do and you have little to risk.*
>
> *Go explore the world and get an education based on experience, not expensive academic theory. Seek opportunities in thriving, frontier markets overseas . . . places like Kurdistan, Mongolia, Botswana, Kazakhstan. Soak up the local intelligence and become the grease guy on the ground who can make things happen.*
>
> *Find people whose lifestyles you want to emulate and make yourself indispensable to them as an apprentice . . this will be the only time in your life that you can afford to work for nothing in exchange for a valuable, first-hand education.*
>
> ***Most of all, stop playing by everyone else's rules.** Refuse to be enslaved by the idea that it's your civic and moral responsibility to pay off the debts of your government's failures. Cast off the yoke of their control . . and summon the courage to live a life by your own design.*
>
> *The path to prosperity in the Age of Turmoil depends on this ability to reject the old system, declare your economic independence, and carve your own path.*
>
> – Simon Black, Young people: get ready to grab your ankles www.sovereignman.com/expat/young-people-get-ready-to-grab-your-ankles

Nonetheless, millions of Americans are still locked within this vortex of eventual failure. You'll know them by these complaints:

"But nobody can raise a family on minimum wage!"

That is certainly true, but so what? Nobody can summer vacation in the south of France on minimum wage, either.

> *During their biannual minimum wage push; Democrats and Obsessive Compulsive Compassion Disorder (OCCD) sufferers love to point out that it's all but impossible to raise a family on the minimum wage in the United States.*
>
> *Well, guess what? It's all but impossible to own and maintain a 150-foot yacht on a middle-class salary in today's economy. . . . Don't buy a yacht if you can't produce the income to afford it.*
>
> *DON'T HAVE A FAMILY IF YOU CAN'T AFFORD DIAPERS.*

> *Now what part of that is difficult to understand?*
> — Neal Boortz, *Somebody's Gotta Say It* (2007)

Those who so far cannot command more from the market than minimum wage should not be trying to raise a family! A wife and children are expensive, and the wise young man will have first raised up his savings (this takes diligence and time) and earnings (*i.e.*, skillset, which takes effort over time) *before* becoming a family man.

> *Question: If your job skills are such that you can only earn the minimum wage, what in the hell are you doing with children?*
> *At $5.15 per hour, and with two weeks off per year, you're going to be able to parlay your incredibly pathetic job skills and work ethic into a whopping $185,400 during those first eighteen years of your child's life . . .* [add up to about] *$50,000 short of what you need to raise your child . . . with no extras!*
> *You are fifty grand short, and you haven't even purchased a carton of cigarettes and a case of beer yet. And you're going to beget a child?*
> *What in the world are you thinking?* (p.163)
> — Neal Boortz, *Somebody's Gotta Say It* (2007)

Minnesota Governor Jesse Ventura was once accosted at a college by a single mother student complaining about the high cost of tuition. Ventura replied, "*Why didn't you become educated before you became a mother?*" Precisely. Don't let your hormones snare you into that trap! Cease or greatly limit your sexual activity, always use a condom, and (just in case) don't sleep with any woman who would not make for you a very good wife and mother of your children.

"Yeah, but taxes and cost of living are high where I live!"

In the documentary film "Waiting for A Living" a CNA complained that she received an insufficient wage for "doing God's work" and that her job is not appreciated by the market. (This was knowable before she chose that career.) A divorced mother of two with no marketable skills beyond waitressing will lose her car and home.

All of these people live in the ruinously high-tax and burdensome regulation state of New Jersey. The state income tax there alone is 11%! If where you live sucks, move! Pennsylvania is right next door, and worlds better. I know of a doctor who happily left, and now makes 50% more out West — not to mention sloughing off that confiscatory N.J. state income tax. (Seven states have no state income tax: Washington, Florida, Texas, Wyoming, South Dakota, Nevada, and New Hampshire).

People leave their home countries for America, but Americans whine that they "can't" move because of jobs, family, etc. This is far too often just an excuse. We are the most internally mobile society on earth. Move to a more favorable state, get trained in a new and better trade, and start over. To remain in a place like New Jersey is just senseless.

"Yeah, but I'm living on a fixed income!"

Yeah, well who *fixed* it? The real danger of the minimum wage racket is that it has effectively become the *maximum* wage for too many people. Why? Because, given a minimum wage, they have been bought off to never increase their skillset. Their laziness is carved in stone with every minimum wage paycheck.

> *There are three keys to avoiding poverty: Stay in school, don't get pregnant, and take any job you can get and work hard at it until you can move to a better one. It's just that simple.* (p. 155)
>
> ***The failure to develop a marketable job skill or work ethic is the very definition of self-destructive behavior.*** *Those who constantly drone on about minimum wage increases or "living wage" ordinances are their enablers. In every sense they help unskilled individuals avoid the consequences of their self-destructive behavior. This isn't evidence of love or compassion. More often than not, it's evidence of either complete ignorance of the consequences of your actions, or of political gamesmanship.* (p. 166)
>
> – Neal Boortz, *Somebody's Gotta Say It* (2007)

And when the dollar has devalued enough to make their paycheck buy even less, then they clamor to Congress to raise the minimum wage. So, instead of looking to themselves for their own needs, they are trained to look to the Government. What losers! Instead of being responsible for their own lives, they see life as a combination of inexplicable and dangerous forces requiring outside help to deal with. In short, they are kept as virtual children, with Government as the parent. By the time they reach their 20s, the cycle and the relationship are nearly impossible to break. (I hope that you're reading this book early enough to make a difference!)

> *For most working people around here, the world outside . . . doesn't exist in any meaningful sense. Sure, there's the trip to Orlando or Branson, Missouri, . . . but if you spend your days at a soul-numbing repetitious job, your evening rotating your tires, rewiring your house, or hauling your aging mother a load of firewood – . . . or recovering on the couch from said job while*

> *contemplating the late fees on your credit cards, when are you supposed to find the time or wherewithal to grasp the implications of global warming? You are brain dead, so a couple of evenings a week you . . . pour beer on the dead brain. A while back I watched a bar full of people stare at a game of Afghani dead-goat polo in silent rapt, attention. If that isn't brain dead, I don't know what is.*
>
> — Joe Bageant, *Deer Hunting with Jesus*

Your rewards in life come as a direct result as to how valuable you are to others. You decide the lower limits of that value. You'll never be able to sell a higher value than that which you can consistently provide. This is why you must start young to continually increase your skillset, which increases your value to others (and even yourself). **Your earnings are merely the measure of your service to others.** This is why I've no sympathy for any capable adult earning only "minimum-wage". Bageant believes this too harsh:

> *A wage earner's only asset is his willingness to give a day's work for a day's pay, the price of which he does not determine. So where does he get the wherewithal to improve his circumstances? He gets that wherewithal from the wages he earns. But in the neocon environment, that wage does not support savings. It does not support higher education. It only allows the wage earner to survive from paycheck to paycheck, hoping he doesn't lose his job and feeling like a loser down inside.*
>
> *Right now, even by the government's spruced-up numbers, one-third of working Americans make less than $9 an hour. A decade from now, five of the ten fastest-growing jobs will be menial, dead-end jokes on the next generation — mainly retail clerks, cashiers, and janitors, according to the Bureau of Labor Statistics.*
>
> — Joe Bageant, *Deer Hunting with Jesus*

These people did not become uneducated and poor overnight. Every town has a library, and there is free Internet everywhere. I've read of many black ghetto youths who learned and battled their way out of their neighborhood hells. I encountered a tour-guide in Chile who taught himself sufficient English over the Internet.

As far as "*a day's pay, the price of which he does not determine*" goes, Bageant is only partially correct. Yes, the "minimum wage" is politically determined, but nobody has to accept it as their *maximum* wage! Just as every war is won or lost before it is ever fought, every wage offer is set before a worker gets hired — based on what that he *already* has in skills, experience, and reputation. If he wants to make more money, he will have to increase his perceived value to employers.

Better still, he should work some kind of side business to supplement his wage. Oh, but Bageant knows why few working-class Americans will ever better themselves:

> *. . . most native hometown kids* [in Winchester, Virginia] *are not concerned with upward mobility at all. They could give a rip about school, and they care even less what educated upscale people think of them. This is a terrible and silent crisis.* ***Working-class passivity, antipathy to intellect, and belligerence toward the outside world start early.*** *They begin at home and continue in grade school.*
>
> — Joe Bageant, *Deer Hunting with Jesus*

Mindset, mindset, *mindset.* It all really boils down to attitude. He spoke of a homeless woman (kicked out by her slumlord): "*All she ever wanted was to eat Lance peanut-butter crackers and watch TV in her own funky bliss.*" Look, if such were the height of her goals, then there was no way that she could have attained even that! Living is hard, and one must become a stronger and better person than merely wanting to eat junk food and stare at the TV, or else you won't be able to coast with even that. (Your crappy diet will cause a health spiral. Your choices — good or bad — will combine to create a syndrome, and the earlier you can catch yourself from practicing poor choices the more quickly you can grow a prosperity syndrome.)

> *What a lot of people are saving for a rainy day is somebody else's umbrella.*
>
> — Caroline Clark, Saturday Evening Post, (good quote for ObamaCare!)

It's not that the working-class are lazy. They most certainly are not. They work long and hard hours. They cannot afford to be lazy, as many are only one trailer payment away from homelessness. Bageant described workers commuting hours a day from West Virginia for their jobs at the Rubbermaid factory:

> *One vanload of workers commuted almost seven hours a day, taking turns driving while the rest caught what sleep they could. Some slept on couches and in sleeping bags at Tim's when the snow was too deep to drive home, . . . Most were family men, some older, some barely out of high-school, living in mobile homes and modulars. They were decent and quiet men who always left the place clean, stepped politely out onto the frozen porch to smoke a cigarette, and did not drink. All seemed worried to death about a possible plant move overseas and about bills, medical bills in*

> *particular. Their wives worked, yet they barely kept their heads above water.*
>
> — Joe Bageant, *Deer Hunting with Jesus*

(Rubbermaid soon after caved into Wal-Mart's demand for lower prices through foreign factories, and thus have so far closed down over a third of its 400 American plants.) Look, if you were born into a poor working-class family or town, you have no choice but to fight your way out of that quicksand before you end up like every other middle-aged guy with adult-onset diabetes and blownout L-5 lumbar disks. Well, as Bageant quipped, "*If you are doomed to eat shit, you may as well bring your own fork.*"

There *will* be a helping hand up and out, *if* you keep striving to better yourself. Whether it's an upper middle-class uncle, or a friend's businessman father, or a private scholarship — find a rope and start climbing. People *will* notice your efforts and goals, and they will help you up and out. (Remember that African bush boy who walked out of Africa to attend an American college with donations?) Americans still root for the hard-climbing underdog, but you can't park your lazy ass at the Rusty Udder every night drinking $2 Schlitz, whining about how "unfair" life is. Man up. Climb up and out.

choose your career by defining your Ideal Day

If you don't like the days, then you'll hate the weeks and years. (However, keep in mind that there's a shovel of shit in every job.) Shadow your potential job by auditing it for a few days. Learn if you like the people, the rhythm, the building, etc.

your 1st job interview with a potential employer

Disclosure: I've had very few jobs in my life (less than a half-dozen), so I'm no expert on how to land a job. However, there are several key things that you must do and do right:

- dress appropriately (clean and ironed shirt is essential)
- quality dress watch (I recommend a Citizen Eco-Drive model)
- clean, dry, moderately firm handshake
- eye contact and smile
- exude confidence
- know the company (research them first!)
- anticipate questions — practice answers
- ask the right questions
- avoid asking about: salary, hours, vacation, sick leave, etc.
- show interest, but don't be too eager
- send a thank-you card or email

Michael Masterson's 5 Habits of Successful Employees

working longer hours
understanding your responsibilities
working harder
working smarter
helping your boss do better

First, you must become a better employee. And second, you must make sure that everyone who matters knows you are better.
— Michael Masterson, *Automatic Wealth*

Each field of endeavor has a bunch of tricks, shortcuts, best practices, rules, whatever you want to call them. If you want to succeed in that field, you must learn them and master them.
— John T. Reed

To earn more, you will have to *do* more. Why else would anybody pay you more than they do now? It's really just that simple.

if you have a job hold onto it by:

Becoming an invaluable employee with a superior attitude.

Volunteering for extra work and showing great interest in what's profitable for the business.

Helping your company cut costs and waste.

Contributing to your company's goal of bringing in revenue or new customers.

Being a source of revenue, not expense, to your company.

choose a job with a *very* short commute

I know of people who commute three (or more) hours every day. which is 19% of normal waking hours. Unless they are effectively getting paid for these hours, it is dead time. Books, study CDs, etc. can help reduce the loss, but only so far. Find a job that you can be home from in less than 30 minutes. This will also save you big money on fuel and car repairs. Use the time saved in commuting for a side business. As Dan Bellack said, "*Life is too short for traffic.*" Amen.

don't be afraid to change careers, and often

One-third of Americans say, "I hate my job."
Two-thirds of your fellow citizens labor in the wrong career.
Others find employment success, but no satisfaction.
Most suicides occur on Sunday nights.
Most heart attacks occur on Monday mornings.
— Max Lucado, *Cure for the Common Life*, p. 96

> *Americans have a completely different attitude towards work* [than Europeans]. *They regard a job like acting in a play. You know that the play is going to come to an end at some time. When the audiences start to dwindle and the box office takings begin to decline, you make plans to move on to another play. The average American has seven careers in his/her lifetime. The key word in America is "employability" rather than "employment". Acting experience and the ability to play a variety of roles – from comedy to tragedy – land you the next part.*
>
> — Clem Sunter, *The High Road*

If you're not into owning your own business, then at least stay flexible for the job market. Mine a particular career until it or you approaches burnout, then morph into something else.

John T. Reed's earmarks of dishonest industries:

high amount of political contributions
sophisticated people dealing with unsophisticated laymen (stockbrokers, insurance agents, financial advisers, etc.)
politics
advertising
commissioned sales
many repair/technical fields

According to him, in the military and corporate world, most superiors were "*a bunch of pompous incompetents who used large organizations as a place to hide from the real world*".

John T. Reed's ways to make an honest living:

tiny companies
clearly measurable job in any size company
honest industries
use your talent (which should be impossible to overlook)
independent unit of a large company

"*No man can be more honest than his boss.*" Reed recommends that you avoid lying, stealing, or kissing ass for a living. Work for yourself, on straight commission, or for small companies run by an honest boss.

the entrepreneurial model

Becoming your own boss will allow you three things over any job. First, is the flexibility to make your own schedule. It is often said that entrepreneurs gladly work 12 hours a day so that they don't have to work for others 8 hours a day. (For some, this is a great deal. I've done this my entire adult life, and cannot even imagine having a job.)

> *It took me 15 years, working in a large organization, to realize that in our society you work 8 hours a day for survival, and if you work only 8 hours a day, all you do is survive . . . Everything over 8 hours is an investment in your future.*
> — a millionaire, quoted by Dr. Thomas Stanley

> *The first man gets the oyster, the second man gets the shell.*
> — Andrew Carnegie

Second, you are selling your labor at *retail*. Your employer marks up your labor cost in order to make a profit. Why not retail yourself? You'll have a few more costs, but you'll still make more of a profit this way. Third, is the opportunity to create *manufacturable* products which are designed once and sold forever. When you work for hourly wages or annual salary, you are only paid for your time. A good book about this is Claire Wolfe's *How To Kill the Job Culture Before It Kills You — Living a Life of Autonomy in a Wage-Slave Society.*

the two secrets to actual wealth

(Making a doctor's salary is not it, but such can provide a very comfortable living.) **The first secret is capital gains.** Buy something for $100 and sell it for $250. I call it BLASH (Buy Low And Sell High). You can do this in your spare time to supplement other earnings. Pay with cash and sell for cash. Simple. Private. Lucrative. You can flip items for a profit at garage sales, flea markets, eBay, CraigsList, etc. (I would not recommend the stock market these days, as you would enter a perilous environment as an amateur. Stay out of what you do not understand.) I know a guy who's had an army surplus business for over thirty years, and he's made a fortune selling "*rags and bags*". He turns over his capital about 5x/year (which is fantastic velocity), and at 200+% each time. Now, he's got to drive all over the country picking up his wholesale inventory and then hawking them at flea markets and gun shows, but he enjoys the travel.

The other secret to wealth is to *multiply* your time. This is done by creating a work that can be produced in volume, such as a music CD, book, software, franchise, or invention. Having your own business allows you to become a *creator*. Creators don't sell themselves by the hour or by the year; they create things which can sell even after their death. My eight working titles now earn enough that I don't have to work full-time if I don't want to.

earnings: linear vs. residual

Linear earnings are wages and salaries. (You make the money.) Residual earnings are profits, capital gains, franchising fees, and royalties. (The money makes the money.)

> *To create a* [working] *lifestyle that does not require my presence.*
> – ultimate goal of cartoonist Gary Trudeau

YOUR OWN SMALL BUSINESS

> *A vision without a task is a dream; A task without a dream is drudgery; A vision and a task is the hope of the world.*
> – anonymous

> *To love what you do and feel that it matters – how could anything be more fun?*
> – Katherine Graham

> *The ideal personality can see reality for what it is, act according to what is best, and believe that things will work out fine.*
> – Michael Masterson, *Automatic Wealth*

> *One of the chief reason for success in life is the ability to maintain a daily interest in one's work, to have chronic enthusiasm, to regard each day as important.*
> – William Lyon Phelps

By the year 2020, the largest employer in America will be Self. We will have to be self-employed in order to survive. Not every small business is in the creation business, and yours may not be. That's OK, because at least you are ❶ selling your labor for retail and not wholesale, and ❷ you have become reliant upon your own self and not some corporation.

> *There is a tide in the affairs of men, which, taken at the flood leads on to fortune. Omitted, all the voyage of their life is bound in shallows and in miseries.*
> – Shakespeare, *Julius Caesar*, IV, III

While everybody has a skill or knowledge which could be sold in the entrepreneurial model, only 12% have the *personality* to be an entrepreneur. (If you work hard only when forced to, forget self-employment.) However, if you are not terrified of taking some risks, if you can motivate yourself, and if you are tenacious about getting what you want — you have what it takes. If you are young, sign up for Junior Achievement (a sort of entrepreneurial Boy Scouts).

> *Whatever home-based business you select, try to pick a product or service that's essential, or is perceived as essential, by a large and very motivated segment of society.*
>
> — Robert G. Allen, *Multiple Streams of Income*

total freedom comes only with total responsibility

> *A free man can legitimately say to an un-free man, "You may be jealous, but, my ass is on the line 24 hours a day." Want to make consulting rates? Then take consulting risks and stop bitching "What about my health insurance!"*
>
> — Terence Gillespie, www.mcgillespie.com

"But, I've never had my own business before!"

> *Life is the art of drawing without an eraser.*
>
> — John Gardner

> *Why not go out on a limb? Isn't that where the fruit is?*
>
> — Frank Scully

> *People who know, and know that they know, can speak with authority that has no comparison. The world makes way for people who know what they are doing and have earned the right to be doing the thing that they are doing.*
>
> — Grant G. Gard, *Don't Just Talk About It — Do It!*

> *Always take a job that is too big for you.*
>
> — H.E. Fosdick

> *80% of success is showing up.*
>
> — Woody Allen

The most certain road to success is to do the *opposite* of that which causes failure (Robert Ringer). Thus, in order to succeed you must first study the causes of failure. To do that, look for some examples of failure. They will not be hard to find. If you have a desirable product or service, acquire enough savings capital to make it widely enough known to the market, and reinvest your profits back into your business . . . you almost cannot fail.

> *The most important thing about getting somewhere is starting right where we are.*
>
> — Bruce Barton

"What if my business flops and people laugh?"

I'll tell you who will never laugh: other entrepreneurs. They understand the guts it takes to start a new business. They will have great respect for your attempt, and many will say so.

> *What's more important—your goal or others' opinions of your goal?*
> — John-Roger & Peter McWilliams, *Do It!*, p. 159

The only people who may laugh if you don't succeed are the ones who never had the courage to try it themselves. They were — from Day 1 — jealous that you escaped the job trap, and secretly wished for your failure — secretly wished for you to return to their miserable world.

> *Mean-spirited criticism doesn't ever come from someone who's doing valuable art themselves.*
> — Liza Matlack, as told to Michael W. Dean, *A User's Manual For the Human Experience*

Failing is not falling down.
Failing is not getting up again.

You've probably heard that before, but don't dismiss it for sounding trite.

> *Far better it is to dare mighty things, to win glorious triumphs even though checkered by failure, than to rank with those poor spirits who neither enjoy nor suffer much because they live in the gray twilight that knows neither victory nor defeat.*
> — Theodore Roosevelt

> *Success is 99% failure.*
> — Soichiro Honda

how will you know your limits without occasional failure?

> *Virtually nothing comes out right the first time. Failures, repeated failures, are finger posts on the road to achievement. The only time you don't fail is the last time you try something, and it works. One fails forward toward success.*
> — Charles Kettering, inventor

> *Do a little more each day than you think you possibly can.*
> — Lowell Thomas

If you have a dream or an idea, and don't see anybody else doing it (or doing it as well as you can), then you've a *duty* to yourself to give it your best try. And, if it doesn't succeed, analyze the reasons *why* it did not.

True success is overcoming the fear of being unsuccessful.
— Paul Sweeny

ignore the envy of others

Mediocre people will be intimidated by your success. That's because they haven't been willing to do what it takes to achieve their dreams, so their retaliation is to attack you for doing what they haven't been willing to do. A lot of them are convinced that, because you are successful, you have used up some of the success that is available for them. You have stolen some of what they could have had if they had only gone after it. They have no idea there is plenty available for all who choose to participate. They are convinced there is a limited supply and you have taken more than your share and robbed them of their share.

It's not that they don't want you to be successful. It's just that they don't want you to be more successful than they are.

However, the biggest fear people have is fear of themselves. They are afraid that they don't have the ability or the guts to do what you have done. They are scared to death to go to the mirror and take responsibility for their lives or to take the action they know is necessary to turn their situation around. And they channel this self-fear and doubt into criticism of you.

— Larry Winget, *Shut Up, Stop Whining, Get A Life!*, p. 183-184

Dr. Dobson on the 6 essential components of your work

It must be something:

you genuinely like to do
you have the ability to do
you can earn a living by doing
you are permitted to do
that brings cultural affirmation
you feel God approves of.

the "ideal" business

In his *"Uncle Eric" Talks About Personal, Career & Financial Security* (from www.bluestockingpress.com), my friend Richard Maybury lists the following excellent guidelines for selecting the "ideal" business:

❶ Can sell anywhere in the world
❷ No employees – if you need it, contract for it
❸ No accounts receivable
❹ All variable costs, no fixed costs (no overhead)
❺ Fast payback (in one year or less to reduce risk)

❻ No inventory (*e.g.*, programmers, consultants, writers)
❼ Easy exit. Business folding cost should be low to reduce risk
and ❽ Cash and cash-like receipts (this is my own addition)

All *excellent* advice. Dr. Gary North offered a great suggestion:

> *Is there any occupation today that is virtually guaranteed, given competence and honesty? I have thought it over, and I think there is one.* ***If you have the skills, become a locksmith.*** *Invest in a trade that has subsidies, 24 hours a day. The skills are portable, the demand is growing, and it combines both sales and repairs. There are locks to match every many's skills, and buyers of services at each level. I'd rather have a locksmith for a son than a sociologist. I want to eat in my old age, not read the result of surveys.*
>
> — *How You Can Profit From the Coming Price Controls*, p. 153

The only trouble I see with purely service businesses (❻) is their inability to "clone" one's time. There are only 24 hours in a day, and we're awake for only 16-18 of them. The writing business is a wonderful cloner; write it *once,* sell it *forever*. The downside (if you publish your own work) is the rather expensive up-front press runs (to achieve low unit cost of the books). On-demand publishing has greatly reduced this, and an online digital product (such as e-books) eliminates sweaty and expensive fulfillment.

A great business is selling self-produced CDs and DVDs. You could contract out the actual production. The disks themselves can be duped in small batches and still have a low unit cost. Wait until orders total a few dozen disks and *then* have them made. (This is why TV offers require 4-6 weeks for delivery. They have no disk inventory on hand, but will run off a batch once the orders pile up.)

always *create value*, not just make a profit

There are many ways to "make money" which neither create value nor improve life for others. The chief example would be pure speculation in the market of currency, stocks, and bonds. The mere act of "buying low and selling high" may indeed make you rich, but what will you have truly *accomplished*? It's just a form (however well-researched) of gambling.

Why not instead *produce* something? *Improve* something?

running a successful business

Every successful start-up business is one that has quickly and correctly answered two very simple questions:

1. What is the most cost-effective way of attracting customers?

2. What is the best way to keep those customers buying?

When problems arise — no matter what they are — the solutions must address one or both of two objectives:

1. *Lowering the cost of acquiring new customers*
2. *Increasing the lifetime value of each existing customer*

— Michael Masterson, *Automatic Wealth*

selling bargains vs. high quality

When times get tough, people gravitate to either price or quality. Don't get stuck in the middle. That's a sure formula for disaster.

— Robert G. Allen, *Multiple Streams of Income*, p. 34

There is hardly any product in the world that someone cannot make a little worse and sell for a little less, and he who makes price his only concern is the natural prey of this man.

— Jeff Cooper

If you sell "bargains" you'll attract only the bargain-hunting poor for your clients (who are exhausting to deal with). Rather, deal in quality goods, which attract customers of quality. There is not enough quality in this world, so do your part to add to it!

some various John T. Reed tips:

if you have inhibitions, use the Internet and an alias
an industry which doesn't care what people think: writing
beware those who represent a big percentage of your earnings
train your customers: what you demand, you get
what you tolerate, you encourage
never "retire" as it's more stressful than marriage or children

Only when you have significant sales and are forced to, kicking and screaming, should you buy furniture. Only when operating out of your home is really screwing up your business should you rent or buy office space. Only when you can see that the lack of a secretary is making you unacceptably inefficient should you hire one — and she would probably just be part-time to start. You should only hire an employee if you cannot get your spouse or children to do the job.

— John T. Reed

7 (+ 1) BASIC SKILLS & KNOWLEDGE

Richard Maybury continues with the following list of the vital skills and knowledge you and your family need:

❶ Austrian economics and Common Law
❷ how to sell
❸ accounting (or bookkeeping)
❹ uniform Commercial Code, especially contracts
❺ typing
❻ how to use a computer
❼ opportunity costs
and ❽ good communication skills

I learned them by the time I was 19 years old, which largely explains my entrepreneurial life history.

Selling I first learned in Kindergarten when I packaged chocolate powder in folded *Big Chief* notebook paper to sell at recess for 3¢. Later I collected, by farmers' permission, unharvested onions in fields and sold them door-to-door for 10¢. In junior high-school, I sold silver and turquoise jewelry at the local mall from card tables. In high-school, I rented space at the flea market to hawk stuff I'd bought the week before.

Typing I learned in the 8th grade (a most useful class!). Anybody can two-finger "hunt and peck" but being able to type 50 words/minute will vastly redeem your time (look into the Dvorak keyboard). By 18 I'd "invented" basic double-entry **bookkeeping** on my own, to my later surprise that it had been around for only a hundred years. I tested out of **Contract Law** with a B+ in college, as I had already owned a successful business for several years before college. **Computers** I learned in high school and college. Therefore, I had to chuckle at Maybury's fine list as I recalled each skill and when I first learned it. Trust me on this; you *must* have and hone these skills and knowledge.

I would add an eighth skill: **how to communicate** clearly and effectively. Learn to write basic letters of introduction, thanks, invitation, proposition, inquiry, complaint, and argumentation. Joining an online forum is a good way to learn and practice your writing style. And, it's anonymous if you choose it to be. Join Toastmasters to hone your public speaking.

EARLY TO RISE

Early to bed, and early to rise, makes a man healthy, wealthy, and wise. Dig deep while sluggards sleep.
— Ben Franklin

Walk into your bedroom right now and set your alarm clock one hour earlier. From now on, you are going to wake up and get to work an hour earlier.

Getting to work early is such a common virtue of successful people that I'm tempted to call it the single most important thing you can do to change your life.
— Michael Masterson, *Automatic Wealth*

Though I've yet to fully master this wisdom in practice, I do know it to be true. It indeed matters that you start your work early. You will accomplish less during eight late hours than during eight *early* hours! Some people are "night owls" by nature, but I'm beginning to think that some of it is just morning laziness. (This is personhally painful to accept, and I try to justify my hours as the eccentric needs of a professional author, but that goes only so far!)

The earlier you start, the more productive you will be. (It is claimed that every hour of work before midnight is 2-4x as productive as any hour afterward.) There are fewer distractions in the dark morning hours. And, you will every day conquer your body's first laziness. Nobody you can name ever slept in for success.

SUCCESS

The highest reward for man's toil is not what he gets for it, but what he becomes by it.
— John Rushkin

Success means accomplishments as the result of our own efforts and abilities. Proper preparation is the key to our success. Our acts can be no wiser than our thoughts. Our thinking can be no wiser than our understanding.
George S. Clason, *The Richest Man in Babylon* (1926), p. ix

K + A = S (Knowledge + Action = Success)
— Bernard Baruch

The way to wealth, if you desire it, is as plain as the way to the market. It depends chiefly on two words, industry and frugality; that wastes neither time nor money, making the best use of both.
— Ben Franklin

It's not success if you don't earn it.
— Michael W. Dean, *A User's Manual For the Human Experience*

The toughest thing about success is that you've got to keep being a success.
— Irving Berlin

Success has made failures of many men.
— Cindy Adams

Victory goes to the player who makes the next-to-last mistake.
— chessmaster Savielly Grigorievitch Tartakower

Success is whatever *you* say it is for yourself. You can measure success in many different ways: material things, travel, social set, or a private feeling of satisfaction. If you believe yourself to be successful, then you *are*. Don't worry about others' standards.

In describing the process of good work, Robert Pirsig once wrote, "I think that when a concept of peace of mind is introduced and made central to the act of technical work, a fusion of classic and romantic quality can take place at a basic level within a practical working context. I've said that you can actually see this fusion in skilled mechanics and machinists of a certain sort, and you can see it in the work they do . . . They have patience, care and attentiveness to what they are doing, but more than this, there's a kind of inner peace of mind that isn't contrived but results from a kind of harmony with the work in which there's no leader and no follower. The material and the craftsman's thoughts change together in a progression of smooth, even changes until his mind is at rest at the exact instant the material is right."

My advice? Homebrew your own quality life, and work for others in your spare time. It works for me.
— Will Groves

common denominators of the successful

1. could only see the good in people.
2. hard and long working hours
3. willingness to risk
4. "*have cultivated a concentration unknown to most people*" (George Will)

5. "*they touch a heart before they ask for a hand*"
   (John C. Maxwell)
6. they love their work (David Sarnoff, of RCA)
7. had great desire (passion fuels the will)
8. attitude more important than heredity, talents, or IQ
9. they know how to get along with people
10. they take on responsibility
11. they finish what they commit to
12. strong personal discipline

Again, some basic, classic advice:

earn little by little
save 10% or more
share 10% or more
steer clear of debt
to move from failure to failure without losing enthusiasm

There is no dignity quite so impressive, and no independence quite so important, as living within your means.
— Calvin Coolidge

Make all you can, save all you can, give all you can.
— John Wesley

failures on the way to success

The future belongs to the discontented. Good things don't just happen. Usually they come to people who are bothered by problems. Grow or go.
— Grant G. Gard, *Don't Just Talk About It — Do It!* (1974)

Learn how to fail intelligently, for failing is one of the greatest arts in the world.
— C.F. Kettering

I will prepare, and some day, my chance will come.
— Abraham Lincoln

paraphrased from Brian Tracy's *The Great Big Book of Wisdom*

There are no extra human beings; you are here on this earth to do something special with your life.

You must decide exactly what it is you want in life; no one can do this for you.

Decide exactly what you want in every area of your life; you can't hit a target you can't see.

Wisdom is an equal combination of experience plus reflection. Take time to think about your life.

What is really your heart's desire? What are you really meant to do with your life?

Idealize! Define the ideal future vision of your life in every detail.

The one thing over which you have complete control is your thinking; use it well.

If your happiness is dependent on someone changing, you are bound to be disappointed.

Thoughts are causes and conditions are effects. You are creating your current life with present thinking.

The more you do of what you've done, the more you'll get of what you've got.

Your life today is the result of all your past choices. New choices create a new future.

If you were starting over today, what would you do differently? Well, start doing that right now!

Imagine no limitation; decide what's right and desirable before you decide what's possible.

To discover new continents, you must be willing to lose sight of the shore.

Where do you want to be in 5 years? Is what you are doing right now going to get you there?

Anything you can hold in your mind on a continuing basis, you can have.

Be prepared to reinvent yourself every year. Imagine starting over with no limitations or encumbrances.

The people you choose to associate with will determine your success as much as any other factor.

Learn from the experts; you will not live long enough to figure it all out for yourself.

Invest 3% of your earnings back into yourself in the form of continuous education.

Self-confidence is an attitude, and attitudes are more important than facts.

Ask yourself continually, "What can I and only I do that, if done well, will make a real difference?"

The average have wishes and hopes. Confident achievers have goals and plans.

Which goal, if you accomplish it, will do more to help you achieve all your other goals?

What is the biggest single obstacle that stands between you and your goal, right now?

The only limitation on your ability is your level of desire; how badly do you want it?

What one great thing would you dare to dream if you knew you could not fail?

Your key to success is to make a lifelong habit of doing the things you fear.

There are no unrealistic goals, only unrealistic deadlines.

Make every goal clear, specific, measurable, and time bounded.

Your subconscious mind cannot distinguish between a real experience and imagination. Fool it.

The natural tendency of all human behavior is toward the path of least resistance. Fight this in yourself.

Whatever you really believe, you will consistently practice.

Ask yourself regularly, "What is the most valuable use of my time right now?"

Once you start an important job, stay with it until it's 100% complete.

Develop the mindset of peak performance. Repeat "Back to work!" over and over again.

Develop a bias for action, a Sense of Urgency, to get things done.

There are no shortcuts. To succeed, start earlier, work harder, and stay later.

Remember, you only have to succeed the last time.

Look for something beneficial in every event that you can turn to your advantage.

Success equals [accomplished] *goals; all else is commentary.*

WEALTH

Wealth is a store of something valuable.
– Michael Masterson, *Automatic Wealth*

Wealth is not his that has it, but his who enjoys it.
– Benjamin Franklin

My riches consist not in the extent of my possessions but in the fewness of my wants.
– J. Brotherton

Status used to be reflected by external things, but is more and more being reflected by experiences. Did you know that 10 million Japanese go ballroom dancing over the weekend? They prefer that to buying fancy cars. In fact, there is a backlash against mass-produced hard objects because they are the antithesis of individuality and self-expression. People want experiences which are emotional and full of personal meaning.
– Clem Sunter, *The High Road*

A man knows nothing if he knows not
That wealth oft begets an ape.
— Norse mythology proverb

The point of these quotations is to illustrate that wealth and money are not synonymous. Sometimes they are very closely related — sometimes not. Money is not wealth. In fact, too much money can be a form of *un*wealth, if such riches destroy your family or sour your soul.

For example, if a loser miraculously wins $2,000,000 in the lottery, he has money but not wealth. A wealthy person has money because he *is* wealthy — he is not wealthy because he has *money*. **Wealth is the ability to earn, save, invest, and keep money.**

Wealth is when small efforts produce big results.
Poverty is when big efforts produce small results.
— George David

If you want to know whether you are destined to be a success or a failure in life, you can easily find out. The test is simple and it is infallible. Are you able to save money? If not, drop out. You will lose . . . You will lose, as sure as you live. The seed of success is not in you.
— James J. Hill

wealth, in and of itself, is not wrong

There is nothing wrong when men possess riches but the wrong comes when riches possess men.
— Billy Graham

My central experience was how people got rich. It seemed to me to explain poverty, you first had to understand wealth; and as I was interviewing poor people, I repeatedly came upon the notion [they cling to] *that wealth came from taking — that the source of wealth is really taking — and therefore the way to overcome poverty is to take it back and redistribute it. When I began to examine just how wealth is created, it seemed to me plain that it arises not from taking, but from giving. People get rich by giving rather than by taking, and this seemed to me to be a very important perception, because the reason for the crisis in capitalism today, it seems to me, is not its practical achievements, but rather the perception of its moral character.*

. . . It's a fact that capitalism has difficulty defending itself as being in accord with Judeo-Christian values that underlie the good society. And the more I examined capitalism in anthropological terms, or even in its contemporary manifestations, the more it became clear that capitalists give. That is to say that they make

investments without a predetermined return; and a gift is not something given necessarily without any return.
— George Gilder, *On The Firing Line*, p. 296

No-one would remember the Good Samaritan if he had had only good intentions. He had money as well.
— Margaret Thatcher

Don't hate the rich. No poor man ever gave me a job.

wealth, however, does have its dangers

No servant can serve two masters, for either he will hate the one and love the other, or he will be devoted to the one and despise the other. You cannot serve God and money.
— Jesus, Luke 16:13

But woe to you who are rich, for you have received your comfort already.
— Jesus, Luke 6:24

Without some sense of helplessness, we risk not seeking God. As Nazi Propaganda minister Josef Goebbels put it, "*Those with the ability to move mountains needn't faith to move mountains.*" Achieving a godlike power through wealth is a perilous thing:

For whoever wants to save his life will lose it, but whoever loses his life for my sake will save it. For what does it benefit a person if he gains the whole world but loses or forfeits himself?
— Jesus, Luke 9:24-25

Certainly God is good to Israel, and to those whose motives are pure! But as for me, my feet almost slipped; my feet almost slid out from under me. For I envied those who are proud, as I observed the prosperity of the wicked. For they suffer no bondage; their bellies are stout and well-fed. They are immune to the trouble common to men; they do not suffer as other men do. Arrogance is their necklace, and violence their garment. Their prosperity causes them to do wrong; their thoughts are sinful. They mock and say evil things; they proudly threaten violence. They speak as if they rule in heaven, and lay claim to the earth. Therefore they have more than enough food to eat, and even suck up the water of the sea. They say, "How does God know what we do? Is the sovereign one aware of what goes on?"

Take a good look! This is what the wicked are like, those who always have it so easy and get richer and richer. I concluded, "Surely in vain I have kept my motives pure and maintained a pure lifestyle. I suffer all day long, and am punished every morning."

If I had publicized these thoughts, I would have betrayed your loyal followers. When I tried to make sense of this, it was troubling to me. Then I entered the precincts of God's temple, and understood the destiny of the wicked. Surely you put them in slippery places; you bring them down to ruin. How desolate they become in a mere moment! Terrifying judgments make their demise complete!

— Psalm 73:1-19

wealth is not happiness — wealth cannot buy happiness

If money is your hope for independence you will never have it. The only real security that a man can have in this world is a reserve of knowledge, experience and ability.

— Henry Ford

Look around in your community and find some man who you know lives for the purpose of accumulating money. . . . Observe this man. Look for warmth in his soul; you will not find it, unless the subject of discussion is money. Watch for a warm, human welcome in his smile; you will not see it — he smiles like a shark. Notice how little he displays an enjoyment of life. Oh, he may go through various expensive motions of enjoyment, but that is something else again.

— Napoleon Hill, *Grow Rich with Peace of Mind*

If great riches are your goal, you will be shocked to learn what *real* misery is after unlimited spending proves powerless to give you peace of mind. You squandered precious early years (when you were emotionally more malleable) getting money, and it will be *very* difficult reorienting yourself later in life to proper priorities. Almost no rich person can do it, and the ones who do usually have to first lose their riches.

Few rich men own their own property. The property owns them.

— Robert G. Ingersoll

White men with their ridiculous civilization lie far from me.
No longer need I be a slave to money.

— Scotsman safari hunter "Karamojo" Bell

Thousands and thousands are yearly brought into a state of real poverty by their great anxiety not to be thought poor.

— William Cobbett

never let your net worth become your self worth

One day a rich man of a miserly disposition visited a rabbi, who took him by the hand and led him to a window. "Look out there," he said. What do you see?" The man replied, "I see men and women and children."

Again the rabbi took him to a mirror. "What do you see now?" The man answered, "I see myself."

"Behold, in the window there is glass and the mirror is glass also. But the glass of the mirror is covered with silver. No sooner is silver added than you cease to see others and see only yourself."

There are indeed very beguiling things and places in this world, and if you become financially very successful it will be very difficult to resist all that you can then easily afford.

There is also a surprisingly high cost to some lucrative careers, such as having to own the "right" car (Mercedes-Benz), wear the "right" clothes, go the to the "right" restaurants, and mix with the "right" social set. I know many wealthy people in Manhattan, and I'd bet that few of them actually sat down and calculated what their $400,000/year salaries really cost them. With local/state/federal taxes, they take home half of that at most. Then, all their expected accoutrements absorb half of the $200,000 left. So, for their remaining $100,000, they have slaved for 60 hours/week. Sure, they fly domestic First Class and international Business Class during their annual luxurious holiday, but so what? They've no ability to enjoy the beach or the ski slope, due to their staying glued to their Blackberry. For them, work never ends. Relaxation is a foreign concept, and they often can't wait to wrap up their holiday and get back to the office!

Their children — poor souls! — have "parents" in name only, are treated like expensive pets and farmed out to nannies and private schools. (I heard of a college-age daughter of a tycoon who had to fly home for Christmas. The family jet wasn't available, so this Princess for the first time had to board a commercial airline. *Gasp!* What's worse, First Class was full so she had to sit in Economy. The horror! It will take months of expensive therapy to get over it, I'm sure.)

Do not accumulate for yourselves treasures on earth, where moth and rust destroy and where thieves break in and steal. But accumulate for yourselves treasures in heaven, where moth and rust do not destroy, and thieves do not break in and steal. For where your treasure is, there your heart will be also. The eye is the lamp of the body. If then your eye is healthy, your whole body will be full of light. But if your eye is diseased, your whole body will be full of darkness. If then the light in you is darkness, how great is the darkness! No one can serve two masters, for either he

> *will hate the one and love the other, or he will be devoted to the one and despise the other. You cannot serve God and money.*
>
> – Jesus, in Matthew 6:19-24

The Bible speaks of how to handle money and possessions in over 2,350 verses, more than any other single subject.

> *The one who loves money will never be satisfied with money, he who loves wealth will never be satisfied with his income.*
>
> – Ecclesiastes 5:10

> *For the love of money is the root of all evils. Some people in reaching for it have strayed from the faith and stabbed themselves with many pains.*
>
> – 1 Timothy 6:10

when money is not the answer, but the *problem*

> *The human race has had long to experience and a fine tradition in surviving adversity. But we now face a task for which we have little experience, the task of surviving prosperity.*
>
> – Alan Gregg

> *Golden shackles are far worse than iron ones.*
>
> – Mohandas Gandhi

Yes, money indeed solves many problems, but money also creates problems of its own. The odd danger of excessive money is that it can lead you into a new set of troubles out of which money cannot rescue, such as psychic deficits, loneliness, betrayal, and despair. Somebody who is used to waiving their no-limit AmEx card around to make problems disappear will likely find himself in a unique trap by having used wealth to buy their way out of things better solved elsehow (*i.e.*, through personal growth, better dealing with people, facing up to unpleasantries, etc.). Now, they've bought themselves into a place which doesn't accept AmEx or VISA, and they will be confounded.

An analogy might be helpful here. I learned to drive a 4x4 from a real expert, and the advice which really stuck with me was to never start out in 4-wheel drive. Begin with 2-wheel drive and go as far as you can, keeping your 4x4 as a reserve if needed. (You will also become a better offroader in 2x2.) See, if you offroad everywhere in 4x4, you have less sense of worsening conditions, and this will lead you into a trap where you finally can't get out even in 4x4.

I see excessive wealth as like 4x4, and regular middle-class living as 2x2 drive. A normal life forces you to deal with stress, waiting, nasty folks, social disputes, disappointments, etc. (You grow as a person that way. Money comes and goes, so you want to always be able to get through a temporary setback as a strong individual, vs. a wealthy weakling.) Now, by living normally but holding 4x4 wealth in reserve, you can bust through sudden and serious problems with money if you ever need to. You haven't daily used your 4x4 wealth to escape necessary personal introspection and growth, and so you will never be caught in that odd place where money cannot help you.

> *I would urge you to see the truth of the situation you're in, Counselor. That is my advice. It is not for me to tell you what you should have done or not done. The world in which you seek to undo the mistakes that you made is different from the world where the mistakes were made. You are now at the crossing. And you want to choose, but there is no choosing there. There's only accepting. The choosing was done a long time ago.*
> — from the movie *The Counselor*

According to artist Picasso, "*living like a poor man, but with money*".

> *The rich who are unhappy are worse off than the poor who are unhappy, for the poor, at least, can cling to the hopeful delusion that more money would solve their problems.*
> — Sydney J. Harris

There is a scene from *Investment Biker* by Jim Rogers. He and his girlfriend rode their own BMW motorcycles around the world, and got delayed in the African countryside by some highway bandits. He and his tall, pretty, blonde Tabitha Easterbrook were in a very tight spot (it was all but a kidnapping). Rogers (an extremely wealthy stockbroker) tried to throw money at the problem by bribing the leader. The more money he offered, the less persuasive it was because the gang leader sensed his power over them growing by the hour. By the end, Rogers was all but begging on his knees. You see, he hadn't much 2x2 living experience, and his 4x4 wealth nearly didn't free him. They could have easily been violated and murdered, never to be found.

I know of a Manhattan yuppie who stoops for no menial task. Her idea of success is to have people shop for her groceries, and then come to her apartment when she's at work to stock her kitchen pantry. She hates to shop, and buys nearly everything online, delivered by mail order. All her housekeeping and laundry are done by others. She has two cars, so as to never be without wheels. Taxis are beneath her; she contracts with a private limo service. As long as all this *works*, there's no inconvenience, but she's well poised for a rude awakening someday. She will have driven her 4x4 wealth into an emotional swamp, bereft of answers.

Every excess causes a defeat; every defeat an excess. Every sweet hath its sour; every evil its good. Every faculty which is a receiver of pleasure has an equal penalty put on its abuse. It is to answer for its moderation with its life. For every grain of wit there is a grain of folly. For everything you have missed, you have gained something else; and for everything you gain, you lose something. If riches increase, they are increased that use them. ***If the gatherer gathers too much, nature takes out of the man what she puts into his chest; swells the estate, but kills the owner.*** *Nature hates monopolies and exceptions. The waves of the sea do not more speedily seek a level from their loftiest tossing than the varieties of condition tend to equalize themselves.* ***There is always some leveling circumstance*** *that puts down the overbearing, the strong, the rich, the fortunate, substantially on the same ground with all others.*
— Emerson, *Compensation*

There are people who have money and people who are rich.
— Coco Chanel

Harvard professor Michael J. Sandel's *What Money Can't Buy*, describes the "skyboxification" of American society. Sandel believes democracy "*requires that we share enough of a common life to think of ourselves as engaged in a common purpose*". I think he's got a point worth considering. Moral: Don't let weath buy off your soul and your humanity. Stay, as the Germans would say, *echt* ("real").

the frugal billionaire

The more you get, the more you got to take care of.
— Alice K. Dormann

Not every "9" (for the 9 zeroes of their $x,000,000,000 net worth) lives in a 66,000 square foot $147.5 million dollar mansion as does Bill Gates. Many (such as Warren Buffett and Carlos Slim) live in homes that are today valued less than $500,000. Also, they:

walk or bicycle, and drive regular cars
buy their clothes off the rack
cut their own hair
skip most luxury items

As Warren Buffet observed, "*Most toys are just a pain in the neck.*" He's right; they are. After a while, you don't own your stuff — your stuff owns you.

now is the best time ever to build wealth

Now is the best time ever to build wealth.

Why? Because now is always the best time.

Now is always the best time to start anything. Results take time, and time is a limited resource. The sooner you begin, the faster you'll get where you want to go.

Remember, every dollar you earn today is more valuable than a dollar you earn tomorrow.

Every day that passes is 24 hours of opportunity you won't have again.

— Michael Masterson, *Automatic Wealth*

Too many of us wait to do the perfect thing, with the result we do nothing . . . we discover that those who have gone fearlessly on before, have . . . traveled a considerable distance. If you start now, you will know a lot next year that you don't know now, and that you will not know next year, if you wait.

— The William Feather Magazine

beware where your treasure goes

For where your treasure is, there your heart will be also.

— Jesus, in Matthew 6:19

I find it very interesting that Jesus did not say the reverse: "*Where your heart is, there your treasure will be also.*" While such is certainly true, it's not as useful. Jesus issued us a warning, that where you spend your treasure (usually money, but also time, energy, and affection) will change your heart without you knowing it.

RECOMMENDED MOVIES

determination, swallowing pride, providing for family	*Cinderella Man*
a love story based on faith and hard work, community	*Sweetland*
grit, determination, hard work, thick skin	*The Iron Lady*
a man who would not quit	*Men of Honor*
not all that glitters is gold, lessons of fake wealth	*Wall Street* (1 and 2)
relentless struggle of a single black father	*Pursuit of Happy-ness*

18

SAVINGS & DEBT

To know that you have enough is to be rich.
— Lao-Tzu

Why Poor People's Bad Decisions Make Perfect Sense

If there is a general mindset that *Modules of Manhood* is written to help you avoid, it is described below. Poverty is merely a matter of finances, but being poor is a vortex of thinking that will almost always keep you trapped. "*We know that the very act of being poor guarantees that we will never not be poor. It doesn't give us much reason to improve ourselves.*" Here is being trapped:

> *What we know about poverty is often academic. It's rare to have a poor person actually explain it on their own behalf. So this is me doing that.*
>
> *There's no way to structure this coherently. They are random observations that might help explain the mental processes. But often, I think that we look at the academic problems of poverty and have no idea of the why. We know the what and the how, and we can see systemic problems, but it's rare to have a poor person actually explain it on their own behalf. So this is me doing that, sort of.*
>
> ***Rest is a luxury for the rich.*** *I get up at 6AM, go to school (I have a full courseload, but I only have to go to two in-person classes) then work, then I get the kids, then I pick up my husband, then I have half an hour to change and go to Job 2. I get home from that at around 1230AM, then I have the rest of my classes and work to tend to. I'm in bed by 3. This isn't every day, I have two days off a week from each of my obligations. I use that time to clean the house and soothe Mr. Martini and see the kids for longer than an hour and catch up on schoolwork. Those nights I'm in bed by midnight, but if I go to bed too early I won't be able to stay up the other nights because I'll f*ck my pattern up, and I drive an hour home from Job 2 so I can't afford to be sleepy. I never get*

a day off from work unless I am fairly sick. It doesn't leave you much room to think about what you are doing, only to attend to the next thing and the next. ***Planning isn't in the mix.***

When I was pregnant the first time, I was living in a weekly motel for some time. I had a minifridge with no freezer and a microwave. I was on WIC. I ate peanut butter from the jar and frozen burritos because they were 12/$2. Had I had a stove, I couldn't have made beef burritos that cheaply. And I needed the meat, I was pregnant. I might not have had any prenatal care, but I am intelligent enough to eat protein and iron whilst knocked up.

*I know how to cook. I had to take Home Ec to graduate high school. Most people on my level didn't. Broccoli is intimidating. You have to have a working stove, and pots, and spices, and you'll have to do the dishes no matter how tired you are or they'll attract bugs. It is a huge new skill for a lot of people. That's not great, but it's true. And if you f*ck it up, you could make your family sick. We have learned not to try too hard to be middle-class. It never works out well and always makes you feel worse for having tried and failed yet again. Better not to try. It makes more sense to get food that you know will be palatable and cheap and that keeps well. Junk food is a pleasure that we are allowed to have; why would we give that up? We have very few of them.*

Nobody gives enough thought to depression. You have to understand that we know that we will never not feel tired. We will never feel hopeful. We will never get a vacation. Ever. ***We know that the very act of being poor guarantees that we will never not be poor. It doesn't give us much reason to improve ourselves.*** *We don't apply for jobs because we know we can't afford to look nice enough to hold them. I would make a super legal secretary, but I've been turned down more than once because I "don't fit the image of the firm," which is a nice way of saying "gtfo, pov." I am good enough to cook the food, hidden away in the kitchen, but my boss won't make me a server because I don't "fit the corporate image." I am not beautiful. I have missing teeth and skin that looks like it will when you live on* [vitamin] *B12 and coffee and nicotine and no sleep. Beauty is a thing you get when you can afford it, and that's how you get the job that you need in order to be beautiful. There isn't much point trying.*

I smoke. It's expensive. It's also the best option. You see, I am always, always exhausted. It's a stimulant. When I am too tired to walk one more step, I can smoke and go for another hour. When I am enraged and beaten down and incapable of accomplishing one more thing, I can smoke and I feel a little better, just for a minute. It is the only relaxation I am allowed. It is not a good decision, but it is the only one that I have access to. It is the only thing I have found that keeps me from collapsing or exploding.

I make a lot of poor financial decisions. None of them matter, in the long term. I will never not be poor, so what does it matter if I don't pay a thing and a half this week instead of just one thing? It's not like the sacrifice will result in improved circumstances; the thing holding me back isn't that I blow five bucks at Wendy's. It's that now that I have proven that I am a Poor Person that is all that I am or ever will be. It is not worth it to me to live a bleak life devoid of small pleasures so that one day I can make a single large purchase. I will never have large pleasures to hold on to. There's a certain pull to live what bits of life you can while there's money in your pocket, because no matter how responsible you are you will be broke in three days anyway. When you never have enough money it ceases to have meaning. I imagine having a lot of it is the same thing.

Poverty is bleak and cuts off your long-term brain. *It's why you see people with four different babydaddies instead of one. You grab a bit of connection wherever you can to survive. You have no idea how strong the pull to feel worthwhile is. It's more basic than food. You go to these people who make you feel lovely for an hour that one time, and that's all you get. You're probably not compatible with them for anything long-term, but right this minute they can make you feel powerful and valuable. It does not matter what will happen in a month. Whatever happens in a month is probably going to be just about as indifferent as whatever happened today or last week. None of it matters. We don't plan long-term because if we do we'll just get our hearts broken. It's best not to hope. You just take what you can get as you spot it.*

(Linda Tirado is a completely average American with two kids and two jobs. She also writes essays on poverty and class issues, which is really a skill she only realized she had a week ago.)

—http://www.alternet.org/economy/why-poor-people-make-bad-decisions, November 23, 2013

As you can see, the main problem is short time horizons and lack of long-term planning. And bad decisions (such as getting pregnant before financial comfort) will often throw you into a quagmire. You must develop marketable skills, work hard, and save wisely to not become one of the poor.

With the previous chapter on working and selling, you'll begin to make money. However, more important than increasing your earnings is being wise in your use of money.

live *beneath* your means, always!

I'd like to live like a poor man — only with lots of money.

— Pablo Picasso

g beneath your means (no longer the American way!) is the only way to allow for savings, and without savings you will always live hand-to-mouth, like an animal. Saving also forces you to "delay gratification" which is very important.

needs/necessities vs. wants/luxuries

Before you can even begin to save, you must thoroughly understand the difference between a need and a want — between necessities and luxuries. A need is something that you *cannot* do without (air, water, food, shelter, and psychological essentials). A want is something you would *rather not* do without.

America is a very prosperous country, and therefore everybody pretty much already has what they *need* (food and shelter). Very few Americans are in lack of necessities. **Needs are limited, but wants are *infinite*.** Most of what we spend money on is wants. Our "consumer" economy is *designed* to produce wants. (Economists call them "luxuries.") Credit card debt is the American way of trying to have everything we want, and right now. This is why *you* must only pay with cash, because it forces you to spend responsibly.

> *Most wonderful of all, the virtues of thrift and temperance, and even of ordinary intelligence, are sale-resistance.*
> — C.S. Lewis, *The Abolition of Man*

constantly reduce your wants

> *When you are poor, you are surrounded by things you think you would like to own but cannot afford to buy. After a while, you equate the feeling of unsatisfied desire with poverty. And when desiring begins to feel poor, having seems like it will make you feel rich.*
> — Michael Masterson, *Automatic Wealth*

stop buying crap!

What is "crap"? Crap is junky stuff which you don't need. It adds up, and always needs replacing.

stop watching TV!

Go to the poorest trailer park in town, and I guarantee that most trailers will have a sat dish on the roof and a big screen TV inside. They're not poor because they live in a trailer. They are poor because they spend on video entertainment what should be savings. Worse still, that "amusement" (a-muse, not to think) sucks up time for personal education or side income. It's the "perfect storm" of bad choices. Poor spending also buys off valuable free time.

They would be better off if they instead bought $100/month of lottery tickets: they might win, and even if they didn't win they'd still have all that time left that they hadn't watched TV!

Oh, the benefits of little/no TV compound in other ways. Since you don't know who won which game, or dropped out of the Survivor show, you can't talk about it with those losers who live through TV shows. Thus, the losers will spend less and less time with you because you have so little in common. What a bargain!

before every purchase, ask yourself:

Is this a need or a want?

If it is a need – *Do I need something else more?*

– are my long-term financial goals more important?

If YES, then buy the other necessity.

If NO – will I still want it next week?

If YES – *Can I afford it with cash?*

If NO – *Will credit purchase pay for its own interest?*

If NO, then do not buy it.

If a want, ask: *Will this enhance my earning potential?*

If NO, then probably not buy it.

If YES, then ask: *Can I afford it with cash?*

If YES, then buy it.

You'll find that it gets easier and easier to say no to your wants.

stop buying retail!

Poor people spend money trying to make themselves appear richer than they are. Rich people spend money making themselves richer.

– Michael Powell, Mind Games

Start haunting thrift stores, garage sales, and flea markets. The value of anything is only what it fetches at such venues. Let the suckers pay retail and eat the instant depreciation from having walked out to the car with their new purchase.

Some excellent bargains I've found over the years:

new dark green dress shirt	$ 1	($ 50 retail)
ZIP drive for Mom's old computer	$ 3	($ 75 retail)
Gore-Tex hiking boots	$20	($125 retail)
Finnish *puukko* knife	$40	($200 retail)
books	$ 1	($ 20+ retail)

write down a list of *every penny* you spend

Your car has an odometer to keep track of every mile down to tenths. Where is your *financial* odometer?

> *If you can manage the pennies in your life, then you'll be ready to manage the millions that will soon be flowing into your life. If you can't manage the pennies, even though millions may come, you won't be able to hang onto them.* (p. 15)
>
> — Robert G. Allen, *Multiple Streams of Income*

Why do you need one at all? So that you can understand the difference between your needs and your wants. Much of what you spend money on is for your wants.

> *You can have anything you want, but you can't have everything you want.*
>
> — John-Roger & Peter McWilliams, *Do It!*, p. 161

OK, back to writing down your expenses. If you don't write them down, then seemingly "extra" dollars in your wallet will get spent. Money is made to be spent, and that's a powerful inertia to overcome.

> *Expenditure rises to meet income.*
>
> — C. Northcote Parkinson

Meaning, people will tend to spend everything they make. This is called "*living from hand to mouth.*" Robert G. Allen describes "The 10 Leaks" of money, and recommends having manilla folders for each:

10% to charity
10% to savings
taxes
shelter
household/food
auto
fun and entertainment
insurance
debt/misc.
business

Get receipts for everything, and place them into their correct folder. Once you tabulate every penny spent, you can identify certain wants that not only can wait, but *should*. The point of doing so is to:

live on 90% of your earnings

Except for the utterly destitute, nearly anybody — no matter how "poor" — can live on 90% (or even less). How? Because almost nobody's earnings are spent 100% on needs. You *need* food, water, shelter, and that's it. Everything else is a *want*. OK, but *why* live on just 90%? What's money for if not to spend? Because the other 10% you must set aside. There is a famous Aesop's fable called the "Ant and the Grasshopper":

> *In a field one summer's day a Grasshopper was hopping about, chirping and singing to its heart's content. An Ant passed by, bearing along with great toil an ear of corn he was taking to the nest.*
>
> *"Why not come and chat with me," said the Grasshopper, "instead of toiling and moiling in that way?"*
>
> *"I am helping to lay up food for the winter," said the Ant, "and recommend you to do the same."*
>
> *"Why bother about winter?" said the Grasshopper; we have got plenty of food at present."*
>
> *But the Ant went on its way and continued its toil. When the winter came the Grasshopper had no food and found itself dying of hunger, while it saw the ants distributing every day corn and grain from the stores they had collected in the summer. Then the Grasshopper knew:*
>
> *It is best to prepare for the days of necessity.*

Earnings are not guaranteed and sudden needs will always arise. This is the ebb and flow of Life. Living on 90% (or less) will allow you a "cushion" for emergencies. (Always have at least $1,000 in cash tucked away. This is emergency money to pay for a sudden car repair, etc. $5,000 is better, and $10,000 is real peace of mind. 95% of emergencies can be solved for less than $10,000.)

save 10% of your earnings *without fail*

> *There are only two things that you can do with your money:*
>
> 1. *You can save it.*
> 2. *You can spend it.*
>
> *Saving your money increases your wealth. Spending it makes you poorer.*
>
> *To develop a saver's mindset — a wealth builder's mindset — you must change the way you feel about spending. You must teach yourself to feel the truth: that every time you buy a depreciating asset, you become poorer.*
>
> *Remind yourself that most of the junk you buy (1) becomes unused after a few months and (2) doesn't provide you with that*

much value anyway. Remember that the best things in life (time with others) are free, or nearly so.

Before buying something, ask yourself, "Will this make me richer or poorer?"

– Michael Masterson, *Automatic Wealth*

There is more pleasure in running up such a surplus than there could be in spending it.

– George S. Clason, *The Richest Man in Babylon* (1926), p. 116

To save means to preserve wealth (*i.e.*, capital), not "invest" or speculate. To save means only to "break even" (goods to goods) over time. That doesn't sound very sexy, but anybody who manages to "only" break even after many years within an inflationary economy is a true winner. Think of your savings as liquid, and your form of savings as a water/airtight container.

There can be no growth without a prior surplus, and such a surplus cannot exist unless you create one through savings. Guys, there is just no way around this; it is a natural law. Unless you consistently save, you will never become wealthy.

"Well, what if I win millions in the lottery?" You'll piss it away, that's what you'll do, because what it takes as a person to *retain* wealth is almost directly related to what it takes to *earn* wealth. If you have no experience in earning wealth, you won't likely be able to hold onto (or make grow) any lottery fortune. If you cannot save money, the seeds of greatness are not in you.

saving for car repairs and tires

A 25mpg car driven 10,000 miles/year will use 400 gallons of gas. At $4/gallon, that's $1,600/year. Typical repairs, tune-ups, oil changes, and tires will cost about that. So, every time you fill up the gas tank, match that $60 fuel cost with an identical $60 into your repair envelope. (This is difficult to do with a credit card. Yet another reason to use cash, which can be saved.) Your car is consumed as you drive it, so you must set aside cash as you go for its repair. Then, you're never having to scramble for money when it breaks down.

how I saved my way into success

I built up my writing and publishing business through hard work and savings. I lived on *far* less than 90% of my earnings by housing myself in a 28' travel trailer for eight years, driving *very* used (though reliable) cars, and buying clothes at thrift stores. At the beginning I sometimes had to borrow funds to pay for book reprints, but after my fourth year I could afford reprints from my earnings. It still took some short-term debt to afford *new* titles, but today my writing/publishing business is financially self-contained. I can afford to publish a new title every year, which is my goal (since a new book per year was as hard as I want to write). It took 15 years to reach that goal, but I did it.

Now, I can afford to take off months at a time in foreign travel, which was long my dream. For example, much of this book was written in 2008 when I spent two months in Africa hunting plains game. The law of savings *works*. If you put 10% or more away from every paycheck, it will increasingly grow over time. Trust me that you'll never hurt by living on 90%.

$1 bills add up!

At every day's end, remove all the $1 bills from your wallet and save them in some container. You'll never miss them, and they will add up to over $1,000 in just a year.

when you enjoy a discount, put it aside in cash as savings

When the checkout clerk says "*You saved $8.35,*" be sure to quickly pay that $8.35 into your savings.

reduce your snacks, treats, and entertainment

That $5 espresso and $2 muffin every morning means $140 each working month. Why go so regularly to the movies for $10 when two months later you can rent new release DVDs for $1? Cutting these kinds of treats by half will easily pocket you over $1,000 a year.

"*The Richest Man in Babylon*"

This is an old book, written by George S. Clason in *1926*. I learned of it recently from a good friend who rereads his copy every year. Only 144 pages, but its style takes a bit of getting used to. The lessons are priceless, such as: *Lo, Money is Plentiful for Those Who Understand the Simple Rules of its Acquisition:*

❶	Start thy purse to fattening	(saving at least 10%)
❷	Control thy expenditures	(spend only by budget)
❸	Make thy gold multiply	(investing your savings)
❹	Guard thy treasures from loss	(beware paper assets)
❺	Thy dwelling a profitable investment	(own your home)
❻	Insure a future income	(insurance, investing)
❼	Increase thy ability to earn	(add to your skillset)

Masterson's 3 Savings Goals

First saving goal:
Pay yourself 10% off the top before you pay any other bills.

Second saving goal:
Every year to save more dollars than the previous year.

Third saving goal:
Every year to increase the income percentage of saving.

The reason you want to start saving now, even if your income is small, is that you want to create the _habit_ of saving. When saving becomes habitual, it becomes easier. And anything that you can do easily, you'll do better, more often, and longer term.
— Michael Masterson, *Automatic Wealth*

SAVING $ ON WHAT YOU BUY

A penny saved is a penny earned.

Actually, a penny saved is more like 1.3¢ earned (before taxes). It is much easier to control your expenses than it is to increase your earnings. The greater your time horizon, the deeper the discount you can find. Procrastination (laziness) forces you to pay full retail. This is just silly. Saving money through smart shopping is an easy way to effectively "make money." This only works, however, if that money is saved. Any money you save on a purchase (*i.e.*, that you otherwise would have spent) should be added into that pile where your routine 10% goes. Meaning, don't get used to spending it.

do not pay interest on things which don't make a profit

Whatever you're paying interest on must carry its own weight with offsetting profit. If it cannot, then it's a net loss.

Everybody you know is paying credit card interest on transitory pleasures, such as dining out. This is just insane. Such people simply do not understand the laws of money, and they will never get ahead in Life. They will always be in debt. Pay with cash, or wait until you can. Learn to deny yourself.

avoid retail whenever possible

The masses sell their labor at wholesale and buy goods at retail (with interest!), and then wonder why they never get ahead in life!

Your secret is to sell your labor at retail and buy your goods at wholesale. This is a very powerful dynamic!

Buy used (garage sales, flea markets, auctions, etc.). Also, wholesale buying co-ops exist for nearly everything, and you should join them. (Another advantage of owning your business is being able to buy at wholesale.)

buy out of season: *Umbrellas: $10. When raining, $20.*

Billionaire J. Paul Getty used to say, "*I buy my straw hats in the fall* " — *i.e.*, after the warm season when they were unpopular and cheap. You may wonder why a billionaire would think that way, for he could buy hats at any price. However, you've got it in reverse: he's a billionaire because he thinks that way! He values money, even to the lowly level of pocket change.

I recently bought some snowshoes in May, for 25% off their winter price. My mom shops for bargain Christmas gifts all year round, and by December she already has them.

> *The more scheduled you are into the future, the cheaper your life is going to become. If you want to learn to control your money, you have to learn to control your time. And the key to controlling time is to extend your planning horizon.* (p. 24)
>
> — Robert G. Allen, *Multiple Streams of Income*

STORING YOUR SAVINGS

Money is very much like water, and that's why finance has so many terms of water metaphor: currency, bank (like on a river), liquidity, income stream, cash flow, etc. Money flows like water, it goes through your fingers like water, and it evaporates like water. If you were trying to store water, would you put it into a leaky bucket, or in a sealed container? Your form of savings must be in a container without holes, with a lid on top, and hidden away.

why you should avoid banks and paper money

> *Banking was conceived in iniquity and was born in sin. The bankers own the earth. Take it away from them, but leave them the power to create money, and with the flick of the pen they will create enough deposits to buy it back again. However, take it away from them, and all the great fortunes like mine will disappear and they ought to disappear, for this would be a happier and better world to live in. But, if you wish to remain the slaves of bankers and pay the cost of your own slavery, let them continue to create money.*

— Sir Josiah Stamp, Director of the Bank of England (appointed 1928), then reputed the 2nd wealthiest man in England

In order to preserve wealth, the form of savings must not be in — *even indirectly* — paper currencies (which are intentionally debased by politicians). The value of paper evaporates, *always*. Why? Because those who print paper money (the Government and its pals) cheat by printing more and more of it for next to nothing. (Each bill costs only 2¢ to print, regardless of what the face value is.) If you are holding stocks, bonds, CDs, etc. you are not only holding an evaporating paper asset (this is called "inflation"), you are also a *creditor* hoping that your borrower will repay you. (Even if he does, it will be with deflated paper currency. For example, 401(k)s have lost 30+% of their value in the past decade.) Famed economist Dr. Franz Pick called paper currency "*certificates of guaranteed confiscation of wealth*".

Gold is the antidote for the poison of paper currencies and their destruction.

> *If the American people allow private banks to control the issuance of their currency, first by inflation and then by deflation, the banks and corporations that will grow up around them will deprive the people of all their property until their children wake up homeless on the continent their fathers conquered.*
>
> *Paper is poverty, . . . it is only the ghost of money, and not money itself.*
>
> *I sincerely believe that banking establishments are more dangerous than standing armies*
>
> — Thomas Jefferson

> *History records that the money changers have used every form of abuse, intrigue, deceit, and violent means possible to maintain their control over governments by controlling money and its issuance.*
>
> — James Madison

> *The paper-money system and its natural associations — monopoly and exclusive privileges — have already struck their roots too deep in the soil, and it will require all your efforts to check its further growth and to eradicate the evil.*
>
> — President Andrew Jackson

> *It is well that the people of the nation do not understand our banking and monetary system, for if they did, I believe there would be a revolution before tomorrow morning.*
>
> — Henry Ford, industrialist and inventor, (1863-1947)

The Federal Reserve definitely caused the Great Depression by contracting the amount of currency in circulation by one-third from 1929 to 1933.
— Milton Friedman

Regarding the Great Depression. You're right, we did it. We're very sorry. But thanks to you, we won't do it again.
— FED Chairman Ben Bernanke to Milton Friedman, 8 Nov. 2002
www.federalreserve.gov/boarddocs/speeches/2002/20021108/default.htm

So, what is the best form of non-paper currency savings? Commodities (*i.e.*, things with inherent value due to scarcity and/or actual utility). Food, alcohol, tobacco, fuel, quality tools, guns, and ammunition are fine examples of usable commodities.

gold and silver coins are superb for savings

If investors had bought gold when the Dow first closed above 10,000 in March 1999, they'd be up almost 280%. Put another way, Dow 10,000 a decade ago "cost" 36 ounces of gold, treating each Dow point as $1. When the Dow revisited that level Wednesday, it was worth only 9.276 ounces of gold. In oil terms, the Dow has gone from 609 barrels to 133.
—www.seekingalpha.com/article/167098-dow-10-000-show-me-the-real-money?source=email

They are the best example of a scarce commodity. (The 140,000 tons of mined gold translates to barely one ounce per person on the earth.) Wealth comes only from human labor and natural scarcity. Although there are still trillions of ounces of gold in the earth and in seawater, it is very costly to mine. Every potential ounce of gold still requires (even with modern technology) several hundred dollars of effort to capture. This is why gold has "built-in" (or "intrinsic") value. It's because there is *no cheating* with gold. (It's the same with silver, another "precious metal".)

With paper, however, there *is* cheating, and *lots* of it! Paper dollars are Government's way of stealing from you. (For a great overview on this, read *The Golden Rule* compiled by Jim Gibbons. I was honored to contribute a chapter in the company of Ron Paul, Doug Casey, Franklin Sanders, Peter Schiff, and other such luminaries.) Betting against gold is the same as betting on Government.

He who bets on governments and government money bets against 6,000 years of recorded human history.
— Dr. Gary North

Quite interesting to me is that in the days of the republic, Roman coins portrayed mythical figures, like gods and goddesses, and ideal concepts. They changed to portraits of the emperor after Caesar. In the U.S., 1913 – which was a pretty bad year overall, with the initiation of the income tax – was the year the first coin with a dead president's head on it was introduced, the Lincoln penny. Before then, we only had things like Liberty, Indians, buffaloes, etc. on our coins. Since then, all our coins have had dead emperors on them. We started out with semi-mythic figures like Washington and Jefferson. But now we do the recently dead – Roosevelt, Kennedy, Eisenhower. It's simply wrong to put the features of your rulers on the coinage. And the Romans, before Augustus, agreed. And, of course, gold was taken out of daily circulation in 1933, silver in 1965, and copper from the penny in 1982. Nothing new.

– Doug Casey, "Casey on Rome; Conversations with Casey"

In the absence of the gold standard, there is no way to protect savings from confiscation through inflation . . . The financial policy of the welfare state requires that there be no way for the owners of wealth to protect themselves.

– Alan Greenspan, "Gold and Economic Freedom"
The Objectivist, 1966

"But gold and silver are now too expensive!"

You may think that $40 silver and $1,800 gold was too expensive in 2012; that you missed the boat back in 2001 when the prices were $4 and $300. OK, you did miss an extra bit of potential profit to be had later (because the dollar was overvalued in terms of precious metals), but that's only an issue of investment, not savings. It is never too late to begin saving!

The price of gold and silver measures the value of paper money, not the other way around. In those nine years of 2001-2012, gold did not go up 5x — *the dollar lost 80%* of its purchasing power. But the gold:goods equilibrium remained the same. **That same ounce of gold buys the same goods (or more) in 2012 as it did in 2001.** Meaning, wealth capital was perfectly preserved, which is the entire point of savings. That same gold also bought the same goods in 1901. There is a great saying, "*An ounce of gold will always buy you a good handgun or a nice suit.*" That was true in 1901, it's true today, and it will be still true 50 years from now (assuming the Government has not prohibited you from owning a handgun — and you tolerated that).

"Expensive is when the product is not worth the money."

Gold and silver are always worth what they cost, and thus can never be "expensive." Let's fast forward the same 10 years to the year 2021. If the paper dollar continues to lose its value at the same rate as it did since 2001, gold in 2021 will be over $5,000 an ounce. Will you have wished then that you'd bought $1,500 gold today? You bet! This shows why it is never too late to buy gold and silver coins. You can only begin to preserve your wealth capital when you buy your *first* bullion coin, and it is never too late to begin to preserve your wealth capital. In short, forget all about the "price" of bullion coins in terms of an increasingly worthless paper dollar. **The urgency is to *immediately* begin to transform at least 10% of your labor into nondepreciating hard assets.**

You can't go back into the past and buy in earlier; that opportunity has already been lost. Thus, pay no attention to it. **The only power you have over time is what you do *today*.** Begin to save wisely and regularly, and you will have no regrets tomorrow. Today is always a "clean slate."

begin precious metals savings with silver bullion coins

Silver is often called the "poor man's gold" because it is easier to afford. An ounce gold coin in Summer 2011 was $1,500, but that same $1,500 would buy you about *37 ounces* of silver. (The downside is that silver is also 37x bulkier as a form of wealth.)

Non-numismatic .999 ounce coins (called "rounds") are the other recommended way to own silver. They sell for "spot" price plus a small premium (usually 50¢-$1). They are privately minted, often in 39mm diameter, with many pleasing designs. They are stored in 20-coin clear plastic tubes.

The U.S. Silver Eagle coins of modern minting are very beautiful ounce coins, but which command a higher premium.

Non-numismatic pre-1965 U.S. dimes, quarters and halves (which are 90%), or "junk" silver, and it sells for X times face value. (Note: To calculate the face value multiplier of 90% junk silver coins, figure 72.34% of spot price. For Morgan and Peace dollars, 77.34%.) So, $40 spot silver means about 29 times face for junk silver — thus, a 90% silver dime will sell for about $2.90.

Probably 20-50% of your precious metals stock should be in junk silver. This will serve as your post-crash trading money once events calm down. (Remember, people will have to be gradually *educated* that silver coins are worth more than copper-clad coins.)

Where do you buy such coins? At your local coin shop, pawn shop, or gun show. Compare prices, however, as the premiums between sellers vary widely.

You should do some research on how to legally avoid sales tax on your precious metal purchases. Many states either do not charge sales tax at all, or at least on purchases over $1,000. If you do not live in such a state, chances are that one of them is a neighboring state. It would probably be worth the time and gas to drive over and buy your coins there.

As you gain knowledge of these coins and the precious metals market, you could even advertise in your local paper as a buyer and thus purchase these coins for no higher than spot (saving you the coin premium). Get a table at a local gun show or flea market to buy coins.

pure silver content of U.S. coins

Dimes, 1916-1964	.07234 oz.
Quarters, 1916-1964	.18084 oz.
Halves, 1916-1964	.36169 oz.
Kennedy 40% Halves, 1965-1970	.14792 oz.
Peace & Morgan Dollars, 1878-1935	.77344 oz.
Eisenhower 40% proofs Dollars, 1971-1976	.31625 oz.

fineness and karat weight of precious metals

Fineness is the actual gold (or silver) content in a coin or bar and is expressed in grams or troy ounces. Each karat weight is a unit of fineness for gold equal to 1/24th part of pure gold in an alloy (usually copper or silver). For example, pure gold, which is .9999 fine, is 24 karat; a fineness of .750 is 18 karats. Gold and silver coins meant for circulation as money are usually 90%/10% copper (an alloy which is much more durable than 100% precious metal).

Below are the standard karat weight to fineness conversions. (Only jewelry is less than 21 karats, usually 9-14k.)

24 karats	=	1.0000 fine	(Maple, Kangaroo, Philharm.)
22 karats	=	.9166 fine	(Britannia, Eagle, Krugerrand)
21.6 karats	=	.9000 fine	(95+% of all gold money coins)

buying gold bullion coins

Bullion coins have no collector ("numismatic") value are perfect for savings. If, however, you ever want gold or silver coins for *investment*, you must buy numismatic coins. This is another world in itself, and too involved for this book. By the time you're ready for numis, you'll be able to do your own research. (I have an entire section on them in my book *Boston on Surviving Y2K*.)

OK, back to bullion coins. South African **Krugerrands** have the lowest premium (by only $10/oz. vs. Eagles), so they'll give you the most gold for your money.

My other favorites are the **American Eagles**. These are beautiful coins which are minted in tenths, quarters, halves and ounces. One *theoretical* catch is their $50/ounce face value. In a coercive buy-back, the government *could* pay you mere face value and claim that you were "compensated." (Funny how you can't go to a bank and *buy* Eagles for $50 in cash!) Anybody who *settles* for that *deserves* it, that's why I described the catch as *theoretical*. Nobody's getting *my* Eagles for $50 an ounce.

The **Canadian Maple Leafs** are *pure* gold (meaning no copper is added to harden the coin) and will thus bend or melt at a harsh word. For durability's sake, I'd pass on all such .999 coins — such as: Chinese Pandas (.999), Australian Kangaroos (.9999), Austrian Philharmonics (.9999), and Isle of Man Persian Cats (.9999).

British Britannias (.917), Mexican (.900), and other foreign bullion coins (all ounce based) are not as well known as Krugs and Eagles, and you don't want to have to educate traders (although fineness and weight *are* clearly marked).

Stick with Krugerrands and Eagles. They both have a durable fineness of .917 (22k) and fit in common plastic tubes.

Just in case you run across some other gold bullion coins, consult the table at chapter's end to learn of their pure gold content. **OGR** means Official Government Restrike (modern copies of older date coins — no numismatic value), **B** means bullion, and **N** means numismatic with premiums over 20%. (Notice how nations had gold coins until the early 1900s, but not much later? Thus began the decline of the Western world. Nations go the way of their money.)

buy valuable survival goods *before* gold and silver

People accept gold because they can trade (spend) it later. Comparatively little gold is actually consumed by industry. Gold money is traded and that's what it's for. On this point, the miser Scrooge McDuck has transposed the means with the end. Although gold money indeed has intrinsic worth, its main value is exchangeability. The miser deceives himself that, by having a pile of gold, he is rich. But can he eat, wear, or live in his gold? No. Unless the miser trades some of his gold for food, clothes and shelter, he will die. That's how the infamous miser Hetty Green lived and died in abject squalor despite her $100 million estate. The miser is an illiterate fool collecting books.

> ***Money is a tool.*** *Like any tool, if money is not used, one might as well not even have it. Clearly, money is meant to be traded (spent), not hoarded in a mattress.* ***Wealth is not money. Wealth is bought with money. Wealth is things and profit-generating assets.***
> — Boston T. Party, *Good-Bye April 15th!*, p. 3/4

Moral: Don't go crazy hoarding gold and silver coins. Get your food, guns, and energy first. Remember, to buy something you must first have a *seller*. Sellers must have a *surplus* of the desired goods. Do you *really* believe that after a currency collapse there will be scads of sellers with the necessary surplus of firearms, food, and fuel that you waited too long to purchase? Walk before running — get your basic and intermediate survival goods *before* you concentrate on stockpiling gold/silver coins.

> *Before you buy gold . . . buy what you'll need the gold for.*
> — Terence Gillespie, www.youroptimal.com

other commodities as savings

Gold and silver bullion coins are a form of money, something that you will eventually trade for a useful good or service. If you anticipate (as I do) future shortages of food, alcohol, tobacco, fuel, quality tools, guns, and ammunition (remember New Orleans after Katrina?), then a large portion of your savings should include these items. You will thus ensure enough not only for yourself and your family, but friends and neighbors (for trade or charity).

My other recommended form of savings is to stockpile things on sale that you routinely use. That way, you beat future price inflation and likely supply shortages. (*The Alpha Strategy* by John Pugsley is the best book on how to buy in bulk and through co-ops.) Having several months of common supplies for self-sufficiency is great insurance in case you lose your job or run into hard times.

TITHING

Christians are commanded to "tithe" 10% of their earnings to the Lord's kingdom. There are many Scriptures on this. (It is actually a kind of investment, as tithers are promised a 700% return! It apparently works even for non-believers.) So, start living on 80% of your paycheck. This allows the Lord to bless you, and you to bless others!

INVESTMENTS

Until you have saved (in the form of cash, gold, and silver that you physically control) at least 3-6 months of living expenses, don't worry about investments. After that, invest carefully and wisely.

at first, the best investment is increasing your skillset

Invest in your own education (not necessarily college!) and tools. Useful relationships are also worthy of time and money.

return *of* investment vs. return *on* investment

"Return of" investment means you got your money back; "return on" means that you made a profit as well. These days, you're fortunate to merely get the return of your investment. Gold and silver guarantee a return of your capital, and when bought/sold with good timing can also act as an investment.

never borrow money for investments

Debtor interest is concrete; investor return is theoretical.

understand *exactly* what you're getting into

Where will your money go? Who has the obligation to pay you back and when? Have these people checked out.

never invest more than 50% of savings in a risky venture

There is never a "sure thing" investment, so don't bet more than half of your nest egg on any one gamble. For example, over half your savings in the stock market (regardless of owning many different stocks) is unwise. Diversify.

risk only what you can comfortably lose

Will your normal routine of life be disturbed by losing the investment? If so, beware! I know of a guy who actually fell for that email scam about getting a share of money from some Nigerian finance minister's account. He raided all his own savings, took out a second mortgage on his home, and flew to London with $75,000. He lost it all, naturally, by breaking all of the above rules. (I even warned him at the early stage of the scam, before he'd gotten on a plane!)

DEBT

There are two kinds of people: those who *earn* interest, and those who *pay* interest. Those who lend and those who borrow.

Debt is almost always a trap. Debt should terrify you, and if it does not it's because you don't yet understand debt. Think of every dollar of debt as being a foot underwater. The deeper you go, the darker and colder it gets, and the more pressure you will feel.

debt is not income, it is an expense!

Debt does not represent income, but a claim *on* future income. Never, ever forget that! Besides that, it is a claim to an additional portion of that future income, which is called "interest." And, besides even that, you will pay interest upon the interest after a year. Soon, the total interest can exceed what was purchased! Here are the figures for a $200,000 mortgage at 7% annual compounded interest, over different periods:

$2322/month over 10 years = $ 78,660 in interest
$1798/month over 15 years = $123,579 in interest
$1551/month over 20 years = $172,144 in interest
$1331/month over 30 years = **$279,016** in interest

Over a 30-year $200,000 mortgage at 7%, you'll pay *$79,000 more* in interest than for the house itself! (Such a mortgage is really more like buying debt than buying a house.) It is nearly impossible to keep up with compounded interest, which is the entire reason for it – to lock you into debt slavery.

If you must buy a mortgage, then at least buy the shortest one you can *painfully* afford. **Avoid any *comfortable* mortgage, because you will spend the excess on luxuries.** For example, find a way to earn only $117/week more (that's only $15.57/day, much of which can be trimmed out of luxuries, such as your $6 fancy coffee). That extra $467/month added to your mortgage payment will cut a 30 year mortgage in half to only 15 years, saving you $155,437 in interest!

Pay more now, and enjoy more later.

Pay less now, and enjoy less later.

There is no escaping this law. By the way: never, *ever* sign for a *variable*-rate mortgage – only a fixed-rate. We are soon due for rampant inflation, and the current 4% rate of Fall 2012 will not remain for much longer. A variable-rate mortgage will be like a string following a helium balloon.

If you can still get a low 4% rate on a *fixed* basis, this may be a way of dumping an increasingly worthless "dollar" on the banksters (who created it out of thin air in the first place). Wages and earnings will go up over time, but your mortgage payment will remain the same, making it cheaper by the year.

never pay interest on depreciating assets

Credit is a form of leverage, and whatever you're borrowing for must make enough profit to pay the interest.

beware credit cards!

As long as you religiously pay off the balance every month, you won't have any trouble. However, if you start to send in just the minimum payment required, your balance will balloon with the interest charges. This is the situation for most Americans.

If you get caught in large credit card debt, do whatever it takes to chew down the balance. Consolidate the higher APR cards into a lower rate card. Borrow against your home to pay off the card.

And, obviously, pay off debts in order of their highest interest rate. (There are some credit cards which kick into 20 or 25% due to *any* late payment. Pay these off first!)

if in debt, start paying it off with 10-20% of your earnings

This 10-20% is in *addition* to that 10% you're already "paying yourself" through regular savings. This is the painful price you must pay for having something now versus saving up for it and buying it later (and without the unnecessary interest). Instant gratification costs very dearly! Learn this right now.

never co-sign for another

> *Do not be one who strikes hands in pledge, or who puts up security for debts.*
>
> — Proverbs 22:26

If you believe that strongly in somebody, lend or give them the money. But don't obligate yourself to their debts, because half of all co-signers end up repaying themselves the debt of others. (If the borrower defaults, the creditor can skip him and directly go to the co-signer.)

student loans

Guys, a college degree is no guarantee of future employment! While it can often help (or serve as a sort of filter for employers), what people are interested in is what you can *do*. While a teenager you should be acquiring a toolbox of useful skills, such as carpentry, construction, welding, auto mechanics, computers, sales, and entrepreneurial experience. Don't arrive at your high-school graduation without a means to immediately pay your own way in life as an 18 year-old adult.

Those who have no skills believe that college is their only answer, thus requiring a student loan. OK, you get a $60,000 student loan, get your college degree, and then what? You're on the hook for about $1,000/month in debt, and in bewildered anger why you're still unemployed. "*But I have a B.B.A.!*" Yeah, so what? So does everyone else! And all of you haven't anything to offer an employer but that. (Search youtube for the "Honest University Commercial".)

5 fundamental and Godly money principles

From *Game Plan for Life,* Ron Blue offers this timeless list:

❶ Live within your earnings.
❷ Avoid debt, or use debt wisely.
❸ Save.
❹ Set long-term goals.
❺ Understand that God owns it all.

From somewhere else (origin forgotten, sorry), is a similar recap:

The need for work:	You value it, because you earned it.
The need for accountability:	Because you value it, you control it.
The vitality of giving:	paying the Lord the first 10%
The importance of saving:	paying yourself the second 10%
The need for risking:	investing, shielding, sharing

www.multiplestreamsofincome.com keyword: God and money
MoneyTracker

Catherine Austin-Fitt's financial detox plan

http://solari.com/blog/

1. - Save Time

Cut out TV and corporate media. They're a brainwashing waste of time. You've got better things to do and think about. Get radical about cutting this out and save 5-10 hrs a week of "bad training".

Get corrupt people and enterprises out of your life. They get access to your data and money. Consider carefully the banks, brokerage houses or institutions you do business with.

Control personal data. There is no privacy. Think through who you do business with and who has access to your data.

Compliance - be impeccable with compliance. In a situation with highly complex rules and no privacy it's easy to get caught up in a dragnet.

Simplify. The less things you're responsible for the better.

2. - Get Smart

Implementing 1. gives you time for 2. and 3.

See things as they truly are.

The greatest wealth creating entity of all time is the family. Think strategically about your family and friends.

If you're not in a conspiracy you need to start one. Conspiracy means to breathe together. Start a conspiracy with your family to benefit each other and keep corrupt institutions out of all your lives. Network with other people who know what's going on. Nobody is as smart as all of us.

If you have time, understand history. What's happening today is logical if you understand the history of things like narcotics trafficking, mortgage fraud, etc.

3. - Reposition Your Assets

The goal of the games of economic warfare are control and equity. Build your equity. Invest in your health and your knowledge. Think strategically about managing these key assets.

We're leaving a large bubble and now people want hard assets. Shift out of phony financial instruments into securities and hard assets with solid economics.

Stick with long term trends. Follow the tapeworm. Don't be confused by economic nonsense into investing into anything that is not long term and high quality like food, water, gold, Precious metals.

Demonetize. We put money into financial assets, get yield, then buy things. This is a losing proposition.

pure gold content of the more common non-ounce coins

	Type	Fine	Content
Austrian 1 Ducat	OGR	.9866	.11090 oz.
Austrian 4 Ducats	OGR	.9866	.44380 oz.
Austrian 10 Coronas	OGR	.900	.09800 oz.
Austrian 20 Coronas	OGR	.900	.19600 oz.
Austrian 100 Coronas	OGR	.900	.98020 oz.
Belgian 20 Francs (1866-1882)	N	.900	.18670 oz.
Chilean 100 Pesos (1926-)	N	.900	.58850 oz.
Colombian 5 Pesos (1913-1930)	N	.9166	.23540 oz.
Danish 10 Kroner	N	.9166	.12860 oz.
Danish 20 Kroner	N	.9166	.25920 oz.
Dutch 10 Guilders (1911-1933)	N	.900	.19470 oz.
English Sovereigns (1871-1984)	N	.9166	.23540 oz.
English £5	B	.9166	1.17700 oz.
Finnish 20 Markaa	N	.900	.18670 oz.
French 20 Francs (1861-1915)	N	.900	.18670 oz.
Hungarian 20 Krona	OGR	.900	.19600 oz.
Hungarian 100 Krona	OGR	.900	.98020 oz.
Italian 20 Lire (1861-1897)	N	.900	.18670 oz.
Mexican 2 Peso	OGR	.900	.04822 oz.
Mexican 2½ Peso	OGR	.900	.06028 oz.
Mexican 5 Peso	OGR	.900	.12057 oz.
Mexican 10 Peso	OGR	.900	.24113 oz.
Mexican 20 Peso	OGR	.900	.48230 oz.
Mexican 50 Peso	OGR	.900	1.20570 oz.
Norwegian 20 Kronor	N	.900	.25920 oz.
Peruvian 1 Libra	N	.900	.23540 oz.
Russian 5 Ruble	N	.900	.12440 oz.
Swedish 20 Kroner	N	.900	.25920 oz.
Swiss 20 Francs (1897-1935)	N	.900	.18670 oz.
U.S.A. $1 (1849-1889)	N	.900	.04830 oz.
U.S.A. $2½ (1840-1929)	N	.900	.12090 oz.
U.S.A. $5 (1866-1929)	N	.900	.24187 oz.
U.S.A. $10 (1866-1933)	N	.900	.48375 oz.
U.S.A. $20 (1877-1933)	N	.900	.96750 oz.

MTB (800-221-5240) sells a $5 color booklet on these coins.

19

MONEY & INFLATION

This chapter is not about making money, or even wealth. Rather, it's about the definition of money.

WHAT IS "MONEY"?

Of course money is a "store of value" and a "unit of account", but what money does for people is often forgotten:

> ***Money is an information system we use to deploy human effort.***
> – Michael Linton, Local Employment and Trading System (L.E.T.S.)

"Deploy" is the *precise* word for what money does to human effort. It's derived from the Latin (*dis*, apart + *plicare*, to fold), and means *"to spread out so as to form a wider front."* Read Linton's quote in my expanded form:

> *Money is an information system we use to spread out human effort so as to form a wider front.*

"To form a wider front" against *what*? **Against the relentless forces of *Nature*, of course.** Her formidable regiments are Gravity, Age, Decay, and Entropy. Humans are in eternal war with these forces, and we use money to spread out our effort so as to form a wider front against Nature.

Why do I accept Federal Reserve Notes from readers for my books? Because I am confident that I can directly trade with others for what I want. Money deploys more than human effort in principle — more specifically, money deploys the human effort of *strangers*. This point is not understood nearly widely enough.

We forget what gives money its value — that somebody exchanged work for it.

— Neal O'Hara

Earlier, I clarified why people exert effort for others at *all*: out of *Love* (as favors), out of *Force* ("pay taxes or go to jail"), and out of *Trade* (this for that). Only Trade can deploy the effort of thousands of distant strangers to work in concert for my benefit, and there can be no such Trade without money.

The novel *The White Plague* provides an indirect example. A deranged man needs some "vector" to spread his concocted plague throughout Ireland. He is one man working totally alone, trying to infect millions of Irishmen. How does he do it? He sent by mail £5 notes to thousands of strangers, with a note reading *"Here's that £5 I owed you."* Those infected notes quickly multiplied their contagion as they frequently passed from hand to hand. Clearly, he understood the deployment of human effort *amongst distant strangers* as money's highest purpose.

Whenever money, that information system for deployment, is suddenly *lost,* then human effort cannot be effectively deployed. **People then become *unemployed.*** Money is the *mortar* of all civilization. A collapse of civilization has always followed the collapse of its money. When there is no money, *when there is only barter*, there can be only *primitive* society. That is why I cannot accept a purely barter economy in defiance of the Federal Reserve banksters. (In fact, the term "barter economy" is more of an oxymoron than not.)

Think of money as an army's communications. If communications are interrupted, then squad leaders cannot report up the chain of command. Very soon, the commanding officer is without vital information and cannot deploy his troops. To destroy an army, destroy its communications.

To destroy a *civilization,* destroy its *money.*

"FEDERAL RESERVE NOTES"

Issued by the Federal Reserve, these FRNs circulate (by force of law) as money. Three vital things to understand about FRNs:

they are not "federal"
there is no "reserve"
they are not promissory "notes"

The Federal Reserve system went online in 1914. The "Fed" is not a branch of government, but a *private corporation* (it's in the Business pages of the phone book) which Congress gave the monopoly power to circulate its FRNs as the nation's currency. Before the Federal Reserve, the government used to directly circulate (without interest) U.S. Treasury Notes into the economy. This was possible because each dollar was a sort of bearer claim check on an amount of silver or gold, and fully redeemable at banks.

For the past century, however, FRNs (what you mistake for "dollars") have been *lent at interest* into circulation.

Here's an example of how the scheme works: Let's say that you are the economy and I am the Federal Reserve. You need $100 in money for the economy to function. I have the government print up $100 in Treasury debt (at interest, collected by the government at gunpoint from the People/taxpayers), direct the U.S. Mint to print up $100 in FRNs and trade them for the Treasury debt. (Note that the Federal Reserve creates nothing to sell, and doesn't even own the printing presses.) The government now spends (through the banking system) that $100 to you, the economy.

With me so far? OK, now let's say that the interest is 10%, and it's due in one year. The year is up; you owe $110. But you have a problem: there is only $100 in currency circulating. *I.e.*, the $10 in interest you owe does not even exist yet. What must you do? Yep, *borrow* it from the Federal Reserve! But that $10 in interest will cost you 10% ($1) in further interest the next year. And so on, and so on.

The scam is this: if a monopoly power issues credit-based currency, it is mathematically *impossible* to ever pay off the national debt with that same currency! And that was the scheme all along.

What happens when the Federal Reserve refuses to lend you additional currency to pay the interest? Well, you bring in some chickens, or your car, or your company. (Or your car company! This is now beginning to happen.) The whole purpose of this fraudulent banking scheme was to eventually steal all the assets of the American People. This began in 2009 with the government (on behalf of the Federal Reserve) "repossessing" large U.S. corporations such as General Motors, investment houses, and mortgage firms.

why not just use somebody else's currency?

Good idea, but the Federal Reserve already thought of that and enacted "legal tender" laws. Only their FRNs are the legal currency of the USA for debt payment. (There is some dispute about whether "debt" means actual trade or merely debt, and thus the "legal tender" laws are deservedly coming under attack.)

It is even against U.S. law to mint your own gold or silver coins and trade them as money!

currency inflation (*i.e.*, reduction in value)

In any monopoly currency that is lent out at interest, currency inflation is a given because the borrower (the entire economy) must constantly borrow into circulation new currency to pay past interest. Inflation is an intentional part of the scam. That's bad enough, but inflation works against you in another way. Remember, money (including all currencies) is an *information system*. That system is only as valid as the reliability of its information.

Government and the central bank (the Federal Reserve) control how much currency is created, and they get to spend it *first*. Since they spend it first, each newly created batch of currency is accepted in the marketplace at full value compared to the existing currency (which had previously formed a price equilibrium with goods and services). But that newly created batch of currency adds to the total amount of currency and thus changes the price equilibrium. That's because now there is more currency chasing the same amount of goods and services, but it takes a while for the market to realize this. The government wins, however, because it paid for goods and services with new currency at a (lower) price it did not deserve. The last thing to readjust its price equlibrium from currency inflation is the working man's paycheck. Wages go up *last*.

most "money" is not in coin or bills, but in e-credit

Bank credit is some 92% of the "money" supply. This deploys 92% of human effort, most of it very far away and even overseas. Right now, your very *life* depends on the organized — *deployed* — effort of *thousands* of strangers. If there is ever a problem with bank credit due to a currency crash or electronic collapse, not only will you have up to *11½ times fewer* people to help you, but the 8% remaining will have to be predominantly *local* since post-crash *money* (cash, cash-like, and commodities) will be local.

Remember, an economy is only as wide as its money, for the issuer must in turn accept his own money.

Since 2006 the Federal Reserve has refused to publish growth figures for "M3" banking credit currency. They don't want you to understand how quickly they're inflating it!

from gold money to worthless paper

Regarding the Great Depression. You're right, we did it. We're very sorry. But thanks to you [Milton Friedman], *we won't do it again.*

— FED Chairman Ben Bernanke to Milton Friedman, 8 Nov. 2002
www.federalreserve.gov/boarddocs/speeches/2002/20021108/default.htm

In 1929, the bank credit portion of the "money" supply was artificially made to collapse on 29 October (Black Tuesday). This was done by (in August) increasing the price of credit and (on 24 October) by calling in the 24-hour call loans to stockbrokers. Investors began to dump stocks overnight and the speculative balloon popped.

Before we go further, it's vital to understand that those who held gold/silver coin (or redeemable certificates for such) were not hurt, because they had real money. Gold/silver is a storehouse of wealth because it's not a mere paper promise to pay, and its price equilibrium to other goods remains constant.

However, those who had "invested" in the stock market had no real money, but only paper promises to pay. (Investors are always creditors.) These promises to pay had been intentionally inflated in paper value because the Fed had *doubled* the amount of banking credit between 1921 and 1929. A balloon cannot be popped unless it's been blown up first.

Then, between 1929 and 1933 the Fed *contracted* bank credit money by *one-third*, which turned a survivable corrective deflation into an economic implosion — creating on purpose the very thing the Fed had been chartered in 1914 to *prevent*. Remember, money is an information system which deploys human effort. By contracting bank credit, the Fed intentionally caused increasing unemployment until 1933. Until Franklin Delano Roosevelt (the banksters' White Knight) was elected President.

Until 1933, the public could redeem their paper gold certificates (coupons) for gold coins. They did so in droves, and this came to be falsely blamed for the depression as the people were accused of "*hoarding*" gold. (What caused the Depression was that the Fed had been hoarding bank credit after 1929.) Just two days after FDR was in office, he closed the banks (temporarily preventing the people from redeemed their paper coupons for gold). Then, a month later, FDR's 5 April 1933 Executive Order read:

By virtue of the authority vested in me by Section 5(b) of the Act of October 6, 1917, as amended by Section 2 of the Act of March 9,

> *1933, entitled "An Act to provide relief in the existing national emergency in banking, and for other purposes," in which amendatory Act Congress declared that a serious emergency exists, I, Franklin D. Roosevelt, President of the United States of America, do declare that said national emergency still continues to exist and pursuant to said section* ***do hereby prohibit the hoarding of gold coin, gold bullion, and gold certificates within the continental United States*** *by individuals, partnerships, associations and corporations and hereby prescribe the following regulations for carrying out the purposes of this order:*
>
> *Section 1. For the purposes of this regulation, the term "hoarding" means the withdrawal and withholding of gold coin, gold bullion or gold certificates from the recognized and customary channels of trade. The term "person" means any individual, partnership, association or corporation.*
>
> *Section 2. All persons are hereby required to deliver on or before May 1, 1933, to a Federal reserve bank or branch or agency thereof or to any member bank of the Federal Reserve System all gold coin, gold bullion and gold certificates now owned by them or coming into their ownership on or before April 28, 1933, except the following:*

Exempted was the industrial, professional and artistic uses, and:

> *(b) Gold coin and gold certificates in an amount* (of face value) *not* ***exceeding in the aggregate $100.00*** *belonging to any one person, and gold coins having a recognized special value to collectors of rare and unusual coins.*

Back in 1933, a $20 gold coin contained 0.9675 ounce of gold. (Thus, one ounce of gold bought $20.67.) The $20 bills back then were *coupons* for 0.9675 ounces of gold, until President Franklin Roosevelt forbade Americans to cash in their paper coupons for gold, and forced them to use irredeemable Federal Reserve Notes as if they were money. (A similar theft of our silver coinage happened in 1964-1971.)

It would be like you closing your checking account, and then forcing at gunpoint your neighbors to accept your now uncashable checks in payment. **This has been our "money" since 1971.**

The theft was upheld by the Supreme Court in the *Nortz* case, but only by a 5-4 majority. Speaking for the minority in an acidic tone was Justice McReynolds:

> *The Constitution, as we have known it, is gone. This is Nero at his worst. It seems impossible to overestimate what has been done here today. The guarantees which men and women heretofore*

> *have looked to protect their interests have all been swept away. There are some responsibilities attaching a man on this bench, to reveal to the bar, in all its nakedness, just what has been done. We are confronted with a condition in which the dollar may be reduced to 50 cents today, 30 cents tomorrow, 10 cents the next day.* (NOTE: Today's 2013 dollar has the 1934 purchasing power of 2¢.) *Loss of repudiation for honorable dealing will leave us ruined. The impending legal and moral chaos is appalling.*

As soon as FDR was in office, the Fed reversed course and injected $100,000,000 of new bank credit money into the system, which was used . . . to deploy human effort as money always does. Thus, FDR's gold theft was seen as successful.

Here's a simplified account of what happened to the typical American family:

FATHER
to 1933 – U.S. currency was redeemable in gold coins
1933 on – gold coins confiscated
Gold Certs confiscated, discontinued, irredeemable

SON
never had gold coins
never had redeemable Gold Certificates
by 1971 – Silver Certificates discontinued for barren FRN's
silver coins discontinued for cupronickel slugs

GRANDSON
today – never had gold coins
never had redeemable Gold Certificates
never had silver coins
never had redeemable Silver Certificates
left with worthless paper scrip and cupronickel slugs

President Lyndon Johnson declared in 1964 that silver was *"too valuable to put into coins"* – which was like saying that nutritious calories are too valuable to put into food. The whole *point* of precious metal coin money *is* their intrinsic value.

The cleverness of it all is wonderful to contemplate. The Father lost his gold, the Son lost his silver – leaving the Grandson without any real gold/silver money whatsoever to safeguard his wealth. None of this was by accident.

Here's a true story from one of my readers:

> **Father:** [explaining how counting money works, coins, paper, etc.]
>
> **9 y/o Son:** *What? How could the paper be worth more than metal?*
>
> **Father:** [brief explanation on fiat currency and token coinage]
> *So, do you understand now?*
>
> **9 y/o Son:** *I think so Dad, but it's going to take me awhile to get used to something so stupid!*

the coming gold confiscation attempt

From 1933 to 1975 Americans could not own more than five ounces of gold. Then, the restrictions were removed (though the dollar is no longer backed by precious metals).

Today in 2015, the American Eagle ounce gold coin will fetch over $1,200 on the free market, but since its *face* value is only $50 that is all the Government will oblige itself to "reimburse" us the next time they steal our gold. Just as in 1933, they will say, "*Here's a $50 bill — what are you complaining about? You still have purchasing power. That's all you cared about, right?*"

the intentionally devalued dollar

The Federal Reserve Note has served its purpose as a multi-generational vehicle of wealth confiscation, and so the banksters are soon to implement their next phase: a North American Union (NAU) currency for Canada, the U.S., and Mexico. (Perhaps the "Amero"?) But first the dollar has to sink quite a bit more. It's plummeting at least 1%/month *and* (which is really shocking) is already worth less than the Canadian dollar. Even the Iraqi dinar has a lower inflation rate than the dollar. Wow.

If you are holding dollar-denominated paper assets, you should quickly transform them into gold or silver coins (I describe this in the chapter *Savings & Debt*), or at least into stronger foreign currencies. (Japan and China are now beginning to dump the dollar. A famous fashion model made big news for renegotiating her contracts to be paid in Euros instead of dollars. When *fashion models* are figuring it out, the dollar can't last for too much longer!)

I highly recommend the free video presentation from www.surviveinplace.com/stansberry.

now you cannot easily protect yourself from inflation

Let's look at the rest of the story, and how a depreciating paper currency is used with a progressive "*income*" tax. The two work hand-in-hand to rip you off in a very sly and silent way.

"*INCOME*" TAXES AND INFLATION

The industrial revolution did not arise because the ruling class wanted to free their serfs – but rather because they realized how additional "liberties" could make their livestock astoundingly more productive. When cows are placed in very confining stalls, they beat their heads against the walls, resulting in injuries and infections. Thus farmers now give them more room, not because they want to set their cows free, but rather because they want greater productivity and lower costs.

The next stop after "free range" is not "freedom".

***The rise of state capitalism in the 19th century was actually the rise of "free range serfdom".** Additional "liberties" were granted to the human livestock not with the goal of setting them free, but rather with the goal of increasing their productivity. Of course, intellectuals, artists, and priests were – and are – well paid to conceal this reality.*

– Stephan Molyneux, video "The REAL Matrix"

A repeat disclaimer: Nothing contained herein is to be construed as legal, accounting, or professional advice. While all information is believed to be accurate, the author and publisher disclaim any responsibility for any liability or loss incurred as a consequence of the use and application, directly or indirectly, of any material presented herein.

some taxation fallacies

"*Taxes are the price we pay for civilization.*"

No, they are not.

The premise is faulty: that government (*i.e.*, coercive monopoly of force) is responsible for civilization. Government is a *parasite* upon civilization, because government *steals* for a living and theft is alien to the notion of civilization. (That *some* of these stolen dollars is spent on civilization is irrelevant.)

My friends, the "*income*" taxes we pay don't go to schools or roads. The system is a wealth distribution scheme to reward nonworking people (*i.e.*, the extremely rich and the extremely poor) who *vote* for a living. And it's we middle-class suckers who are letting it all happen.

"*You have a duty to pay your fair share of taxes.*"

No, you do not. Legal tax avoidance is permissible.

> *There is nothing sinister in arranging one's affair as to keep taxes as low as possible . . . for nobody owes any public duty to pay more than the law demands.*
>
> – Judge Learned Hand

> *Over time government spending has gone from about 5% GDP in the early 1900's to 40% today. This roughly translates into your overall tax rate being 40% for state, federal, and local taxes. (the chart below only shows Federal data, not state or local which are roughly an additional 10-15% GDP depending on the state).*
>
> *However, not all 40% of your money goes to other people. Some of it goes to roads, infrastructure, defense, schools, etc., all of which are considered "public goods" and not income transfers. These budgetary items account for a whopping 30% of the federal budget and roughly the same for state and local budgets. In other words, 70%, SEVENTY PERCENT OF YOUR TAX MONEY GOES TO OTHER PEOPLE, meaning the government is not an agent of governance as much as it is an agent of wealth-redistribution.*
>
> *So if 40% of your income goes to a budget where 70% of it is spent on other people, that means 28% OF YOUR TIME IS SPENT BEING A SLAVE OR HOST TO OTHER PARASITES. More if you're foolish enough to "try hard" and "become successful." Out of a 50 year career that's 14 YEARS OF VACATION you could have had, but instead you were literally a slave to somebody else for those 14 years.*
>
> – *Enjoy The Decline*

Your two only duties are to ❶ honor your agreements and ❷ not encroach upon other people and their property. Since government creates nothing and can only distribute stolen wealth, a huge part of your not encroaching upon others (because you now understand that wealth was coercively taken from people) is not to accepting government checks.

Taxes in America are levied differently than in other countries. In America (as I will explain) taxes are levied only on *voluntary* activities and conditions. It is theoretically possible for a man to exist solely off the land, earning no taxable income, and paying little in excise taxes. Thus, he would not legally owe any taxes whatsoever, and none morally. He takes nothing *from* government and therefore owes nothing *to* government.

only two kinds of taxes: direct and indirect

The only thing the Constitution twice declared was that direct taxes must be apportioned:

> *. . . direct taxes shall be apportioned among the several States ...*
> — U.S. Constitution, Article 1, Section 2, Clause 3

> *No capitation, or other direct, Tax shall be laid, unless in Proportion to the Census or Enumeration herein before directed to be taken.*
> — U.S. Constitution, Article 1, Section 9, Clause 4

In times of crisis, the Constitution allows direct taxes on people and property to be levied against Americans by the USG, through their state governments. All direct taxes must be apportioned equally person to person. (When you see a semi trailer with a license plate that reads "Apportioned" it means that it is taxed based on weight.) However, the USG was not designed to be funded with direct taxes, but *indirect* taxes. These are called imposts, duties, and excises. In *The Federalist* #21, Alexander Hamilton explained how it was to work:

> *Imposts, excises, and, in general, all duties upon articles of consumption, may be compared to a fluid, which will, in time, find its level with the means of paying them.* ***The amount to be contributed by each citizen will in a degree be at his own option, and can be regulated by an attention to his resources.*** *The rich may be extravagant, the poor can be frugal; and private oppression may always be avoided by a judicious selection of objects proper for such impositions.*
>
> *. . . It is a signal advantage of taxes on articles of consumption, that they contain in their own nature a security against excess. They prescribe their own limit; which cannot be exceeded without defeating the end proposed, that is, an extension of the revenue . . . .*
>
> *If duties are too high, they lessen the consumption; the collection is eluded; and the product to the treasury is not so great as when they are confined within proper and moderate bounds.* ***This forms a complete barrier against any material oppression of the citizens by taxes of this class, and is itself a natural limitation of the power imposing them.***

Excises are levied on avoidable activities because the Constitution requires indirect taxes to be voluntary and evadable. For example, you can legally avoid duties by not buying imported goods. You can legally avoid excises by not making or buying domestic goods so taxed.

> *Excises are taxes laid upon the manufacture, sale, or consumption of commodities within the country, upon licenses to pursue certain occupations and upon corporate privileges; the requirement to pay such taxes involves the exercise of privilege.*

— ***Flint v. Stone Tracy Co.***, 220 U.S. 107 (1911)

Excise tax. *A tax imposed on the performance of an act, the engaging in an occupation, **or the enjoyment of a privilege**. Rapa v. Haines, Ohio Comm.Pl. 101 N.E.2d 733, 735. A tax on the manufacture, sale, or use of a good or on the carrying on of an occupation or activity or tax on the transfer of property.*

— Black's Law Dictionary, 6th Edition, p. 563

The terms 'excise tax' and 'privilege tax' are synonymous. *The two are often used interchangeably.*

— ***American Airways v. Wallace***, 57 F.2d 877,880

a new tax on business profits

The passage of the bill will mark the dawn of a brighter day, with more of sunshine, more of songs of birds, more of the sweetest music, the laughter of children well-fed, well clothed, well housed. Can we doubt that in the brighter, happier days to come, good, even-handed, wholesome Democracy shall be triumphant?

— Congressman David A. De Armond of Missouri, about the 1913 income tax bill

Up until 1913, the wealthy paid very little indirect tax as a proportion of their earnings, because excise taxes are regressive in effect. (Meaning, the more money you have, the less fixed costs matter to you.) So, there became a clamor (largely fomented by the elite) to create a federal excise tax on business profits ("income"). This required a constitutional amendment, reportedly ratified in 1913. When the income tax came online the next year, only 85,000 of the 65,000,000 Americans were effected because the beginning tax bracket was placed very high (at about $100,000 in today's dollars).

It has been absolutely established by the U.S. Supreme Court in many decisions (beginning with ***Brushaber v. Union Pacific***, 240 U.S. 1 of 1916) that the federal "*income*" tax is an indirect tax. Conceptually, it must therefore be levied on privileged activities. The "*income*" tax cannot be levied on any personal exercise of your inalienable rights, since that would be an unconstitutional direct tax (because direct taxes must be equally applied to everybody through "*apportionment*"). This is why the Constitution twice stressed that direct taxes must be apportioned.

The 16th Amendment was written so that the 1894 federal "*income*" tax (overturned by the Supreme Court in 1895 ***Pollock***) would be construed as an indirect tax on privileged and/or profit-generating activities vs. an unapportioned direct tax on property.

The 16th Amendment of 1913 clarified the federal government's power to tax (indirectly) "*incomes, from whatever source derived.*" It cannot (without apportionment) directly tax the source, but only any "*income*" derived from that source. (It cannot tax the "parent", so to speak, but only the "child".)

> *When a court refers to an income tax as being in the nature of an excise, it is merely stating that the tax is not on the* [source] *property itself, but rather it is* ***a fee for the privilege*** *of receiving gain from the property. The tax is based upon the amount of the gain, not the value of the property.*
>
> – John R. Luckey, Legislative Attorney for the Library of Congress, "*Frequently Asked Questions Concerning The Federal Income Tax*" (C.R.S. Report for Congress 92-303A (1992)) www.taxhistory.com/crs/toc.html

example:

Buying a house for $200,000 and selling it for $200,000 is an untaxable event because no profit is derived. An income tax applied to that sale would be an unconstitutional direct tax on property. However, if you sold that house for $300,000, then a $100,000 profit would be derived from that source, and an income tax (theoretically) could be levied as an indirect excise on real estate speculation.

Most of the 1913-1930 tax cases regarded the feds trying to illegally tax gross receipts ("everything that comes in") vs. net profits *derived*. The famous *Drexel* case of 1922 was quite explicit:

> *. . . all that Congress would need to do, hereafter, in seeking to take over to its control any one of the great number of subjects of public interest, jurisdiction of which the states have never parted with, and which are reserved to them by the Tenth Amendment, would be to enact a detailed measure of complete regulation of the subject and enforce it by a so-called tax upon departures from it. To give such magic to the word 'tax' would be to break down all constitutional limitation of the powers of Congress and completely wipe out the sovereignty of the states.*
>
> – ***Baily v. Drexel Furniture Co.***, 259 U.S. 20 (1922)

Well, how could an excise tax behave as a direct tax — *i.e.*, how could an indirect tax actually go beyond that $100,000 profit and take some of the original $200,000 equity? How could an excise tax actually tax the *source*, if under the Constitution, such is forbidden? Naturally, the Government had a nice trick:

inflationary currency

inflation partners with taxation, against you

Please follow me very, very closely here because this is one of the most important things I have to explain to you.

example:

Two identical homes in different towns are $200,000. Years later, Homeowner A likes the identical home in town B, which is now for sale. Market value on both homes is now $300,000, solely because of currency inflation of 150%. (Meaning, new currency has outpaced new homes, changing the $:home equilibrium by 150%.)

Homeowner A sells for $300,000 and buys home B for the same amount. Basically, the homes effectively traded out at parity. But according to the IRS, Homeowner A made a $100,000 profit and thus got taxed 40% of it.

That $40,000 in "*income*" taxes is more than just 40% of his (artificial) profit, it really constitutes 13.3% of the equity of his home — equity which no indirect excise tax is legally able to touch! Inflationary currency coupled with an "*income*" tax allows the Government to effectively tax property you already paid for years ago, thus reducing your net worth!

Had the two homeowners simply traded homes, there would have been no accounting profit at all. Or, had the dollar:goods equilibrium (called "prices") remained stable (like it used to be with gold/silver $s), then there also would have been no accounting profit.

However, because we are forced to use a depreciating currency no longer backed by precious metals, if we sell something for more than we paid, it only *appears* that we make a profit. Actually, we make no profit at all because the goods-to-goods exchange equilibrium (which is what really matters) never changed.

An analogy: imagine a tax system that taxed adults based on height — $100 per foot. That would be a stable tax rate, unless the Government monkeys with the measurement standard by declaring that 1 foot now = 11 inches. This would overnight increase everyone's taxes by 8.3% (1/12).

Another analogy: let's say the highway speed limit is 75mph. If Government changed the definition of a mile from 5,280 feet to 4,400 feet, then the velocity that was formerly described as 75mph will hereafter be described as 90mph. The highway patrol now writes you a ticket for doing 90 in a 75, even though your true velocity never increased. You're not going any faster, but the Government will fine you as though you are!

This is precisely what has happened over the past century. "*Income*" taxes are calculated by dollar figures, but the definition of a dollar was allowed to become elastic as its supply was increased (inflated). **This was *no* accident.** It was a most clever way to circumvent constitutional apportionment of direct taxes by making the "*income*" excise tax effectively direct in a very murky way. (To my knowledge, this issue has never been taken to court.)

An inflationary currency also coupled with progressive tax rates (which increase as a percentage, vs. being a flat rate) has the inevitable effect of artificially moving the middle-class into higher tax brackets which were allegedly imposed only on the wealthy. Few understand this because it's the dirty little secret never taught in civics class.

This evil system explains why the American middle class has no longer (since 1973) been able to increase its net worth. We are being taxed not just on our salaries, but effectively on property we've owned for years. This is why post-1973 Americans are the first generation *not* to live better than their parents! This is why grown, working children with families must often move back in with mom and dad.

All because 1 foot = 11 inches. Then 9", then 4", and finally ½" Oh, c'mon, ½"? Yes, that's right. Since the 1913 "*income*" tax the dollar is worth but one-twentyfourth (or less) of its original value. (Since even I was a boy the dollar has been devalued by 60%.)

> *Taxation, with its offspring inflation, is the vital weapon to displace the system of free enterprise.*
>
> – Karl Marx (founder of modern Communism)

20

GOVERNMENT and YOU

Government should do only those things the people cannot do for themselves.
— Ronald Reagan

The greatest menace to freedom is an inert people.
— Louis D. Brandeis

Governments are historically the most destructive thing in human history. In the last century alone, governments killed 170,000,000 people.

All governments have a codependence problem. They hate anything they cannot control. Yet governments try hard to control things, despite the futility.
— Michael W. Dean, *A User's Manual For the Human Experience*

You need only reflect that one of the best ways to get yourself a reputation as a dangerous citizen these days is to go about repeating the very phrases which our founding fathers used in their struggle for independence.
— C.A. Beard

To be GOVERNED is to be watched, inspected, spied upon, directed, law-driven, numbered, regulated, enrolled, indoctrinated, preached at, controlled, checked, estimated, valued, censured, commanded, by creatures who have neither the right nor the wisdom nor the virtue to do so. To be GOVERNED is to be at every operation, at every transaction noted, registered, counted, taxed, stamped, measured, numbered, assessed, licensed, authorized, admonished, prevented, forbidden, reformed, corrected, punished. It is, under pretext of public utility, and in the name of the general interest, to be placed under contribution, drilled, fleeced, exploited, monopolized, extorted from, squeezed, hoaxed, robbed; then, at the slightest resistance, the first word of complaint, to be repressed, fined, vilified, harassed, hunted down, abused, clubbed, disarmed, bound, choked, imprisoned, judged, condemned, shot, deported, sacrificed, sold, betrayed; and to crown all, mocked, ridiculed, derided, outraged, dishonored. That is government; that is its justice; that is its morality.

— P.J. Proudhon

Government is the enemy of all well-intentioned, decent, industrious men.

— H.L. Mencken

Since when have we Americans been expected to bow submissively to authority and speak with awe and reverence to those who represent us?

— William Douglas

NATURAL LAW vs. POLITICAL LAW

I'd like to begin this lengthy chapter with a few words about . . . my grandmother. Not that she has won some kind of prestigious award, or is renowned for some great achievement. She is a pretty typical elderly woman in her late 80s, but ironically this would seem to make her story unusual.

My elderly grandmother has been required, since 2000, to have her Social Security Number on her driver's license. Why must she give a formerly private federal number on state documents as a national identifier? Because of the so-called "Deadbeat Dads Database" legislation which alleges to track fathers who are delinquent on their child-support payments.

Hmmm. My grandmother is in a Deadbeat Dads Database. Well, she's a she, and can't be a dad. Not only that, being nearly 90 she can't have any more children. Furthermore, even her youngest child is post-menopausal!

If my grandmother spends more than $3,000 in cash she is then required to fill out a federal Currency Transaction Report allegedly designed to uncover drug-dealing money launderers.

If my grandmother cashes someone's check at their bank, she must submit her fingerprint to the teller even though she can produce ID. This is to allegedly thwart fraudulent checks.

When my grandmother boards a commercial airliner, she must remove her shoes and walk in stocking feet through a magnetometer. If she's lucky, she avoids being groped by some "security officer." This is allegedly for everyone's safety, even though the historic hijacker has been a Middle Eastern male, someone we're now officially prohibited from profiling. (It is against public policy to search more than 2 Arabs per flight, and airlines have been fined $150,000+ for doing so.)

If my grandmother goes to purchase a handgun for personal protection, the transaction must first be approved by the FBI in a computerized background check with a notoriously flawed database.

If my grandmother wants a report of the health records that she herself was responsible for generating, she will be told that she has no access to such records, but that nearly any government agency does.

Folks, we're no longer presumed innocent, we're presumed guilty. We're no longer punished for what we've done, but for what we might do. This "prior restraint" is a slap in the face of our Common Law heritage, and is carried to such ridiculous extremes that 90 year old ladies are now automatically presumed to be people of aggression, theft, and fraud. My point is this: if my elderly grandmother,

> who has no underage children to support
> who does not pass hot checks
> who does not launder drug money
> who has never committed any crime
> who has a right to her own health records, and
> who never carries bombs on airliners

. . . has been caught up in the dragnet of modern federal police power allegedly constructed for criminals, then how can you or I ever expect to become free of it?

We can't.

We can't become free of it. We can't become free of it, because federal police power was subtly grafted onto the constitutional DNA in Philadelphia back in1787. And this was completely intentional.

The primary source of America's ills is her rejection of the Natural Law. There are just Two Rules in life. Encapsulated by my colleague Rick Maybury in just 17 words:

> **Do all you have agreed to do, and**
> **Do not encroach on other persons or their property.**

The first covers civil law; the second criminal. Civil and criminal matters, all neatly contained within those 17 words. This is the law which the Apostle Paul spoke of in Romans Chapter 2 Verse 15 as being written in our hearts. Meaning, the capacity for Natural Law was issued to us as universal inventory, along with the rest of our vital organs. It is in our very nature to recognize and wish to obey the Natural Law. This is why every major religion in history is in accord with those 17 words:

> Do all you have agreed to do, and
> Do not encroach on other persons or their property.

If a stranger hasn't a "right" to any of your time, your earnings, or your property — society (a collection of strangers) hasn't the right, either. You have no "duty to society" but this:

> To pull your own weight.
> To produce no less than you consume.
> To honor your agreements.
> To not hinder others as they do the same.

The Western world codified this over time and called it the Common Law. Common Law was the system for discovering and applying Natural Law in human affairs. I say "was the system" because we don't have it any more. It's been stolen from us. Since law contains the guidelines for the use of force, governments want control of these guidelines to make themselves exempt. This is why governments hate the Common Law, and always nationalize the justice industry in order to implement their preferred system, Political Law. The Natural Law was stolen from us by government, and replaced with legal positivism, in which the law is no better than the source of its authority.

This substitution was the ulterior motive of the "Founding Lawyers" of 1787 during the constitutional convention at Philadelphia. The American Revolution was a war over the difference between Scientific Natural Law and Political Law. After six years of war, the colonial forces fighting for Natural Law prevailed against the British in 1781 at Yorktown. Yet, the forces desiring Political Law had not been totally defeated. By 1787, they had successfully clamored for a constitutional convention "for the sole and express purpose of revising the Articles of Confederation."

That was their *ostensible* goal.

Of the 55 delegates, 41 were politicians and 34 were lawyers. Only 8 had signed the Declaration of Independence, and 6 the Articles of Confederation. The famous revolutionaries were *not* delegates. Jefferson and John Adams were in Europe, Patrick Henry had refused outright, while Thomas Paine, Sam Adams, and Christopher Gadsden were not even chosen. My point here is this: we had *two* sets of Founding Fathers: one which fought the Revolution, and a second which foisted upon an unsuspecting nation a new constitution chock full of Political Law. The first set of Founding Fathers fought for the rule of Natural Law.

The second set of Founding Fathers organized to demolish the Natural Law and erect a system of legal positivism. Their true goal was to scrap the Articles of Confederation entirely and replace it with a new government combining various elements of a republic, democracy, federation, and mercantilistic state. And what kind of system did the Constitution ordain? Alexis deTocqueville understood what kind back in 1825: "*an incomplete national government*".

Not, as we've been taught in school, a federal government but an incomplete national government, one which would be gradually completed over time through the clever clauses of "*necessary and proper*" and "*supreme law of the land*" which energized the treaty and interstate commerce sections. A new government not based on Natural Law, but on Political Law. The Constitution was the "settlement of the American Revolution."

The forces behind Natural Law had won the American Revolution, only to lose it within a single decade. The so-called anti-Federalists of the day were highly incensed. Patrick Henry warned in 1788 that "*Congress, from their general powers, may fully go into the business of human regulation .... By this Constitution some of the best barriers of human rights are thrown away .... That paper should have declared the common law in force.*"

After the anti-Federalists failed to prevent the Constitution's ratification in 1789, they did manage to push through two years later what we now call the Bill of Rights. It was their attempt to reassert at least some Natural Law. While the Bill of Rights has helped to limit government, it sadly hasn't lasted over time.

With the help of the federal courts, the 10 Amendments have been reduced to little more than speed bumps in the road of Tyranny. Our 2nd, 4th, and 5th Amendment rights, for example, are 80% gone. We no longer have rights, we have permissions. Permission to speak, permission to publish, permission to own weapons for self-defense, permission to own a business and keep (perhaps) half the profits.

We are being regulated to death, as deTocqueville described:

> *The will of man is not shattered but softened, bent and guided; men are seldom forced by it to act, but they are constantly retrained from acting. Such a power does not destroy, but it prevents existence; it does not tyrannize, but it compresses, enervates, extinguishes, and stupefies a people, till each nation is reduced to be nothing better than a flock of timid and industrial animals, of which government is the shepherd.*

Does anybody truly believe that your Government is dedicated to freedom and flourishing of every American? America is not the freest country in the world. We are merely the healthiest patient in the cancer ward. And to cure the patient would kill the doctor.

All indices show that America's standard of living peaked in about 1973, and has fallen ever since. Those born in the 1990s are the first generation who cannot be expected to live better than their parents. And why is that? Because we have lost the Natural Law, that device which makes justice and prosperity possible. Because Force and Fraud are, due to government regulation, inherent in nearly every transaction, the *laissez-faire* Win-Win scenario is generally a faint and fond memory. Thus, through millions of transactions involving guaranteed loss, America is sliding backwards. Such has been the course of all collectivist nations in history.

Because the scientific Common Law has been stolen from us, we no longer have the tool necessary to discover legal principles in such divisive matters as:

abortion
animal rights
assisted suicide
child theory and the age of majority
euthanasia
genetic engineering
ownership of ancient archeological sites
ownership of extraterrestrial materials
ownership of orbits
ownership of scenic views
reproduction rights of mental incompetents
space junk
surrogate motherhood
thermal pollution

Now, these things are left up to random, ever changing democratic persuasion, assuming such can still prevail against the entrenched hierarchy. Because of the inherent turbulence of opinion, we'll never arrive at wise, stable answers to the above dilemmas.

Even though the 2nd Amendment clearly states that your right to keep and bear arms "shall not be infringed," (which is strong, unequivocable verbiage that no other Amendment enjoys), Political law applied to your right to keep and bear arms has made illegal:

rifles too short
handguns too long
rifles too military-looking
guns too powerful
and all guns too quiet

You'll go to jail if your gun has a muffler, and if your car does not. Because of the rule of Political Law, in Vermont it is illegal to whistle under water. Well, has that become a problem?

BIRTH AND DEATH OF A REPUBLIC

Most of the trouble in the world is caused by people wanting to be important.
— T.S. Eliot

When planning for posterity, we ought to remember that virtue is not hereditary.
— Thomas Paine

Imagine that the 50 States are sovereign, Independent Households — each with their own families. These Independent Households live next to each other within a geographical area — a few blocks on State Street.

A rash of vandalism and crime descends upon the neighborhood. Also, the city wants to put a toxic-waste dump nearby. The Independent Households now have a definite *common* interest — to stop local crime and prevent the proposed toxic-waste dump. They realize they will work more effectively together as a republic, rather than separately. So, the Independent Households form a neighborhood security force and representative body to the city called **United Households of State Street (UHSS).**

The *only* purpose for UHSS is to combat foreign vandals and prevent the toxic-waste dump. The Independent Households finance UHSS for those purposes only, and none other. The Independent

Households choose Jeff R. Son as their UHSS representative. Remember, the Independent Households remain sovereign, meaning that each Household runs itself without any outside interference. The family matters within each Household are for *that* Household's government (parents) to decide.

the beginning of the end for the Republic

> *Only a virtuous people can be free. Freedom can survive only if the people are inwardly governed by a moral law.*
> — John Courtney Murray

Things work well for about 70 days. UHSS reduces burglaries, thwarts the dump, and stays out of the Independent Households' affairs. However, the city has grown frustrated with the Households' successful union and tries the old "divide and conquer" ploy.

There happens to be some bitter Northern Household animosity over an activity practiced in the Southern Households. The Northern Households want the Southern Households to stop and the Southern Households want the Northern Households to butt out. The city secretly antagonizes this friction. Also, the city funds the successful election of candidate B.R. O'Crat over Jeff R. Son.

Things become so tense that the Southern Households threaten to secede from UHSS if the Northern Households don't back off. The Northern Households claim that UHSS cannot be split apart. The Southern Households secede and form their *own* security force; **Confederate Households of State Street (CHSS).**

Fighting begins between the Northern and Southern Households and lasts four days. This is the **"War Between the Households."** The Northern Households and the UHSS win. The CHSS is dissolved and the Southern households are forced back into the UHSS. The war decided that the Union of the households took precedence over their sovereignty.

unlimited democracy = unlimited *kleptocracy*

> *1. The undermining of the dignity and sanctity of the home, which is the basis for human society.*
> *2. Higher and higher taxes: the spending of public money for free bread and circuses for the populace.*
> *3. The mad craze for pleasure, with sports and play becoming more exciting, more brutal, and more immoral.*
> *4. The building of great armaments when the real enemy was within – a decay of individual responsibility.*

> *5. The decay of religion, whose leaders lost touch with life and their power to guide.*
>
> – Edward Gibbon, 1788, *Decline and Fall of the Roman Empire*

The households were so busy getting their lives back in order, they forgot all about B.R. O'Crat. First, he demands money from the households for a neighborhood beautification program. Even though this isn't in the UHSS charter, the households agree. Next, B.R. O'Crat issues rules on how the households are to maintain their lawns. The households fuss about it, but go along with the new lawncare regulations. Then, the UHSS demands that a *percentage* of each household's income be "contributed" into a neighborhood insurance program to protect the households in case of property damage. Though also not within the UHSS charter, the households grudgingly support the "Neighborhood Insurance" program.

Because of roving vandals (secretly funded by the UHSS), the UHSS strengthens the neighborhood security force and establishes a curfew while demanding more household "contributions" to meet the "vandal threat." The fearful households agree. Then, the UHSS decrees a free allowance given to any child who cannot find "suitable" odd jobs for pocket money. Household "contributions" rise again to pay for these allowances.

A few days later, the UHSS decrees that the children will *also* have the right to vote in the upcoming UHSS election. B.R. O'Crat is retiring; running in his place is Moe Uvda Saym, who promises more gardeners and security guards, higher allowances for kids, and subsidized candy. The working parents within the households are alarmed at the high cost of maintaining the UHSS, and nominate Les Taxes as their candidate. Les Taxes promises lower "contributions" and reduced UHSS authority. Soon, he is leading in the polls. A very important election is held, and working parents are shocked that Moe Uvda Saym wins. It is later learned that agents of the UHSS tinkered with the voting software and rigged the election so that Les Taxes would lose.

Realizing that democracy has been subverted, the parents arm themselves to kick out Moe Uvda Saym and his cronies, and restore the UHSS to its original limited charter.

(Except for the last paragraph of the story, you've just read a history of the United States of America.)

> *When a country works reasonably well - when the schools teach algebra and not governmentally mandated Appropriate Values,*

when the police are scarce and courteous, when government is remote and minds its business and works more for the benefit of the country than for looters and special interests, then pledging to it a degree of allegiance isn't foolish. Decades back America was such a country, imperfect as all countries are, but good enough to cherish.

As decline begins, and government becomes oppressive, self-righteous, and ruthless yet incompetent, as official spying flourishes, as corruption sets in hard, and institutions rot, it is time to disengage. Loyalty to a country is a choice, not an obligation. In other times people have loved family, friends, common decency, tribe, regiment, or church instead of country. In an age of national collapse, this is wise.

— Fred Reed, "Bail",
http://archive.lewrockwell.com/reed/reed210.html

tyranny by the tax-consuming masses

Envy implies ill will, spite, and hostility toward others, of wanting what others possess (or appear to have). ***If the object of envy cannot be possessed, it should be destroyed so that no one else can have it either.***

—Robert P. Vichas; *Annotated Handbook of Biblical Quotations, Verses, and Parables*

It is difficult to conceive of a more worrisome relationship than that between ignorant voters and highly knowledgeable, well-organized political activists.

— Ilya Somin

How can a nation survive when a majority of its citizens, now dependent on government services, no longer have the incentive to restrain the growth of government?

— Congressman Jim DeMint (SC)

Wrath is cruel, and anger is outrageous; but who is able to stand before envy?

— Proverbs 23:17

the rope-pulling experiment

In the 1930s a sociologist named Ringelmann had a brilliant idea to test his theory that collective action is weaker than the sum of its energy parts. He selected eight men, each with identical rope-pulling strength. However, when teamed together these men did not pull at their full individual strength: 3 pulled with the strength of 2.6, 5 pulled as 3.5, and 8 pulled with the strength of 5. *I.e.*, much of each individual's potential might went unused in a collective effort. This "social loafing" is just human nature: why pull 100% when others are on the same rope? Reimann concluded that this experiment demonstrated the inherently wasted energy in public projects. Politicians pander to this phenomenon.

> *If the 2012 election showed us anything it was just how blindly committed the American electorate is towards fundamentally changing the United States from a country of freedom and individualism to one of mediocre egalitarianism and commune. For a spectacular failure like Barack Obama to get re-elected with such a pathetic message only proves just how delusional the people are and how hopeless the situation is.*
>
> *A large hurdle many Real Americans will face is jettisoning their moral and ethical code when it comes to independence, self-reliance, and hard work. It has been ingrained in us genetically, it has been reinforced socially, and it is part of what we value and pride ourselves on. Unfortunately such honorable ethics are not only obsolete, they are a liability.*
>
> *With government spending accounting for 40% of GDP and half of all Americans collecting a government check, the rules of the game have fundamentally changed. The social contract between producers and parasites is no longer one of temporary, emergency assistance, needed solely to ensure an economic parasite returns to production as quickly as possible. It is now a political class of slave-masters that purposely, knowingly, and actively vote to live off of the producers. This requires all Real Americans have the courage to acknowledge and accept this fact, as well as change their behaviors accordingly.*
>
> – *Enjoy The Decline*, "Captain Capitalism"

By a multiplication of despots, the taxpaying parents are democratically outvoted by their tax-consuming children and the UHSS employees. The children get their higher allowances and candy. The UHSS security force keeps the parents in line, who toil the rest of their lives as indentured servants for the UHSS and its patrons. This is *always* the end result of unlimited majority rule; virtual slavery of the productive citizens by those who live on government favors and welfare. Ultimately, the fleas, the heartworms and the ticks overwhelm the dog.

> ***A democracy cannot exist as a permanent form of government.*** *It can only exist until a majority of voters discover that they can vote themselves largess out of the public treasury.*
>
> – Alexander Tytler

> *The democracy will cease to exist when you take away from those who are willing to work and give to those who would not.*
>
> — Thomas Jefferson

> *We no longer believe that it is just for one man to govern two men, but we have yet to outgrow the absurd belief that it is just for two men to govern one man.*
>
> — Charles T. Sprading; *Liberty and the Great Libertarians*

> ***Special interest politics is a simple game.*** *A hundred people sit in a circle, each with his pocket full of pennies. A politician walks around the outside of the circle, taking a penny from each person. No one minds; who cares about a penny? When he has gotten all the way around the circle, the politician throws fifty cents down in front of one person, who is overjoyed at the unexpected windfall. The process is repeated ending with a different person.* ***After a hundred rounds everyone is a hundred cents poorer, fifty cents richer, and happy.***
>
> — David Friedman; *The Machinery of Freedom*

Everyone is fifty cents poorer, *while the politician is fifty dollars richer!* Think about that.

> *Government is a broker in pillage, and every election is a sort of advance auction of the sale of stolen goods.*
>
> — H.L. Mencken

> *The day will come* [in the United States] *when a multitude of people will choose* [through universal suffrage] *the legislature. Is it possible to doubt what sort of a legislature will be chosen? On the one side is a statesman preaching patience, respect for rights, strict observance of public faith. On the other is a demagogue ranting about the tyranny of capitalism and usurers and asking why anybody should be permitted to drink champagne and to ride in a carriage while thousands of honest people are in want of necessaries. Which of the candidates is likely to be preferred by a workman? . . . . When society has entered on this downward progress, either civilization or liberty must perish.*
>
> — Thomas Macualay, his 1857 prediction

> *A government that robs Peter to pay Paul can always depend on the support of Paul.*
>
> — George Benard Shaw

> *Let us always have in mind that every attempt in the history of the world to establish a loafer's paradise has wound up a dictator's hell-hole.*
>
> — Harold E. Stassen

We must put an end to this, *not* by eliminating the democratic election of public officials, but by amputating the ravenous grasp of *envy and laziness* within the democratic process.

> *It only stands to reason that where there's sacrifice, there's someone collecting the sacrificial offerings. Where there's service, there is someone being served. The man who speaks to you of sacrifice is speaking of slaves and masters, and intends to be the master.*
>
> – Ayn Rand

Before the tax on wages, the tax-consumers had little to grasp, since the federal government agent had little to confiscate. Now that the federal government steals, at gunpoint, one-third of this nation's production, there is plenty for it to pass along to its voting welfare clientele. Whenever envy and laziness can be *politically cultivated and rewarded* through the democratic process, that nation is on its deathbed.

The vote cannot be allowed as a financial substitute for working.

We no longer have a limited, Republican form of government as required by the Constitution (IV:4:1). We have a *de facto* national government of democratic socialism.

> ***It is bad to be oppressed by a minority, but it is worse to be oppressed by a majority.*** *For there is a reserve of latent power* (envy) *in the masses which, if it is called into play* (and it always is), *the* [productive] *minority can seldom resist. But from the absolute will of an entire people there is no appeal, no redemption, no refuge . . . .*
>
> – Lord Acton; *The History of Freedom in Antiquity*

> *. . . the principle that comfort trumps democracy underlies society today. We have the trappings of election, the theater of close counts, the excitement of watching the polls – that is, the emotions associated with a tight football season. But what real influence do we have? Can we divert the remotely chosen path of our children's education, alter or even speak against the flow of immigrants across our borders, question racial preferences? No. These things are decided for us. We can lose our jobs for speaking of them. The more things matter, the less we can say about them.*
>
> *. . . We can exercise any freedom that doesn't endanger the status quo. We can live where we want, change jobs, watch*

> *pornography, read seditious books and even write them (provided we don't seek a wide circulation), and buy endless things we don't need or much want. But we can't speak our minds.*
>
> *. . . the satisfaction of the drives for food, comfort, sex and entertainment* [misdirects us from important issues]. *Satiety breeds indifference.*
>
> — Fred Reed, *Nekkid in Austin*, p. 215

> *1. You cannot legislate the poor into prosperity by legislating the wealthy out of prosperity.*
> *2. What one person receives without working for, another person must work for without receiving.*
> *3. The government cannot give to anybody anything that the government does not first take from somebody else.*
> *4. When half of the people get the idea that they do not have to work because the other half is going to take care of them, and when the other half gets the idea that it does no good to work because somebody else is going to get what they work for, that my dear friend, is the beginning of the end of any nation.*
> *5. You cannot multiply wealth by dividing it.*
>
> — Adrian Rogers

I *do* believe in the democratic election of public officials, only if one first recognizes the potential dangers of democracy. In the hands of a lazy, envious, self-righteous majority, democracy is the most *vicious* tyrant of all. Norman Thomas (1884—1968) was a leading American socialist, pacifist, and six-time presidential candidate for the Socialist Party of America. As a 1944 candidate for President, Thomas said:

> *The American people will never knowingly adopt socialism. But, under the name of "liberalism", they will adopt every fragment of the socialist program, until one day America will be a socialist nation, without knowing how it happened.*

Years later, he went on to say: "*I no longer need to run as a Presidential Candidate for the Socialist Party. The Democratic Party has adopted our platform.*" Well, gosh.

> *Kleptocrats throughout the ages have resorted to a mixture of four solutions:*
>
> *1. Disarm the populace, and arm the elite.*
>
> *2. Make the masses happy by redistributing much of the tribute* [theft by taxes] *received, in popular ways.*
>
> *3. Use the monopoly of force to promote happiness, by maintaining public order and curbing violence.*
>
> *4. Construct an ideology or religion justifying kleptocracy.*
>
> — Jared Diamond, *Guns, Germs, and Steel*

Arguing over who should have their hands on the levers of centralized power totally ignores the point that those levers shouldn't exist (to be eventually abused) in the first place.

— Tom Baugh, http://militantlibertarian.org/2010/10/27/a-plus-b-equals-your-worst-nightmare/

OUR MODERN HERD

I define evil, then, as the exercise of political power — that is, the imposition of one's will upon others by overt or covert action — in order to avoid extending one's self for the purpose of nurturing spiritual growth. Ordinary laziness is nonlove; evil is antilove.

— Dr. M. Scott Peck

I used to haunt a small-town Colorado microbrewery for its weekly burger parties. Once, a friend joined me at one of them. We stood at the periphery of this young, dredlocked, dog-owning, happy throng in mute amazement at their conviviality and camaraderie. I turned to my friend and asked, "*Hey, Dave, why don't we have anything like this?*" He replied they were herd animals, and libertarians like us were not.

Herd animals. It explained a lot, succinctly. But why were they herd animals? What compelled them to clump in groups? Author Michael Crichton, as usual, had an insight:

Over the last thirty years, scientists had studied predator-prey interaction in everything from the lion to the hyena to the warrior ant. There was now a much better understanding of how prey defended themselves. Animals like zebras and caribou didn't live in herds because they were sociable; herding was a defense against predation.

. . . [C]oordinated group movements made it harder for predators to pick out a single individual. Predators were drawn to attack an animal that was distinctive in some way. . . . So the message was simple. Stay together. Stay the same.

— Michael Crichton, *Prey* (2002), p. 287-8

A light went on inside my mind. I now had a new and valuable revelation about my philosophical and political foe: the collectivist. Stay together and the same, and you'll stay alive.

. . . Those studies agreed on one thing. Whether you modeled warrior ants or Serengeti lions, the studies confirmed one major dynamic: left to their own devices, predators would kill all the

> *prey until none remained – unless there was a prey refuge. In real life the prey refuge might be a nest in a tree, or an underground den, or a deep pool in a river. If the prey had a refuge, they'd survive. Without a refuge, the predators would kill them all.* (p. 306)

But who or what is *our* predator? Well, Nature, for one. However, some people (such as farmers and mountain men) are equipped in psyche and spirit to deal successfully with Nature. But not every human being must join a pack for sheer survival. Nature alone is not the entire answer. Another component of predation must still exist. It does: intra-species predation. It is highly unusual in Nature — except for *Homo Sapiens*.

Without meaning to, Crichton pointed the way to a new understanding of collcctivist politics. Liberals and neocons alike view a society with free individuals as (in one of two different ways) a brutal state of nature. To the liberals, greedy businessmen would (without regulations) pay us all 25¢ an hour as they raped the environment. To the neocons, without a different set of regulations, humanity would speedily reduce itself to rampant immorality and chaos. As Joseph Sobran quipped:

> If you want government to intervene abroad, you're a conservative.
> If you want government to intervene at home, you're a liberal.
> If you want government to intervene everywhere, you're a centrist.
> If you want government to intervene nowhere, you're an extremist.

So, both camps of collectivists busy themselves in "protecting" the rest of us from their own respective fears. Both camps endeavor to create their own unique "prey refuge." Greed is the predator of the liberals — of the neocons, depravity. (I often wonder about the probable psychological "projection". Perhaps liberals are instrinsically more greedy than they can admit, and the neocons more skanky. It seems a fair question.)

It boils down to this paradigm: we libertarian, free-enterprise types have had to endure intergenerational political battles (waged by others) to determine *which* prey refuge will be imposed on us — when we never naturally considered ourselves to be prey, much less those in need of a refuge.

And we certainly don't consider ourselves to be predators, but that is how the collectivist prey see us. For their own warped sense of protection, those prey become our predator. It is truly an odd world.

BE *VERY* SKEPTICAL OF GOVERNMENT

> *Government has one unique power that we, as mere citizens, do not have: the power to use force to accomplish its goals. This should make us suspicious of government at all times.*
>
> – Neal Boortz, *Somebody's Gotta Say It*

> *All governments are run by liars and nothing they say should be believed.*
>
> – I.F. Stone

> *They have given us into the hands*
> *of the new unhappy lords,*
> *Lords without anger and honour,*
> *who dare not carry their swords.*
> *They fight by shuffling papers;*
> *they have bright dead alien eyes;*
> *They look at our labour and laughter*
> *as a tired man looks at flies.*
> *And the load of their loveless pity*
> *is worse than the ancient wrongs,*
> *Their doors are shut in the evenings;*
> *and they know no songs.*
>
> – G.K. Chesterton, *The Secret People*

> *Power corrupts, and absolute power corrupts absolutely.*
>
> – Lord Acton

> *. . . the Government will only make use of these powers in so far as they are essential for carrying out vitally necessary measures.*
>
> – Adolf Hitler, explaining the Enabling Bill of 1934, allowing him executive order privileges

In 1945 Berlin, with the German collapse just weeks away, a young girl declared to her family that the war was lost, and the Nazi Propaganda minister's claims of an imminent military reversal were false. Her mother, horrified, replied, "*Would Herr Doktor Goebbels lie to us at a time like this?!*" Well, duh.

All governments, including ours, are run by liars, with agendas far behind the public scenes:

> *Once the ruling members of the Council on Foreign Relations have decided that the U.S. Government should adopt a particular policy, the very substantial research facilities of CFR are put to work to develop arguments, intellectual and emotional, to support the new policy, and to confound and discredit, intellectually and*

> *politically, any opposition. The most articulate theoreticians and ideologists prepare related articles, aided by the research, to sell the new policy and to make it appear inevitable and irresistible.*
>
> — Rear Admiral Chester Ward, former Judge Advocate General of the U.S. Navy and a member of the CFR for sixteen years, in his book *Kissinger on the Couch* (1975)

> *To acquire immunity to eloquence is of the utmost importance to the citizens of a democracy.*
>
> — Bertrand Russell

Here is a hard, realistic rule that will serve you quite well:

Presume government *guilty*, until proven innocent.

Remember, government produces nothing — it only takes from producers. Government is a parasite which never shrinks on its own, and will do anything to remain on its "host", the American people. Government steals, and will easily lie to keep you from realizing how much is daily stolen from you.

> *Only the vigilant can maintain their liberties, and only those who are constantly and intelligently on the spot can hope to govern themselves effectively by democratic procedures. A society, most of whose members spend a great part of their time, not on the spot, not here and now and in the calculable future, but somewhere else, in the irrelevant other worlds of sport and soap opera, of mythology and metaphysical fantasy, will find it hard to resist the encroachments of those who would manipulate and control it.*
>
> *In their propaganda today's dictators rely for the most part on repetition, suppression and rationalization—the repetition of catchwords which they wish to be accepted as true, the suppression of facts which they wish to be ignored, the arousal and rationalization of passions which may be used in the interests of the Party or the State. As the art and science of manipulation come to be better understood, the dictators of the future will doubtless learn to combine these techniques with the non-stop distractions which, in the West, are now threatening to drown in a sea of irrelevance the rational propaganda essential to the maintenance of individual liberty and the survival of democratic institutions.*
>
> — Aldous Huxley; *Brave New World Revisited*

the Tuskegee Institute syphilis experiment

From 1932 to 1972 the U.S. Public Health Service (forerunner of the Center for Disease Control) deliberately withheld effective treatment of poor black men in Alabama for their syphilis. They were lured into the study by a government letter that read:

REMEMBER, THIS IS YOUR LAST CHANCE FOR SPECIAL FREE TREATMENT.
BE SURE TO MEET THE NURSE.

This was an "open secret" experiment, widely known throughout the medical community. No doctor protested, until Dr. Irwin Schatz wrote a scathing letter in 1965:

> *I am utterly astounded by the fact the physicians allow patients with a potentially fatal disease to remain untreated when effective therapy is available.*

Dr. Anne Yobs of the U.S. Public Health Service privately commented:

> *This is the first letter of this type we have received. I do not plan to answer this letter.*

Finally, an outraged federal employee, Peter Buxton, leaked details to the *Associated Press*. The federal government later settled a class action suit for $10,000,000 to the victims.

no more precious metal in our money

Just before President Lyndon Johnson removed all silver from our coinage in 1968, he promised the public that the government would never do such a thing. This is typical of politicians.

the embarrassing truth about 9/11

The legal and economic history of our nation's decline I quite well understand. But the sociological foundation required for this patent squandering of our Common Law rights escapes my comprehension.

By some process not entirely clear to me, we have developed into a people unable to hear the truth, and thus have achieved a government incapable of telling the truth.

Be they schools, airliners, or post offices — the fact that mandatory "gun-free" zones get defenseless people killed is the truth which can neither be heard nor told in this country.

What is the core truth about 9/11 Americans cannot hear and their Government cannot tell? The only one which no major newspaper can dare report? That 9/11 happened because of American cowardice. According to the official story, our airplanes were hijacked by 5-man teams. Outnumbered by 20 to 1, and armed with only boxcutters, our airplanes were apparently hijacked and flown into buildings by 5-man teams.

First, we submit to 30 years of unilateral in-flight passenger disarmament. Then, when a pack of rabid, opportunistic losers take notice of such a ripe vulnerability, what does America clamor for? To become even *more* defenselessness! The airport confiscation of their tweezers and nail clippers! (And let's put up a fuss about arming pilots, too!) One definition of insanity is the repetition of action with the expectation of different results. Unilaterally disarmed passengers invite hijackings. Yet what was the national response to 9/11? Disarming passengers even further.

That is nothing short of insanity.

Terror, like dancing, requires two participants: one to lead, the other to follow. Manhattan lost several prominent skyscrapers and over 3,000 people because Americans gave up their dignity to remain armed. They chose the likelihood of terror. Now, we've regressed to the pitiful state of children, whimpering for Sky Marshals on every flight. *Daddy, protect us from the Bad Men!*

> *It is inevitable that eventually the people will demand absolute security from the State. And absolute security is absolute slavery.*
>
> — Taylor Caldwell

I'm not talking about merely being afraid. I'm talking about being terrorized — terrorized to the point that dozens of grown men will allow themselves to be herded like cattle to the back of a Boeing by a few guys with boxcutters. I'm talking about dozens of grown men being so terrorized that they will helplessly watch a stewardess get her throat slit before their very eyes.

This is the price — this is the result — of cowardice. Whatever happened to the Men in this country? In the event of a water landing, your removable seat cushion will serve as a flotation device? How about: in the event of a terrorist hijacking, your removable armrest will serve as a club! Hijack us now, Mohammed Atta!

Government regulations got 3,000 people killed on 9/11, and *then* reduced your freedoms further with the "PATRIOT" Act.

> *No one can point to a single incident where national security was impaired because someone insisted on their right to free speech or their right to privacy or their right to due process.*
>
> — Judge Andrew Napolitano

America is an entrenched culture of the lie; little wonder that our government so rarely tells the truth. Our masters insist that exchanging liberty for security is necessary during the (Forever) War On Terrorism. Well, that lie has been hawked by every government supremacist in history. As William Pitt commented in the 1770s:

> *Necessity is the plea for every infringement of human freedom. It is the argument of tyrants; it is the creed of slaves.*

our government's wars

> *The world is governed by very different personages from what is imagined by those who are not behind the scenes.*
>
> — English Prime Minister Benjamin Disraeli

> *What luck for the rulers that men do not think.*
>
> — Adolf Hitler

> *Taxes are not raised to carry on wars, wars are raised to carry on taxes.*
>
> — Thomas Paine

> *If Tyranny and Oppression come to this land, it will be in the guise of fighting a foreign enemy.*
>
> — James Madison

> *The purpose of the State is to secure power through a war on the people. The purpose of war is to defeat a people in order to establish a* [new] *State. The State is a never ending war on the domestic population; war is a temporary aggression on a foreign people.*
>
> — Per Bylund

the 2009 economic meltdown

When investors began to lose confidence in the stock market, Treasury Secretary Paulson urged the public not to sell because of some imminent recovery. It soon came out that this was *intentionally* bad advice, but the government tried to defend their lies as necessary:

> [T]*he Treasury Department said that any review of* [patently misleading and false] *announcements last year must be considered in light of the unprecedented circumstances in which they were made.*
>
> — www.nytimes.com/2009/10/05/business/economy/05bank.html

Translation: when our elected representatives and their appointed officials believe we need to be manipulated, they rationalize their lies based on whether they think we need them at the time.

In this specific case, the Treasury Department's lies (via Hank Paulson) encouraged people to hold their investments. Therefore, if you listened to Paulson et al, you literally lost your hard earned money and life savings. Last time I checked, citizens should not expect to get fiscally hosed by their Treasury Secretary.

— www.sweetness-light.com/archive/shocker-bailed-out-banks-werent-healthy

Learn to daily think for yourself, refuse to take government propaganda as truth, and research matters with your own mind. The more you see a particular issue being hammered in the news, the more suspicious you should become. (Remember the 2009 hysteria over getting your flu shots? It turns out that more people got sick from the *shots* than those who refused the shots! Ask around.)

There is ample evidence in our view (on the Internet) that the powers-that-be seek continued global convergence and control. Most conspiracy theories in fact deal with ways that the elite plans to create and increase this control. The Daily Bell itself is an outgrowth of this phenomenon, pointing out on a regular basis how elite fear-based promotions are initiated and configured to permeate Western culture. Each of these promotions has as its goal, in our opinion, (cumulatively, anyway) the formation and expansion of world government. The pattern is not hard to detect, we believe. One does not have to be "paranoid" to do so.

—http://www.thedailybell.com/1307/10-Credible-Conspiracy-Theories.html

the Supreme Court upholds ObamaCare

Am I surprised at this morning's news? No. The only thing that is the least bit surprising is that it was Roberts, who was heretofore considered a "constructionist", and not Kennedy, who finally put the last nail in the coffin of the First American Republic. The corpse inside said coffin has been dead for years. Let's call GWB's administration the terminal illness, Obama's usurpation in November of 2008 as the actual moment of death of the First American Republic, the last 3.5 years as one long funeral dirge, and today as the final graveside interment service. The First American Republic done got low, and now is taking the long dirt nap. It's all over except for the rotten, rotten descendents sniping over the estate like buzzards.

Bottom line: since I fully understand and accept that the Republic is dead and the Constitution is no longer in force, and that the Rule of Law is dead, nothing surprises me.

Not an iota of ObamaCare will be touched, much less repealed. The republicans want it every bit as much as the democrats. They're all gunning for that power. They will NEVER turn loose of that power voluntarily. We are now to the point where the only way we get rid of these people and re-establish a lawful government is through involuntary removal. In short, we are either going to have to have a junta, or an all-out hot civil war. I strongly, strongly advocate a junta at this point. A junta would be, by far, the least bloody solution. Sadly, there are no men of integrity left in the flag officer corps to do it – the U.S. military is populated by vile, power-hungry, money-grubbing Marxist degenerates just as much as the three branches.

Which circles us back to the root problem of personal integrity in this nation. ***We are a nation of godless cowards and self-worshiping trash, and we will have the government we deserve as such.***

Why do I bother saying anything at all? Because I want there to be some sort of digital record showing that not every single person in this godforsaken country was a coward and an imbecile. I don't want the people who are living on this continent ten or twenty years from now to be able to whine and deflect responsibility for their sorry, sorry state by claiming that "no one ever told us" or "no one ever explained anything to us." No, you were told. You were warned. And it wasn't just me doing the warning and explaining. You will accept your suffering in SILENCE. You will blame nothing and no one except YOURSELVES. You will own the tyranny that you live under, because you begged for it. You bought it with your own stupidity, and you nurtured it with your own squealing cowardice.

– Ann Barnhardt

be very skeptical of corporate media

By diligently avoiding Truth — about nearly everything — America has fully become the People of The Lie. Lies sell better than truth by a 30 to 1 margin — the sales ratio of Fiction to Nonfiction.

For example, the entertainment industry is, at its core, in the business of selling lies. I once worked on a movie set. What struck me was that there are so many more people behind the camera than in front of it. The viewer cannot truly appreciate this because the viewer is watching the actors. And what are the actors doing? Ignoring dozens of production people and stacks of equipment in order to say words they didn't write, conveying emotions they don't own. Actors must ignore what is real to sell the viewer what is not. Actors are professional liars, and this is a multi-billion dollar industry.

Even historically based films are invariably saturated with lies. Who saw *Schindler's List*? OK, now who also read the book? I read the book. It contains many things left out of the movie. Director Steven Spielberg chose to omit one of the most important events at Schindler's camp in Czechoslovakia:

> [Oskar Schlinder] *rode day and night, not only to purchase food for the Jews in Brinnlitz camp, . . . but to buy us arms and ammunition in case the SS conceived of killing us during their retreats.*
>
> *During the winter, Oskar built up an independent arsenal . . . . Most of the weapons . . . came from a flawless source, from Obersturmbannführer Rasch, SS and police chief of Moravia. The small cache included carbines and automatic weapons, some pistols, some hand grenades.*
>
> *. . . Once Oskar had the weapons, he appointed Uri Bejski, brother of the rubber-stamp maker, keeper of the arsenal.*
>
> *. . . Having selected a small body of prisoners for training, Uri took one at a time into . . . the storehouse to teach them the mechanisms of the Gewehr 41Ws. Three commando squads of five men each were formed.*

As a shooting instructor and gun collector, I can tell you that the Walther G41W rifles mentioned were technologically quite extravagant and expensive. Very few were manufactured, and they fetch about $5,000 today. Oskar Schindler always purchased the best!

So, what did you miss in the movie? Jews with guns then disarmed the camp guards and *SS Kommandant* Motzek, who pleaded for his life — that's what you missed! Not only was this an important historical event, it would have made a fantastic scene! Who here wouldn't have enjoyed watching formerly helpless Jewish prisoners, now armed, stripping the *SS Kommandant* of his pistol and the guards of their rifles?

Yet director Steven Spielberg, himself Jewish, chose not to film this vital part of the story. He chose to lie by omission. He chose not to tell you the vital truth about the Holocaust, that it occurred solely because millions of Jews were unarmed. The few times they *did* arm themselves and resist were greatly rewarded, such as the Warsaw uprising, Sobibor, and Treblinka. Those heroic Jews not only had guns, they had unregistered guns. So should we:

> *A registered gun belongs to whomever is in political power, even temporarily. The only defense that the citizen has against tyranny is the unregistered gun.*
>
> — Jeff Cooper

Oskar Schindler bought his Jews unregistered guns! Spielberg had not only the opportunity, but the duty to tell you this truth in *Schindler's List*, but chose not to. This is all the more incredible when you learn that he has one of the largest automatic weapons collections in America. When chided for the apparent hypocrisy of his well-known support of gun-control, Spielberg is said to have replied, "*That's for them!*" Meaning, no unregistered guns for you and me.

If historically-based films are not truthful, then what about documentaries? Well, beware what poses as a "documentary" as Michael Moore's films have proven. His atrocious *Bowling For Columbine* was chock full of outright falsehoods, such as banks directly dispensing shotguns to new customers in the lobby.

UNCLE SAM IS NOT YOUR "SANTA"

> *For I mean not that other men be eased, and ye burdened...*
> — II Corinthians 8:13

> *The problem isn't a Congress that won't cut spending or a president who won't raise taxes. The problem is an American public with a bottomless sense of entitlement to federal money.*
> — P.J. O'Rourke; *Parliament of Whores*

> *In proportion as you give the State power to do things <u>for</u> you, you give it power to do things <u>to</u> you; and the State invariably makes as little as it can of the <u>one</u> power, and as much as it can of the other.*
> — Albert Jay Nock; *Memoirs of A Superfluous Man*

You have no right to complain about high taxes or government intervention in the economy while living off "Uncle Sam." Earn your own living; do not steal through the vote. Government benefits are paid for with stolen money. If you do nothing else, at least get off the taxpayers' backs!

NEVER TALK TO POLICE

> *. . . nor shall any person...be compelled in any criminal case to be a witness against himself . . .*
> — Fifth Amendment to the Constitution

> [Confession under American law must be] . . . *Free and Voluntary . . . not be extracted by any sort of threats of violence, nor obtained by any direct or implied promises, however slight, nor by the exertion of any improper influence.*
> — *Bram v. U.S.*, 168 U.S. 532 (1897)

"self-incrimination"

Because of TV shows portraying sleazy criminals who "plead the 5th" with a sneer, this vital Constitutional right seems something only the guilty would use. After all, what does an honest man have to hide? The answer is that an honest man has nothing to hide from honest men! The 5th Amendment is there to protect an honest man from *dishonest* government!

The government has a propaganda campaign to confuse the public about their 5th Amendment right to not be a witness against themselves. You've probably heard the catch phrase "*self-incrimination*" — as if your 5th Amendment right extends only to personal testimony that is "incriminating." The feds are trying to transform a *broad right* into a *limited privilege*. According to them, if you're innocent and your testimony is not "incriminating" then the 5th doesn't apply. Read the 5th Amendment yourself. It says *nothing* about "*self-incrimination*." Perhaps you still don't see the danger of an innocent man speaking freely to the police because he's not guilty of anything. He figures there's no harm; he's innocent. What can the police do to an *innocent* man?

But suppose this scenario: an armed robber was spotted fleeing in a blue Ford from the shopping mall. Ten blocks away, a policeman pulls over Mr. N.O. Cent for speeding. N.O. Cent *also* drives a blue Ford. RADIO FLASH! Suspect fled from Northgate Mall in a blue Ford. "*Were you just at Northgate Mall?*," the officer asks. N.O. Cent has no idea what's going on, but he naturally wants to be helpful to the officer. He's an honest citizen who gladly assists the police. And because of it, N.O. Cent is about to be arrested. He *was* at the mall, and says so. **N.O. Cent has just "incriminated" himself without even knowing it.**

RADIO FLASH! Suspect is described as white male, six feet tall, 200 lbs., blond hair, jeans and T-shirt. Obviously, thousands fit that description. But that's not what the police officer is thinking. He's thinking that N.O. Cent is looking more and more like his man. The officer calls in and asks where the suspect was last heading. The answer comes back; south on 12th Avenue. N.O. Cent is handcuffed, read his rights (maybe) and hauled off to jail. (This sort of thing happens every day.)

At this point, N.O. Cent, who's never committed a crime in his life, has a felony arrest record. Presumably, this horror story will all be cleared up when the police catch the real robber. But, the police are no longer searching — they've already "found" him. The police are not looking to clear N.O. Cent — they're looking to convict him. **The best thing for him to do right now is to *shut up* and call his attorney.** But N.O. Cent is so stunned about all this that he keeps trying to convince the detectives of his innocence. He unwittingly confirms tiny pieces of circumstantial evidence as his activities bear a striking similarity to those of the robber. Mall employees recall N.O. Cent near the store which was robbed, a parking lot witness seems almost positive that N.O. Cent was the guy, etc.

This is enough for the D.A. He files charges against N.O. Cent for armed robbery. It's the evening's big news story. His neighbors make snide comments like "*just when you thought you really knew somebody . . .*" Because of Channel Zero's sensationalist and misleading coverage, the public believes that N.O. Cent is an outwardly normal citizen who has a hidden dark side. A Dr. Jekyll and Mr. Hyde, if you will. (Anybody charged with a notorious crime goes through *two* trials: the one before the *press*, and the one before the *court*. The verdict of the first trial will influence the verdict of the second.)

The trial is a disaster. N.O. Cent is so embittered over all this that he doesn't make a good witness. His court-appointed attorney is resplendent in mediocrity. But N.O. Cent doesn't need mediocrity — he needs Perry Mason. And who is "Perry Mason"? The District Attorney! Uh, oh. N.O. Cent is found guilty of armed robbery and sentenced to twelve years hard labor. (Meanwhile, the real robber is in another state, laughing at his own good fortune.)

His conviction is sustained on appeal. N.O. Cent's marriage breaks up and his family leaves him, convinced that Dad is a crook. Forlorn, abandoned and emotionally destitute, N.O. Cent hangs himself with his prison bedsheet. The next month, the real robber is caught (he had drunkenly bragged about the whole episode in a bar). Finally, the very TV station, Channel Zero, which helped convict N.O. Cent in the public's mind, does an Geraldo-type special, damning the criminal justice system. The end.

True story? Yes and no. This exact incident did not happen, but this kind of thing has. And still does. In every State. Innocent people, sadly, sometimes slip through the cracks in the system. What's my point? It is this: just as the guilty are not assured of *prison,* the innocent are not assured of *freedom.* The innocent must KNOW their rights as solidly as the criminals do. N.O. Cent was not arrested because he was a criminal; he was arrested because he was ignorant of his 5th Amendment right to remain silent. (The police are only required to "Mirandize" a suspect *after* his arrest, not before.) His own mouth sent him to prison.

using your 5th Amendment right

Think how much differently this story would have turned out had N.O. Cent known of his 5th Amendment right to not give testimony about himself. When the policeman asked if he had just been at the mall, N.O. Cent's defenses would have gone up. He would have then asked, "*Officer, are you asking me that in connection with some crime committed at the mall?*" The officer would have had to admit this was so. Then, Mr. N.O. Cent would have replied, "*Since I am a criminal suspect, I will consult with my attorney before speaking. Based upon my Fifth Amendment right, I will make no further statement at this time.*" **And then he clams up. He says absolutely *nothing* else.**

Under this scenario, N.O. Cent would certainly *not* be arrested. All that can happen is that his name and address would be taken down. N.O. Cent then immediately calls his attorney. In the meantime, since nobody has been arrested, the police are still actively searching for the robber. This time, he doesn't get away. The police catch him in his blue Ford with the stolen goods. Had N.O. Cent talked his way into being arrested, the police would have probably called off the city-wide BOLO (be-on-the-lookout) for blue Fords with blond male drivers.

The moral of the story is don't talk to the authorities. Not even one word. One never knows what might or might not be "incriminating" evidence. You are not required to help the police in constructing a chain of evidence against you. The Founding Fathers were concerned about forced testimony, no matter what kind it was. Snow White, Satan, or anybody between — nobody can be *compelled* to be a witness against himself.

still not convinced?

Go to www.startpage.com (never use Google; they keep track of all your search activity) and find the video "Don't Talk to the Police" by Professor James Duane of the Regent University. In this very entertaining presentation (followed by officer George Bruch), you'll learn why it's always best to remain silent:

1. There's no way talking can help you.
2. You may admit guilt with no benefit in return. No need to rush.
3. A little lie or mistake is guaranteed of even the innocent.
4. Police don't have to use your exculpatory comments in court.
5. The police could misinterpret or misremember your comments.
6. You won't likely recall perfectly.
7. If true statements are later mistaken as false, it's incriminating.

using your 5th Amendment right

If you are ever in a situation where you wish to use your 5th Amendment right in response to a question, say:

I respectfully decline to answer that question on the grounds of the Fifth Amendment.

You cannot make *blanket* objections under the 5th. To properly use the 5th, you must apply it to each question *individually*. If the authorities get snotty and ask if you're going to answer *all* their questions that way, replying "Yes" constitutes a blanket objection. Instead, reply, "*I don't know, because I don't know what you're going to ask me next.*"

> *The Fifth Amendment is an old friend and a good friend. It is one of the greatest landmarks in man's struggle to be free of tyranny, to be decent and civilized.*
> — Justice William O. Douglas

DUE PROCESS OF LAW MEANS:

- no execution on life / liberty / property without a judgment
- no judgment without a unanimously guilty verdict
- no guilty verdict without a jury of your peers (equals)
- no trial without a jury
- no trial without indictment
- no indictment without admissible evidence
- no admissible evidence via your compelled testimony, and
- no admissible evidence without lawful search / seizure

- no lawful search/seizure without a warrant
- no warrant without probable cause
- no probable cause without consent of a judge or grand jury
- no judge without a court
- no court without jurisdiction
- no jurisdiction without authorization
- **no authorization without either the Constitution or YOU!**

THE 4th BRANCH OF GOVERNMENT: A FULLY-INFORMED JURY

Formerly we suffered from crimes; now we suffer from laws.
— Tacitus

Quis custodiet ipsos custodes?
(Who will guard the guardians themselves?)
— Juvenal, VI. 347-8

tyranny stops with the informed jury

Although all three branches of government have colluded to deny us our right to life, liberty, property and pursuit of happiness, we can still thwart this tyranny. If an American is arrested for exercising his Constitutional liberties, denied due process, and railroaded through a show "trial" in some "kangaroo court," the government is powerless to put him in jail or take away his property unless the jury also participates in this fraud. Bad law and bad government are powerless without ignorant, cooperating jurors. (A judge can overturn a verdict of guilty, but *not* a verdict of innocence.)

You see, the "buck stops" with the jury. Our jury system is the *last* possible block to tyranny. The Founding Fathers knew this, of course. That's why you have the Constitutional right to a trial by jury before your peers (equals) in *any criminal case*, and in any civil case where the dispute exceeds $20. If you stop and think about it, the only sensible purpose for a jury *is* to judge the *law*. A court judge is a professional at weighing the evidence of a case — that's what he does every day. **However, a judge, because he works for government, cannot be an *impartial* judge of the *law*.** To judge the law requires a jury of one's peers, a group of people who have no vested interest in the law itself, as do the police and the courts. **To**

judge the *law* is the whole point of our jury system! *This* is why your right to a trial by jury is the only right mentioned *three* times in the Constitution.

The government understandably views the jury system as a threat and does everything it can to make jury service an unpleasant, undignified experience. Members of a jury pool are crammed in uncomfortable chairs in hot, stuffy rooms and forced to wait for hours in sheer boredom. (When I was there, they even prohibited us from reading to pass the time!) As a result, Americans dislike jury duty. If you admit to going you'll usually be kidded for not having found some way to get excused. This attitude is *exactly* what the government wants. After this chapter, you'll not only understand why, but you might even look forward to serving as a fully-informed juror someday.

a juror judges both facts *and* law

> ***Every jury in the land is tampered with and falsely instructed by the judge*** *when it is told it must take (or accept) as law that which has been given to them, or that they must bring in a certain verdict, or that they can decide only the facts of the case.*
>
> — Lord Denman, C.J. O'Connel V.R., 1884

> *The people themselves have it in their power effectually to resist usurpation, without being driven to an appeal to arms. An act of usurpation is not obligatory; it is not law; and any man may be justified in its resistance. Let him be considered as a criminal by the general government, yet only his fellow citizens can convict him; they're his jury, and if they pronounce him innocent, not all the powers of Congress can hurt him;* ***and innocent they certainly will pronounce him if the supposed law he resisted was an act of usurpation.***
>
> — Theo. Parsons, 2 *Elliots's Debates*, 94; Bancroft

The jury is actually more powerful than the judge. In a jury trial, the judge is merely the referee. Contrary to the TV courtroom-drama crap where the judge admonishes the jury to "*apply the law only as I give it to you*," the jury is the judge of both facts *and* law. If any juror feels the law to be unConstitutional or oppressive (or even just plain unfair), or the defendant's rights to have been violated, or valuable evidence withheld, or any other like reason, **that juror can vote his conscience *against* the evidence.**

> *The jury has a right to judge both the law as well as the fact in controversy.*
>
> — John Jay, 1st Chief Justice Supreme Court

The jury has the right to determine both the law and facts.
— Samuel Chase, U.S. Supreme Court Justice, 1796,
Signer of the Declaration of Independence

The law itself is on trial quite as much as the cause which is to be decided.
— Harlan F. Stone, 12th Chief Justice U.S. Supreme Court, 1941

The pages of history shine on instances of the jury's exercise of its prerogative to disregard instructions of the judge . . .
— *U.S. v. Dougherty*, 473 F. 2nd 1113 (1972)

Jurors should acquit even against the judge's instructions . . . if exercising their judgement with discretion and honesty they have a clear conviction that the charge of the court is wrong.
— Alexander Hamilton, 1804

The jury has the power to bring a verdict in the teeth of both law and fact.
— Oliver Wendell Holmes, U.S. Supreme Court Justice, 1902

We recognize, as the appellants urge, the undisputed power of the jury to acquit, even if its verdict is contrary to the law as given by the judge and contrary to the evidence. *This is a power that must exist as long as we adhere to the general verdict in criminal cases, for the courts cannot search the minds of the jurors to find the basis upon which they judge. If the jury feels that the law under which the defendant is accused is unjust, or that exigent circumstances justified the actions of the accused, or for any reason which appeals to their logic or passion,* ***the jury has the power to acquit, and the courts must abide by that decision.***

Concededly, this power of the jury is not always contrary to the interests of justice *. . . freedom of the press was immeasurably strengthened by the jury's acquittal of John Peter Zenger of seditious libel, a violation of which, under the law as it then existed and the facts, he was clearly guilty.*
— *United States v. Moylan*, 417 F.2d 1002

Without a unanimous guilty verdict from the jury, the judge must declare a mistrial and free the defendant. It only takes one juror in twelve to stop a "kangaroo court" proceeding in its tracks. Since a juror is a judicial officer (even if only for a day) he tacitly swears an oath to uphold the Constitution. That oath is his overriding duty. A juror's first priority is to judge the law — judging the facts is second. For a juror to vote in favor of the Constitution and acquit, even against the evidence, is called **jury nullification.**

Jury nullification was used before and during the Civil War by Northern juries who refused to convict runaway slaves. It was used during Prohibition ("War Against Booze") to such an extent that the law collapsed and Congress had no choice but to repeal it. (Many Americans, in fact, even *began drinking on principle!*) Jury nullification is used today by freedom-loving jurors who refuse to convict honest, nonviolent, hard-working Americans of "tax crimes." If only one out of twelve (8%) voters knew their right to acquit noncriminals, government tyranny in that area could be *wiped out*.

putting bad law "out of business"

Bad laws are the worst sort of tyranny.
– Edmund Burke

I asked one of their members of Parliament whether a majority of the House could legitimize murder. He said, No. I asked him whether it could sanctify robbery. He thought not. But I could not make him see that if murder and robbery are intrinsically wrong, and not to be made right by decisions of statesmen, that similarly all actions must be either right or wrong, apart from the authority of the law; and that ***if the right and wrong of the law are not in harmony with this intrinsic right and wrong, the law itself is criminal.***
– Herbert Spencer

I like to think of jury nullification as putting bad law "out of business." The lawyers and politicians will tell you that even if a law *is* unconstitutional or unfair, you must tolerate and obey it until it's either repealed or struck down by the courts. That's total B.S.

All laws which are repugnant to the Constitution are null and void.
– *Marbury v. Madison*, 5 U.S. 137, 176

Where rights secured by the Constitution are involved, there can be no rule making or legislation which would abrogate them
– *Miranda v. Arizona*, 384 U.S. 436 (1966)

The general rule is that an unconstitutional statute, though having the form and name of law, is in reality no law, but is wholly void, and ineffective for any purpose; since unconstitutionality dates from the time of its enactment, and not merely from the date of the decision...

No one is bound to obey an unconstitutional law and no courts [or juries] ***are bound to enforce it.***
– *16th AMERICAN JURISPRUDENCE*

To quote the Latin phrase; *Lex mala, lex nulla*, "A bad law is no law, is to no effect."

Do you eat in a bad restaurant until it finally goes out of business? Do you keep taking your car to a lousy mechanic until his garage folds up? Of course not, you *avoid* those places! A poorly run business will stay open as long as it has sufficient, regular patrons. You don't *have* to *help* it remain open. But when you obey an unjust law, you help keep that bad law in force. The people are the "customers" of a law. When we encounter an unjust law and refuse to "shop" there — it goes "out of business" for lack of "patrons."

You see, lawmakers are terribly insecure. When their ridiculous laws are treated to jeering noncompliance they lose their feeling of authority. Lawmakers *can't stand* for us to guiltlessly flaunt their laws. If we can't be intimidated into submission, then they will repeal the law just to save face. This is exactly what happened with the 55 mph speed limit. Most of us drove at 70+, without feeling guilty, Congress franticly scrambled to ditch the absurd 55. It's another example of "*Where's-the-crowd?-I'm-their-leader!*"

A law is *never* overturned until at least one person *challenges* it, and is never repealed until enough people *ignore* it. One legal challenge can get a law overturned, and a handful of noncompliants can force the legislature to repeal it to save face. Without the resistance of at least *one* individual a law will *never* go away. And why *should* it? Why would the courts or the legislature strike down a law obeyed by everybody? Why would they repeal such a "successful" law? Only the *people* can initiate a law's death!

A bad law will *stay* on the books as long as it's generally *obeyed*.

Obedience keeps bad law in "business."

"Legal" is not necessarily right! "Illegal" is not necessarily wrong!

taking the law into your own hands?

This might sound like a radical concept to some. "*Why it's taking the law into your own hands!*" they would exclaim. But they forget (or never knew) that individuals are sovereign. Our government's power comes *from us* who delegate it *to* the government by consent. We *are* the law! **We *delegate* powers to the government which are *ours* to begin with.**

We allow the government *to act as our agent* in the writing, enforcement and administration of law. It is a *revocable* arrangement: if our agent abuses its stewardship of our law, *we have not only the right, but the duty* to strip it of that stewardship. We have the right to "take the law into our own hands" because it's our law in the *first* place! When the government defaults on its assigned, contractual duty to uphold the Constitution or guarantee a Republican form of government, it also gives up its concomitant power. I am *not* advocating anarchy or lawlessness, but the restoration of power our government servant has stolen from us.

Wouldn't you, if you had the chance, thwart a burglary in progress, apprehend a purse-snatcher or stop a street-punk from robbing an old lady? Of course you would. But, wouldn't you be "taking the law into your own hands"? Absolutely. Moral, ethical law is to be enforced *whenever* it is being broken, by whomever is at hand if the police are not available. Law enforcement begins with the *people*. Would you let your neighbor's house burn down because you didn't want to "take fire-fighting into your own hands?"

governing the governments

Eternal vigilance is the price of liberty.
– Thomas Paine

A watched pot never boils.
– old American proverb

The Constitution has 9 techniques for governing our governments:

1) election and non-election;
2) petitioning for redress of grievances;
3) ignoring and refusing to obey unjust laws and orders;
4) demanding due process of law;
5) **using the power of trial by jury to vindicate innocent victims of oppression;**
6) impeachment or removal from public office for unsatisfactory or criminal activity;
7) taking legal action against violators of life, liberty and property;
8) withholding financial support; and
9) the use of arms for the defense of life, liberty and property.

What if the bureaucrats wrote a "law" that you must send your children to a government summer camp (which is, of course, in the "national interest") and applied stiff jail terms if the parents didn't comply? Parents are outraged, refuse and are tried in court. You are a juror in one of those trials — what will you do? *Convict* parents for not turning over their children's minds to the government, or *acquit* them as your American heritage demands? Remember this:

No victim, no *crime*. No crime, no *punishment*.

Has the accused actually *harmed* somebody, or was he accused of simply not being a perfect government robot?

> *I consider trial by jury as the only anchor yet imagined by man, by which a government can be held to the principles of its constitution.*
>
> — Thomas Jefferson

> *People who are taught God's law will enforce that law over the man-made laws, and the system will work as intended.* ***If, however, the people will not stand against injustice, they will certainly fall to it.*** *If the government becomes oppressive, there is nobody to blame but the jurors for giving the government its power.*
>
> — George T. Radovich

> *If a juror accepts as law that which the judge states then that juror has accepted the exercise of absolute authority of a government employee and has surrendered a power and right that once was the citizen's safeguard of liberty.*
>
> — *Elliot's Debates*, Bancroft, 1788

Jury nullification is *legal*, it's *moral* and it's *necessary*. Disagreeing with this vital American principle is like *not* stopping the day-care people from abusing your child because it would be "*taking baby-sitting into your own hands.*" If Congressmen can vote themselves a pay raise, then *you* can vote us all a *tax cut* by acquitting untax patriots. (If one can't go to jail for not paying *property* taxes, then why should *anybody* go to jail for not paying *income* taxes?)

The Fully Informed Jury Association
www.fija.org

be an American juror and nullify bad law

> *To be born free is an accident.*
> *To live free is a responsibility.*
> *To die free is an obligation.*
>
> — Brig. Gen. Bill Halley, USMC

The first thing is to register to vote so you can get on a jury. When you *are* called for jury duty, show up. You want to serve on that jury! The government will be looking for people who appear to be impressionable, loyal believers. You want to look a little wide-eyed at being in the presence of such important officials in such an impressive courtroom. Let the government believe that you're awed by the whole experience and that you'll accept the law exactly as the judge gives it to you. When they say the law is not on trial, you'll agree. When they ask if you will judge nothing but the facts you tell them what they want to hear. (Gosh, you couldn't even *imagine* judging anything else!) If they ask you if you've ever heard about FIJA, you could say you're not sure but you think it's an island in the South Pacific (Fiji). You want to appear as one of the common sheep. If you give them absolutely *no clue* that you know your juror rights, you'll get on that jury! (I've even read of a case where the judge asked the jury panel what *bumper stickers* they had on their cars. You *must* be on your toes.)

This sort of thing is *not* lying. It's like telling a burglar that you have no hidden jewelry. Government is trying to steal your jury vote. Don't feel guilty about using mental reservations for liberty's sake.

A FULLY-INFORMED JURY IS JUSTICE BY THE DOZEN!

During the trial, pay very close attention to the proceedings. If the defendant is prohibited from using the Constitution in his defense, you'll know why. It will be no mystery why the judge denies most of his objections. You'll know you are in a kangaroo court. Say very little to the other jurors until the jury actually begins its deliberations.

If the defendant has harmed no one and is on trial for breaking an unjust law, then you *must* put that law on trial in front of the other jurors. Explain how a jury has the absolute, but unadvertised, power to judge the law itself. Point out that a juror's duty is, *first,* to judge the law, and *second,* to judge the facts. Since they probably never heard any of this before, they might think you're crazy. Stay calm and polite. Don't become emotional! You have a fantastic opportunity to make a profoundly positive difference in the lives of eleven Americans. You can be their very first eye-opener to the federal mythology.

At the very least, you will single-handedly deadlock the jury and the judge/referee must declare a mistrial. The government then will either drop the whole matter or seek a retrial. If you are successful in educating those eleven others of their power, duty and rights as American jurors, you can all unanimously vote to acquit. The judge/referee can never overturn a *not-guilty* verdict. Either way, mistrial or acquittal, is a victory for our freedoms.

If you're not called for jury service, perhaps you can help educate those who are. Find out when the juries report for service and distribute FIJA flyers on the courthouse steps! Concentrate your efforts at the federal courthouse, since that's where the worst forms of injustice occur. (The government *loathes* this sort of thing, so avoid actual jury tampering.)

A final word on jury nullification. Use your jury power *responsibly*. Acquitting one who is clearly guilty of technically breaking a law should *only* be done when you have a serious moral disagreement with:

❶ the fairness of the law, or

❷ the fairness of the proceedings and presented evidence, or

❸ the fairness of the likely punishment

GETTING BACK TO SANITY

In *Conspiracy,* Dr. Gary North outlines the four general stages that we all must reach:

1) the will to ethics

— to act morally in terms of the information you receive.

> *Patriotism is supporting your country all the time, and your government when it deserves it.*
>
> — Mark Twain

2) the will to resist

— to despise evil and injustice and swear active resistance to such until we achieve victory.

> *Freedom is never voluntarily given by the oppressor, it must be demanded by the oppressed.*
>
> — Martin Luther King

> *Let them march all they want, so long as they pay their taxes . . .*
>
> — General Alexander Haig

> *The history of liberty is a history of resistance.*
>
> — Woodrow Wilson

The spirit of resistance to government is so valuable that I wish it to be always kept alive.
— Thomas Jefferson

Until they become conscious they will never rebel, and until after they have rebelled they cannot become conscious.
— George Orwell, *1984*

In the beginning of a change the patriot is a scarce man, and brave, and hated and scorned. When his cause succeeds, the timid join him, for then it costs nothing to be a patriot.
— Mark Twain

And yet no weapons, no matter how powerful, can help the West until it overcomes its loss of will power. In a state of psychological weakness, weapons become a burden for the capitulating side. To defend oneself one must be ready to die, and there is little such readiness in a society raised in the cult of material well-being.

It is not simply a question of checking the encroachments of totalitarianism; we must first overcome our own lack of resolve.
— Solzhenitsyn

The time is now near at hand which must probably determine, whether Americans are to be, Freemen, or Slaves; whether they are to have any property they can call their own; whether their Houses, and Farms, are to be pillaged and destroyed, and they consigned to a State of Wretchedness from which no human efforts will probably deliver them. The fate of unborn Millions will now depend, under God, on the Courage and Conduct of this army. Our cruel and unrelenting Enemy leaves us no choice but a brave resistance, or the most abject submission; that is all we can expect. We have therefore to resolve to conquer or die.
— George Washington,
to his troops before the Battle of Long Island

An oppressed class which did not aspire to possess arms and learn how to handle them would deserve only to be treated as slaves.
— V. Lenin (quoted in *The Gulag Archipelago* by Solzhenitsyn)

We should not forget that our tradition is one of protest and revolt, and it is stultifying to celebrate the rebels of the past . . . while we silence the rebels of the present.
— Henry Steele Commager

Es mejor que morrir en las pies que vivir en las rodillas.
(It is better to die on your feet than to live on your knees)
— Emiliano Zapata

> *Live free or die. Death is not the worst of evils.*
> — 1809, Revolutionary War general John Stark

> *And how we burned in the camps later, thinking: What would things have been like if every Security operative, when he went out at night to make an arrest, had been uncertain whether he would return alive and had to say good-bye to his family? Or if, during periods of mass arrests, as for example in Leningrad, when they arrested a quarter of the entire city, people had not simply sat there in their lairs, paling with terror at every bang of the downstairs door and at every step on the staircase, but had understood they had nothing left to lose and had boldly set up in the downstairs hall an ambush of half a dozen people with axes, hammers, pokers, or whatever else was at hand? . . . The Organs would very quickly have suffered a shortage of officers and transport and, notwithstanding all of Stalin's thirst, the cursed machine would have ground to a halt!*
>
> *If . . . if . . . We didn't love freedom enough. And even more we had no awareness of the real situation . . . . We purely and simply deserved everything that happened afterward.*
> — Alexander Solzhenitsyn, *The Gulag Archipelago*

> *If there must be trouble, let it be in my day, that my child may have peace.*
> — Thomas Paine

3) the will to self-education

— to embark upon fruitful study on this and related issues, at the expense of TV viewing. To stubbornly resist the brainwashing by the powers that be, which desire to hold your mind in captivity.

> *Knowledge will forever govern ignorance; and a people who mean to be their own governors must arm themselves with the power which knowledge gives.*
> — James Madison

> *At least once every human being should have to run for his life, to teach him that milk does not come from the supermarket, that safety does not come from policemen, and that news is not something that happens to other people.*
> — Robert Heinlein

> *Once the principle of government—judical monopoly and the power to tax — is incorrectly accepted as just, any notion of restraining government power and safeguarding individual liberty and property is illusory.*
> — Hans-Hermann Hoppe

If a nation expects to be ignorant and free it expects what never was and never will be . . . . The people cannot be safe without information. Where the press is free, and every man is able [and willing] *to read, all is safe.*
— Thomas Jefferson

4) the will to dominion

— not merely to overthrow evil in high places, but to *replace* it with ethical authority. Unless replaced with godly, constitutionally-minded men and women, merely "throwing the rascals out" is futile.

The state is what it is because the citizens are what they are. We may not expect better states until we have better men.
— Plato

General Washington did not defeat the British Army with freedom of speech. He shot them.
— author unknown

That rifle on the wall of the labourer's cottage or working class flat is the symbol of democracy. It is our job to see that it stays there.
— George Orwell

This republic was not established by cowards; and cowards will not preserve it.
— Elmer Davis

www.oathkeepers.org

This is a very timely group with a vital mission: to convince American soldiers and police to not participate in tyranny:

1. We will NOT obey orders to disarm the American people.

2. We will NOT obey orders to conduct warrantless searches of the American people

3. We will NOT obey orders to detain American citizens as "unlawful enemy combatants" or to subject them to military tribunal.

4. We will NOT obey orders to impose martial law or a "state of emergency" on a state.

5. We will NOT obey orders to invade and subjugate any state that asserts its sovereignty.

6. We will NOT obey any order to blockade American cities, thus turning them into giant concentration camps.

7. We will NOT obey any order to force American citizens into any form of detention camps under any pretext.

8. We will NOT obey orders to assist or support the use of any foreign troops on U.S. soil against the American people to "keep the peace" or to "maintain control."

9. We will NOT obey any orders to confiscate the property of the American people, including food and other essential supplies.

10. We will NOT obey any orders which infringe on the right of the people to free speech, to peaceably assemble, and to petition their government for a redress of grievances.

http://oath-keepers.blogspot.com/2009/03/oath-keepers-declaration-of-orders-we.html

pray for America

Some trust in chariots, and...in horses: but we will remember the name of the Lord our God.

— Psalm 20:7

For we wrestle not against flesh and blood, but against principalities, against powers, against the rulers of darkness of this world, against spiritual wickedness in high places.

— Ephesians 6:12

If my people, which are called by my name, shall humble themselves, and pray, and seek my face, and turn from their wicked ways; then will I hear from heaven, and will forgive their sin, and will heal their land.

— II Chronicles 7:14

Fret not thyself because of evildoers, neither be thou envious against the workers of iniquity. For they shall soon be cut down like the grass, and wither as the green herb.

Rest in the Lord, and wait patiently for him: fret not thyself because of him who prospereth in his [evil] way, because of the man who bringeth wicked devices to pass. Cease from anger, and forsake wrath: fret not thyself in any wise to do evil. For evildoers shall be put off: but those that wait upon the Lord, they shall inherit the Earth.

> *The wicked have drawn out the sword, and have bent their bow, to cast down the poor and needy, and to slay such as be of upright conversation. Their sword shall enter into their own heart, and their bows shall be broken.*
> — Psalms 37:1-2, 7-9, 14-5

> *The first thing to recognize in this cosmic struggle is that those who seek power through manipulation or through execution* [of force] *have in principle lost the battle. They lost it almost 2,000 years ago* [following the resurrection of Jesus]. *They hold power temporarily. Although they are accomplished power manipulators, power is not the issue; ethics is the issue. God and His law are the issue.*
> — Dr. Gary North, *Conspiracy*

Always keep in mind that the struggle for life and freedom is a *spiritual* battle — *not* an earthly one. The *war* itself is over; Jesus won it 2,000 years ago. What we are currently involved in is a mopping-up operation. The enemy has *already lost.* It is Satan's illegitimate power over God's kingdom that we are to roll back. God has a very clear plan for America in this battle, and we must pray for her. Christians have lost much of America through spiritual default — by not praying. No significant change will occur in America unless we return to the fundamental, *spiritual* arena; unless we return to *prayer* that God "root out the wicked."

www.FreeStateWyoming.org

I refuse to accept the proposition that a police state is the price we must pay to live in a free country. I refuse to be daily treated like a criminal while evil is allowed to flourish. I refuse to live in fear of my government when it is supposed to be my servant protector. In response to this growing totalitarianism, many are moving out West.

Of those, many have chosen, for many good reasons, Wyoming, where we may live as adults, not as terrorized and helpless children. Where we may look to ourselves and to our neighbors for help, not to the government which must necessarily plunder others first. Where life exists without a preponderance of government supremacists. Where our local Sheriff is our friend and neighbor, not some functionary of a faraway tyranny. Where we may enjoy our rights, unless we abuse them at another's expense.

> *A well disciplined society needs few laws; but it needs strong mores.*
> — William F. Buckley

Where we are not domesticated to the point of docility. Where we don't cower before street criminals; they cower before us because we with our skill at arms outnumber them 50 to 1 everywhere we go. Where we do not give up our personal weapons at any time or for any reason, because to do so would be to place ourselves under the physical power of armed strangers whose intentions and mercies can never be known in advance.

I'm looking for people who are tired of living under government supremacists and their irrational, confiscatory Political Law. I'm searching for people who live by Courage and Truth, and not under Fear and Fraud.

To help facilitate this migration, I founded the Free State Wyoming. Who may join? Anybody who will formally renounce fraud, theft, and aggression as political and social expedients and pledge to be good neighbors for the goals of political liberty, free trade, and voluntary cooperation is welcome to join the Free State Wyoming.

This isn't about race, religion, creed, or anything else. It's about reinstating the rule of Natural Law in at least some portion of America. Thomas Jefferson wrote:

> *Rightful liberty is unobstructed action according to our will within limits drawn around us by the equal rights of others.*
>
> . . . [A] *wise and frugal government, which shall restrain men from injuring one another, which shall leave them otherwise free to regulate their own pursuits of industry and improvement, and shall not take from the mouth of labor the bread it has earned.*
>
> *This is the sum of good government.*

I have already moved to Wyoming because I want to live peaceably amongst good neighbors who believe in that just as strongly as I do. Amongst those who will not plunder each other through the ballot box. This is what my novel *Molôn Labé!* is about: what life could be like in a free society, and how we might achieve that in Wyoming.

We don't want a lawless society, rather one that is free of *political* law. We desire to live under the scientific, Natural, Common Law, because the rights of each of us are equally protected. We yearn for a locale where personal integrity is the norm, not the exception.

Do you know what integrity is? It is loyalty to those . . . *not* present. I want to help rediscover, in Wyoming, what it once meant to be an American. A person with specific and definable principles. A person who exuded character and honor. Who obeyed the common law even when no police were around. Who did not steal, aggress, or encroach on his neighbor through the vehicle of government. Who showed flawless loyalty . . . to those not present. In "The Covenant" Rudyard Kipling wrote:

We thought we ranked above the chance of ill.
Others might fall, not we, for we were wise—
Merchants in freedom. So, of our free-will
We let our servants drug our strength with lies.

The pleasure and the poison had its way
On us as on the meanest, till we learned
That he who lies will steal, who steals will slay.
Neither God's judgment nor man's heart was turned.

We don't have to be the People of the Lie, besetting ourselves with a government that steals and slays. This isn't about Democrats vs. Republicans. Both parties violate the Two Rules:

Democrats infamously encroach on your property.
Republicans infamously encroach on your person.

No moral political party would encroach on either, which is why I am a libertarian.

As the old Indian put it, "*The first step in a successful life is the conquest of fear. Once that has been achieved, everything else falls into place.*" Those who live in fear are incapable of consistently doing the right thing. They can act neither bravely nor honorably — not for themselves, not for their families, and certainly not for America. We don't suffer in this country for lack of knowledge, but for lack of *courage*. We know what the right thing to do is. We just don't have the guts to do it. We are no longer brave enough to think and act for ourselves.

We have lost our liberties and our nation because we have chosen to reject courage for cowardice. We have chosen to live in fear. In fear of asking the right questions, thus in fear of knowledge, thus in fear of responsibility, and thus in fear of action. In George Orwell's *1984,* one line stands out:

Freedom is the freedom to say 2 + 2 = 4.
If that is granted, all else follows.

I proclaim that 2 + 2 = 4, not 3 and not 5. What you do with that is up to you. In closing, I hope that you will live by what you value, and never by what you fear. I hope that you will show the courage to consistently do the right things in life — to live by the Two Rules and their 17 words.

> Do all you have agreed to do, and
> Don't encroach on other persons or their property.

I hope you are, or will become, a person of integrity, always showing loyalty to those not present . . . even if you must move to Wyoming to do so.

21

TAXES

I predict future happiness for Americans if they can prevent the government from wasting the labors of the people under the pretense of taking care of them.
– Thomas Jefferson

HISTORY OF THE "*INCOME*" TAX

The Internal Revenue Code (IRC) is constitutional, but sly. Some people do indeed make "*taxable income*" – others do not. It's quite a tale!

"*income*" is undefined by Congress and the IRS

The Congress shall have power to lay and collect taxes on incomes, from whatever source derived, without apportionment among the several States, and without regard to any census or enumeration.
– 16th Amendment to the Constitution (1913)

First, understand that the 16th Amendment did not change a thing. It did not allow direct and unapportioned taxation on capital or property:

[The 16th Amendment] *does not justify the taxation of persons or things previously immune . . . it does not extend taxing power to new or excepted subjects . . .*
– ***Evans v. Gore***, 235 U.S. 245 (1920)

The 16th Amendment allows for the taxation of *"income"*, however:

The general term "income" is not defined in the Internal Revenue Code.
– ***U.S. v. Ballard***, 535 F2d 400, 404 (1976)

That's right: the term "*income*" is not defined in the Internal Revenue Code (IRC). Not once. Why not? Because:

"*income*" is a constitutional term

Since the term "*income*" has been a constitutional term since 1913, Congress has no power to define it. "*Income*" means today what it meant in 1913. The one thing the IRC cannot define (because Congress isn't allowed to) is "*income*". Well then, what is "*income*"? Since the IRS doesn't define it, who did? The Supreme Court, from 1913 to 1920. Here's a key early case:

> *. . . it becomes essential to distinguish between what is, and what is not "income". . . Congress may not, by any definition it may adopt, conclude the matter, since it cannot by legislation alter the Constitution, from which alone it derives its powers to legislate, and within whose limitations alone, that power can be lawfully exercised.*
>
> – ***Eisner v. Macomber,*** 252 U.S. 189, 206 (1920)

A Senate report on H.R. 8300 (the proposed 1954 tax code) had something very illuminating to say about section 61 "*gross income*":

> *This section corresponds to section 22(a) of the 1939 Code* (which corresponded to Article 4(a) of the 1913 Code – KWR).
>
> *Section 61(a) provides that gross income includes "all income from whatever source derived."* ***This definition is based upon the sixteenth amendment*** *and the word "income" is used as in* ***section 22(a)*** [of the 1939 Code] ***in its constitutional sense. It is not intended to change the concept of income that obtains under section 22(a).***
>
> – Section 61. Gross income defined, Report on H.R. 8300

That is, the term "*income*" is not to be construed in a dictionary or conversational sense! It does not mean "all that comes in".

> ***We must reject*** *in this case, as we have rejected in cases arising under the Corporation Excise Tax Act of 1909* [citations omitted], *the broad contention submitted in behalf of the government that all receipts – everything that comes in – are income within the proper definition of the term "gross income," and* [thus we must also reject] *that the entire proceeds of a conversion of capital assets, in whatever form and under whatever circumstances accomplished, should be treated as gross income.*
>
> ***The true function of the words "gains" and "profits" is to limit the meaning of the word "income".***
>
> – ***Southern Pacific Co. v. Lowe***, 247 U.S. 330, 335 (1916)

"*Income*" must first be a net profit or gain — it is not gross receipts. Yes, the Internal Revenue Code defines "*gross income*" and "*adjusted gross income*" but only as types of "*income*". You must first know what 16th Amendment "*income*" is before you can understand what "*gross income*", etc. are. The noun "*income*" must first be defined before adjectives come into play.

4 key words: "*from whatever source derived* "

> *The Congress shall have power to lay and collect taxes on incomes,* ***from whatever source derived,*** *without apportionment among the several States, and without regard to any census or enumeration.*
>
> — 16th Amendment to the Constitution (1913)

The entire key to understanding our federal "*income*" tax system is the phrase "*from whatever source derived*". The word "*derive*" comes from the Latin *de rivus*, or "from the river". Put another way, fish are taxed no matter the river from which caught — *but the river itself* cannot be taxed (without apportionment among the states).

"*derive income*" is NOT a legal synonym of "make money"
"*gross income*" = "total net profits", not "gross receipts"

The "*income*" tax touches only on any gain/net profit that is *derived from* its source, but *not* the capital, property, or labor source itself (because that would be a direct tax, and unconstitutional without apportionment). Here,, from the *Income Tax Act of 1913*, is a perfect example of "*income*" not being equal to gross receipts (original emphasis underlined):

> *Art. 4. Gross income includes all gains, profits, and income derived from –*
>
> *(d) Gains or profits and income derived from any source whatever,* ***including the income from, but not the value of,*** *property acquired by gift, bequest, devise or descent.*
>
> *– Income Tax Act of 1913*

Read the seminal case ruling on deriving "*income*" from its source. (The original emphasis is underlined.)

> *The government, although basing its argument upon the definition as quoted, placed chief emphasis upon the word "gain," which was extended to include a variety of meanings;* ***while the significance of the next three words was either overlooked or misconceived. "Derived from capital;"*** *"the gain derived from capital," etc. Here, we have the essential matter: not a gain accruing to capital; not a growth or increment of value in the investment; but a gain, a profit, something of exchangeable value, proceeding from the property, severed from the capital, however invested or employed, and coming in, being "derived" – that is, received or drawn by the recipient (the taxpayer) for his separate use, benefit*

and disposal — <u>that</u> is income derived from property. Nothing else answers the description.

The same fundamental conception is clearly set forth in the Sixteenth Amendment — "incomes, <u>from</u> whatever <u>source derived</u>" — the essential thought being expressed with a conciseness and lucidity entirely in harmony with the form and style of the Constitution.

— ***Eisner v. Macomber***, 252 U.S. 189, 207 (1920)

does a paycheck = "*net profits*" and "*income*"?

In 1913 the new "*income*" tax was clearly understood to be levied only on U.S. business profits (and federal pay). Not gross receipts, but gains and profits. If you convert (*i.e.*, sell) a capital asset for $100, is that a profit? Only if you had less than $100 invested in it (purchase, maintenance, etc.).

Now, if you sell your *labor* for $100, did you make a profit? This is truly the question. The most recent and inclusive definition of "*income*" comes from a 1955 ruling (to embrace punitive damages):

*. . . **undeniable accessions to wealth**, clearly realized, and over which the taxpayers have complete dominion . . .*

— ***Commissioner v. Glenshaw GlassCo.***, 348 U.S. 426, 431 (1955)

accession
3. increase by something added; augmentation from without

When you sell your labor property, do you have an "*augmentation from without*" (as with a profit or capital gain), or merely a trade? Let's try a mental exercise to understand labor vs. "*income*":

A potter makes a coffee mug for himself. (no "*income*")

There is no accession to wealth from without, as he was the creator (who made something from skills within). Not even the IRS taxes somebody making his own stuff for his own use. Although the mug has economic value, creating it in the first place is not "*income*". Creation is neither accession nor "*augmentation from without*". Now, let's introduce a barter transaction:

Potter trades mug to farmer for 20lbs. of apples. (no "*income*")

Still, no accession to wealth, as they merely traded property, right? Instead of making clay mugs, the potter could be growing his own apples — what's the difference? None. The trade is not "*income*" and Congress cannot transform it into "*income*".

The Treasury cannot, by interpretive regulations, make income of

> *that which is not income within the meaning of the revenue acts of Congress, nor can Congress, without apportionment, tax as income that which is not income within the meaning of the 16th Amendment.*
>
> – ***Helvering v. Edison Bros. Stores***, 133 F2d 575 (1943)

However, according to the IRS, if he sells the mug for *any* amount, such is magically a "*gain*" and thus "*gross income*" (less expenses). But what if:

> Potter sells mug for $10, and buys 20lbs. of apples with $10.

The IRS would still consider this $10 "*gross income*" regardless that the $10 was used to buy the same goods he could have simply traded for evenly. Here we've arrived at the paradox that illustrates why a direct tax on labor (unless apportioned) is unconstitutional. The initial manifestation of human labor is the original source of all property. A direct tax on that actually taxes property itself, the vehicle by which we stay alive. The lower courts, however, have sneeringly ruled that you have a "*zero-basis*" in your labor, thus any pay you receive is a taxable gain:

> *Appellant's contention that the amounts he received from his employers constituted an equal, nontaxable exchanges of property rather than taxable income is clearly without merit. . . . Merely raising the argument . . . justifies the imposition of sanctions.*
>
> – ***Casper v. Commissioner***, 805 F.2d 902, 906 (10th Cir. 1986)

Oh, *really*? Ponder this scenario: two guys fix cars for a living – a salaried mechanic making $50,000 from a shop, and a self-employed mechanic grossing $50,000. The mechanic entrepreneur writes off shop expenses (*e.g.*, tools, training, rent, electricity, advertising, etc.) to offset "*gross income*", but the mechanic employee cannot and is taxed in full?

How can the same $50,000 be taxed so differently? Especially since the putative rationale for the 16th Amendment was to tax business profits, not paychecks? A good synopsis of this paradox is at:
www.constitutionalincome.com/first_chapter.php

from taxing business profits to paychecks

History can be a fascinating tool when it serves as a time machine to learn the truth before truth got blurred, scrambled, and forgotten. Did the "*income*" tax acts of 1894 and 1913 embrace the working man's wages? Let's begin with the Attorney General of 1894:

> ***A second reason for the income tax was the desire to equalize in some degree the burdens of taxation.*** *The prior taxes,*

> *customs, duties and internal revenue alike, being laid on consumption, they bore more heavily on the poor and what is sometimes called the lower middle class of the population.*
>
> *A flagrant injustice to the poorer class of contributors unless compensated by the existence of other taxes* ***from which, as from the present income tax, they are altogether exempt.***
>
> — Attorney General Olney, addressing the Supreme Court in 1894 during oral argument of the first **Pollock** Case, 157 U.S. 427

The common man's labor was not touched by the "*income*" tax of 1894, as admitted by the U.S. Attorney General! This had not changed by 1913. (Most telling is the historical fact that *not once* was the possibility raised during public discussion of the proposed 16th Amendment that it could embrace the common paycheck. A thorough search of the *Congressional Record* proves that it simply never came up!) The issue then was all about the wealthy "fat cats" who were seen not to be suffering under any real tax burden. Now read from the man who *wrote* the 1913 Revenue Act:

> *The Treasury regulations soon to be prepared will make it clear to every taxpayer the requirements of the law* ***and its application to income derived from the various kinds of business****. To any person who keeps familiar with* ***his business affairs*** *during the year to the extent that at its end he knows with reasonable accuracy the amount of* ***his aggregate annual profits****, the matter of executing his tax return would be both simple and convenient.*
>
> — synopsis of the first income tax implemented under the 16th Amendment, by Judge Cordell Hull the person responsible for writing the Revenue Act, found at *Congressional Record* of October 16, 1913 (page 5679, Volume 50, Part 6)

The Revenue Act author repeatedly wrote only of "*business*" and "*business affairs*" and "*annual profits*" — never about a worker's paycheck itself. If the states and the people of 1909-1913 believed that common paychecks could be taxed, would the 16th Amendment have been ratified? No way.

> *The purpose of the framers of the Act in only permitting deductions for the expenses actually incurred in carrying on any business, and excluding personal, living and family expenses, was for the reason that* ***the specific exemption of $4,000 from*** *taxable income was supposed to be sufficient to provide* ***personal, living and family expenses.***
>
> — Thomas Gold Frost, *A Treatise on the Federal Income Tax Law of 1913* (1913), Section 37, page 28

$4,000 in 1913 was 200 $20 gold pieces (which, at 0.9675 oz./coin contained 193.5 ounces of gold — today worth over $200,000). Quite the exemption! No wonder why the common man of 1913 never feared the "*income*" tax because it was (ostensibly) not intended to crowd into "*personal, living and family expenses*". Neither the numbers nor the letter of the law applied to him! Furthermore, neither did the legislative record of the 16th Amendment support the post-1930s belief that private-sector paychecks were to be taxable as "*income*". One researcher has proven that:

> *Since 1996* [Phil] *Hart has made two trips to the Library of Congress and the Supreme Court's library in Washington, D.C., and has visited about a half dozen other libraries. He has researched every Congressional Record entry and relevant Congressional documents during the period of time where the income tax amendment to the Constitution was being debated and ratified. He has also accumulated in his files an impressive body of newspaper articles, law and economic journal articles, books, essays and letters* ***that capture the intent of the income tax from the first congressional debate in 1909 through the time it was implemented in 1913.***
>
> *The purpose of this area of research was to discover what the intent of the American People was when they lobbied Congress and their state legislatures for an income tax amendment to the Constitution. Hart believes an objective review of the record proves that* [non-government] *wages are not income and that the 16th Amendment does not empower Congress to levy a new kind of tax not authorized by the Constitution. According to Hart,* ***"The purpose of the 16th Amendment was to bring tax relief to wage earners."***
>
> — http://proliberty.com/observer/20020413.htm

Until 1913 it was the common man who funded the Government through indirect taxes (duties, imposts, and excises). The large corporations and investors of the day paid very little in indirect taxes, and thus were seen to be getting a free ride. Hence the contrived clamor (which is a story in itself) to tax their huge net profits. In no way did the public realize then that the "*income*" tax would grow in 30 years to cunningly embrace their common paycheck! Here's how that happened.

"*gain derived . . . from labor*"

> *. . . "income" may be defined as the* ***gain derived from*** *capital, from labor, or from both combined, . . .*
>
> — ***Stratton's Independence v. Howbert***, 231 U.S. 399, 415 (1913)

"*Income*" is neither capital nor labor itself, but gain "***derived from***" (out of, and thence separated from) capital and/or labor. Being an employer is the primary example of "*deriving income from labor*", and taxes are due on the net profits from that employment. A private-sector paycheck can indeed be a *source* for taxable "*income*" – for the profitable *employer*!

the federal government "*employee*" tax

> *The 'Government' is an abstraction, and its possession of property largely constructive. Actual possession and custody of Government property nearly always are in someone who is not himself the Government but acts in its behalf and for its purposes. He may be an officer, an agent, or a contractor.* ***His personal advantages from the relationship by way of salary, profit, or beneficial personal use of the property may be taxed . . .***
>
> – ***United States v. Allegheny,*** 322 US 174 (1944)

Must the IRS wait until a federal employee "*derives income from*" his salary? Nope. His federal salary is not a source of derived "*income*" — it is deemed taxable in itself. Also, it is linguistically simple to directly and clearly tax federal salaries, as Congress did in 1862:

> *Sec. 86. And be it further enacted, That . . .* ***there shall be levied, collected, and paid on all salaries*** *of officers, or payments to persons in the civil, military, naval, or other* ***employment or service of the United States*** [government], *including senators and representatives and delegates in Congress, . . . a duty of 3 per centum on the excess above . . . six hundred dollars . . .*
>
> – *Revenue Act of 1862*

Pretty straightforward, huh? No "*gains derived from*" language in there! Taxes were directly levied on federal salaries. (They still are.) Now, compare that section 86 with section 90, which imposed the first tax upon:

> *the annual gains, profits, or income of every person residing in the United States whether* ***derived from*** *any kind of property, rents, interest, dividends, salaries, or from any profession, trade, employment, or vocation . . .* (Section 90)

Here appears the first tax statute use of "*derived from*", to separate taxable gain/net profits from their "*income*"-producing sources.

Now — follow me closely here — if section 86's federal "*salaries*" were identical to section 90's business "*income derived from salaries*", then there would have been no need for a section 86 tax on federal salaries. While tax laws may be confusing, they are never redundant. (Re-read these two sections until you fully grasp this vital point, for the past is our key.)

As you've previously read, a salary is just a salary until you "*derive in-*

come from salaries" by reselling labor for profit. **Section 90 taxed business profits and capital gains — not paychecks themselves. Section 86 taxed only federal paychecks.** Congress could not tax private-sector paychecks, and didn'tt attempt to, not even through murky language.

In 1894, Congress re-enacted the 1862 "*income*" tax on federal employees to explicitly require the inclusion of:

> *the salary or other compensation paid to any person in the employment or service of the United States* [government] . . . *in the calculation of* [taxable] *total gains, profits, or income . . .*
> — *Income Tax Act of 1894*

Again, this is a straightforward taxation of federal salaries, which had no "*gains derived from*" language. Federal salaries were never explicitly called "*gains, profits, or income*" but simply included in their calculation — lumped in as "*income*" yet without outright calling them that. It's as if *Revenue Act of 1862* section 86 were absorbed into section 90, yet without expanding the scope of *whose* salaries were taxed. This 1894 verbiage was the beginning of the sneakiness: to include in the calculation of net profit/"*income*" that which was not technically so. Yet again, in 1913, only federal salaries were taxed:

> ***Art; 5. The following items should not be included as gross income:***
> *(e) The compensation of all officers and employees of a State or any political subdivision thereof, including public-school teachers, etc.* ***When such State officers or employees are compensated by the United States, they must include such income as taxable.***
> — *Income Tax Act of 1913*

The clever "*include such income as taxable*" language led to the misperception by 1942 that "wages are income". Since WWII, the common man's paycheck has become — both conversationally and through the lower courts — directly tar-babied to taxable "*income*". People no longer speak of "earnings" (a tax neutral word) but of their "*income*" (which has tax implications).

private-sector paycheck: "*income*" itself, or source of "*income*"?

If you carefully read the *Income Tax Act of 1913*, you'll see some curiously different language regarding private-sector salaries:

> *Art. 4. Gross income includes all gains, profits, and income* ***derived from*** [the following sources of] —
> *(a)* ***Salaries, wages, or compensation for personal service*** *of whatever kind and* ***in whatever form paid.***

Article 4(a) considers the perspective of businessmen paying salaries and deriving net profit ("*income*") from such payment. The cost of a salary is certainly a business expense to the employer, but is it inherently "*income*" to the worker? Well, if 4(a) meant that salaries are themselves "*gains, profits, and income*" to the worker, then it would have read "*in whatever form **received***" — not "*in whatever form **paid*** [by the business as expenses]".

In 1913, what followed Article 4 was clearly a list of sources from which "*income*" could be derived. (The 1942 code was even more clear: "*Income* [derived] *from the following **sources**: salaries, wages, compensation for personal services*".) "*Income*" from all sources is taxed, but not the sources themselves. Arguably, nothing has changed today (although the lower courts, being either confused or complicit, so far disagree).

<u>1913's</u> <u>article 4(a)</u>	<u>Today's</u> <u>section 61(a)(1)</u>
*Gross income includes all gains, profits, and income **derived from** -* *(a) salaries, wages, . . .*	*gross income means all income **from whatever source derived** including (but not limited to) the following items:* *(1) compensation for services, . . .*

However, today's 26 USC § 61 version of 1913's Article 4 was intentionally muddled to be readable *two* different ways: "*the following items*" can be read as either examples of "*income*" themselves — *or* of sources which produce "*income*". (Since Congress may tax all "*incomes, from whatever source derived*" what would be the point of listing types of "*income*" as is alleged of section 61?) **This ambiguity could not have been accidental.** Also purposeful was the removal of the 1913 language "*gains, profits*" to make "*income*" seem synonymous with gross receipts — so that the casual reader more readily assumes that "*compensation for services*" was taxable "*income*" by itself, without gain/profit derivation. (To "*derive income*" is not a synonym of "make money".) Remember, "*income*" must be separated from its source just as a baby is from its mother. **No source "mother" is taxable — but every profit "baby" is.** SCOTUS again made this abundantly clear in 1939:

> ***A source of income is not income, and the source is not subject to income tax** . . .* [A] *tax on income is not economically or legally a tax on its source.*
>
> — ***Graves vs. People of the State of New York***, 59 S. Ct. 595

So, does the 16th Amendment embrace a private-sector salary itself as "*income*", or is a tax due only on any business "*income derived from*" paying salaries? **It is your responsibility to learn who "*derives income*" from salaries – the worker or his employer?** To help you understand this, let's revisit how federal employees were taxed under the Code.

Historically, since 1862 until today, the pay of federal employees was subject to "*income*" taxation, but in a way different from the business net profit "*derived from*" having paid salary expenses to employees. For example, from 1932 to 1939, federal employment compensation was "*included in gross income*" while private employment was not. Yet another smoking gun. Here is section 22(a) of the 1939 IRC:

> *(a) "Gross income" includes gains, profits, and income* ***derived from salaries, wages,*** *or compensation for personal service . . .*
>
> *In the case of Presidents . . . and* [federal] *judges taking office after June 6, 1932,* ***the*** [entire] ***compensation received as such shall be included in gross income;*** *. . .*

Do you see the distinction? Private-sector salaries were not directly taxed (only their gain/profit/"*income*" as sources), but federal salaries *were* taxed in their entirety. The 1942 *Revenue Act* § 466(a) took the subterfuge further:

> *There shall be withheld, collected, and paid upon all wages of every person,* ***to the extent that such*** [section 465(d) government "*employee*"] ***wages are includible in gross income,*** *a* [5%] *tax . . .*

The illuminating qualifier "*to the extent that such wages are includible in gross income*" was removed from the IRC in a 1943 "*clerical amendment*". (Yeah, you bet it was!) The "*wages of every person*" was shrewd because it seems to embrace anybody making a paycheck. However, section 465(a) "*wages*" were not paid to "*persons*" — but to "*employees*" (previously defined in section 465(d) as government workers). Sneaky, huh? And just months after Pearl Harbor, who would have dug into this and challenged it?

The tricky goal was to gradually make Americans believe that wages were directly taxable by including federal "*wages*" within taxable "*income*", but without outright asserting that private wages (in the conversational sense) are "*income*". (Tax cases prior to WWII were corporate cases because the IRS was not yet imposing the "*income*" tax on private-sector paychecks.)

Since 1862 the wages of federal employees have always been directly subject to "*income*" taxation. However, if your private paycheck were directly taxable (as is federal "*compensation*"), then Revenue Acts would read that way! They would have dispensed with any "*income derived from salaries, wages, and compensation*" language, **as they have *always left out this phrase* when directly taxing federal pay.** A side-by-side comparison of how government wages are taxed vs. business "*income derived from* [the employer having paid] *wages*" is striking:

government "*wages*"	"*income derived from wages*"
1862 [A 3% tax] *shall be levied, collected, and paid on all salaries of officers, or . . . persons in the . . . service of the United States, including* [Congress]	**1862** *the annual gains, profits, or income of every person residing in the United States whether* ***derived from*** *. . . salaries, or any profession, trade, employment,*
1894 [Includible in "*gains, profits, or income*"] *is the salary or other compensation paid to any person in the employment or service* ***of the United States***	**1894** *gains, profits, and income . . .* ***derived from*** *. . . salaries, . . . profession, trade, employment*
1913 *When such State officers or employees are* ***compensated by the United States****, they must include such income as taxable*	**1913** *Gross income includes all gains, profits, income* ***derived from*** *salaries, wages, or compensation for personal service of whatever kind in whatever form paid*
1939 *Presidents* [and federal judges], *the* [entire] *compensation received as such shall be included in gross income;*	**1939** *"Gross income" includes gains, profits, and* ***income derived from salaries****, wages, or compensation*
1942 [A tax of 5%] *upon the wages of every person, to the extent that such* [§ 465(d) government "*employee*"] *wages are includible in gross income* *an officer, employee, or elected official* ***of the United States****, a State, Territory, or any political subdivision thereof, or* [D.C.], . . .	**1942** *income* **[derived]** ***from the following sources****: salary, wages, compensation for personal services*
1986 (today's IRC) *an officer, employee, or elected official* ***of the United States****, a State, Territory, or any political subdivision thereof, or the District of Columbia, or any agency or instrumentality*	**1986 (today's IRC)** *gross income means all income* ***from whatever source derived*** *including (but not limited to) the following items (1) compensation for services, . . .*

What were *never* directly taxed in any of those Revenue Acts were salaries of those not working for government. While subsequent "*income*" tax acts increased the rate and then added progressiveness, the limited scope of what *could* be taxed (federal pay and U.S. net profits) has never changed. **Making a "*salary*" is not the same thing as "*deriving income from a salary*" (as an employer).**

The only real difference between the tax acts of 1862, 1894, 1913, 1921, 1928, 1939, 1942-1944, 1954, and 1986 was the increasing vagueness and slipperiness of the language. What was clear in 1862 had very purposely become muddied by 1954. By then, IRC codewriters had completely mastered the linguistic trick of turning your private-sector pay into "*income*" — by way of calling them federal government "*employee wages*" which have been legally taxed since the Civil War. (According to IRS apologists IRC § 3401(c) term "*employee*" embraces private-sector workers. I am not convinced.)

Supreme Court never ruled labor = "*income*"

The below cases are trotted out by government supremacists to "prove" that all paychecks are automatically taxable as federal "*income*".

> ***Stratton's Independence, Ltd. v. Howbert***, 231 U.S. 399 (1913)
> ***Eisner v. Macomber***, 252 U.S. 189 (1920)
> ***Lucas v. Earl***, 281 U.S. 111 (1930)
> ***Steward Mach. Co. v. Collector***, 301 U.S. 548 (1937)
> ***Helvering v. Gerhardt***, 304 U.S. 405 (1938)
> ***Graves v. New York***, 306 U.S. 466 (1939)
> ***Central Illinois Public Serv. Co. v. U.S.***, 435 U.S. 21 (1978)

For brevity, I'll address only the first two. Just as "tax protestors" are (often rightly) accused of quoting cases out of context, the same is true of those who believe that the IRC conveys (hah!) "plain meaning".

Stratton's Independence v. Howbert, 231 U.S. 399 (1913)

> [T]*he* [net profit] *earnings of the human brain and hand when unaided by capital . . . are commonly dealt with as income in legislation.*
> — ***Stratton's Independence v. Howbert***, 231 U.S. 399, 415 (1913)

This was not a case which ruled that "labor compensation is a taxable gain". ***Stratton's*** "'*income' may be defined as the gain derived from capital, from labor, or from both combined*" regarded a mining corporation objecting to the taxation of selling its own mining property (as a mere "*depletion of capital*"). The Court ruled that since they had mixed in labor with their mined ore, that the ore had increased in value (vs. remaining in the ground) "*and here we have combined operations of capital and* *labor*". That ruling in now way declared that salaries and wages were 16th Amendment taxable "*income*" — only that a net gain/profit/"*income*" could be "*derived from labor*". That's all it said.

It is one thing to be a laborer, yet quite another to "*employ labor*". A company resells labor (usually bundled with capital investment) at retail and makes a profit, whereas the laborer is the source of labor (sold at wholesale to his employer). ***Stratton's*** merely compared the mining company to other companies, not to laborers. This was in no way a wage case, but is tragically mistaken as the foundational "wages are gains and profits" case from the early era of the 16th Amendment. ***Stratton's*** has become utterly misread by many to mean that working for a paycheck constitutes a 100% gain, thus taxable. Many lower courts have fallen for it (***Tornichio v. United States***, ***Gavigan v. United States,*** and ***U.S. v. Buras***), ignoring the vital "*derived from*" qualifier (which is now totally misunderstood to mean merely "*from*" vs. its correct "*separated from its ______ source*").

Basically, the courts don't comprehend the meaning of "*derive*".

Eisner v. Macomber, 252 U.S. 189 (1920)

> *Income may be defined as the gain derived from capital, from labor, or from both combined, including profit gained through sale or conversion of capital.*
>
> — ***Eisner v. Macomber***, 252 U.S. 189 (1920)

Greatly stretched as a wage case when it was not, ***Eisner*** certainly did not rule that a paycheck is "*income*". The case decided that "*income*" did not include a stock dividend which merely added value to the stock (vs. a profit dividend of cash value). Everyone needs to internalize page 207 of case, which hammered out (note the original emphasis in underlines!) the full meaning of "*derive*":

> *Here, we have the essential matter: not a gain accruing to capital; not a growth or increment of value in the investment; but a gain, a profit, something of exchangeable value, proceeding from the property, severed from the capital, however invested or employed, and coming in, being "derived" — that is, received or drawn by the recipient (the taxpayer) for his separate use, benefit and disposal — that is income derived from property. Nothing else answers the description.*

"*Income*" and sources of "*income*" are two different things. After years of research into this subject, I have found no compelling evidence that private-sector paychecks were meant in 1913 to fall under the 16th Amendment's "*income*". Here was the proper sentiment well understood back in the day:

We favor an income tax as part of our revenue system, and we urge the submission of a constitutional amendment specifically authorizing Congress to levy and collect a tax upon individual and corporate incomes (profits), ***to the end that wealth may bear its proportional share of the burdens of the federal government.***

— Democrat Party Presidential Platform of 1908

IRS admits: only federal "*employees*" pay

Want a real "smoking gun" on all this? Here is a copy of an IRS notice often sent out to scare the uninformed private-sector worker:

Urgent !!

We intend to levy on certain assets. Please respond NOW.

(To avoid additional penalty and interest, pay the amount you owe within ten days from the date of this notice.)

Our records indicate that you haven't paid the amount you owe. The law requires that you pay your tax at the time you file your return. This is your notice, as required by Internal Revenue Code Section 6331(d), of our intent to levy (take) any state tax refunds that you may be entitled to if we don't receive your payment in full. In addition, we will begin to search for other assets we may levy. We can also file a Notice of Federal Tax Lien, if we haven't already done so. **To prevent collection action, please pay the current balance now.** If you've already paid, can't pay, or have arranged for an installment agreement, it is important that you **call us immediately** at the telephone number shown below. Current balance may include Civil Penalty, if assessed.

Notice the suspicious (intentional) gap above the large paragraph?
Now, here is the full notice with the vital text intact:

Urgent !!

We intend to levy on certain assets. Please respond NOW.

(To avoid additional penalty and interest, pay the amount you owe within ten days from the date of this notice.)

As a current or retired federal employee, you must pay your federal taxes as required by law.

Our records indicate that you haven't paid the amount you owe. The law requires that you pay your tax at the time you file your return. This is your notice, as required by Internal Revenue Code Section 6331(d), of our intent to levy (take) any state tax refunds that you may be entitled to if we don't receive your payment in full. In addition, we will begin to search for other assets we may levy. We can also file a Notice of Federal Tax Lien, if we haven't already done so. **To prevent collection action, please pay the current balance now.** If you've already paid, can't pay, or have arranged for an installment agreement, it is important that you **call us immediately** at the telephone number shown below. Current balance may include Civil Penalty, if assessed.

"*As a current or retired federal employee, you must pay your federal taxes as required by law.*" Little wonder why this crucial phrase was left out by the IRS! You must be able to understand the defined terms of IRC § 3401, such as "*wages*" and "*employee*". This notice is connected to IRC section 6331, which is often sent to employers but omitting its subsection (a). One citizen wrote his Congressman E. Clay Shaw asking for clarification, to learn that the "*income*" tax levy was authorized only upon salary and wages of **federal** employees and officials:

E. CLAY SHAW, JR.
22ND DISTRICT, FLORIDA

COMMITTEE:
WAYS AND MEANS
SUBCOMMITTEES:
CHAIRMAN
TRADE
SOCIAL SECURITY
OVERSIGHT

CHAIRMAN
FLORIDA CONGRESSIONAL DELEGATION

Congress of the United States
House of Representatives
Washington, DC 20515–0922

1236 LONGWORTH HOUSE OFFICE BUILDING
WASHINGTON, DC 20515
[illegible]

DISTRICT OFFICES:
BROWARD COUNTY
1512 EAST BROWARD BOULEVARD
SUITE 101
FORT LAUDERDALE, FL 33301
[illegible]

PALM BEACH COUNTY
222 LAKEVIEW AVENUE, #235
WEST PALM BEACH, FL 33401
[illegible]

WEB SITE
www.house.gov/shaw

January 24, 2005

Mr. Gary A. Fennell
[redacted]
Boca Raton, Florida 33431-5926

Dear Mr. Fennell:

Thank you for contacting me with a question regarding your troubles with the Internal Revenue Service (IRS). While responding as best I can, please understand that I am not giving any legal advice. I would strongly advise you to seek counsel on this matter.

U.S. Code, Title 26, Subtitle F, Chapter 64, Subchapter D Part II, Section 6331 (a) states:

If any person liable to pay any tax neglects or refuses to pay the same within 10 days after notice and demand, it shall be lawful for the Secretary to collect such tax (and such further sum as shall be sufficient to cover the expenses of the levy) by levy upon all property and rights to property (except such property as is exempt under section 6334) belonging to such person or on which there is a lien provided in this chapter for the payment of such tax. Levy may be made upon the accrued salary or wages of any officer, employee, or elected official, of the United States, the District of Columbia, or any agency or instrumentality of the United States or the District of Columbia, by serving a notice of levy on the employer (as defined in section 3401(d)) of such officer, employee, or elected official. If the Secretary makes a finding that the collection of such tax is in jeopardy, notice and demand for immediate payment of such tax may be made by the Secretary and, upon failure or refusal to pay such tax, collection thereof by levy shall be lawful without regard to the 10-day period provided in this section.

This particular provision does not appear to extend to private sector employees. If a form was given to an employer that omitted section (a), this form could be considered misleading.

I hope that this is helpful to you. Again you may wish to seek help from an attorney or tax professional.

Sincerely,

E. Clay Shaw, Jr.
Member of Congress

ECS:cd

So, what's been happening is that the IRS uses on private-sector workers Code section 6331(a) regarding the levy of federal "*salary and wages*". When they do so, they omit subsection (a) – which limited the scope of 6331. That certainly is "*misleading*" as Congressman Shaw observed.

THE 16th AMENDMENT

Who controls the past controls the future.
Who controls the present controls the past.
— George Orwell; *1984*

As long as the 16th Amendment is in place, the odds are slim that we can restore a constitutional republic dedicated to liberty.
— Ron Paul to the U.S. House, 29 January 2003
www.lewrockwell.com/paul/paul76.html

16th Amendment ratification funny business

To ratify the Income Tax Amendment of 1913 required the approval of three-fourths (36) of the 48 states. In *The Law That Never Was,* authors Beckman and Benson traveled to the capitals of all 48 states for certified copies of the votings. The states must pass any proposed amendment exactly as written by Congress without any changes whatsoever. (Not even a misplaced comma can be tolerated, for it might significantly change the law's intended meaning.) Of the 36 states which allegedly passed the 16th, at least 32 committed grievous departures from the mandatory strict procedure. The legislative journals of Oklahoma, Missouri, and Washington prove that those states intentionally amended the language (which was not allowed, but Secretary of State Knox nevertheless counted such as *assent* to the proposed amendment).

Most outrageously, Kentucky voted 22 to 9 *against* the 16th, but was fraudulently recorded as one of the *ratifying* states. (Also rejecting the amendment were Connecticut, New Hampshire, Rhode Island, and Utah. Visit www.jeffdickstein.com and www.thelawthatneverwas.com)

The certified record of all this is irrefutable, which is why both the Congress and the Supreme Court (every member having received a copy of *The Law That Never Was*) have ignored this timebomb. Congress says it's a *judicial* matter. The courts claim it's a *political* matter, relying on Revised Statute 205 (the "Enrolled Bill Rule" creating a conclusive presumption of ratification). They know that to recognize the 16th's ratification record would make it null and void overnight, and thus kill the modern "*income*" tax.

Though the matter seems stagnant, I think it's revivable. If millions of Americans suddenly learned of this, we could at last force the issue. Given the universal unpopularity of the "*income*" tax, this issue is ripe. (Aaron Russo's groundbreaking film *From Freedom to Fascism* touches on the matter, although with some variously faulty information regarding taxes.) This political remedy could work if the country were competently told of it.

FINAL THOUGHTS ON "*INCOME*" TAXES

Truth certainly exists.
But it is very hard to put together.
It's always an assembled truth.
Truth must be assembled.
– Heinrich Boll

If the Legislature were to attempt, by taxing all occupations, practically, to annul the prohibition against a poll tax, the question made might arise. ***But there is a clear distinction between a tax upon certain specified businesses, where the skill of the operator is a source of profit,*** *or where the public are appealed to for patronage and protection of a fixed and regular business,* ***and a tax covering all persons, whatever may be their occupation.*** . . . [The opinion then refers to taxes on lawyers, doctors, etc. and continues:] *The skill, or education, or tact, which is the source of profit in these* [taxable] *occupations,* ***is clearly distinguishable from that capacity which is in every man to work for his support with the hands which God has given him.***
– TAXING THE EXERCISE OF NATURAL RIGHTS,
John MacAurthur Maguire, Harvard Legal Essays (1934), p. 286

Maguire touches precisely on why a direct, unapportioned tax on common labor is unconstitutional. "Wages = '*income*'" has become a very entrenched myth, supported by hundreds of millions of paying Americans, and the lower courts. Many Americans, however, do not believe that there is any legal or historical issue with the "*income*" tax applied to common earnings. They tend to call those who seek the truth "tax protestors".

Neo: <awakening from a coma> *Why do my eyes hurt?*
Morpheus: *Because you've never used them before.*
– *The Matrix*

Cornell University (well-known for its law school) has a very thorough website on every aspect of the Constitution. In its page on the 16th Amendment, nowhere does this prestigious university support the claim that a private-sector paycheck is itself "*gross income*":

Income Subject to Taxation
Building upon definitions formulated in cases construing the Corporation Tax Act of 1909, the Court initially described income as the "gain derived from capital, from labor, or from both combined," inclusive of the "profit gained through a sale or

*conversion of capital assets"; **in the following array of factual** situations it subsequently applied this definition **to achieve results that have been productive of extended controversy.***
— www.law.cornell.edu/anncon/html/amdt16_user.html

("*Productive of extended controversy*", indeed!) I applaud Cornell for telling it straight, and not adding to the smoke and mirrors.

Lastly, what is most encouraging is that IRS employees are beginning to quit, out of principle, such as former IRS C.I.D. Special Agent Joseph Banister. Read his stirring story of integrity and courage at www.freedomabovefortune.com. The enforcers cannot be totally counted on! Tectonic news!

Here ends my layman's nonprofessional overview of 16th Amendment "*income*". Whether or not a private-sector paycheck received by the worker is taxable "*income*" to him is a question you may want to answer for yourself. (Beware of many bad, misleading, and irrelevant opinions on *both* sides of the matter. **I am recommending *no* action of yours but vigorous study and discussion.** Retain your focus on what is 16th Amendment "*income*".) Nothing in this chapter is "*aiding and abetting the understatement of tax liabilities, promoting abusive tax shelters and/or hindering the proper administration of the Internal Revenue Code*." Do not email me with questions — conduct your own personal research on the Web.

A searchable IRC (Title 26 U.S. Code) can be downloaded from:

http://uscode.house.gov/lawrevisioncounsel.shtml
www.law.cornell.edu/uscode/
www.findlaw.com/casecode/uscodes/

and the IRC's associated regulations can be downloaded from:

www.access.gpo.gov/cgi-bin/cfrassemble.cgi?title=200526
http://ecfr.gpoaccess.gov/cgi/t/text/text-idx?c=ecfr&tpl=%2Findex.tpl

IRC definitions can be downloaded from:

www.law.cornell.edu/uscode/html/uscode26/usc_sec_26_00007701----00-.html

Most Supreme and lower court rulings can be downloaded from:

www.findlaw.com
www.supreme.justia.com
www.law.cornell.edu/supct/index.html
www.supremecourtus.gov/opinions/boundvolumes.html

historical federal income tax acts

www.losthorizons.com
www.famguardian.org/PublishedAuthors/Govt/HistoricalActs/HistFedIncTaxActs.htm

contrary portrayals (some quite clever, so use caution!):
http://home.hiwaay.net/~becraft/deadissues.htm
http://www.netaxs.com/~evansdb/tpfaq.html
http://www.fraudsandscams.com/tax.htm
http://docs.law.gwu.edu/facweb/jsiegel/Personal/taxes/IncomeTax.htm
http://www.quatloos.com/tax_scams.php

> *I apprehend no danger to our country from a foreign foe . . . Our destruction, should it come at all, will be from another quarter.* ***From the inattention of the people to the concerns of their government, from their carelessness and negligence****, I must confess that I do apprehend some danger.*
>
> — Daniel Webster

> *. . . the best way* [for statists] *to exhaust the spirit of people who might otherwise mobilize that spirit in order to acquire freedom is to keep them working as much of the time as possible simply to stay biologically alive.*
> [To which his guest James Michener replied:] *Give people less and less food till they reach the breaking point, then feed them more so they can work, but be sure then to diminish the food so they go back to the breaking point. The gulag formula . . .*
>
> — William F. Buckley, Jr., *On The Firing Line*

When enough Americans are well informed on this matter, then a groundswell for political and legal change can occur. Verily, the Supreme Court needs to squarely analyze the legislative history of the 16th Amendment and finally resolve the question of whether the people, the states, and Congress of 1909-1913 intended to apply an "*income*"/net profit tax to common paychecks. Do your part to demand an answer!

WHAT ABOUT SOCIAL SECURITY?

Here is the standard reply from SSA should you inquire if you are required by law to have an SSN to live and work. SSA has been sending this letter from at least 1948 to 1998, as this copy shows:

> ***The Social Security Act does not require a person to have a Social Security number to live and work in the United States,*** *nor does it require a Social Security number simply for the purpose of having one.*
>
> — http://home.hiwaay.net/~becraft/ScottSSNLetter.pdf
> http://en.wikipedia.org/wiki/Social_Security_(United_States)
> www.famguardian.org/Subjects/Taxes/ChallJurisdiction/YourRightsAndSSNs.htm

Here is more evidence that the SS program is voluntary:

> . . . *Individuals who are ineligible for* ***or do not wish to participate in the benefits of the social security program*** *shall nevertheless obtain a social security number if they are required to furnish such a number* . . . [if they otherwise come under IRC tax jurisdiction].
>
> — 26 CFR 301.6109-1(d)(1)
> http://law.justia.com/cfr/title26/26-18.0.1.1.2.1.54.96.html

The federal regulation itself confirms that the Social Security program is voluntary. Your "participation" is up to you. Since its inception in 1935, the SSA has been a completely voluntary program for private-sector workers. In fact, the USG published advertisements urging Americans in the 1930s to join up! With words like "*join*" and "*application*" it read like a credit card ad! It also spoke of "*who is eligible*" — not "who is required".

A A government poster about the Social Security Act, which began to provide Americans with some financial protection against unemployment, illness and old age.

An SSN is required of every federal "*employee*" making "*wages*" — however, you do not have to work for the Government or sign a "*voluntary withholding agreement*" under § 3402(p).

Social Security is a voluntary welfare program acting as a very lousy insurance policy. You don't have to join, and the U.S. Congress exempted themselves (and other federal workers) from the scam until 1984 due to public ridicule. (Once you're in, however, getting out is nearly impossible, even if you renounce irrevocably all claims to any future benefits.) Now, if you are a "*taxpayer*" under the IRC and "*liable*" to file returns and pay "*income*" tax, then the use of an SSN is mandatory. But only if you are first an IRC section 7701(a)(14) "*taxpayer*". And as you've just learned, you may not be. (Search for a business in Houston named "Arrow Plastics" and learn how they dealt with SS "requirements".)

"Must My baby Have A Social Security Number Now?"

Go to www.ssa.gov/pubs/10023.html (an official government site), and read line 20:

> *No! Getting a Social Security Number for your baby is strictly voluntary.*

Now, hospitals are rarely aware of this, and will earnestly try to automatically issue one at birth. Know the law; know your rights!

the Two Rules of Life

Do all you have agreed to do, and
Do not encroach on other persons or their property.

The first covers civil law; the second criminal. The primary source of America's political and economic ills is her rejection of the Natural Law.

The American Revolution was a war over the difference between Natural Law and Political Law, and it did not end in 1783 with the defeat of Great Britain. It is still being fought. It began as a tax revolt, and, after a 130 year general ceasefire (from 1783-1913) it continues today. In 1936 less than 1 American in 25 suffered IRS wage withholding. Today, nearly every worker is painfully familiar with the IRS tax bite.

> *"Reality," after all, is what is socially accepted. When the Sixteenth Amendment was passed, a proposed amendment was rejected that a 10 percent ceiling should be imposed. Rejected on the grounds that merely mention the figure "10 percent" might encourage Congress to levy a usuriously high tax. A 10 percent tax was then a* reductio ad absurdum.
>
> — William F. Buckley, Jr., *On The Firing Line*

What happened these past seven decades? **If the "*income*" tax has truly applied to all paychecks since 1913, then why were so few Americans paying it until WWII?** Quite a bit has happened, actually. Our originally limited federal government has become a *de facto* national government with nearly unlimited powers. And all within the lifetime of your grandparents. In *The Covenant* Rudyard Kipling wrote:

> *We thought we ranked above the chance of ill.*
> *Others might fall, not we, for we were wise —*
> *Merchants in freedom. So, of our free-will*
> *We let our servants drug our strength with lies.*
> *The pleasure and the poison had its way*
> *On us as on the meanest, till we learned*
> ***That he who lies will steal, who steals will slay.***
> *Neither God's judgment nor man's heart was turned.*
>
> *Yet there remains His mercy — to be sought*
> *Through wrath and peril till we cleanse the wrong*
> *By that last right which our forefathers claimed*
> *When their law failed them and its stewards were bought.*
> *This is our cause. God help us, and make us strong*
> *Our will to meet Him later, unashamed!*

Our government began to lie, and we *let* them.
Then it began to steal, and we *let* them.
Now it slays, here and abroad. And we *let* them.

They may be (for now) out of our control, but at least we do not have to continue paying for it. We don't have to continue feeding the hand that bites us.

This chapter was as simple as I could write it. It is sufficient to broadly understand the issues involved, and to form a framework for further study. And further study is urged of all Americans. Is there still time? Does enough of our national home remain unburned? Enough to live in while we restore the rest? I do not know, but it seems obvious that the alternative is unthinkable. We cannot let the government fire continue to consume our home around our ears. If enough of us will demand the promise of liberty originally granted us over 225 years ago, we can restore America's constitutional republic and its system of limited taxation.

But it's up to us. It is up to *you*.

> *Find out just what any people will quietly submit to and you have the exact measure of the injustice and wrong which will be imposed on them.*
> — Frederick Douglass (a self-freed slave), 1857

Thomas Jefferson wrote:

> *Rightful liberty is unobstructed action according to our will within limits drawn around us by the equal rights of others.*

> . . . [A] *wise and frugal government, which shall restrain men from injuring one another, which shall leave them otherwise free to regulate their own pursuits of industry and improvement, and shall not take from the mouth of labor the bread it has earned.*
>
> *This is the sum of good government.*

LEGAL TAX AVOIDANCE

Tax *avoidance* is legal. Tax *evasion* is not.

They say that "*taxes are the price of civilization.*" While some tax revenues actually go to building roads and libraries, most do not. Mostly, taxes are the way the parasite class can get a free ride on the productive class. You must always keep that in mind. Taxes should be vigorously avoided (legally) whenever possible. With ample study and firmness, this is easily done. Some methods of tax avoidance may come very close to illegal tax evasion. What is legal is not always moral, and what is moral is not always legal. It is up to you to first form your own moral base.

own your own business

Business expenses are deductible against "*income*" taxes, and you'd be surprised the extent of what can be written off to offset your annual net profit. If your business requires much travel, many of your daily expenses (which provide you a comfortable lifestyle) are fully deductible. You might even be left with a profit that falls beneath "*income*" reporting requirements.

barter

Also, trading goods-for-goods may keep you clear of "*deriving income*" in such transactions — unless and until you finally cash out and "*derive*"/"realize" the instrinsic profit into monetary form. The IRS hates barter, so be careful what you do, and how.

working for cash

Cash is the enemy of the parasite class, because it is anonymous. So, they have tried to make cash suspicious in modern life, where only drug-dealers use cash. ("Normal" people pay by check or credit card.) This is a sham, however. There is nothing evil or wrong about cash. In fact, cash is moral because it gives Government less information about the People and their private lives. Cash is also moral because it does not feed the banking system (which creates "money" out of thin air, and then charges you interest on the privilege that Government gave them).

Start using cash and insisting on cash wherever possible! You could offer a 10-15% discount for cash because it "*reduces your paperwork and bookkeeping requirements*". (You are responsible under relevant law, however, to report all "*income*" that is legally subject to federal tax.)

Do not bank your cash, but store it at home. Cash is unregistered wealth, and if you deposit it in the bank you not only effectively "register" it with the Government, but that cash is now in the control of the bank (nearly a branch of Government these days). They can limit your withdrawals or even freeze your account anytime they are told to do so.

must you collect "*sales tax*"?

That depends. You must *very* carefully study your state's sales tax regulations and squeeze the true meaning out of such terms as "*sale*" and "*retail* " and "*goods*" and "*vendor*" and "*business*". (How your business is organized may also be a factor in whether "*sales tax*" applies to you. Occasionally selling your own household goods may not constitute a "*business*" through garage sales and flea markets.)

lawful avoidance of the "sales tax" racket

Sales tax can apply only if the buyer sells a product for dollar currency (cash or check). Sales tax cannot apply to goods traded. (If you trade in your car for a newer one, its trade-in value is nontaxable.) Well, what if the buyer hasn't anything you want in trade? OK, then this might work for you, depending on your state.

If you are at a show (gun show, flea market, etc.) and the local sales tax vulture is about, asking "*vendors*" if they have a sales tax license, you might reply that you are not "selling" but *trading*. All your "prices" are in silver ounces. Well, where would a potential buyer conveniently get silver in order to trade with you? Why, from your buddy the next table over, who happens to be selling silver bullion. But wouldn't he have to collect sales tax on his silver sales?

Not if your state *exempts* precious metals. Many states do. (Have a copy on hand of the relevant law exempting precious metals.) It is important that somebody else sells your customer the silver. If you do it yourself, then there is probably not sufficient distinction between your having sold vs. traded your goods. This will make the sales tax vulture go nuts, as there's *nothing* he can do about it. If he really gets horsey, calmly reply that if he doesn't quit pestering you, you will inform everybody of this legal way of circumventing the *mala prohibita* of imposing tax collection obligations on occasional private sellers.

Tax *avoidance* is legal. Tax *evasion* is not. Besides, if you're selling used goods, the state already got its tax at the original retail level, so how much can the state rightfully insist on taxing the same thing again later?

"The charges, your Honor, are concealment of identity, possession of a dangerous weapon, and we're waiting to hear from the Bureau of Weights and Measures."

22

FIGHTING

[In today's "safe society"] *aggression has become a bad word and testosterone a banned substance. Danger is something to be avoided . . . something to be neutered.*

— Jon Wertheim

In other walks of life, maybe you can get away with pretending, but not in fighting. You have to honor your true nature. Fighting forces honesty down your throat.

— Sam Sheridan, *The Fighter's Mind*, p, 279

If you've never been in a fight, how much can you really know about yourself?

— *Fight Club*

The essence of life is struggle and its goal is domination. There are higher goals and deeper meanings, but they exist only within the mind of man. The reality of life is war.

— *The Way and The Power*

Everybody is fighting something.

— Brazilian jui-jitsu master Renzo Gracie

All you need to do to achieve peace is to give up.

— Jeff Cooper

There are two very important things that most young men cannot do with confidence: defend themselves, and dance. Dancing credibly is easier, and a few months of lessons will suffice. After that, practice. However, becoming a deadly fighter — a warrior — takes stern commitment and years of hard training.

Everybody is fighting something. It's an immutable part of Life. Even if you're boxing in a ring, or grappling on a mat, or defending yourself in a dark alley, you are still in some kind of fight. Although this chapter is about physical fighting, anybody can drink from the metaphoric well.

Besides, men love to fight. Or should. It's in our genetic design. You've a wildman within. (Or should.) He's there for a reason, and you're not complete without him. Discover the Warrior within you, and train him. You need him, and so does your family and country.

A male who cannot fight (and usually prevail) is not yet a Man.

For a more philosophical exposition on the significance of fighting, we need look no further than Plato's Republic.

For those who haven't read it, in the Republic Socrates explores the concept of justice through examining both the just society and the just individual, and then he goes on to delineate their common elements. On the societal level he notes that a just community is made up of a number of vital component parts: rulers who govern, workers who labour, and an army that functions to protect them both. In the individual he finds a similar configuration - the mind that governs the body, the limbs that do the work, and the "themos" (which is often translated as "temper" or "aggression") that plays a parallel role in protecting the individual. Justice in the Republic consists in having all of the component parts (in either individual or society) being present and working together properly.

In the wisdom of the ancient Greeks then, the "themos" is the vital third component in the human constitution, along with the mind and the body. Without the "themos", no individual is complete, and at a social level, no society will ever achieve a true state of justice.

It is my opinion that one of the negative legacies of feminism in Western culture has been an attempt to deny the "themos", which seems to be more strongly present in men than in women. This has been for the most understandable of reasons - because of the excesses of male violence. But perhaps it's time that we realised that trying to eliminate "themos" from society altogether is like trying to eliminate spiders and snakes because we find them distasteful. We soon discover that the created order needs all of its creatures - even those that some of us find ugly - if it is to function properly.

My experience with a vast number of men is that they tend to be either functioning as doormats to their wives and girlfriends, or they're beating up on them. This is a reflection of the same crisis in dealing with the themos". When we attempt to repress the themos', it often spurts out in the most horrible and destructive of forms. When we successfully repress it, we emasculate our men, so that they're no longer able to stand up for anything. Ironically, of course, such modern day men are not only unable to offer any strength to society. They're no longer even attractive to the women they sought to please.

The only constructive alternative is for us to reharness the "themos" and channel it creatively. We need to get in touch with that distinctive male energy - recognise it, affirm it, and then learn to bring it under control so that it can be put to good use.

I do seriously believe that our community would be greatly served if every teenage boy, when he reached the age of say 16 or 17 was obliged to train for a fight.

(Fighting' Father Dave Smith - Parish Priest, community worker, professional fighter, father of three. Dave is the only Australian in Holy Orders to turn pro boxer to help fund his work. He is Parish Priest in Dulwich Hill, has a sixth-degree martial arts black belt, and has received numerous awards for his work with young people. Get a free preview copy of his book, 'Sex, the Ring & the Eucharist' when you sign up for Dave's newsletter at www.fatherdave.org.)

— www.winyourmmafight.com

THE WIMP MINDSET

One who places safety first is, quite specifically, a coward. We do not go to war to be safe, neither do we climb mountains, or race cars, or hunt buffalo, to be safe. We hear commentators explain that we should not resist violent crime because we may get hurt. This is the advice of the rabbit people who live all their lives in fear and never know the joy of danger. There are people like that, and while we may feel sorry for them, we must never take their advice seriously.

— Jeff Cooper

Statistically, fighting back is safer than giving in.

— Curt Rich

Unless we keep the barbarian values, gaining the civilized ones will be of little avail.

— Theodore Roosevelt

In my 2004 novel *Molôn Labé!* I composed what I supposed was an over-the-top, outrageous satire on the "*never fight back!*" mindset. My goal was to take nondefensive reasoning to its logical extremis, and thus perhaps inoculate the random non-warrior against the infection of wussiness. Here it is:

Submissive Inviting the Sharing of Suppressed Yearnings (SISSY)

Our goal is to expose once and for all the real cause of criminal violence. Crimes are violent only because the "victim" might resist. If the initiator could *peaceably* get what he wanted, he would *forsake* any violence in doing so. Makes sense, doesn't it?

The root of "coercion" is one party not willing to *share*.

Let us therefore go directly to the heart of the matter. We must simply *outlaw resistance*. Those who "defend" themselves are *willing partners* in the deadly dance of violence. It takes *two* to Tango!

Self defense has no defense!

By mandating submission, we remove the reason for violence. Do you see the elegant simplicity of this? Eliminate resistance and you eliminate violence!

Make a fist — Go to jail!

We propose the registration of all Carnally-Generous men ("rapists"). Thereafter, all Carnal Gifts shall take place by random selection. The Carnally-Generous simply chooses his preferred Receptor, who reports for Submission Duty. (This is scheduled at *mutual* convenience — fair is fair.) No fuss, no muss. "Rape" without violence is merely sex, and any woman's reluctance to accept a Carnal Gift is *elitism*, pure and simple.

No more "rapist." No more "victim." *No more violence!*

The Submission Program can also be applied to "muggings" and all other so-called "crimes of violence."

A nonviolent society through submission!

Imagine the tax savings from closing down all the unnecessary "Sex Crimes" police units. This would free up law enforcement to investigate *real* crimes such as: hate speech, homophobic discrimination, unregistered gun trafficking, suspicious cash transactions, underground homeschooling, spanking, vaccination evasion, sedition, and hooliganism.

There can be no peace until we embrace the will of others.
The only real evil is *not sharing*.
Join SISSY today!

I could not have dreamed that 10 years later that such silliness would be actually expected in an official school pamphlet (later withdrawn due to overwhelming public disgust). Quoted verbatim:

Refuse to get mad. Anger is a feeling we have toward our enemies, not our buddies. When you get angry, you are treating them like they are your enemy. Besides, if a bully finds out he can get you angry, you become their puppet and the bully controls you.

Treat the person who is being mean as if they are trying to help you. No matter how insulting or mean they may sound, be grateful and think they really care about you. (This does not mean you have to believe what they tell you.)

Do not be afraid. Fear is something we feel toward enemies, not buddies. When you are afraid, you are treating the bully like an enemy. If you [are] afraid, you are automatically putting the bully in the stronger position, and you automatically lose, and since the bully wants to keep winning, he will continue doing things to make you feel afraid.

Do not verbally defend yourself. We defend ourselves from *enemies*, so we are treating the other person as an enemy not a friend. When one person attacks and the other is the defender, the attacker is in the stronger position, so the defender is automatically the loser. If we defend, we lose.

Do not attack. We attack enemies, not friends. If I attack you back, I am treating you like an enemy, so the bully will in return, treat you like an enemy. It takes two people to fight, so it's the person who retaliates or responds, who actually starts the fight.

If someone physically hurts you, just show you are hurt; do not get angry. If someone hurts you, you want them to feel sorry and apologize. If you get angry, they won't feel sorry.

Do not tell on bullies. The number one reason bullies hate their victims is because the victims tell on them. Telling makes the bully want to retaliate. Tell an adult only when a real injury or crime (theft of something valuable) has occurred. Would we keep our friends if we tattled on them?

Don't be a sore loser. No one likes a sore loser. Would you like to play with someone who gets all upset when they lose? Lose gracefully and be a good sport; kids will like you better.

Learn to laugh at yourself and not get "hooked" by put-downs. Make a joke out of it or agree with the put-down. For example:

"*If you think I'm ugly, you should see my sister!*"
"*You're right, and it's going to get worse!*"
"*If you think I look like a nerd, you should see my dad!*"

To recap this toxic swill: never fight back, always remain a victim, and answer insults to include your own family. What evil pap. It will ruin a boy for life, while enriching therapists and psychiatrists. He will never become a Man. And that is exactly their goal.

my 2004 satire:

We must simply outlaw resistance. Those who "defend" themselves are willing partners in the deadly dance of violence. It takes two to Tango!

public school policy of 2014:

If I attack you back, I am treating you like an enemy, so the bully will in return, treat you like an enemy. It takes two people to fight, so it's the person who retaliates or responds, who actually starts the fight.

There is an orchestrated effort to eliminate manly courage, and make us all into quavering women who need the State to protect them. Well, not me, and not you. The rest of the gutless world can go live in the hell of their creation. We, however, will never *start* a fight, but we will always *end* one. That is the Warrior mindset.

THE WARRIOR MINDSET

One bleeding-heart type asked me in a recent interview if I did not agree that "violence begets violence". I told him that it is my earnest endeavor to see that it does. I would like very much to ensure – and in some cases I have – that any man who offers violence to his fellow citizen begets a whole lot more in return than he can enjoy.

– Jeff Cooper

To secure ourselves from defeat lies in our hands, but the opportunity of defeating the enemy is provided by the enemy himself.

– Sun Tzu

My best wrestlers . . . knew how to win [because of their fighting mindset] *before they knew how to wrestle. . . . It's easier to teach the skills than the mentality.*

– Dan Gable, from *The Fighter's Mind*

The advice "choose your battles" implies that you indeed choose some! Fighting consists of (in order of importance): mindset, tactics, skill, and gear. Mindset is absolutely crucial; you cannot win without it. I highly recommend *Living the Martial Way — A manual for the way a modern warrior should think*, by Forrest E. Morgan. Some points:

> The Martial *Way* is not a sport, hobby, or occasional pastime. It's a way of life.
>
> Warriors belong to an elite group — one that knows no cultural boundaries.
>
> Begin by acknowledging your warriorship. Think, feel, and act like a warrior. Set yourself apart from the rest of society by your personal excellence.
>
> Throw away your vanity, and pursue internal objectives. Learn to recognize the difference between internal and external motivations. Train to achieve personal excellence, not certificates and belts.

"*swim the deep waters*" — boxing champ Gabriel Ruelas

The only way to learn how to fight, is to fight. Learning the moves — the *kata* — is necessary, of course, but that's not fighting. Getting your ass kicked until you begin to kick ass . . . is fighting. There is simply no substitute for actual hand-to-hand fighting.

The very odd and intense movie *Fight Club* is built around this very theme. Grown, urban men — disgusted by their own wussy nature and corporate careers — begin to frequent basement "fight clubs". If it's your first time there, you are required to fight. For the first time in their lives, these accountants and salesmen "*swam the deep waters*".

mental toughness

> *There's always a point at which people will break. That's why you train mental toughness. Everyone will break — there's not a man alive that can't be broken. Your job, with all that mental training, that suffering, is to just push your own line of mental breaking so far back your opponent can't find it. Then you take your opponent and get him to cross his line, because once he starts breaking he accepts your dominance, and once he accepts your dominance, you can finish him off.*
>
> — Josh Waitzkin, from *The Fighter's Mind*

This is something developed usually early in Life, and while you can get it later, it's much more difficult then.

the heart of a winner

Two great racehorses, 1930s Seabiscuit and 1970s Secretariat, were both known to be rather lazy off-track. They ate prodigiously and took long naps. They didn't like to train. They were temperamental. Oh, but on *racing* day, they put their entire heart into the run, beating what were otherwise faster and much better conditioned horses.

While I'm certainly not recommending that you slack off on training, I mention heart because it ties into mindset, and heart can often help to overcome a larger or more experienced opponent.

Alain Burrese, J.D. of Your Warrior's Edge

Alain is an attorney in Montana, and martial artist who offered:

> *As for mastering a martial art, yes that can take a long time. However, for basic self-defense, a lot can be learned in short courses such as Bill Kipps FAST courses, or Peyton Quinn's RMCAT courses, etc. (I'm working on more short classes, and Toney Blauer is another who teaches the shorter classes) . . . Learning some basics and mindset is better than nothing, and I did like how you emphasized mindset since that is the most important.*

Alain has several websites and books which I all recommend. Sign up for his excellent free monthly newsletter.

www.burrese.com
www.lostconscience.com
www.yourwarriorsedge.com
www.toughguywisdom.com

Marc "Animal" MacYoung

Great stuff at: www.nononsenseselfdefense.com

quality gear won't make up for a wimpy mindset

Americans have the tendency to try to buy competence through equipment, gear, and gadgetry. As a defensive skills shooting instructor, I see examples of this in nearly every class with students showing up wearing highly-tuned (and nearly unfired) handguns. Oh, and they're *so* interested in being *fast*! Speed only matters after the mind is trained.

A good man with mediocre gear will beat a mediocre man with good gear. Count on it! *Become* a good man, and then you'll *deserve* the good gear. The best man can prevail without optimum gear.

A great book is Paul Kirchner's *Deadliest Men Who Ever Lived*. Containing chapter vignettes from bad-asses throughout history, it makes for inspiring reading. Order it from Paladin Press.

WHICH MARTIAL ART?

I hope martial artists are more interested in the root of martial arts and not the different decorative branches, flowers, or leaves. It is futile to argue as to which leaf, which design of branches, or which attractive flower you like; when you understand the root, you understand all its blossoming.
— Bruce Lee, *Tao of Jeet Kune Do*, p. 23

There are no superior martial arts, only superior martial artists.

Amongst the solid fighting arts, it almost doesn't matter. Karate, tae kwon doe, boxing, grappling — they're all good in their own way. There is no "best" martial art, and any new "tool" in your "toolbox" is welcome. I would recommend a strong hand/feet striking style, coupled with a good ground fighting style (such as Brazilian jui-jitsu). What is more important than your style is your heart, mindset, and commitment to quality training.

Choose each martial doctrine by analyzing the threat you're most likely to face, evaluating your physical and emotional assets, then selecting the doctrine that best fills your needs.

The final ingredient is integration. As you develop skills from a variety of doctrines, you must learn to integrate them into an effective personal arsenal. . . . become a smooth fighter, effective at all ranges, in any situation.
— Forrest E. Morgan, *Living the Martial Way*

begin with avoiding, and then trapping

Meaning, start with foot movement, hand/arm blocks, and traps. Learn to first defend. Then come the strikes. Then combinations of blocks/parries and strikes. I like Jim Grover's Combatives Series on video (www.paladin-press.com).

no weapons

In today's terrorism-paranoid world, it's increasingly likely that you will not be able to enter many buildings or travel with any kind of edged or projectile weapon. Disarmed populations have been the historical norm, especially in Asia (which is why many martial arts originated there). Learn to fight without any weapons. Next, learn to improvise weapons with everyday items (ballpoint pens, a magazine rolled up, a belt with a heavy buckle, broomstick, etc.)

Although boxing is limited in several ways (very basic blocking, no trapping, no foot/leg strikes), it's still a very well understood art and quality training is available in any medium-sized city. I like boxing for its foot movement, sense of timing, and whole-body striking power.

Krav Maga is a synthesis martial art developed by the Israeli Defense Forces, known for its simplicity and effectiveness.

Muay thai is a kickboxing art from Thailand, known for intensive bouts. Not often found here except in larger cities.

with weapons

stick and knife

I like the Philippino martials, such as *Escrima* and *Doce Pares*. By the way, having a quality 4-6" fixed (not folding) blade knife on you often is just good policy. The legal length per state varies (usually about 4-5½"), so know before you carry. (More on knives shortly.)

handgun

For your choice of handgun, choose the largest caliber (9mm minimum) that you can control, in the highest quality semi-auto you can afford. (I recommend the .40, in a Glock, XD, or MSP — or the .45 1911.) Don't skimp on a quality concealment holster. Train well, practice regularly, and wear it daily. (More on handguns shortly.)

WAY OF THE WARRIOR: 7 VALUES

Justice
Courage
Benevolence
Politeness
Honesty
Honor
Loyalty

The trouble with this country is that a man can live his entire life without knowing whether or not he is a coward.
— Barrymore

TRAINING

Every battle is won or lost before it's ever fought.
— Sun-tzu

Civilize the mind, but make savage the body.
— Old Martial Arts Maxim, Survival360.net

The point of training is not just learning how to fight, but to learn it so deeply that your skills — when needed — switch on without thinking. For example, if somebody suddenly tossed you a ball, you'd be able to instantly react and catch it. But remember all the hours as a little boy it took you to learn how to catch at all? Catching became part of you. You have what the Japanese call *mushin* — mind without thinking.

You learn deeply in order to "forget". Once a motor skill is part of you, thinking is no longer required. Doing has become *being*. Only quality training over a long period of time will give you that. Forget about the "instant bad-ass" video programs for sale in magazines, as they cannot replace the real training found only in a *dojo*. Remember, "*tomorrow's battle is won in today's practice*".

"entity" vs. "incremental" learning

Entity skill is that which seems inborn and innate, while incremental skill derives from the hard work of step-by-step training. Entity skill, although real and valuable, foments a brittle psychology that is vulnerable to shattering from defeat.

Incremental skill, however, is not prone to giving up easily. These people "gut it out" even in the face of insurmountable problems.

The man who can drive himself further once the effort gets painful is the man who will win.
— Roger Bannister, first man to break the 4-minute mile

Forrest Morgan's plan for training

Train against unrestrained, realistic attacks.
Make free-sparring an important part of your training.
Become a student of anatomy.
Practice forms with utter seriousness.

perfect practice makes perfect

If someone asked me what a human being ought to devote the maximum of his time to, I would answer, "Training." Train more than you sleep.
— karate master Masutatsu Oyama

I get them to where they can't do it wrong even if they tried.
— legendary boxing trainer Cus D'Amato

Find quality instructors. Commit to regular training over a long time. Do not practice mistakes. Continually focus on your weakest area.

dedicate yourself to *years* of training

> *There are no shortcuts but a lifetime of study. There are no easy ways but obsession.*
>
> *Once you've devoted a lifetime to study, then the important thing is to get out of your own way and not screw yourself up by thinking. The better you get the simpler everything gets.*
>
> – Sam Sheridan, *The Fighter's Mind*

Sheridan makes the vital point that mastery in anything (art, music, fighting, tennis, gymnastics, etc.) generally takes about 10 years of constant study. (Or, as others have calculated, about 10,000 hours for world-class skill.) He's right: there are no shortcuts. There is no secret to competency but to get motivated, get busy, and stick with it for a very long time.

> *It is interesting to differentiate between self-esteem and self-respect. As I see it, self-esteem is a sociological term which assumes to be a sort of inherent, or more properly inculcated feeling of individual merit. Self-respect, on the other hand, must be earned, and a man respects himself because of what he knows himself to be and what he has proved he can do.*
>
> – Jeff Cooper, *Shotluck*

physical conditioning

> *The single best conditioning program for any given activity is the activity itself.*
>
> – Forrest E. Morgan, *Living the Martial Way*, p. 203

Andre Agassi learned this the hard way after a new coach questioned why Agassi had been running marathons for training, since tennis is all about explosive starts and stops.

strength

This is naturally important, but speed and accuracy of the blow is more important (just as in shooting).

speed

Speed plus mass equals force. Practice quality moves as smoothly as possible, and speed will develop on its own.

stamina

Fighting is an exhausting exertion past about 30 seconds. If you've no stamina, train to win your fights very, very quickly.

agility

You must be strong, flexible, and relaxed in a balanced way. All the martial arts masters have profound agility, and move like cats.

coordination

This is more important than the other qualities, which are useless without coordination. (Watch actress Summer Glau's dancing skills pay off in the bar fight scene of *Serenity*. She wasn't a martial artist in real life, but easily trainable due to coordination and agility.)

train with others

This is the only way to *really* push yourself. Training on your own is fine if that's all you've got, but it goes only so far.

my basic workout: a quality Rebounder trampoline

Your body cannot tell the difference between gravitational force and weight. Bouncing vigorously on a rebounder subjects every cell in your body to 2-3Gs of momentary deceleration, and every cell grows stronger. Rebounding is also the most efficient way to move your lymphatic fluid (you've 5x more of it than blood!) through your body to keep cells flushed out. It's much more low impact than jogging, and much more efficient. (Al Carter of www.healthbounce.com pioneered Reboundology, the most efficient form of exercise yet known.)

I strap on 20lbs of leg weights and 10lbs of arm weights, and jump with Tee-Ball bats (to practice my stick fighting). 20-30 minutes of this each day gives me a full-body workout combining strength, CV, and flexibility conditioning. Weeks before going on African safaris, I jump with my hunting rifle, and it pays off in the field.

While I started out long ago with Carter's rebounders, I've since gone to the bungee corded JumpSport (which I prefer over springs).

the enhanced workout

There are many videos avaible, such as P90X, Insanity, etc. The actual choice is less important than your commitment to a daily regimen for the first consecutive 90 days. After that, you've formed an exercising habit that is much easier to keep. Never drop it!

the cultivated warrior

The ancient *samurai* of Japan highly regarded what we today would classify as feminine pursuits, such as painting, writing poetry, calligraphy, playing the flute, and flower arranging. There is nothing unmanly about this kind of balance. *Samurai* strived to refine simplicity, elegance, harmony with nature, and purity of thought.

DEALING WITH FEAR

> *Studies have shown that a sky-high heart rate affects your thinking, vision, and hearing and that the only way to maintain a reasonable heart rate, in a fight, is by living through it. Fighters make peace with the terror of "fight or flight" and learn to harness it. But it takes time.*
>
> — Sam Sheridan, *The Fighter's Mind*

I've an entire chapter on dealing with fear, and the solution is basically to dive in and get over it. You cannot master fear by keeping the object at bay. Stand, face and attack your fears! (There is a good scene in the movie *Red Belt* about this, regarding a rape victim learning to fight.)

> *Well, Bill* [Hickok] *was a pretty good shot. But he could not shoot as quick as half a dozen men we all knew in those days, nor as straight either. But Bill was cool, and the men who he went up against were rattled, I guess. Bill beat them to it. He made up his mind to kill the other man before the other man had finished thinking.*
>
> — Buffalo Bill (Cody) in an interview conducted 10 January 1917 and written up in *Outdoor Life* via W.H. MacFarlane

IN THE RING

> *The time to win a fight is before it starts.*
>
> — Frederick W. Lewis

being "in the zone"

loss of fear — no fear of failure
no thinking of performance
total immersion in activity
narrow focus of attention
effortless performance — not forcing it
feeling of being in complete control
time/space disorientation (usually slowed down)

universe perceived to be integrated and unified
unique, temporary, involuntary experience
– being "in the zone" through peak performance, by Applied Sport Psychology

"*Another man's sword is your sword.*" – Yagyu Munenori

His weapon is your weapon, if you figure a way to use it against him. Every strength is a two-sided coin containing a weakness. A big, strong guy is often slower. An angry opponent will lose his reason. A perceptive guy can be faked out. A confident fighter, if broken in his area of confidence, may fold up quickly. His sword is your sword.

some rules from combat veterans

The important things are always simple; the simple are always hard.

The enemy never watches until you make a mistake.

The enemy invariably attacks on two occasions:
When they're ready. When you're not.

When you have secured the area, make sure the enemy knows it too.

NEVER, EVER GIVE UP!

From a young man [studying Brazilian jui-jitsu] *we go – we believe that if we go until one of us quits it's never gonna be me!*
– Renzo Gracie

This goes back to heart and mindset. The racehorse Seabiscuit broke the heart of War Admiral before the final stretch with a "*That's all you got?*" matching pace. Every opponent has a breaking point; find it and wait him out. Never let 'em see you sweat; that point will come soon.

To develop Kiai, *you must first find your own* kokoro. *Make never giving up a habit. Always attack a challenge; never avoid or simply endure it. . . . Only you can decide whether you will live in triumph, whether facing an opponent or meeting the gut-wrenching challenges of life.*
– Forrest E. Morgan, *Living the Martial Way*, p. 111

THE WARRIOR'S HONOR

Forrest Morgan offers a simple three-step program:

Determine your obligation.
Weigh the situation for justice.
Take courage and act.

For most people, understanding their obligation and the just thing to do is not the problem — taking courage is. As I've mentioned elsewhere, courage is a muscle and it must be exercised. Do what is right, no matter the personal cost. With practice, honor will become an unconscious habit, and you will not even reflexively consider dishonorable alternatives.

the difference between losing face and losing honor

Since honor depends upon your commitment to meet your obligations, honor cannot be taken from you — only you can lose it. However, losing face is something others can do to you. Whether or not to fight for it is your choice — just don't confuse face with honor.

There are people with honor and little face, and people with face and no honor. Being honorable means living well with yourself.

HANDLING DEFEAT

It's easy to do anything in victory.
It's in defeat that a man reveals himself.
— Floyd Patterson

Loss is where you can get better. That's why you learn more when you lose than when you win. When you win you forget.

Life is a continuous experience. You only fail by not learning.
— Renzo Gracie, from *The Fighter's Mind*

Maturity is a big part of success in fighting, because it means you understand the game — that losing is part of the game. It doesn't mean to let yourself get conquered, but to know that you can win again, at the right time you can be great. The key to doing well in competition is to accept.
— Ricardo Liborio, from *The Fighter's Mind*

Successful fighters have things that work for them, and work incredibly well, but the great champions are those who can accept, internalize, and understand defeat.
— Sam Sheridan, *The Fighter's Mind*

Don't let a defeat get you down. Analyze why you lost, and train to eliminate it for the next time. Think about it vs. feeling about it. (Again, this is a trick to avoid corrosive emotions. You cannot analyze something *and* feel about it at the same time. Crowd out the blues by switching on the rational left brain.)

Was it just not your night, or were you untrained and unprepared? Try to negate any holes in your fighting skills. If you still lose, be philosophical about it. Accept that everyone can lose.

BE ARMED, DAILY

To my mind it is wholly irresponsible to go into the world incapable of preventing violence, injury, crime, and death. How feeble is the mindset to accept defenselessness. How unnatural. How cheap. How cowardly. How pathetic.
— Ted Nugent

And he that hath no sword, let him sell his garment, and buy one.
— Jesus, from Luke 22:36

While defensive weapons are not the end-all-be-all, they are often vital "force multipliers" when attacked by stronger or multiple assailants. Weapons all have their strengths and weaknesses, usually based on their effective distance.

a daily carry knife

For arms-length and closer, a knife is superior to a handgun (which is vulnerable to being taken away from you). There are many places (NYC, foreign countries) where you cannot easily bring or lawfully carry a handgun with you, but you could carry a knife.

fixed blade vs. folder?

For your primary knife, I recommend a 3-5" fixed blade. Folders are slower to deploy during stress, can break or fold up on your hand, and have inferior handles and steel. The only advantage of a folder is a bit more carry convenience (and leeway with most state laws), but I'll explain how a fixed blade knife can be comfortably and openly carried.

Alain Burrese of www.yourwarriorsedge.com recommends the modern tactical folders. If I test one I like, I'll post it on my site.

properties of steel

Much is asked of a general purpose knife. It must do many different tasks, such as cutting, chopping, and piercing. And all this while keeping a good edge! It should have decent corrosion resistance. It must flow well in the hand of a fighter.

There are many dozens of knife steels, all of them trying to exploit some good compromise between mutually exclusive properties: such as wear resistance (keeps an edge), strength (it can pry), toughness (it can chop), rust resistance, ability to take an edge. Tough knives are generally not hard, and hard knives are not tough. No steel excels in them all, and most underperform in one area:

steel	great	good-fair	poor
O1	wear resistance	toughness	corrosion resistance
1095	wear resistance	toughness	corrosion resistance
5160	toughness	wear resistance	edge holding
D2	wear resistance	corrosion resistance	
440C	corrosion resist.	toughness	sharpness
CPM-S30V	wear resistance	toughness	

Hardness and toughness are mutually exclusive, so one must compromise. (A scalpel cannot chop, and an axe cannot shave. There is no "one knife" for all needs, but you can come pretty close.) Your blade edge should hardness test at least 58 Rockwell C scale, though 59-61 would be my ideal. (62+Rc is much more prone to chipping.)

which kind of steel?

Your choice is broadly between a "stainless" (with 13+% chromium for rust resistance, at some expense of hardness) or high-carbon (harder/sharper steel, but with much less chromium so they rust more easily). **More than anything else, your desired level of stain resistance will determine the other properties.** Any knife will require maintenance, so it's your choice between often replacing an edge, or often removing a stain. My thought: if you will commit to keeping a high-carbon blade polished and lightly oiled (vs. insisting on a soft stainless steel which needs more frequent sharpening), you will enjoy an inherently superior knife.

Carbon steel is rarely used by anyone but the custom makers, as the big manufacturers cater to the lazy public who demand stain resistant finishes. One exception is Randall's ESSE series made of 1095 (0.95% carbon, 0.4% manganese, but no vanadium) – a hard, tough blade, black coated for stain resistance (keep the edge oiled!).

I used to be friends with a custom knifemaker, and thus became quite the snob, never condescending to carry anything less than one of his $500+ blades made of O1 high carbon tool steel. Today, I no longer fully buy into that hype, and am much more realistic to the fact that quality stain resistant knives are good enough for all but the most extreme needs. Just always have a decent knife on you. (For example, I have a nice custom blade of 5120 and 5160 Damascus laminate that keeps a great edge yet has very good stain resistance.)

There are a few "best of all worlds" steels out there which keep a decent edge while not rusting easily. For a high-carbon blade that has decent stain-resistance, consider D2 or CPM-10V. (Either are perfect for small, thin blades with edge hardness of 60-62 Rc. These aren't as tough as a premium stainless, but sharper.) D2 is a very old steel, difficult to polish out its "orange peel" look, and not a "sexy" alloy — so few knifemakers (Bob Dozier, Benchmade) use it. If you run across a nicely made D2 custom, give it a try.

I also very much like these chrome-vanadium alloys: BG-42 (a favorite, but harder to sharpen), CPM-S30V (dedicated cutlery steel), VG-10 (whips ATS-34 butt), and AUS-10 (akin to 440C, but with vanadium and less chromium). These steels approach an ideal for most users.

I see *no* reason to choose any of the *non*-vanadium stainless steels, such as ATS-34 and 440C (merely OK at best). 420 and 425 (<0.5% carbon) are not worth considering. (Never bother with generic "Stainless", a soft 420 series. If it's at least 440 with 0.75% carbon, or 440C with 1.2% carbon, they'll say so.) 440C was popular in the 1980s, and got displaced by ATS-34/154CM (which was displaced by BG-42, with 1.2% vanadium and twice as much manganese). Any company using 440C only chose it because it's cheap and easy to machine. You can easily find better steel in your knife. If you must have a stainless knife, at least insist on a vanadium alloyed steel for superior hardness and edge-holding ability.

blade length, thickness, and profile

While there are some nice 3½" blades, they are just too short for defense or general field work. Even a 4" blade seems a mite short for me. I prefer a 4½-5½" blade length for my daily carry knife.

Blade thickness should be 3/16th" (4.8mm) stock. 2.5-3mm is too thin, and ¼" is too chunky for a medium-size blade.

A good general-purpose blade profile is the "drop point". (I don't care much for the *tanto* profile in a short knife; it's more suited for swords.) I like a knife to be slightly blade heavy in balance, which moves better in the fighting hand.

A muted or blackened finish increases discretion. Carbon blades can be cold-blued. Stainless blades must be painted or coated.

Overall length should be 8½-10". Weight will be 7-10 oz.

My ideal: 4.9" drop (or clip) point blade, 9½" overall, 8 oz.

handle

It should have a moderate choil (the circular cutout where your index finger goes), and short quillion (the finger guard). Material should be G10, micarta, Kraton rubber, linen, or wood. Plastic is too cheap. No paracord! I like a lanyard hole, just in case.

The handle should be on the short side (4-4½"), with no blocky shape. (Good luck. Most knife handles are very uninspired.)

sheath material

Kydex is the best, followed by thick polypropylene and leather. Cordura nylon frays and absorbs water/sweat, and is crap.

fixed blade length and the law

Generally allowed is between 3½"-5" (check the laws on the maximum length to carry, and these differ for open vs. concealed). Here are some concealed carry maximums from David Wong's *The Traveler's Gun & Knife Law Book.* www.SpartanPressOnline.com

Boston, Mass.	<2½"
D.C.	<3" (folder only; all fixed blades illegal)
Colorado	<3½" (fixed)
Connecticut	<4"
Georgia	<5"
Texas	<5½"

Wherever you go, it is best to carry a hunting blade vs. some wicked looking thing with skull and crossbones logo. Names such as the "Hunter" or the "Outdoorsman" are preferable to the "Avenger". (And, always refer to your blade as a "tool" and not a "weapon". "*Sir, have you any weapons on you?*" "*No weapons, Officer, but I am lawfully wearing a fieldcraft tool knife.*")

Many states (including California) will allow open carry of any length of fixed blade, so long as there is no criminal intent. Blades longer than 5½" (such as the 6" Cold Steel SRK, an otherwise decent choice) and the knife begins to be too obtrusive for carry (and generally illegal to conceal in most jurisdictions). Public nervousness also noticeably increases with such blades. (The trick is to pick a useful length for defense, yet without attracting adverse attention.)

3" fixed blades

Cold Steel Mini Hunter	$25
Boker Plus Dozier Arkansas Traveler	$47

3½" fixed blades

Cold Steel Pendelton Lite Hunter	$ 30
Boker Plus Dozier Anchorage Pro Skinner	$ 47
Muela Kodiak (apparently BG-42 steel)	$130

4" fixed blades

Cold Steel Finn Bear	$ 30
Cold Steel Sisu (much nicer version of above)	$275

These are copies of the classic Finnish *Puukko* designed in the 1950s by the renowned master craftsman/artist Tapio Wirkkala (1915 - 1985) and manufactured by Oy Hackman. (I found an original at a gunshow for just $40. Brookstone sold them in the early 1970s.) These icons were carried daily by most Finnish men, until such masculine habit and cultural heritage was banned in 1977. Still, many men properly ignore the central ban and continue to openly carry this piece of Nordic tradition! (The Swedes have a similar knife, the *Mora*, which are generally thinner.)

Since the *Puukko* has no guard (or "choil") to prevent the hand riding up into the blade, these knives are inherently ill-suited for stabbing, which *may* help you avoid an arrest for carrying a "weapon". This knife is an "everyday" tool, used by everyone in Finland. Cold Steel has revived the Wirkkala *Puukko* for an excellent daily carry knife. The *Sisu* deluxe model is very elegant and well-made of VG-1 San Mai III Stainless steel.

4½" fixed blades

Cold Steel Master Hunter	$100
Katz Adventure A2 and A3 Series	$130
Benchmade Rant Drop point	$
Randall ESSE-4 (1095 high-carbon)	$185
Fällkniven F1 (VG10 laminate)	$125
Doug Ritter RSK® Mk3	$165

5" fixed blades

Cold Steel	$

5½" fixed blades

Cold Steel Kobun (with excellent slip sheath)	$ 40
Katz Adventure A1 Series	$150

carrying your fixed blade knife

While there is nothing wrong with a classic vertical belt sheath, it can seem a bit extreme for some clothes and social situations.

There are some belt sheaths that ride inline on the belt, and worn opposite front (*e.g.*, above left pocket for right-handed person). Such are sleek, but work well only for the smaller knives.

I prefer a slip-sheath (often I can convert the belt sheath, unless I have a custom Kydex made), tucked in the right front of my beltline. It is instantly accessible, yet unobtrusive in daily life. Carry openly, unless hidden by a vest or jacket. (I should warn you that this form of knife carry may seem mildly threatening to some.)

knives under $50

There are decent enough stainless steel fixed blades at any KMart or hardware store for less than $50. While I don't recommend that you stick with such a low-cost knife, it's much better than no knife at all. I picked up several acceptable quality Chinese knives made for Winchester for only $15 each. Every bag has its own knife, and during air travel I can risk TSA stealing it from my checked luggage. Smith & Wesson sells their $15 model S&W640, and it's a surprisingly nice 3¾" blade.

Used bargains abound, if you know where to look. For example, at a recent gun show I spied a perfectly decent used 4" stainless drop point. Only $5. I then applied $1.50 worth of black heat shrink tubing to the handle, and will make a simple Kydex slip sheath to complete a perfect stowaway backup blade.

Sportsman's Guide probably still sells the thin 4" Swedish knives (*Mora Kolstall*, High Carbon) for about $15. While the green plastic handle and sheath are nothing great, the blade itself is good.

Camillus sells a very affordable carbonitride titanium/AUS-8 fixed blade that remains my sharpest stainless steel knife.

Cold Steel's *Kobun* is a 5½" tanto boot knife with versatile Secure-Ex sheath (works as a frontal belt slip sheath). AUS-8A. Only 4.4oz, and a whopping bargain at just $40. If the blade length is not too long for you and your jurisdiction, this is an excellent value as an affordable daily "good-to-go" knife.

Another winner from Cold Steel is their Pendelton Lite Hunter for about $30. The plastic handle and nylon sheath are nothing special, but the 3¾" stain-resistant drop-point blade is great. This is probably the best value for a good, inexpensive knife. Every car and backpack should have one.

$100-150

This will buy you a surprisingly good knife.

The 4½" Cold Steel Master Hunter, which although a field dressing/skinning knife, makes for a fine carry blade. Its triple laminate VG-1 San Mai steel sharpens very well. I've used it in Africa hunting, and like it (though the handle is ½" too long and a bit blocky for my taste). I also just found a used older version in Carbon V at a gun show for just $40, and easily removed the slight tarnish.

The Jeremy 1095 is 59-60Rc for just $110. Custom maker Jay Higgins offers very nice stain-resistant 4½" blades for just $100. The Spanish Muela Kodiak is a 3¾" BG-42 steel and excellent $150 value. The Fällkniven F1 (VG10 laminate) is a superb $125 bargain.

$150-200

I like the Spanish-made Adventure Series (4¼", 4½", 5½" blades — 440C+ steel) from www.katzknives.com. The handle shape is excellent for a production knife (materials are cherrywood, stag, or micarta). These are fine all-purpose knives which will do anything (utility or defense) well enough. A good daily carry blade, though a bit on the heavy/chunky side.

The Doug Ritter RSK® Mk3 for $165 is becoming a real favorite. It's 4½" CPM S30V drop point (58-60 HRC) is perfect for daily tasks. A very well thought out and quality choice for survival and utility. The nylon sheath, however, is cheesy. Have a Kydex one made for yours.

$200+

$200 is where good custom knives usually begin, with much better steel than 440C stainless (merely adequate in edge holding). The better the steel (such as VG-10 or INFI), the more an acute angle of edge it can have for sharpness. Buck Taylor makes nice knives here.

Another way to go is Damascus layered steel. My Higgins custom 4½" drop-point has 416 folds of 5120 and 5160 steel. It is *very* tough, sharpens easily, and keeps an edge. It has mild resistance to corrosion (about on par with D2). Higgins buys Damascus steel and grinds them into shape (called "stock removal"). Handles and guards are as basic or as fancy as desired. Jay's workmanship is very good, and he is pleasant to deal with. I like to support this father & son shop. www.jayhigginsknives.com

knife sharpening

Cro-magnon hunters of 3300 B.C. drug their dull copper axe blades across a rock. Some things just work, and still the best way to maintain a knife edge is to drag it across a rock — an Arkansas whetstone. Yes, there are whiz-bang sharpening gadgets, but first learn to sharpen your knife on a stone like a Real Man.

www.SharpeningMadeEasy.com (good book available)
www.danswhetstone.com

www.ebladestore.com/sharpening_tips.html
www.zknives.com/knives/index.html

knife fighting training

First, train to defend yourself against a knife attack and common lunges, swipes, and stabs. Learn to avoid, trap, and disarm. Only then train with your own carry knife. Learn the "Seven Cuts". Find a qualified instructor (vs. some blowhard with an allegedly "unique" angle or product that he's trying to sell). Train under a guy who has actually been in some knife fights.

If you ever have to defend yourself against lethal harm with your knife, never let him see it coming. (For an illustrative scene, watch Dr. Hannibal Lecter during the Florence street scene in *Hannibal.*)

semi-auto handgun

Before all else, be armed.
– Machiavelli

A pistol is a weapon of astonishing efficiency and versatility when skillfully used, but its skillful use is rare. This is odd, when you think of it, for while the pistol is common-place throughout the "civilized" world, only the merest handful of men – now or in the past – have ever approached the ability to make it do what it can. ***A really good man, wearing a really good sidearm, is a serious, almost insurmountable, problem for any person or group which contemplates his forcible coercion.*** *He may be safely taken with poison gas, a tank, or a precision rifle – under certain circumstances – and that's about all.*
– Jeff Cooper

. . . be prepared to join in the fray with disconcerting alacrity and deadly effect . . .
– Arizona lawman John Clum, 1870s

Across a room, a handgun prevails over a knife. You shouldn't allow dicey characters to get within 20' of you, anyway. Skill usually outweighs choice of gun or caliber, but as you become skilled carry the most increasingly powerful gun you can effectively wield. Any quality, reliable handgun in .40 or .45 will do . . . if *you* will do. (Even a 9mm will generally serve, but I urge you to choose a .40 or .45.) Carry daily.

handgun training

A man is not armed because he has custody of a weapon. He is armed only if he has the skill to use it as well. Gun fighting is one part technique and three parts attitude. The only acceptable response to the threat of lethal violence is immediate and savage counterattack.

A handgun is an interesting artifact, and its mastery is a notable accomplishment. Those who master it achieve a peculiar satisfaction, for they partake in some measure of one of the attributes of the gods — the ability to point the hand and smite at a distance. This idea existed millenia before anyone ever saw a pistol, so it must be an innate human aspiration, independent of technology. It is obviously the basis of the pleasure we take in pistolcraft.

As the handgun has no will of its own, it has no skill of its own; however, in a master's hands its efficiency is almost unbelievable. As with all instruments, it is the man, not the tool, that makes the difference. Skill with a shovel makes less difference than skill with a violin. The handgun lies somewhere between.

— Jeff Cooper, founder of Gunsite shooting academy

In the 1970s, USMC Lt. Colonel Jeff Cooper popularized the "Modern Pistol Technique" (two-handed aimed fire of a .45) at his Gunsite shooting academy, and this doctrine became the core of defensive handgun training. Other recommended schools are Thunder Ranch in Oregon and Bill Rogers' classes in Georgia. Louis Awerbuck is also a very capable instructor. Any experienced NRA-certified instructor in your area can get you started with good basics.

I have trained in such schools, and teach basic/intermediate levels; email me if interested. Also, study my *Boston's Gun Bible.*

open vs. concealed carry

"*I carry a handgun because a cop is too heavy.*" About half of the 50 states actually allow open carry without any kind of permit, though restrictions vary. I believe that open carry is a disincentive on crime, and helps to remind the rest of the public that good guys can (and should) carry a handgun.

"*shall issue*" concealed carry states

Some 35 states have "*shall issue*" permits, meaning that they must issue you a CCW permit if you qualify. While I do not believe in seeking a license for anything which is my peaceable right to do, if getting your permit will cause you to daily carry, then get a permit.

no permit required for concealed carry

To date, these states do not require *any* permit for a non-felon to carry concealed: Vermont, Alaska, Arizona, and Wyoming. Such is called "*Vermont carry*" after the state which never required a permit.

when driving, have a combination lock bag or briefcase

If stopped by the police, I put my knives and handgun in the bag, and lock it before the officer is at my window. Thus, I am no longer armed according to the *Terry v. Ohio* court case (though some oppressive states may disagree — know before you go there). The *McClure-Volkmer* Act protects armed travelers between states through hostile jurisdictions (if the gun is unloaded and locked away).

Even in 2nd Amendment-friendly states, I prefer to lock up my carry weapons during any police stop or checkpoint. It greatly simplifies matters.

the .22LR rifle

Every household should have either a Marlin Papoose (it nicely takes-down to fit in a small bag) or a Ruger 10/22. Either goes for about $250, and are magazine-fed. Good for www.appleseed.org training, plinking, pest-control, or even self-defense in a pinch. Buy boxes of 550 copper-plated rounds for about $20.

in town, a shotgun or .223 carbine

A 12 gauge shotgun (preferably a pump-action, such as the Remington 870) with #6 birdshot is a good choice for apartment dwellers. An affixed tactical light is recommended. If you are recoil averse, then a 20 gauge should be your choice.

Personally, I would rather have a .223 carbine because of increased range, precision, and magazine capacity. An AR-15 is hands-down the best choice, but those on a budget would do fine with KelTec's .223 carbine.

If expense or local laws dissuade you from a shotgun or .223 carbine, then a .22LR is your only option. With training and cool handling, this $200 rifle can be very effective (headshots only). It's a fun plinker, and can take small game. You should have one, anyway.

a bolt-action .308 or .30-06 rifle

There are few problems you can't fix,
with $700 and a thirty-ought six.
— Lindy Cooper Wisdom

As Clint Smith of Thunder Ranch is known for saying, "*You get caught in a fight with a pistol. You go to a fight with a rifle.*" Across the street and beyond, I'd want an accurate rifle in a powerful common caliber, preferably with optics. Visible threats out to 600yds, you can defend against. Hunting bolt-action rifles abound, and you should have one. (For mostly personal reasons, I lean towards the Winchester M70 and Savage over the Ruger and Remington.)

Calibers: there are dozens, not that such a selection is necessary for most of you. Go with either the .308 (makes for a lighter rifle) or the .30-06 (has a bit more power for heavier bullets). While there is nothing wrong with the 6.5x55, .270, .300 Win Mag, etc. — there is no *compelling* reason for most men to choose any of them over a .308 or .30-06. Just trust me on this, and save yourself lots of headspace from almost purely theoretical arguments.

Choose a *quality* scope with ballistic drop compensator reticle to make reliable hits from 300-600+yds, such as the Leupold, Pentax, Nikon, or the Shepherds 310-P2 (hands down my general favorite; visit www.shepherdsscopes.com).

A bargain even today is any **surplus U.S. M1917 bolt-action** in .30-06. Most of these fine WWI-era rifles have been sporterized, and go for as little as $250 as they've lost their collector value. Years ago I found one with a modest Tasco 3-9x scope. With my 168gr handloads it shoots within a nickel at 100yds. Talk about getting my $190 worth! As spares I've found others (without optics) for under $300. Great for friends, or the vacation cabin.

I also recommend a semi-auto "sport-utility rifle" (*i.e.*, military pattern) such as the **.223 AR-15**, or better still something in .308/7.62 such as the M1A, FAL, or HK91. (The only AR-10s I can recommend are the LMT and P.O.F. models. The rest seem to have odd and persistent troubles.)

The WWII/Korean War era **M1 Garand** in .30-06 is still a sleeper of a bargain at under $900. Visit www.cmp.org, or your nearest gun show. (Put a Scout scope mount from www.amegaranges.com on it with a Leupold 2½x Scout scope in Leupold or Warne QD rings, and you've a dandy all-around Man's rifle!) There is no "assault rifle" hysteria surrounding the wood stocked M1 which uses 8-round clips (vs. 20-round mags -- so it's legal nearly everywhere). Ammo is still a relative bargain, but word is getting out. Hurry, and get a real Man's rifle! My *Boston's Gun Bible* has all the info you need to shop for your own.

rifle training

Speed is fine, but accuracy is final.
— Bill Jordan

Owning a rifle does not a rifleman make. This requires *training*. Attend quality courses at Gunsite, Thunder Ranch, and similar well regarded schools. (A good first step that direction is to attend a weekend www.appleseed.org class in your area. Bring any .22LR., even if you've never shot a rifle, and start with that. Basics are basics, and will translate to your .223 and .308.) Developing credible skill with a centerfire rifle takes at least 1,000 rounds. Surplus ammo, until about 2008, was only 15¢/round. Today it's 50¢-$1/round. Tomorrow it may be restricted through new regulations. All American Men should become Riflemen, so get started quickly. It's fun, patriotic, Manly, and could save your Life.

As a life-long shooter, hunter, and dedicated gun enthusiast, I could go on and on. It's easier for both of us if you simply get a copy of my *Boston's Gun Bible* (and *Safari Dreams* for you hunters).

CLINT SMITH WISDOM

My friend Clint is the founder of www.thunderranchinc.com, a superb shooting academy which he runs with his wife Heidi. I've been to his classes, and learned a lot from this great teacher.

The most important rule in a gunfight is: Always win and cheat if necessary.

Don't forget, incoming fire has the right of way.

Make your attacker advance through a wall of bullets. You may get killed with your own gun, but he'll have to beat you to death with it, cause it's going to be empty.

If you're not shootin', you should be loadin'. If you're not loadin', you should be movin', if you're not movin', someone's gonna cut your head off and put it on a stick.

Do something. It may be wrong, but do something.

Shoot what's available, as long as it's available, until something else becomes available.

If you carry a gun, people will call you paranoid. That's ridiculous. If you have a gun, what in the hell do you have to be paranoid for.

Don't shoot fast, unless you also shoot good.

You can say "Stop!" or "Alto!" or use any other word you think will work, but I've found that a large bore muzzle pointed at someone's head is pretty much the universal language.

You have the rest of your life to solve your problems. How long you live depends on how well you do it.

You cannot save the planet but you may be able to save yourself and your family.

Thunder Ranch will be here as long as you'll have us or until someone makes us go away, and either way, it will be exciting.

more excellent gun wisdom from random folks

Don't pick a fight with an old man. If he is too old to fight, he'll just kill you.

If you find yourself in a fair fight, your tactics suck.

I carry a gun cause a cop is too heavy.

When seconds count, the cops are just minutes away.

An armed man will kill an unarmed man with monotonous regularity.

The old sheriff was attending an awards dinner when a lady commented on his wearing his sidearm. "Sheriff, I see you have your pistol. Are you expecting trouble?"

"No ma'am. If I were expecting trouble, I would have brought my rifle."

The true soldier fights not because he hates what is in front of him, but because he loves what is behind him.

-- G.. K. Chesterton

Those who hammer their guns into plows will plow for those who do not.

-- Thomas Jefferson

SELF-DEFENSE TIPS

Wer kaempft, kann verlieren.
Wer nicht kaempft, hat schon verloren.
(Whomever fights, may lose.
Whomever doesn't fight has already lost.)
— Berthold Brecht

self-defense is moral, and a healthy part of life

We have never been able to link gun ownership with crime, so we must wonder just what is the basis for this unending political negativism. Our personal view is that the motivation of those who would disarm us remains upon analysis to be sheer envy. The individual who owns his own personal firearms, and commands the skill necessary to use them well, owns a peace of mind that his adversaries cannot match.

The non-coper has reason to feel inferior to a successful Gunsite graduate, and this annoys him enough to supply him with an indefensible political position. A man who cannot cope envies and therefore dislikes the man who can.
— Jeff Cooper

You have a *right* to respond to aggression with violence. While one may never initiate force, it immoral to not defend yourself from attack.

prepare yourself mentally

One must mentally prepare oneself regarding a willingness to not be a victim of attack. This mental preparation is senior to all else. One must consider what to do if attacked — to punch, shoot and KILL or bite and kill or cut and kill or stab and kill or kick and kill or punch and kill or all of these things together. If one must defend oneself, it is insane to do anything other than go for the most deadly and certain points.
— Mr Jody Hudson,
www.theruralspecialist.com/essays/selfdefenceideas.html

don't be there!

That is, stay away from or get out of dangerous neighborhoods, groups and situations if there is any possible way to do so. Only if cornered or not able to get away or if in your own home or if with a child or elderly person that eliminates the possibility of getting away — should one stand and argue, fight, use any sort of weapon or shoot.
— Mr Jody Hudson

"*How do I win bar fights?*" a student asked his instructor. "*Stay out of bars*" was the reply. The easiest fight to win is the one you avoid. Somebody wise once offered some really great, simple advice:

Don't go to stupid places.
Don't hang with stupid people.
Don't do stupid things.

always maintain erect posture

Posture is the currency of leadership. It's an unspoken language, a tool of command. When a group of people are talking, all fall silent and turn their attention when the man who stands straightest speaks. It's an unconscious reaction, a Pavlovian response. He's the straightest, so he must be the authority. And, believe it or not, regardless of who in the group is the greatest in stature, all usually assume the man who stands the most erect to be the tallest.

Grace is the outward expression of physical and spiritual power. It is the product of confidence, strength, coordination, and perfect balance.

— Forrest E. Morgan, *Living the Martial Way*, p. 266, 280

"*If you look like food, you'll be eaten.*" — Clint Smith

Erect posture, a purposeful stride, fearless eye contact (without staring), and exuded confidence are warning signs to predators.

if there, walk and talk your way out

Most potential attacks can be defused with a calm, certain, non-combative but UN-fearful verbal and physical retreat. If the attack is not likely to be lethal then the only sensible response is to quietly and effectively leave the situation without a comment, . . . and immediate, ready to act, retreat.

— Mr. Jody Hudson

don't get boxed into any corners

By "corners" I also mean metaphorical ones (which will lead to actual physical corners), such as leaving in somebody else's car. Keep your distance, and keep all your options open. Agree to nothing — do nothing — that tactically limits you.

are you *sure* that it is a lethal emergency?

You must be able to convince your jury that the assailant had the proximity, intention, and capability to cause grievous bodily harm. This is called the "reasonable man" defense.

Some jurisdictions actually require you to have retreated as far as you can go. Know the laws of your locality.

if at home, call 911 immediately, before pressing trigger

There could be nothing more advantageous to you later than a 911 recording of "*Get out of my house! Stop! Get away from my child! Stop or I'll shoot! Bang! Bang! Bang!*"

if there's no avoiding the fight, be instantly savage!

> *There should be no warning and no gradient use of force when fighting for one's life. The counter-attack should be surprising, sudden, sequential, continuous, overwhelming, fast, furious, and with each thrust, blow, shot or kick intending to permanently end all fight in the attacker. . . . That is, and it is horrible to contemplate; one must plan and prepare to shoot for the head; punch for the nose; gouge to remove or burst the eyes, kick to break the knee and crush the groin. Fingers, keys, pens, pencils, thumbs or anything handy should be thrust into the eyes, throat, mouth, nostrils, entrails and any soft or delicate part of the body of an attacker – DEEPLY enough to gouge the organs, nerves and even the brain to as far as the finger or implement may reach – several inches deep. Yuck, we don't like to even read this . . . but it is true.*
>
> *And keep shooting, kicking, biting, gouging and punching until the attacker is no longer moving. If one stops, that attacker is likely to shake off your counter-attack and commence something even more torturous and worse than he first planned or had already started.*
>
> – www.theruralspecialist.com/essays/selfdefenceideas.html

This is another purpose of training: to discover the savage fighting beast within you. I've heard it described many ways, such as "*the red glowing eyes deep from a well*" or Theodore Roosevelt's "*wolf in the heart*". When you feel this for the first time, it can be disorienting and scary. Don't shun it; embrace this unfamiliar part of you. You will probably someday need to "go there" for real in order to save your Life.

after you fight and prevail . . .

breathe, seek cover, keep assailant muzzled, and reload
make sure he has no accomplices
call 911 ("*I've been assaulted. I need police and EMT here!*")
change *nothing* at the scene (you'd likely get caught)
do not talk to police after the incident!
keep your mouth shut, and let your attorney speak for you
never boast about having "*blown the bastard away!*"

Consider paying for a prepaid legal service which can provide a quality defense attorney in most cities. It may even be wise to have them phone the police and ambulance for you, which avoids your voice on tape to be later replayed, analyzed, and possibly used against you. (If you use your cell phone, the line will be kept open by 911 services.)

FINAL WORD

And woe thrice over to the nation in which the average man loses his fighting edge.
– Theodore Roosevelt

Go! Confront the problem! Fight! Win!
– Edna Mode, *The Incredibles*

RECOMMENDED MOVIES

honor in the face of lies & betrayal	*Redbelt*
dark and gritty story about awakened manhood	*Fight Club*
tremendous valor under impossible odds	*Zulu*
defending oneself against betrayal and smears	*Fair Game*
struggle, perserverance	*Slumdog Millionaire*
duty, love, courage	*High Noon*
"What we do in life, echoes in eternity."	*Gladiator*
spontaneous, combustible leadership	*Spartacus*
defending family and country	*The Patriot*
sheer heroism	*Braveheart*
victory of the tenacious underdog	*Rocky*
earning what others have sacrificed for you	*Saving Private Ryan*
courage, friendship, self-sufficiency in the wild	*Jeremiah Johnson*
sheer survival between three opposing forces	*Last of the Mohicans*
a wraith discovers honor	*The Last Samurai*
"By protecting others, you save yourselves."	*Seven Samurai*

The Walking Rifleman

by Joe Sledge

When a man takes his rifle a walkin'
it adds not a bit to his load.
It makes him in fact somewhat lighter,
for he walks as a free man, unbowed.

When a man takes his rifle a walkin',
he's master of all he can see.
A good man won't abuse the position,
for a master's a fine thing to be.

When a man takes his rifle a walkin',
he'll keep his eye sharp, his wits keen.
That's not just a tart he's escortin'.
No, that lady beside him's a queen.

When a man takes his rifle a walkin',
its condition doesn't matter to me.
He can load it however he chooses
so long as he lives by Rule Three.

When a man takes his rifle a walkin'
and he needs a second shot quick,
he'll be glad of the time spent on homework,
that he mastered reflexive bolt-flick.

When a man takes his rifle a walkin'
and he's hunting, to feed him and his,
well, he's living the way God intended,
and that's just the way that it is.

When a man takes his rifle a walkin',
as some say he should not be allowed,
well, they'd better be saying it softly,
for a man with a rifle is proud.

So if you take your rifle a walkin',
realize what you're saying, my friend.
You're saying that you are a free man
and woe be to him who butts in.

So let's take our rifles a walkin',
with pride - defiance if need.
If we don't want to be the last riflemen
we've got to re-sow freedom's seed.

Yes, let's take our rifles a walkin',
and we'll walk in the light, so they'll see.
And if they come to tell us we cannot,
then we'll water the Liberty Tree.

23

MOVING

Unless you're in some motorized vehicle (or on a horse), you live in a pre-20th Century 3mph world. I recall a high-school math teacher who walked to and from school every day, about 3 miles each way. Two hours a day of walking. Now, walking two hours a day may seem fun for some, but it's not the optimal form of exercise, and it's certainly not the optimal use of one's time. This teacher was a very austere man (who lived with his mother, no less), so walking two hours a day probably didn't seem like a sacrifice. But he was burning up 400 hours/year walking to school. Mr. K voluntarily chose to live in a 3mph world, and squandered thousands of potentially productive hours of his life.

Much of what is invented, manufactured, and sold is some kind of tool to save you time. If it has wheels or wings, it's a "time machine", and you absolutely need one to maximize your time. Here is the basic range of time machines, compared to hoofing it down the road. (Unless one walks barefoot, I figure $30 for shoes!)

$ 30	walking	3mph		
$ 100	bicycle	21mph	7x walking	$ 10
$ 400	moped	42mph	14x walking	$ 43
$ 700	250cc motorcycle	63mph	21x walking	$ 43
$ 2,000	car or large motorcycle	84mph	28x walking	$ 186
$ 40,000	Cessna 172	132mph	44x walking	$2375
$ 90,000	VANS RV-8	207mph	69x walking	$2000
$250,000	turboprop twin	330mph	110x walking	$3902
$500,000+	private jet	555mph	185x walking	$3333

The $ figures on the right are what each additional multiple of walking speed costs for that next faster time machine. (To keep things simple for this comparison, I don't get into operating costs of fuel, oil, tires, maintenance, insurance, etc.) As you can see, the faster you want to locomote yourself, the more expensive each additional multiple. The bar graph curve quickly steepens, as with any increasingly qualitative good. At some point, the earning power of your time will not afford the next faster time machine. This is why most Americans can afford a car, but not a private airplane (not even a Cessna), and why most pilots stop at a Cessna and can't afford a 200mph $90,000 cross-country ship, much less a turboprop twin or a private jet.

Even a modest $100 bicycle would have multiplied Mr. K's time by 7, and gotten him to school in only twice the time to a car. For another $300 he could have bought a moped and kept up with 45mph small town traffic – *i.e.*, a time machine equal to car for his purposes. He didn't need to even spend $2,000 for a car or full size motorcycle. A moped would have been his optimal solution, redeeming hundreds of hours every year to do something else (either fun or productive). Now, he probably imagined himself wise to have saved money from owning any vehicle, but it was a foolish decision not to own *any* time machine because it guaranteed a waste of much of his own Life.

Before deciding which time machine to buy, ask yourself:

What is my time worth *right now*?
What could my time be worth in *one year*?

Begin to think of time machines by their utility (multiples of speed over walking), and whether the next faster time machine can contribute to increased earnings. (I'm ignoring the "prestige" factor of luxury cars allegedly necessary for certain careers, even though such is another form of utility. Right now, I'm just discussing speed.)

If you're a minimum wage level of worker, your time is not worth much to others, so you don't need a lot of time machine. A bicycle or moped would likely serve you just fine, and you could afford it.

Now, let's say you had a training opportunity in the next town which after a year could double your earnings, and car pooling or bus service was not available. Here would be a case where ramping up your time machine to a small car or 650cc motorcycle would make sense because it would pay for itself by getting you to this training. Get into the best bargain of the next necessary level of time machine. Let it fully pay for itself before you think of anything faster.

full-size motorcycles (600+cc)

A fast, comfortable, cross-country 1000cc street bike can be found used for $1,000-$5,000. Fuel consumption will be 35-50mpg, but tires last only 10,000 miles. (Get a used1990s BMW shaft-drive and save money over the long haul replacing chains and sprockets.)

cars

If you're frugal and don't care about owning a "chick magnet", focus on a used Japanese wagon (I recommend Toyota or Mazda, but not really Subaru) with a 5-speed. Japanese because they simply are more reliable than a VW, Ford, or GM. A wagon because it offers double the utility (holds a lot of stuff, and you can even camp in it) for little extra cost. (I once bought a used Honda Civic wagon for $1,000, drove the hell out of it for a year and then sold it for $1,300. Gee)

If you're not frugal, then I still recommend a sporty wagon over a sedan for their amazing utility. The Dodge Magnum is a very unique wagon, and some are AWD with a V-8.

Avoid problem or extinct brands: Saab, Mitsubishi, Saturn, etc.

misc. driving tips

In traffic, see "through" the car ahead to discern what he must react to — you'll gain an extra 1-2 seconds of warning. Look at the front tires of an object car to know where it's going. When stopping behind another car, stay far back enough to see its rear tires — this will give you enough room to go around a stalled vehicle. When parking, pull through to the forward slot (saving a later backing up to get out).

go to a quality driving school, such as Bondurants

And read the book *Drive To Survive* by Curt Rich.

trucks

If you live anywhere near back country, get a 4x4. A half-ton is usually sufficient, unless you plan on often towing something heavy. I think that a Yukon/Tahoe/Suburban is a great rig, better than a truck with topper. Mileage will be in the high teens, and perhaps even 20mpg at 70mph on the highway. Smaller foreign SUVs don't often do any better, so you might as well get a larger GM.

small airplane (Cessna 172, Piper Cherokee 160)

Used all over the world since the 1950s, this is a 4-place (pilot + 3 passengers and no baggage, or just one passenger and 200 lbs. of baggage). With no headwind, its ground speed cruise is about 132mph with an endurance of about 3.5 hours (~460 miles). And since it can fly almost directly from A to B, bypassing traffic, winding roads, etc. Cessna pilots use a 2/5ths rule of thumb for comparing travel times vs. a car. An average five hour road trip can be flown in about 2 hours. (It takes some time to check the weather, file a flight plan, and pre-flight the airplane, but with practice this all takes just 30-45 minutes.)

A road trip of 2 hours isn't much longer than flying in a Cessna (120 min. driving - 30 min. preflight + 48 min. flying = 42 min. saved). That 42 minutes saved will cost you about $80 in flying costs (Cessna 172s are about $100/hour including fuel) vs. $30 to drive. Now, if it meant making some critical deadline, that extra $50 might be worth it.

For certain trips over mountain ranges or endless dull highways, a small airplane is the way to go! If you have *any* desire to fly, I very, very strongly recommend that you begin taking lessons. Flying costs about $100/hour (3-4x more per mile as driving), but the fun, utility, and satisfaction are tremendous. (There are ways to keep costs manageable. You could go into partnership for a plane, or rent. Sharing costs and landing at small fields with no tiedown fees make flying as cheap or cheaper than driving an SUV.)

fast cross-country single engine airplane (Mooney M20C)

At 170mph, this will cruise much faster than a Cessna Skyhawk 172, with twice the range, and some can be had for the price of a 172. (While they hold 3 passengers, the backseat is very cramped.) The increase in cruise speed and range for a $40,000 airplane is quite a bargain, as long as you don't land on corrugated grass strips.

Airplanes faster and bigger than this begin at $100,000+, so unless the extra speed or capacity is important to you, such ships are not worth the greatly increased cost. What a 250cc motorcycle is to a car, a $25,000 Tailwind is to a Beech Baron twin. As you can see from my chart, stepping up within the airplane class is *very* expensive. $25,000-$50,000 will buy you a *lot* of winged time machine, and most pilots needn't spend much more than that.

FLYING COMMERCIALLY

A must read: *The Travel Detective*, by Peter Greenberg, which contains all the inside scoop of how to book and fly like a pro.

I am old enough to have accomplished a lot of travel before the post-9/11 security" silliness, and remember when passengers were treated with general respect and dignity vs. as terrorists and criminals. Thus, I don't recommend commercial air travel, and became a pilot partially in order to avoid outrageous TSA screening policies.

From 1996 to 2001 was the "Computer Assisted Passenger Prescreening" program run by the FBI and FAA. CAPPS selected passengers for additional screening of any checked luggage for explosives. (Such selected passengers did not undergo any additional security screening at checkpoints.) Although CAPPS had selected 8 of the 19 hijackers on 9/11, it failed to prevent their actions.

Shortly after 9/11, CAPPS II was unveiled, a profiling system (fed by airline data) which ranked passengers by security risk score for additional screening. Congress killed it in the summer of 2004 due to public outrage. The DHS didn't give up, and has since tried to roll over CAPPS II into another program called "Secure Flight". After DHS lied to Congress about the existence of pre-approval testing and that American Airlines had provided 1.2 million passenger records for prototype testing, Congress postponed its implementation until the DHS could pass 10 tests for accuracy and privacy protection. (Folks, this is just window-dressing.)

the DHS future of air travel

Even the new "Secure Flight" program will not assuage the paranoia of the DHS. What they are interested in is new shock bracelet technology to immobilize onboard passengers at the whim of the cabin crew. I wish I were making this up:

> *An official with the Department of Homeland Security says the U.S. should consider having airline passengers wear electronic bracelets that could track their movements, hold personal information and be triggered like a Taser to stun them into immobility.*
>
> ***Paul S. Ruwaldt of the DHS Science and Technology Directorate wrote the inventor of "the immobilizing security bracelet,"*** *a Canadian company, saying he looked forward to receiving a written proposal, according to Washington Times columnist Jeffrey Denning.*
>
> ***"It is conceivable to envision a use to improve air security, on passenger planes,"*** *said Ruwaldt's letter, posted on the website of the company, Lamperd Less Lethal.*
>
> *The video says passengers could be fitted with "electronic ID bracelets" they would wear until they disembark their flights. The device would replace a ticket, carry passenger information, track passengers through terminals and track carry-on luggage.*
>
> ***But the key feature is that the bracelets could be discharged, as a gun, and leave the wearer "immobile for several minutes" although without causing "permanent injury."***
>
> *"For a businessman on his way home, to a young family going south for a winter holiday, wearing an EMD bracelet during flight is a small inconvenience to assure their safe arrival," says the company. "Many, if not most, passengers would happily opt for the extra security."*

> *The U.S. government has expressed interested in such 'bracelets' for air travelers.*
>
> *The company acknowledged on its website the negative response to Denning's story about its product: "It is amazing how much controversy our new research project has created."*
>
> **[DHS] *Ruwaldt wrote in his letter to the company, 'To make it clear, we* [the federal government] *are interested in the immobilizing security bracelet, and look forward to receiving a written proposal."***
>
> *The Canadian company responded to the publicity about its proposal with a website statement:*
>
> *"We wish to clear up any misconceptions regarding the EMD Safety Bracelet for Airline Security," the company said. "The bracelets remain inactive until a hijacking situation has been identified. At such time a designated crew member will activate the bracelets making them capable of delivering the punitive measure -— but only to those that need to be restrained. We believe that all passengers will welcome deliverance from a hijacking, as will the families, carriers, insurance providers etc. The F-16 on the wingtip is not to reassure the passengers during a hijacking but rather to shoot them down. Besides activation using the grid screen, the steward/stewardess will have a laser activator that can activate any bracelet as needed by simply pointing the laser at the bracelet -- that laser dot only needs to be within 10 inches of the bracelet to activate it."*
>
> *Lamperd, of Sarnia, Ontario, Canada, also provides training and designs specialized civil defense-related equipment. It boasts of expertise in "less-lethal tactics and equipment" used by military and police departments around the world for crowd control and "peacekeeping."*
>
> — "Shock bracelets for all airline passengers"
> July 08, 2008, WorldNetDaily
> www.lamperdlesslethal.com/news/upload/pg2HomelandSecurity7_06.pdf

So, forget all about low-tech passenger intervention (as with the attempted shoe-bomber, and allegedly Flight #93). No, the DHS wants us all strapped in our "ConAir" seats, and ready to be wrist-tasered by some stewardess guard. (This is about the most *warped* thing I've heard in years.) Why not just put all passengers under general anesthesia during the flight, and revive them at their destination? Wouldn't that be safer still? I mean, a really clever terrorist just might remove his bracelet in-flight *before* he tried to take over the plane. *Duh.*

What really gets me is how stunned those cretins at Lamperd, Inc. really are at the public outrage. Their website response was absurd: "*Oh, don't worry, the stewardess won't shock you unless you really deserve it! And the F-16 won't shoot down your plane unless it has to!"*

If "Secure Flight" and all the passenger security screening were so effective, then why would DHS be so fascinated by "Electro-Muscular Disruption" bracelets? Conversely, if DHS is so insecure about the effectiveness of airport screening, then why are we submitting to such a worthless hassle?

Every stupid TSA procedure just broadcasts the fact that TSA doesn't believe in what they claim they are doing.

Remember the silly "*Take Shampoo Away*" excitement? The limitation of carry-on liquids and gel was a *sham*. Ostensibly, the TSA is worried that Liquid A and Gel B can be mixed to form a binary-component explosive. So, what's their brilliant safety plan at the airport? To seize your Liquid A and Gel B and toss them into the *same* trash barrel, along with everybody *else's* — many of them *leaking*. That the American public believes this sham is a disgrace. (The rules have relaxed since 2006, and 3oz clear containers in a 1-quart ZipLoc are permitted in carry-on bags. *Oőooh, thanks!*)

TSA "Selectee" and "No Fly" lists

> *Imagine a list of suspected terrorists so dangerous that we can't ever let them fly, yet so innocent that we can't arrest them - even under the draconian provisions of the Patriot Act.*
>
> *This is the federal government's "no-fly" list.*
>
> *There is no recourse for those on the list, and their stories quickly take on a Kafkaesque tone. People can be put on the list for any reason; no standards exist. There's no ability to review any evidence against you, or even confirm that you are actually on the list.*
>
> *And, for most people, there's no way to get off the list or to "prove" once and for all that they're not whoever the list is really looking for. It took Kennedy three weeks to get his name off the list. People without his political pull have spent years futilely trying to clear their names.*
>
> *There's something distinctly un-American about a secret government blacklist, with no right of appeal or judicial review. Even worse, there's evidence that it's being used as a political harassment tool: environmental activists, peace protesters, and anti-free trade activists have all* [been listed].
>
> — www.papersplease.org

Being on the TSA Selectee list gets you a secondary screening. Being on the TSA No Fly list prohibits you from U.S. commercial air travel. During airline check-in, if you get a boarding pass, you're clear. If your boarding pass and bag tags have an "SSSS" on it, then prepare yourself (and luggage) for "Secondary Security Screening Selection" (which means hand inspected carry-on, explosive detectors, and hand-held metal detectors).

The TSA will not divulge if you're on the list, and is trying to threaten the airlines with a $25,000 fine per disclosure to passengers. The number of names on the list is rumored to be in the hundreds of thousands, though this was denied:

> [DHS secretary Michael Chertoff claimed in October 2008] *the No Fly list contained only 2,500 names, with an additional 16,000 "selectees", who "represent a less specific security threat and receive extra scrutiny, but are allowed to fly."*
>
> —www.cnn.com/2008/TRAVEL/10/22/no.fly.lists/index.html

The Canadian government has its own version, which they charmingly call "Passenger Protect". It contains 500-2,000 names, incorporated from domestic and foreign intel data, including the TSA No Fly list.

these TSA lists legally apply only to international flights!

> *The* [TSA] *No Fly* [and Selectee lists are] *disseminated to airlines on a daily basis to be used as a watchlist for comparison against* ***passenger manifests for all flights that enter or depart U.S. airspace.***
>
> — *The Federal Bureau of Investigation's Terrorist Watchlist Nomination Practices*, Appendix II, p. 70
> U.S. Department of Justice, Office of the Inspector General, Audit Division, Audit Report 09-25, May 2009
> www.usdoj.gov/oig/reports/FBI/a0925/final.pdf

Although these lists are applied to domestic flights, I may be the first author to point out that they are apparently limited in law only to flights "*that enter or depart U.S. airspace*".

what TSA lists really say to the public

If these TSA lists were limited only to those wanted for questioning or arrest, that could be understood. But it's much more than that because people are prohibited to fly — without reasonable suspicion or probable cause. You cannot know why you were placed on the list, and there is no quick or reliable protocol for being removed. (The courts have so far ruled that since you are not guaranteed any right to commercial air travel, no constitutional injury occurs.)

What really gets me about this stupid list is that it proves the TSA is *not confident* about their own airport security procedures. For example, even if an individual were on the list (yet without any warrant for his arrest), search him more thoroughly if need be, but after that why not let him fly? What's the risk, unless the security screening is lousy? In fact, if I were the Government, I'd *want* such "watched" people to fly, because it places them in a controlled environment (where their behavior and associates can be monitored), and more can be learned about their travel habits than if they drove (which can still be quite private, even today).

what will likely get you on the TSA Selectee list

Since neither the TSA nor the airlines run a background check at the time boarding passes are issued, immigration status and criminal records do not come into play here.

The list criteria for being on "double-secret probation" (unavoidable reference to the movie *Animal House*) by the TSA are deemed too sensitive to disclose:

> *The criteria for No Fly list is defined by the Homeland Security Council Deputies Committee. The original criteria were established by the committee on October 21, 2004. On February 8, 2008, this committee established revised criteria for the No Fly list which are not listed here because the criteria has* [sic] *been deemed sensitive by TSA.* (p. 70)
>
> — DoJ report (op cit.)

. . . but here are some pretty good guesses:

having a one-way reservation
paying cash for your ticket (that got me snagged once)
booking a flight on the day of departure
being a "no show" for any leg of your flight
flying to countries like Iran
random selection (admitted by TSA agent Amy Von Walter)

what could get you on the TSA No Fly list

Any significant kind of public dissent (done in your own name) will probably land you on the No Fly list.

> *Walter F. Murphy, McCormick Professor of Jurisprudence at Princeton, reported that the following exchange took place at Newark on 1 March 2007, where he was denied a boarding pass "because I* [Professor Murphy] *was on the Terrorist Watch list."* ***The airline employee asked, "Have you been in any peace marches? We ban a lot of people from flying because of that."*** *"I explained," said professor Murphy, "that I had not so marched but had, in September 2006, given a lecture at Princeton, televised and put on the web, highly critical of George Bush for his many*

> *violations of the constitution." To which the airline employee responded, "**That'll do it.**"*

This is just more proof that the whole DHS/TSA thing is really about cementing our national compliance to government. "*Have you been to any __________? We ban a lot of people from flying because of that.*" The No Fly list is supposedly for people who are a credible threat to civil aviation, not political dissidents. If anybody gets turned away at the counter subsequent to having attended an April 2009 "Tea Party", please let me know. Those who suspect being on the No Fly list ought to digitally record the ticket counter check-in procedure.

Adopting the Muslim religion can also apparently get you on the TSA No Fly list:

> *Yusuf Islam, a singer and pop star formerly known as Cat Stevens. Author of song "Peace Train." His flight from London was diverted and forced to land in Maine once the government realized he was aboard, and he was barred from entering United States.*
>
> —http://abcnews.go.com/2020/News/story?id=139607&page=1

Diverting an international flight because *Cat Stevens* was onboard? Just insane.

Having a very common name like "Gary Smith" or "John Williams" will greatly increase your odds of being listed.

All that aside, the TSA No Fly list includes (or has included) serving members of Congress, airline pilots, Saddam Hussein (while in U.S. custody!), and 14 of the 19 hijackers of 9/11 (*after* 9/11!). This kind of junk data only inconveniences innocent travelers, and wastes security assets and time. Not one terrorist has been caught because of the TSA No Fly list.

watch out for *SPOT!*

Not the dog Spot, but the TSA's "Screening Passengers by Observation Techniques":

> *Select TSA employees will be trained to identify suspicious individuals who raise red flags by exhibiting unusual or anxious behavior, which can be as simple as changes in mannerisms . . . . Those who are identified as suspicious will be examined more thoroughly; for some, the agency will bring in local police to conduct face-to-face interviews and perhaps run the person's name against national criminal databases.... If such inquiries turn up other issues* [such as] *countries with terrorist connections, police officers can pursue the questioning.*
>
> —www.time.com/time/nation/article/0,8599,1195330,00.html

Try not to look "*anxious*" making a tight connection, or you may be SPOTted by an overzealous "*select TSA employee*".

packing for privacy, comfort, & convenience

This should be done with great forethought, especially if you lawfully fly with a firearm. In Chapter 11 of my *You & The Police!* I explain how to do this. Make *absolutely sure* no stray ammo or spent brass are left in your luggage or pockets.

I strongly urge against the carrying of any sensitive paperwork, receipts, business cards, etc. While computer data can easily be encrypted and hidden, papers are vulnerable to inspection and being copied. Business travellers take a great risk by often carrying with them company documents that contain proprietary, legally privileged, or trade secret information. FedEx such materials ahead, if feasible.

what to wear

Your goal is to be comfortable, yet not draw attention to yourself. Americans are the poorest dressed passengers in the world, so if you dress down a bit you'll fit right in. A good wardrobe is chino-type slacks and a simple button-down shirt. It's informal, comfortable, yet has at least a *bit* of style. Avoid flashy shirts, hand-tooled leather boots and expensive jewelry. Ladies, if you'll dress up a bit you'll be less bothered by officials.

Make sure that you've removed all telling personal items from your wallet and pockets, such as business cards, lists, etc. Carry a digital voice recorder for any confrontation with airport cops. (Many cell phones will work nicely for this.) If you don't tape the Scene, they can claim that you consented to a search.

the travel vest

I wear one most commercial flights. In it go *all* metallic pocket items (leaving me to walk through the metal detector without a beep, because a second beep garners a secondary screening), copies of your necessary travel info, a USB drive (containing color photos of your bags in case they are lost), and any personal comfort items. For example, here is what I stuff in mine for Africa:

toothbrush, small tube of toothpaste
earplugs in a 35mm film can (flying is ear-damagingly noisy)
inflatable neck pillow
blindfold (for sleeping on the plane)
safety razor

travel First-Aid kit (Imodium A-D, aspirin, band-aids, etc.)
antibacterial towelettes or gel
Ziploc bag of unscented baby wipes
eyedrops
coughdrops
Ziploc bag with latex gloves
energy bars
paperback novel
small notepad and pen
digital camera, spare batteries
spare memory card for camera (cheapest in USA)
cell phone, and charger (wall USB)
folder with copies misc. paperwork (insurance, passport, etc.)

Yes, you *could* keep these things in your day pack, but accessing it frequently from the overhead bin is a hassle. Also, a worn vest is less likely to become lost or stolen. If a belt pack isn't your style, then a good travel vest would work well.

neck wallet (an absolute *must*)

Protect your passport, international DL, travelers' checks, backup credit card, and some cash. Wear that neck wallet *everywhere* — without exception. If empty of anything metallic, you can even wear it through the magnetometer.

ankle wallet

This contains travelers' check receipts (always keep separate from the checks!), a spare credit card and drivers license, some cash, copies of passports (yours and your friend's) and any other vital paperwork. If this seems redundant to your neck wallet, trust me that it is not. Modularity and multiple "baskets" for your "eggs" is what protects you against Murphy.

slip-off shoes

Given the shoes-off silliness of airport "security" you will enjoy travelling in easily slipped off footwear, such as Roper walking boots. Such can also serve as your about-town shoes, casual or dress-up. Some quality replacement insoles can really make a comfort difference. Try out the gel-packs.

And have a pair of sacrificial slippers or spare socks for the shoeless shuffle. Public airport floors are filthy. TSA used to provide slippers, but no longer (although you should still insist, firmly).

non-metallic belt buckle

Be able to wear your belt through the metal detector, versus holding your pants up like an idiot.

pack intelligently

You want to be able to comfortably survive with what you have *with* you, because checked bags are frequently delayed (though rarely lost permanently), or you could be stuck at an airport for many hours. Your carry-on bag should have enough to sustain you, such as a change of clothes, hat, spare batteries, some books, and personal hygiene items. (Readers of *Safari Dreams* have thanked me for this tip!)

Get a *quality* nylon backpack with 2500-3500 cubic inch volume — about the maximum size allowable in overhead storage bins. If there's some local disturbance while you're traveling, you may be on your own for a while, and a good pack (no bright colors) then becomes tactical gear. It should have wide and thickly padded straps, at least one outside pocket, an organized interior, and a *very* rugged bottom. REI and other quality outdoors stores will have good choices. (Most will be made in Asia, but avoid packs made in Communist Vietnam. Chinese products may be nearly unavoidable these days, but you've no excuse supporting *Hanoi*.) I like the Kelty Redwing 3100. The Vaude Seattle 65 Travel Pack is versatile choice (www.eigerequipment.com), as it looks like a small suitcase, but has hidden shoulder straps. Whatever you choose, walk twice around the block with at least 30lbs of weight for comfort trial.

Leave your carry-on 20% empty in case your checked bag is overweight and you need to empty it of some things. Know your airline's weight limits, and actually weigh bags at home.

scour and secure your laptop, PDA, etc.

This is especially true for any international travel because CBP agents are now overtly permitted to read and copy your data. With 400 million travelers entering the country each year, secondary inspections generally occur only from lookout lists or agent suspicion. (More on that later in this chapter.)

luggage tags and locks

It is suspicious to *not* have tags on your baggage. Use the kind, however, which cannot be publicly read. Have secure luggage tags on the outside *and inside* of all bags (including carry-on). Reliable contact info (such as a prepaid cell phone) is a must, yet can still be private. Your address should match the one you gave the travel agent.

Use TSA locks for your checked luggage; at least you'll know if they pawed through them. Have a spare set inside just in case the original pair are mistakenly cut off, or damaged.

checking in

Your goal is to get your boarding pass and check your bags without being remembered. Get there early enough to avoid looking harried, and have your stuff ready (bags tagged, ticket ready, etc.) Do not act furtive. You're on vacation and you're happy, remember? You're merely a grain of passenger sand on an airport beach. Request a forward, window seat. You'll exit the plane more quickly and you can unobtrusively doze against the bulkhead. (I use foam earplugs and sleep perfectly.)

confirm your flight and reservation within 48-72 hours

Some airlines require this. Your travel agent will advise. Do not skip this vital step, as your flight could have been cancelled or merged into another, or your reservation lost.

at the airport, *verify* boarding/departure times

One international flight left 20 minutes earlier than ticketed, and I barely noticed it in time. (*That* was exciting.)

board *early*

The masses arrive late and wait. Breeze through earlier. This also gives you plenty of time to unravel any snags, especially if they're related to being on the TSA No Fly list.

showing ID at ticket counter

Ever since the Unabomber's threat to down a 727 out of LAX in spring 1995, passengers have been obliged to show ID during check-in. (This was *supposed* to be, of course, "temporary" just like the WWII 5% "Victory Tax" on wages. This kind of crap is never temporary; it's merely the latest click of the tightening ratchet.)

The real reason wasn't to prevent terrorism, but so the airlines could kill the unused ticket resale business (called "bucket shops"). I once flew from Europe to the USA on a bucket shop ticket in the 1980s, and was even upgraded to First Class by the counter agent (so that a family in Economy could all sit together).

> [W]*hile the photo ID requirement is presented as an antiterrorism security measure, it is really an airline-business security measure* [to kill sales of unused tickets].

So business is why we have the photo ID requirement in the first place, and business is why it's so easy to circumvent it. Instead of going after someone who demonstrates an obvious flaw that is already public, let's focus on the organizations that are actually responsible for this security failure and have failed to do anything about it for all these years. Where's the TSA's response to all this?

The problem is real, and the Department of Homeland Security and TSA should either fix the security or scrap the system. What we've got now is the worst security system of all: one that annoys everyone who is innocent while failing to catch the guilty.

– "The Boarding Pass Brouhaha", Bruce Schneier
www.wired.com/news/columns/0,72045-0.html

Until 2008, you could still check-in for a flight without ID if you accepted secondary screening (*Gonzales v. Gilmore*). That wasn't widely known, and few who knew about it tried it.

The public didn't complain loudly enough about the "*Your papers!*" environment, so today the TSA generally will not process you without government ID:

Effective June 21, 2008, adult passengers (18 and over) are required to show a U.S. federal or state-issued photo ID that contains the following: name, date of birth, gender, expiration date and a tamper-resistant feature in order to be allowed to go through the checkpoint and onto their flight.

Passengers who do not or cannot present an acceptable ID will have to provide information to the Transportation Security Officer performing Travel Document Checking duties in order to verify their identity. Passengers who are cleared through this process may be subject to additional screening. Passengers whose identity cannot be verified by TSA may not be allowed to go through the checkpoint or onto an airplane.

Acceptable IDs include:

** U.S. passport*

** U.S. passport card*

** DHS "Trusted Traveler" cards (NEXUS, SENTRI, FAST)*

** U.S. Military ID (active duty or retired military and their dependents)*

** Permanent Resident Card*

** Border Crossing Card*

**** DHS-designated enhanced driver's license***

** Drivers Licenses or other state photo identity cards issued by Department of Motor Vehicles that meets REAL ID benchmarks (All states are currently in compliance)*

** A Native American Tribal Photo ID*
** An airline or airport-issued ID (if issued under a TSA-approved security plan)*
** A foreign government-issued passport*
** Canadian provincial driver's license or Indian and Northern Affairs Canada (INAC) card*
** Transportation Worker Identification Credential (TWIC)*

Non-US/Canadian citizens are not required to carry their passports if they have documents issued by the U.S. government such as Permanent Resident Cards. Those who do not should be carrying their passports while visiting the U.S.

This standardization of the list of accepted documents better aligns TSA with other DHS components, including Customs and Border Protection, and REAL ID benchmarks.

— ID Requirements for Airport Checkpoints
www.tsa.gov/travelers/airtravel/acceptable_documents.shtm

beware excess baggage weight fees!

You're allowed two checked bags, weight 50lbs each. Between 50-70lbs they will charge you $50, but over 70lbs is a whopping fee. Weigh your bags *before* you leave home, and allow extra space in your carry-on in case you need it.

remove your baggage claim stubs from ticket jacket

Place these *immediately* in your neck pouch. Do not step away from the ticket counter until you've done this!

detach your return ticket and place in neck pouch

If you don't, it can easily become separated and lost.

do not walk about with your passport or ticket in hand

Keep these secured until you must provide them.

airport security tips

Modern airport security installs a steel door on a grass hut, since the airport workers go through far less screening. Also, the *shoes-off, no-shampoo* drill is no doubt calculated to dehumanize and condition passengers. (What indignity will people *not* put up with these days?) While you can't avoid the process, reduce its unpleasantness by packing in this fashion:

front pants pocket

Outbound ticket and ID in one pocket, and most of your cash in the other. Remove all metallic items.

neck pouch inside the shirt

This contains all vital paperwork: passport, baggage claim checks, return ticket, some cash, travelers' checks, and a spare credit card. Have nothing metallic inside so you can wear it through the detector.

travel vest

All pocket metallic items go in here: coins, watch, keys, cell, etc. Your goal is to pass the detector without beeping.

going through the metal detector

I place my things in trays in this order: shoes, belt, vest/jacket, laptop, rucksack. Thus, I am dressing on the other side while they are screening my rucksack (which has the most items and takes the longest to clear). The reverse order begs for trouble, and it's embarrassing to have to wait for your belt, etc. while the TSA agent is opening up your carry-on bag. You also project much more authority and dignity dealing with those people when you're fully dressed. It makes a difference.

opting out of the terraherzian scanners

These are *not* demonstrated to be safe over the long run. I always "opt out" for the patdown. This generally annoys them, but so far it remains your option. During this grotesquely indignant procedure, I like to create doubt in their minds. "*Oh, they don't provide you with dosimeter badges to keep track of cumulative radiation from these scanners?*" The agent will reply that these new scanners don't use radiation. "*Everything in the electromagnetic spectrum is 'radiation', including sunlight. The issue is whether or not it's safe. Only now are they realizing that cell phones can cause brain cancer.*" If they continue to assert their scanners' safety, I inquire if they are a doctor, scientist, or engineer. That usually shuts them up.

your attitude with TSA staff

The most important thing is to always remain calm, even when angry. Be either cheerful or icy (depending on your mood and their disposition), *but never kiss their ass.* While you cannot avoid their shoes-off shampoo silliness, you can avoid stroking their egos with any hint of groveling. If you can pull it off without a whiff of sarcasm, ask questions such as, "*Where can I get such cool blue gloves like yours?*"

Always be prepared mentally to forego your flight and recollect your checked luggage, rather than accept rampant indignities. Remember that you may be just one question away from a cavity search if TSA gets nervous for being inquired about their patently inane procedures or demanding to know if the AirServ dweeb actually works for TSA.

> [T]*he TSA has crafted its procedures so that the demand for identification credentials is made neither by the TSA itself nor the airline, but by a third party whose identity and authority are entirely unverifiable to the traveller, and who is accountable to the traveller neither through government legislative and regulatory procedures nor through enforcement of contractual rights (since they have no contractual relationship to the traveller).*
>
> *To give an added* frisson *of resemblance to countries with corrupt or dysfunctional police and governments, the people in uniform demanding people's credentials are lying about being government employees. The real government employees watching them don't care. And if, like me, you so much as ask a few polite questions about what is going on, you are detained, threatened with arrest, searched, investigated, your papers copied by the government for your permanent (I can only presume) dossier, and the unaccountable third party (and, in the case of an RFID passport, anyone else within range with a reader in their luggage) left with the unregulated legal "right" to use and sell any data obtained from its government-coerced scrutiny of your credentials.*
>
> — Edward Hasbrouck, "Unanswered questions at Dulles Airport"
> www.hasbrouck.org/blog/archives/001066.html

airport behavior

Enroute to your gate, just do what everybody else does. If in a hurry, jog. If you've plenty of time, casually make your way, stopping at the gift shop. Do not go to the bathroom directly before or after clearing security. Such is done by drug couriers who are constantly adjusting the parcels taped to their bodies. You shouldn't be smuggling anything, so don't worry about it.

I advise against making *any* pay phone calls, however innocuous. Airport pay phones are routinely pen registered and even monitored at the direction of a surveilling agent. If cell phones were monitored at airports, it wouldn't surprise me. You should have made your calls beforehand. Your pickup party should know to check your flight number in case it's running late, so you won't be expected to call him.

I prefer to get to my gate straightaway, sit down and read. When I say read, I don't mean just turn the pages — I mean *read*. If you've caught some agent's attention, he will look you over with binoculars across the terminal from behind a mirrored window. He will scrutinize your eye movements, and spot any nervous hand/foot movements. Therefore, pick a seat which is not easily observed, sit down and *read*.

If you need to use the bathroom, by all means do so — but only *once*. Repeated trips to the bathroom are typical of drug couriers. Do not make frequent trips to the water fountain — such implies nervousness.

If accosted by TSA or DEA, they will demand to see your tickets and ID. You are under no legal obligation to comply unless detained or arrested. Start your digital voice recorder. **You should *never* go where *"we can talk more privately."*** Stay put — make a quiet scene if you have to. Demand to see and scrutinize their credentials — write it down. (If they refuse, express disbelief that they are truly officers or agents, and thus powerless to detain you. *Then* they'll show you their badges.) Keep asking if you are free to go. If they claim *"reasonable suspicion"* to detain your luggage and it contains something politically incorrect, state your possessory right to it (so that they can't claim you abandoned it) and excuse yourself to get your lawyer. Leave the airport *immediately*. You should have already read my *You & The Police!*

picking up your bags

Go to baggage claim without delay. At some airports, baggage handling is so efficient that it sometimes beats the passengers. Get there before somebody walks off with it, as stub verification by airport personnel is almost nonexistent.

Pick up your bags, and *leave*. Airports are hazardous environments, full of federal agents. I prefer my party to pick me up *outside* baggage claim and therefore not have to park. You should have arranged this before your flight and not need to call them upon arrival.

Also, I prefer to be dropped off at the curb and not have them come in with me. I like a simple, clean *Bon voyage!* on the outside, so I can concentrate on making my flight.

INTERNATIONAL FLIGHTS

Most of the same tips for domestic flights apply here.

what to take (carry-on bag)

passport
International driver's license
GPS
multiplug adaptor for foreign power outlets
one of your two GMRS radios (your partner has the other)
gifts for foreign friends (organic maple syrup is a real hit)
quality binoculars (Leica, Zeiss, etc., 8x30 or 6x42)
Bose noise-cancelling headphones (a real treat!)
small clear spray bottle mister (very refreshing on long flights)

what to wear

Dress in quality clothes. For myself, I prefer to wear a suit and tie and fly Business Class. I've never had problems. Officials generally don't mess with successful businessmen. (Once, I was even asked if I was a diplomat!)

check-in

Get there *way* early. Relax and act excited about your trip. If you schmooze the ticket agent about this being your — *gosh!* — very first flight on TransOceanic Airlines, she might even upgrade you to Business Class for free. If no upgrade is possible, then ask for an exit row bulkhead seat (they have the most legroom).

clearing foreign Customs and Immigration

They are primarily concerned if you have enough traveling funds to avoid becoming a welfare case in their marvelous Socialist country. For young people, having a gold VISA or American Express card goes a long way in smoothening your way. (And leave your ratty jeans at home, please.)

If asked where you'll be staying, mention an upscale hotel. (If you're *really* serious about your cover story, then you should have already made reservations there, in case they check.)

If you're visiting Israel or some other sensitive country, ask that your passport *not* be stamped, or at least a stamped paper be merely stapled inside. This is a fairly common request.

staying in foreign hotels

The desk clerk will invariably want to see your passport, if not photocopy it — if not keep it during your stay. Do not allow this. Explain that you took it to the Fulmarian Consulate for a visa. Show/give them a photocopy instead.

Do not let the hotel hold your room key while about town. You don't want the front desk knowing precisely when you come and go. If your key is generic (without the hotel's name), then keep it on your person. If not, then hide it somewhere in the hotel, or nearby. I devised a clever way to hide mine, but I can't tell anybody — not even *you*. Sorry.

be nice to the hotel maids

Leave a $2-5 tip every morning for your maid. My mother convinced me of this, calling it inexpensive theft insurance. Neither of us have ever suffered pilfery by the housekeeping staff. Even if you're only staying one night, leave a tip. It's thoughtful, *and* you might leave something in a room one day. Which maid is likely to turn it in — a tipped or untipped?

getting around overseas

Planes, trains and automobiles. Europe, for example, is so compact that air travel isn't really necessary. Take the train. Forget Eurail passes; they force you to stay on the move to get your money's worth. Simply buy your ticket and step aboard.

The *MitFahrGelegenheit (MFG)*

The *MFG* is a neat thing. In German it means "passenger opportunity". *MFG* agencies are in nearly every town across Europe and will (for a fee of $3-12, depending on trip distance) put you together with a driver going your way. With gasoline being $8.00 per gallon, most Europeans can't afford to drive alone for long distances. So, a driver calls up the agency and says that he's going to Munich on the 8th and has room for 2 passengers. He pays no fee to the agency. The passengers pay the agency's fee, and an agreed maximum of roughly 10¢ per mile to the driver. The agency won't ask for your ID. Reserve your *MFG* by phone, drop by, pay the fee, get the driver's name, call him and arrange the price and pickup. The driver doesn't have to know your real name or your address. I prefer to be picked up outside the train station. If you don't care for the driver, the agency will make another introduction for you without charge.

I've used *MFG*s many times, without a hitch. I made some good friends, and never did the drivers charge me the full rate. I've ridden with all kinds of folks, from student musicians to an army captain. The

MFG experience is faster, cheaper and more personable than the train. You might have to wait a couple of days to find a tricky route, but you'll always be able to get close enough to take a short train ride. Take along some fruit to share or a guitar to play, relax and enjoy your trip.

ENTERING THE U.S.

This is real fun. I once returned home through Atlanta, and DEA was there to greet our plane, all suited up in black ninja gear. Barking at us to stand in line and place our bags to the left, our bags were sniffed by two drug dogs. There was no *"Good afternoon, ladies and gentlemen. We are drug enforcement agents and this spot-check is purely routine. We apologize for this delay and welcome you to the United States."* It was like getting off the cattle car train in Auschwitz — an utterly disgusting display of naked power.

In 1997 I opined that customs officials were seemingly trained by the *Sicherheitsdienst*. Now, with the DHS hiring ex-Stasi chief Markus Wolfe as a consultant, I know I was right.

Treasury Enforcement Communications System (TECS II)

The first checkpoint will be the TECS II counter where your passport will be scanned. If you are wanted in the NCIC, suspected/convicted of smuggling, drug dealing, or tax evasion, or wanted for jumping bail you will be detained at the very least. If you are snagged here, remain silent, reserve your rights and state that you wish to speak to your attorney. After two hours, they either have to arrest you for something, or let you in.

clearing U.S. Customs

The one thing to be profoundly aware of is that you have no Bill of Rights at the border (or its "*functional equivalents*" such as international airports).

CBP can review and copy all your laptop data

> *One of our most important enforcement tools in this regard is our ability to search information contained in electronic devices, including laptops and other digital devices, for violations of U.S. law, including potential threats," said Jayson Ahern, deputy commissioner, U.S. Customs and Border Protection, in an online post in June.*
>
> —www.wikileaks.org/wiki/DHS_Report_Says_Leave_Laptops_At_Home

Without probable cause, reasonable suspicion, or even "mere suspicion", CBP agents can review any electronic data. This is a new policy, cancelling a 1986-2007 higher standard requiring PC before material could be copied. (The 1986 directive stated that customs officers "*as a general rule . . . should not read personal correspondence.*")

All that is gone now. Today, if you refuse to boot up or open obviously encrypted files, they can seize your computer and analyze it at leisure over weeks.

> *The policies cover "any device capable of storing information in digital or analog form," including hard drives, flash drives, cellphones, iPods, pagers, beepers, and video and audio tapes. They also cover "all papers and other written documentation," including books, pamphlets and "written materials commonly referred to as 'pocket trash' or 'pocket litter.' "*
>
> *When a review is completed and no probable cause exists to keep the information, any copies of the data must be destroyed. Copies sent to non-federal entities must be returned to DHS. But the documents specify that there is no limitation on authorities keeping written notes or reports about the materials.*
>
> ***Customs Deputy Commissioner Jayson P. Ahern said the efforts "do not infringe on Americans' privacy."***
>
> — "Travelers' Laptops May Be Detained At Border"
> Ellen Nakashima, *Washington Post*
> August 1, 2008; Page A01

CBP policy was upheld by the 9th Circuit Court in the April 2009 ***US v. Arnold*** (www.eff.org/cases/us-v-arnold).

> *As we all know, CBP's data collection capabilities have been widely discussed in the law enforcement community and we have been asked by many various agencies to copy and transmit documentation being carried by travelers for legitimate law enforcement reasons.*
>
> — unnamed CBP agent in a 11 July 2007 email to colleagues

All this has been internationalized thanks to the 2009 *ACTA* ("Anti-Counterfeiting Trade Agreement") treaty regarding pirated movies and music (which allegedly finance terrorism). How the treaty reads we do not know, because the documents are withheld for purportedly containing "*information that is properly classified in the interest of national security pursuant to Executive Order 12958.*" (Classifying treaties affecting passenger luggage? More paranoia. So much for Obama's promise of government "*transparency*".)

Some delegate, however, used his cell phone to photograph the draft text, and sent it to www.wikileaks.org.

> ***Article 2.6: Scope of the Border Measures***
> *3. Where a traveller's personal baggage contains goods of a non-commercial nature within the limits of the duty-free allowance and there are no material indications to suggest the goods are part of commercial traffic,* ***each Party may consider to leave such goods, or part of such goods outside the scope of this section.***

"*May consider*" to not inspect your laptop? Gee, thanks!

> *This probably seems curious if you are not aware there is a consensus among government officials, some industry leaders and liberal think tanks that counterfeiting music and movies is connected to organized crime, which is connected to TERRORISM. So, of course, what is needed is a Piracy Patriot Act.*
>
> *The government officials of the treaty nations are devising ways to monitor the contents of your computer and iPod to prevent such things as downloading through peer to peer networks . Of course, any interesting stuff, incidentally discovered in rummaging through your hard drive, would be referred to the proper law enforcement agency, like the IRS, DEA, your ex-spouse – whatever.*
>
> *However, these government hackers are savvy enough to realize that people will not readily buy the idea that a twelve year old girl, downloading a Hannah Montana Movie bittorrent, is connected to the International Jihadist movement. So they feel it best, for the time being, to hide behind the National Security shield, while they work out ways to efficiently rummage through our hard drives and mp3 players:*
>
> ***The privacy of your laptop is something that has to be forfeited in the New World Order.***
>
> *I guess we will just have to give up some of our quaint American customs in favor of the hip ways of the New World Order. One of those is embracing the culture of surveillance.*
>
> ***In suspicion we trust.***
>
> – Becky C., "Obama's Culture of Surveillance"
> www.girlinshortshorts.blogspot.com/2009/04/obamas-culture-of-surveillance.html

Privacy expert Bruce Schneier has this advice:

> *Encrypting your entire hard drive, something you should certainly do for security in case your computer is lost or stolen, won't work here. The border agent is likely to start this whole process with a "please type in your password". Of course you can refuse, but the*

agent can search you further, detain you longer, refuse you entry into the country and otherwise ruin your day.

You're going to have to hide your data. Set a portion of your hard drive to be encrypted with a different key - even if you also encrypt your entire hard drive - and keep your sensitive data there. Lots of programs allow you to do this. I use PGP Disk (from pgp.com). TrueCrypt (truecrypt.org) is also good, and free.

While customs agents might poke around on your laptop, they're unlikely to find the encrypted partition. (You can make the icon invisible, for some added protection.) And if they download the contents of your hard drive to examine later, you won't care.

So your best defence is to clean up your laptop. A customs agent can't read what you don't have. You don't need five years' worth of email and client data. You don't need your old love letters and those photos (you know the ones I'm talking about). Delete everything you don't absolutely need. And use a secure file erasure program to do it. While you're at it, delete your browser's cookies, cache and browsing history. It's nobody's business what websites you've visited. And turn your computer off — don't just put it to sleep — before you go through customs; that deletes other things. Think of all this as the last thing to do before you stow your electronic devices for landing. Some companies now give their employees forensically clean laptops for travel, and have them download any sensitive data over a virtual private network once they've entered the country. They send any work back the same way, and delete everything again before crossing the border to go home. This is a good idea if you can do it.

If you can't, consider putting your sensitive data on a USB drive or even a camera memory card. Encrypt it, of course, because it's easy to lose something that small. Slip it in your pocket, and it's likely to remain unnoticed even if the customs agent pokes through your laptop. If someone does discover it, you can try saying: "I don't know what's on there. My boss told me to give it to the head of the New York office." If you've chosen a strong encryption password, you won't care if he confiscates it.

Lastly, don't forget your phone and PDA. Customs agents can search those too: emails, your phone book, your calendar. Unfortunately, there's nothing you can do here except delete things.

I know this all sounds like work, and that it's easier to just ignore everything here and hope you don't get searched. Today, the odds are in your favour. But new forensic tools are making automatic searches easier and easier, and the recent US court ruling is likely to embolden other countries. It's better to be safe than sorry.

— "Crossing Borders with Laptops and PDAs"
www.guardian.co.uk/technology/2008/may/15/computing.security

I suspect there will soon come a time when travelers' laptops are simply downloaded as a CBP routine. Schneier's advice is sound, which I supplement with some ideas of my own:

have a spare, inexpensive, sacrificial laptop for border crossings
lean (no data other than necessary during travel)
an OS *not* Windows (Puppy Linux is optimal)
have a CBP and a private pup_save.sfs boot file
a scrubbed (or new/empty) hard-drive (or no HD at all!)
free of any music or video files, even legal archive copies
all data kept in a TrueCrypt volume, and already emailed home
the TC volume backed up on a well-hidden USB drive

The real key to this is learning Puppy Linux, as described in Chapter 14 of my book *One Nation, Under Surveillance*. You'll *never* plug all Windows security holes — not if the feds have unlimited time to analyze your laptop. The Puppy Linux boot sector can be encrypted, and runs from a USB drive. Thus, the box doesn't even *need* a hard-drive, and even if it has one, no data or TrueCrypt installation must reside there. Whether or not you choose to hide a backup USB is your call, but not even that is necessary since you can store the TC volume somewhere on the Web.

You could email home your normal pup_save.sfs — settings file, shred it from your USB, and open the second .sfs — file which is a very basic replacement for the border inspection, containing not even a whiff of any online history. **This *tabula rasa* aspect is impossible with a Windows box** unless you DBANed the entire HD (that takes hours) and reinstalled Microsoft's crappy OS — and even then I still wouldn't trust it. The Puppy Linux *tabula rasa* plan can be done in just minutes, on your arriving flight. You'll have full use of your computer right up until you land, and it is useless to CBP thereafter.

If the CBP agent is naturally astonished over the unusual Puppy Linux box operating by live CD without a hard-drive, explain how you only use the machine to check email and don't download anything. Tell him that a travel vacation to you means little or no computer work (and don't forget to chuckle). Rather than seizing a computer without a storage device, they will likely let you just be on your way.

You've got a proper machine that is sacrificial, without costing you any data or much money, and without possibility of incriminating you. Used laptops are commonly under $200, so just figure this into your trip budget.

Or, you can sell it overseas just before you return, but after you've emailed or FTPed your data back home. (Good used laptops are popular in other countries.) Suffice it to say that there are many ways to "skin this cat". Anybody caught flat-footed on arrival with their brand new $2,000 data-rich Mac PowerBook seized by CBP is simply ignorant.

Oh, and don't forget to either file shred your camera's SD card, and/or swap it out for the "public" version.

if your laptop is seized/returned, never use it again

You would never be sure if a keylogger had been installed to capture and transmit your passphrases. If it's ever seized/returned, DBAN the HD and sell it.

final thoughts on entering Customs

I prefer to bring less than the full allowance, declare nothing and go through the green lane. Focus on the person ahead of you, and walk straight through without glancing at the agents to your side. Flit your eyes about and they'll call you over for a baggage search.

Avoid bringing back certain furs and leathers, ivory, etc. and you'll have no surprises. Also, you're supposed to report over $10,000 in *"cash"* (cash, bearer notes and bonds, blank or *endorsed* checks and M.O.s, etc.), so know that in advance. If they find unreported cash beyond $10,000, it *will* be confiscated and you'll be arrested. It's nice to live in such a "free country".

If detained, don't raise a fuss. Coolly cooperate, but don't forget to record the incident. (Practice covertly activating your digital voice recorder or cell phone. Twelve states require consent of *all* parties to record — know which ones.)

leaving the airport

If you were hassled by the feds or the airport police, do *not* use the pay phones. You should have already arranged for your ride home. If things were really dicey clearing customs, or even if you just have an eerie feeling, beware. The authorities may already have probable cause on you and are waiting for you to charitably lead them to the friend picking you up, or to your car in airport parking. Wave off your ride with a covert signal (*e.g.*, scratching your nose) and take a cab to some prearranged meeting point (*e.g.*, a mall, etc.). Similarly, do not walk to your parked car. Take a cab and come back later for your car.

final thoughts

It's probably obvious that I don't relish commercial air travel. But what's the alternative? Private aircraft. It's a whole other world!

BECOMING YOUR OWN PILOT

It's difficult to imagine a greater and more satisfying skill than learning to fly aircraft. Plus, you've the benefit of traveling like a man, under your own control, with dignity for you and your passengers. No more "*Shoes off!*" commands by TSA, no more radiation scanners, and no more blue gloved groping.

learning how to fly

the Private Pilot course

As a lifelong tutor and instructor of many subjects and skills, I can appreciate a quality program when I see it. Today's flight program is a very effective, efficient, safe, and successful course to transform utter novices into fledgling pilots within 40-75 hours of flying. You'll be far from expert, but you'll be safe enough and competent enough to fly alone and quickly increase your skills and confidence. I was extremely impressed how the course was laid out, and how the foundational skillset was built layer by layer. Flying is not terribly difficult, but it does require feet/hand coordination, good judgment, attention to detail, and a fair amount of courage.

In only 10-15 hours in the air, you will be allowed to fly alone for the first time, doing three takeoffs and landings. This is your first "solo", and it's a great feeling to accomplish it (although it's rather spooky when your CFI gets out of the plane and has you go up alone!). From there, with every additional 10 hours of flying, your skill and confidence increases substantially. With only about 30-40 hours, you'll make your first X-country solo; a heady experience! (At this point, barring bad weather, something weird, or overly strong crosswind during landing, you will begin to really feel like a pilot.)

FAA regulations

Although I am hardly some reflexive fan of government and regulations, most of the FAA's regs seem logical, fair, and engendering of safety. For example, you cannot take up passengers as a student. (Resist the temptation to invite some girl flying with you!) And, as a Private pilot, you cannot take up passengers at night unless you've done 3 takeoffs and landings at night within the past 90 days. (You're on the honor system with your logbook details.) You won't be allowed to fly above 17,999' unless you are Instrument rated with an instrument-equipped airplane. Etc. No real tyranny there.

there is lots of book work!

I was surprised by the ample study materials for aerodynamics, weather, navigation, communications, and regulations. There are some standard FAA books that you'll buy, and I highly recommend supplementing them with Rod Machado's books, and some Internet study videos (especially for understanding the VOR!).

http://www.m0a.com
http://www.thedigitalpilot.com
http://flighttraining.aopa.org

the medical exam

This is required before your first X-country solo (usually done about 15-20 flying hours into your schooling). This Medical Certificate Third Class is also your Student Pilot License. You are now technically an FAA pilot (there are five classes: Student, Sport, Private, Commercial, and Airline Transport Pilot).

The medical exam is brief (about an hour), but quite comprehensive. If you are color-blind, need glasses, have hypertension or poor balance, are a diabetic — such *will* be discovered. If you can't pass such a medical, you can still fly with just a driver's license level of health, but with limitations (as a Sport pilot, in smaller planes which can't exceed 120kts or carry more than one passenger).

learning how to radio like a real pilot

This aspect I enjoyed a lot, but many students don't. I bought a few books just on this subject, and their exhaustive scenarios and sample dialogue helped me immensely. (Also, spending some time listening in at a towered airport is very instructive. Many scanners accept aviation frequencies.) Aviation comm is designed to be utterly clear and efficient. What *can* be said with fewer words — without losing any meaning — *should* be said with fewer words. The airways are a limited and precious commodity. Listen in to www.liveatc.net.

Some tower controllers will seem overly fast talking, so you should preface your first call in as "*Cessna 123YankeeZulu, Student Pilot*". This will almost always get you a slower recitation from ATC. If you didn't understand him, reply "*Say again please, words slower*". **If you are unclear about *anything*, clarify!** I cannot overstress how vital that is. Assume nothing; be *absolutely* sure what you are being told to do, how, and when. Other pilots are trusting you to be where you're supposed to be, landing on runway 16 Right, not Left.

When arriving at a new airport with many intersecting runways, inform the tower that you are "*unfamiliar, request progressive taxi*". Your ego is never in the equation. Admit ignorance; ask for help.

Out West, there are many untowered airports, so we pilots must self-announce within 10 miles. For example: "*Lusk traffic, Cessna 123YankeeZulu is one zero miles west, leaving seven thousand five hundred for five thousand eight hundred, inbound for a left 45, runway 28, full stop, Lusk.*" (*I.e.*, to whom you're talking, who you are, where you are, what you're doing.) Then, as you get closer, you keeping announcing yourself, even while in the pattern. If you've any other traffic going to Lusk, you will coordinate directly with that pilot so that everyone is sure who is where and doing what.

the X-country solo flights

> *All of a sudden, the guy that taught you isn't there any more. And something comes over you. And it's the realization is that it's up to you. Everything you're about to do, is you. So, you remember everything you've been taught."*
>
> — *One Six Right*, on your first solo,
> www.youtube.com/watch?v=qv1khv4M0Lg

These flights for me were a great joy. Flying over beautiful terrain, having "my" Cessna to myself was marvelous. I wanted to keep flying, landing at every new airport along the way.

renting your training airplane

What felt remarkable was that people who had barely met me were fine with letting me take up their $40,000 Cessna after <30 hours of flying time. (Try Hertz with a student driver's license and no credit card!) There is great trust operating within aviation. Earn it.

the written test

After you've done your two X-country solos, you'll begin to study hard for your Written (60 A-B-C multiple choice questions over 2 hours; 70% is passing). Your CFI will give you a couple of practice exams, and I found these very helpful. Some of the questions are a bit tricky, as all of the answers may be technically correct, but you must choose the most *generally* or encompassingly correct answer.

This is a computerized test given by an FAA Proctor in some approved facility (usually at an airport). The 120 minutes allotted is plenty; most finish in 90. Rip through the easy questions first, and flag the work problems for later. You can always come back to recheck and change answers. Your sample sectional maps, diagrams, etc. contain a lot of information that can help you with answers (such as Class B airspace details), so use the test's own materials.

After you have answered all 60 questions, go back and review each one and make sure that you hadn't misread a question and answered too quickly. Flag what you're not sure about, and review them later to finally choose. You'd have to miss 19+ questions to fail, so don't get too stressed out about the test.

Oh, one last thing: many sample questions found in your Jeppesen practice booklet, and also in your CFI practice tests, you will see in the actual Written. Not merely similar, but the *exact* same questions and answers! The FAA has been using virtually the same sample base of 700 questions for years (and your 60 will be randomly chosen by computer). So, pay attention to your practice questions, as you will see about half of them again for real. A comforting notion.

Your results are instantly available, and you'll be able to see which questions you missed (though not why, which requires some remedial study later in those areas.) A certified copy of your test will be given to you. (Immediately take a digital photo of it as a backup, and don't lose the original! You'll have to show it at your checkride.) I flew myself to the testing center (your CFI has to sign off on any solo X-country flights), and it was a great feeling to have flown in, passed, and then flown home. I recommend this, as it's a real confidence booster!

If you flunk the test, it can be retaken. Just study harder!

the flight test "checkride"

While not overly difficult (it encompasses knowledge and skills which any new pilot should own), it is no cakewalk, either. It's an all day affair, lasting 5-6 hours. I heard that about 80% of students pass their first time, and those who don't are not ready to be in the skies alone. The general aviation community is a small one (there are only 600,000 pilots in the USA, and many of them are not current), and we guard our reputation. Society places a lot of faith in us small airplane pilots, so we're not about to certify some buffoon as a Private.

checkride prep

While your CFI is sometimes a Designated Examiner who can give your checkride, he cannot himself sign you off to take it. Another CFI is put in the loop to judge your skills through 3+ hours of flying, and then he will judge you as ready to take your Practical. It is a wise system to interject a second CFI for objectivity. (Just so you know, there are no "rubber stamp" flying schools out there. You are assured of rigorous, quality training from a dedicated cadre of instructors, who try hard to ensure high standards for aviators.)

OK, you're signed off to take your Practical

You have 2 years after your written test to pass your Practical Test. I wouldn't dally; get right to it as soon as you are confident with your skills. (The late Jeff Cooper, shooting instructor guru, was correct in saying that skill is properly measured by what you can reliably do on demand, *right now*. My corollary is that skill is what you can do three times in a row, anytime, graded by the least best.)

First, the Examiner will carefully check all your paperwork, for you and your airplane. (You should have looked all that over beforehand, to avoid any snags. Make sure that your ship is up to date for its annual, transponder, ELT, etc. You should also know how often these inspections are due.)

Then, there will be an oral exam (~90-120 minutes, and it's quite comprehensive). This will generally revolve around your X-country flight planning, so anything on it and your map will open up topics for questions. My Examiner posed as "*I don't know anything about flying, so please explain this to me*".

Next, you'll go out and pre-flight your airplane, and he will ask you about many of the systems. You are expected to know which antennas go to which instruments, what to look for on functioning controls, why the fuel tank vent tube is placed behind the wing strut, etc. "*Why does an engine need oil?*" I was asked. The questions can be that basic. He is trying to expose any holes in your understanding.

Once you both board your airplane, you'll be expected to give a mock passenger briefing. A good template for that is the SAFETY list, which is Seat belts, Air vents, Fire extinguisher, Exits, Traffic, and Your questions.

Finally, there is a specified list of maneuvers which you will have to demonstrate within a narrow range of error (airspeed, altitude, heading, bank angle), and these parameters require practice. I spent probably 15 hours on honing them before my checkride. (Practice your safety clearing turns, as you'll be flunked if you forget them.)

takeoffs (normal, short field, soft field)
landings (normal, short and soft field, forward slip, go-around)
X-country planning, navigation, and diversion
slow flight (constant airspeed: level, turns, climb, descend)
steep turns (level 360° in a 45° bank, left and right)
simulated instrument flying (under the hood)
stalls (power-on, power-off, base-to-final turn)
emergency descents with intention of landing

Few students have all of this 100% down cold; everyone has their own problem area. There are great study books and online videos to help you, so use them. (Landings, especially crosswind, are probably the biggest bane for most.) For a little while, steep turns had me concerned until I learned that I'd misrecalled the bank angle at 60° (difficult, and anything steeper is aerobatic flight) vs. a far easier 45°! (I was just beginning to nail the 60° steep turns when I realized my error, which made 45° no worries.) You'll have to perform a steep turn to the left and to the right, and most students bank one side better than the other, so practice hard to make them equally good.

The regs state that if you fail *any* particular section of the flying, you fail the checkride (though you'll generally receive credit towards the retest for everything you did right the first time). Since, however, the regs state that you may be failed for "*consistently exceeding tolerances*", there seems to be a small grace window for the Examiner. So, if the rest of your checkride has gone well, he may cut you a bit of slack for a slightly flubbed maneuver. "*Well, you lost 50' too much altitude on that one, but with today's brisk downdrafts, I'm going to give it to you.* (Say "*Thank you*" and then shut your mouth.) He may even — but don't count on it! — give you an actual Mulligan: "*OK, that one was obviously just for practice, now do it for real.*" (If you're *that* lucky, you've absolutely got to nail it the second time. You will not get another chance — you miraculously got a do-over at all!)

When I hadn't compensated enough for the crosswind aloft, and let myself get almost pushed out too far from my diversion heading to the alternate airport, he mentioned that the field was not at 12 o'clock but upwind at 1 o'clock. I replied, clearly with tongue in cheek, that I planned it that way to better enter the 45 to a left downwind for runway 33. He laughed at my pluck and passed me on the maneuver. Examiners are people, too. Don't forget that.

About the tolerances of ±10kts/10°/100', what may save you if you go outside these is that you'd made immediate correction when tolerances began to exceed. It's better to bust the altitude range through overcorrecting (which at least shows alertness and diligence) than through absentmindedness or sluggish reaction. Don't, however, stare obsessively at your instruments in fear of these tolerances. He will want to see a *lot* of your looking about the sky. Don't spend more than 20% of your eye time on the panel.

One last thing to remember is that some Examiners will test your ability to shut down distractions in the cockpit. So, if he seems unusually chatty during a maneuver, or is rooting around the floor for a dropped pencil, politely ask him to delay such things until you are on the ground. You are Pilot In Command, so act like one.

choosing an Examiner

You're looking for a guy who is "*out to give you your license*". Somebody who would never pass a bad pilot, but wouldn't cank a good pilot. What you don't want is some overly picky, surly guy who is looking to flunk you. The GA fraternity knows who's who, so ask around. (I was blessed to have a great fellow with a reputation for being fair, and I purposely delayed my checkride for two weeks until he was available.)

learn what your Examiner likes

For example, of the three possible ground reference maneuvers, he chooses only one. (I heard that my guy liked S-turns, and that's what he had me do.) For your X-country nav work, he will probably have a pet route that he likes, so find out what it is and then go practice it beforehand to test your checkpoint choices and see them from the air. (The map is not the territory.) Time your route, and construct a "wind card" that morning to simplify your diversion and WCA.

try to schedule on a day without strong/gusty wind

The test is unnerving enough as it is without going through it in unusually strong winds. Even though you are supposed to be able to demonstrate landings during up to a 15kt crosswind component, I urge you to reschedule for a better day than that!

The normal jitters cannot be totally avoided, so don't squirrel out for merely those, but if you believe yourself not to be ready it's far better to reschedule than flunk. Go get some more practice, if not more training, and come back *owning* these maneuvers.

it's checkride day

I've the same tip here as I do for taking any big international trip: have everything done *two* days beforehand, and use the day before your checkride to *relax* and breezily go over your materials. *I.e.,* don't study until 2A.M. the night before! Instead, just chill out. Go see a movie, or have dinner with friends. Enjoy a hike. De-stress.

What the Examiner wants to see is that you are a levelheaded fellow who can be trusted to make sound and safe decisions up there all by himself. Unless you convince him that you deserve to be rated as a Private Pilot, on the ground is where you will stay in Life. Understand and use the PAVE list of factors (Pilot, Airplane, enVironment, External pressures).

Try to relax as much as you can during this big day, and develop a friendly rapport with the Examiner. He *wants* you to pass, as we in the GA community are always pleased to welcome new pilots.

During the maneuvers, be very sure about what he is asking you to do ("*Sir, which heading and altitude do you want?*"), and voice out loud your thought process and intentions. He wants to understand your piloting thinking, to get inside your head and be comfortable with your decision making. Explain *why* you're doing A and not B or C. Point out anything safe, wise, or conservative that you do. (You're demonstrating that you *know* what is safe, wise, and conservative. Also, he may miss it without your announcement. For example, I mentioned that since an overtaking aircraft passes on the right, I do my first clearing turn to the left. He nodded in approval.)

For my landings, my Examiner didn't tell me which type of landing to do, but rather explained the hypothetical conditions of the runway so that I would choose the appropriate type of landing. I'm sure this is pretty typical, and it's a good way to test one's knowledge. The Examiner will also pose you many different scenarios and ask what would be your decision. Would you continue to your original destination, turn back, divert to another airport, make a precautionary landing in a hay field, request Special VFR, refuel, or not take off? You'll be expected to follow applicable regs as you fly, while such can be obeyed with safety.

congratulations, you passed your checkride!

During mine, I did a nice go-around (even sliding to the side of the runway, as required, which he said only 10% of applicants do). My last landing was the 0 flaps forward slip, which I am pretty good at and didn't fail when it counted. I did a full stop on the runway, and he shook my hand with a "*Congratulations!*" It was hard to process that I had passed, and that all that training and focus was now behind me. Taxiing up he quipped that the only way I could fail now would be to walk away from the plane with the engine running. I replied, "*That, or run over the spotter there!*" (I "flew it all the way to the chocks" and was very careful not to let my joy and relief distract me.)

I was in a lovely daze as we walked into the FBO for him to do the paperwork and cut me my Temp Airman's Cert (good for 120 days while the real license is made and sent — a classy green credit card looking thing with Orville Wright's photo on it). He went over my strong and weak points of my flight, and I agreed with his assessment. Everyone in the FBO apparently knew that it was my checkride day, and folks genuinely welcomed me aboard.

I wish for you such a day. Not since graduating from renowned shooting schools had I such a feeling of accomplishment. It cost me over $10,000 and hundreds of hours of studying, but I'd do it all over again tomorrow. In fact, I sort of did, by soon getting a rotorcraft endorsement. Glider and seaplane were next on the list, followed by complex and high-performance aircraft, and then my instrument rating. Last will be Commercial and multi-engine.

piloting advice

Here, I'm assuming that you're either a current Private Pilot, or at least a Student Pilot far along in your training. I am not (yet!) a high-time pilot, or Instrument rated, and thus certainly am not claiming great experience, but can still offer some good, classic advice.

always, always, *always* get the weather!

While conditions at your homebase may be CAVU (ceiling and visibility unlimited), over the horizon 60 miles away could be a line of thunderstorms spitting hail in your intended path. With a wifi tablet and good weather subscription/flight planning service, it takes only a couple of minutes to have a solid briefing.

If flying through dicey weather, first get a Flight Briefing. If the briefer says "*VFR not recommended* " it's usually wise to heed such. Also, be able to receive weather in the air (XM, or ADS-B). One way to do this is to phone a pilot friend mid-flight for an update (especially on big picture cloud cover).

Summer temperatures will increase your density altitude, and don't get slack with your weight and balance calculations.

Winds aloft will affect your flight time, and thus fuel endurance. On XC trips with headwinds, flightplan enough fuel stops enroute!

use your checklists, *always!*

There are several checklists: exterior inspection, pre-start, runup, takeoff, etc. Almost every time I dispensed with using the relevant checklist, it bit me in the butt. Most of the time I only embarrassed myself, with no harm done. A few times others saw or heard about it. Here's a list of my gaffes as a student pilot:

tried to start engine without having first enriched the mixture
began to taxi without turning on the fuel selector valve – engine died
started takeoff roll with my window not latched shut
often forgot to turn transponder to ON before taking off
once took off with full flaps (prevents climbing above 500' AGL)
left airplane with Master switch on, and totally ran down the battery
once forgot to close my flight plan (got scolded by FSS the next day)

While these were generally not independently dangerous mistakes, most crashes occur through a series of errors which cascade into disaster. You must never assume some condition of your airplane, and never believe that you can remember every checklist item perfectly and in sequence. That laminated placard must be relied upon for every flight! General aviation is risky stuff, and you must leave nothing unnecessarily to chance.

stuff not to gloss over during solo practice

Once your CFI is confident that you can take the airplane up and about by yourself, it's a very liberating feeling. But don't get sloppy and lazy! Practice everything he taught you, as if he were still in the right seat.

your preflight is the easiest way to avoid a problem!

Don't get sloppy about W&B calculations, especially if you're taking on passengers and/or more baggage than normal. In a small plane it's easy to become overweight or out of CG range. You can't just "pile in" who or what you want, like a car. Have an accurate digital scale in the hangar and weigh everybody/thing. Don't forget to take into account that day's density altitude for the entire route. Calculate your takeoff and landing rolls, noting any obstacles to clear. During the walk-around, pay special attention to:

rudder trim tab (not unbent by some well-meaning passenger!)
elevator trim tab (moves with elevator, yet with no free flutter)
free and CORRECT control surface movement
all antennas present
oil filler cap on tightly
fuel caps on correctly, and sumps checked for water
pitot tube not clogged with any bugs or mud daubers

control positioning for wind during taxi

You should develop a sense from where the wind is blowing at all times, and often the wind is more perilous to you on the ground vs. in the air. On the ground, the upwind side requires up aileron (which keeps that wing down). As you taxi and turn, what was the upwind wing becomes the downwind wing, so coordinate your ailerons. Your CFI will show you, but don't slack off on this during your solo work as this issue is a component in your PTS checkride.

Once, during a day of variable winds (variable means changing direction, not speed), I landed nicely in a crosswind, and was rolling out for a full stop, but the wind suddenly turned around on me to a strong left quartering *tail*wind. My plane was lifted on its nosewheel and right main. Very exciting! This is why they say:

Fly the airplane all the way to the chocks!

do not be sloppy on the rudder pedals

Nosewheel airplanes have their center of gravity (cg) in front of the main landing gear, and thus on the ground have superior directional stability over tailwheel airplanes. Thus, it's much easier to taxi, takeoff, and land a NW vs. a TW, and NW pilots tend to stay sloppy with their feet. In a TW, this bad habit will get you a ground loop pretty quickly. Get a TW endorsement; it's worth having the skill.

So, even if you fly only NW ships, practice TW quality of footwork. Taxi *straight down* that yellow line, and with the rudder vs. the brakes. Make it seem as though your airplane taxis on rails.

You're not a real pilot until you've a tailwheel endorsement!

slow flight maneuvers

Practice not merely with "mushy" controls, but with the stall horn warbling. Anything faster is just cheating. Especially concentrate on base-final turns (both left and right traffic) and stall recovery at typical pattern bank angle. (Done right, you'll lose but 50' of altitude and can easily go-around.)

diligent cross-country planning

Never skimp on getting a complete weather report through a standard briefing. Inflight, check on iffy weather ahead, while always having a list of alternate airports at hand to divert to. Know your winds aloft at different altitude levels to minimize headwinds.

Pay close attention to weather, runway, and lighting conditions at your airports (landing and alternate). Compare their actual past weather to what the TAFs predicted: is a front moving in faster or slower than expected?

Work up reasonable fuel consumption estimates for each leg of the flight, and revise these with accurate groundspeed calculations during the actual flight in order not to get caught with less remaining fuel than you'd accounted for. (I'd plan for 60 minutes of daytime and 90 minutes of night reserve, which on a long trip requires at most only one extra fuel stop. Doubling the mandatory time requirements is cheap "insurance" in case you get lost or must avoid bad weather.)

real old-fashioned pilotage

Try not to resort to navaids. Yes, a GPS and autopilot will get you there with about zero hassle, but electronic devices fail often enough to not rely upon them. Fly without their actual help. Your map, plotter, stopwatch, and E-6B mechanical flight computer are all you really need for most VFR flights.

Orient your sectional map in the direction of your flight, and learn to read it upside-down. Keep track of your checkpoints and revise your ETAs with ATA info. When disoriented, slow down to Vx, look for something big and then find it on your map. If *really* lost, climb, communicate, confess, comply with ATC or FSS.

VORs and ADF navaids (vs. GPS)

Yes, they are antiquated and not precise, but relying only on your GPS could cause you a problem someday if it ever conks out. A friend of mine is a CFI and ATP, who mentioned exactly this scenario:

> *I actually ended up shooting an NDB approach in IFR down to minimums in the LearJet one day. That was unexpected. I understand your lack of enthusiasm for the VOR and more so the NDB/ADF work. Maybe it will help knowing that I actually had to use them for more than just practice/training.*

practice making *perfect* landings

Become a diligent student of the perfect landing. It's about the most important part of your flight, and the one which even a novice passenger can appreciate.

I was known to be a fiend for landing practice, sometimes going up for 2 hours, never leaving the pattern for 20+ landings. (My A&P joked that I was spending more time on the ground with my touch-and-go work than actual flying! When I was a 100 hour pilot, I'd already logged 300 landings; a fairly high 3:1 landings:hours ratio.) Watch the yoke of an experienced pilot sometime, and learn from their deft forward/back pressure modulations.

I finally began to film my landings, for a later review and 1-5 star grading (*Poor, Fair, Good, Extremely Good, Outstanding*). I've yet to give myself a 5-star *Oustanding* for what I've filmed, but I've many 4-stars and several 4½-star greasers with a barely perceptible touchdown. The important trend is that I rarely have 1- or 2- star landings anymore. My goal was to average, first, 3-stars, and then 3½-stars. It will take a while to average 4-stars, but I shall eventually get there!

Here are some great tips from the Internet:

* *Fly a perfect pattern — visualize it over the ground*
* *Retrim with every configuration change*
* *Find a final-fix point, a barn, tree, or fence, that is one-half mile from the runway threshold, and be 400' AGL at that point*
* *Aim for the second centerline stripe and land on the third*
* *Be completely stabilized at 300 feet — in the right configuration and at the correct airspeed*
* *Control your airspeed to plus or minus 3 knots of the book*

recommended speed
* *Know when to go around*
* *Carry a little bit of power, as in a soft-field landing*
* *Keep the nose constantly rising to the landing attitude*

That last one is key to making a greaser, especially with a tiny bit of added power given just above stall speed.

Come in high; don't "drag it in" with power and low angle. Always stay high enough in the pattern at all times to be able to land without power.

All takeoffs are voluntary.
Landings are not meant to be saved – go around.
Only a final landing is mandatory.

often practice crosswind landings

These are unnerving for most students, and they were for me. The wing-low approach (upwind wing dipped into the wind for lateral control, with opposite rudder to maintain the runway centerline) takes some getting used to, but I found it fun once I got the knack. Today, hearing "*wind calm*" from the ATIS is almost a disappointment as I won't get crosswind landing practice! (For those calm days, practice your forward slips, short and soft field landings.) Never forget to put full aileron into the crosswind on rollout. A valuable tip:

> *A good way to practice crosswind landings is by making a series of low approaches to a long runway. For the first few, overfly the runway at approach speed, with perhaps the first notch of flaps. Using the ailerons, practice moving the aircraft from one side of the runway, to the centerline, to the other side of the runway (not too far!), and back to centerline. After a few passes, you should get the aileron control part down. On the next series of low passes, use the rudder to keep the nose parallel to the centerline as you maneuver the aircraft. Once you've got these basics down, you're ready to practice a full crosswind landing.*

The strongest crosswind component landing I've so far made was 16kts in a 172, which was much more intense than the ~10kts or so I'd been used to. The Cessna 172 was demonstrated for 15kts, but can take nearly 30. After that, you simply run out of rudder.

My point is to constantly challenge yourself with gradually greater limits. Once you've stretched yourself and expanded an owned skill, maintain it with practice. This keeps up your confidence, which you will surely need on a gusty day.

take weight off the nosewheel as often as you can

My checkride Examiner made a special point of that to me in our debriefing. After touching down, keep the yoke back into your lap, keeping the weight off the NW for as long as possible. And, this helps to practice your soft field technique. "Wheelie" in from the runway for as long as you can. (Nosewheel struts really take a beating otherwise.)

wake turbulence (easy to *pooh-pooh* until you hit some!)

This can easily flip a small plane. Aerobatic training shows you how to continue the roll into upright, vs. pulling back on the yoke and doing a split-S into the ground.

flaps during the landing pattern

some comments about 40° flaps

Full 40° flaps indeed slow the descent and steepen the angle (vital for short fields or landing past an obstacle), but at a potentially high cost. In many airplanes you cannot forward slip with full flaps. And during a balked landing or touch-and-go you'll have to *immediately* (as you're adding full power) re-trim and retract flaps by 10-20° else you will not accelerate to V_x or climb well.

If you don't remember to gradually retract flaps, you'll struggle barely in the air with lots of yoke back pressure. You'll suddenly recall to retract flaps. This is a very dangerous moment, as you're pulling the yoke back into your lap, with full power, and you risk an instant pitch up to a very steep angle for a power-on stall <200' off the ground. Unless you've practiced for this, it will surprise you. It takes great presence of mind to push on the yoke immediately and with judicious force, at once reducing the angle-of-attack and increasing airspeed to V_x. I read of a solo student pilot (with his CFI watching on the ground) who killed himself during his second touch-and-go of the morning. Forgetting to retract flaps before takeoff, he pitched up some 60°, and spin-stall crashed upside-down. (I believe that CFIs should train students to handle exactly the scenario I just described. While *contrived* power-on stalls are practiced, students should also train for the unintentional version from ballooning after tardy flap retraction.)

10° or 20° is often preferable to 40°

40° flaps will reduce C172 stall speed by 6kts, and half of that is achieved with only 10° flaps. From 20° to 40° flaps, you reduce stall speed by only 1kt, while making the airplane more difficult to fly after a rejected landing. All 40° flaps really give you over 20° is a somewhat steeper descent angle (which likely is not a crucial factor to most normal approaches).

I've found 10° or 20° flaps to be much more versatile, safer during balked landings, and preferred for a majority of approaches with ≤10+kts wind. Few days provide truly calm wind on the deck, so a bit of extra airspeed is usually suggested (especially for gusts or significant crosswinds). Many airplanes can forward slip (which is handy to bleed off excessive altitude on final) with up to 20° flaps. And during a balked landing or touch-and-go you haven't so much flaps to retract, and if you're late or forgetful about retracting them, that 20° flaps probably won't cause you too much problem on/above the runway until you retract.

I once had an alternator trip the overvoltage breaker during some touch-and-go work, draining the battery before I could notice. Fortunately, I lost battery power on my downwind before I had reduced airspeed to $<V_{fe}$ (*i.e.*, before I could extend flaps). Had it happened on final, with (electric) full 40° flaps already extended, I could not have retracted them if I had to reject that landing.

So, get a lot of experience with 0-20° flaps landings, and rely on them for windy days. The less the flaps, the less the nose-down trim you'll have to undo during a go-around. (The most reliable flap setting for me greasing a landing is 0°. I had the hardest time learning greasers with 40° flaps, as I tended to balloon — partly because my CFI trained me not to trim after base/20° flaps, as I'll discuss next. It takes a very deft feel for the back pressure during such a flare, slowing down enough to get the stall horn just inches above the deck.)

Those approaches strongly suggesting (or actually requiring) full 40° flaps are not all that common, but do practice your go-arounds with those 40° flaps and get used to handling that unnatural sensation (and avoiding a nose-up departure stall).

trimming during the landing pattern

Some pilots trim for every power or configuration change (meaning for each of the three increments of flaps, 10° downwind/20° base/40° final). While this allows more of a hands-neutral final approach, the disadvantage is that if you've trimmed after the third notch of flaps (*i.e.*, for the full 40° on final), you've created a *lot* of extra nose-down trim to undo during a balked landing or touch-and-go.

My CFI taught me not to trim for 40° flaps, and another CFI confirmed that he also does not trim after the second notch of flaps. It's a good subject to kick around the pilot's lounge.

what's not in the PTS, but *should* be

The Practical Test Standard (PTS) is a very good testing basis for student piloting skill, but I think a few other things should be required.

grass strip takeoff/landings

Grass strips are a different world. No VASI or PAPI glideslope lights, no smooth, long surface, and no pretty centerline stripe. The first time my CFI demonstrated a grass strip landing, I was surprised at how dramatic and intense it seemed. Bumpy, noisy, and with no comfortable hard strip visual cues. I was stunned to imagine that soon I would be confident on grass. Now, I've a habit of making at least two takeoff and landing cycles per session on grass. It's good for the pilot's soul, and the soft field technique (which is a tad funky compared to a normal takeoff/landing) is one to have down cold.

Once I became confident as a student, I thought them a lot of fun and was thus surprised to learn that few pilots practiced them. I think they're shortchanging themselves of an important skill to keep sharp. (I saw a heart-breaking video of a pretty VANS RV-7A flipping over during a grass field takeoff attempt. He didn't even *try* to roll only on his mains, and the nosewheel caught some hole. That accident didn't have to happen. With a metal prop, the FAA requires an expensive engine tear-down to look for crankshaft damage. Ouch!)

Grass strips should be part of the PTS. It seems silly to test one's soft-field technique on a 6,000' concrete runway. There's nothing like the actual experience of landing on a bumpy grass strip, and you will definitely learn to keep that nosewheel up!

Also, I believe that a few actual practice emergency landings should be done on grass. Not just power at idle, but shutting off the engine at altitude, trimming for best glide speed, mock attempts at restart, and gliding into a viable traffic pattern for soft field landing... on grass. "*Train hard, fight easy*" as the famous soldier creed goes.

Furthermore, add an emergency descent (usually because of an engine or cabin fire). A controlled spiraling 45° dive will quickly get you a 2,000 fpm descent, something no Cessna pilot would normally ever experience.

spin recovery (actual vs. mere "awareness")

Stall recovery is taught in flight instruction, but not spin recovery. While the power-off/neutralize aileron/opposite rudder technique is discussed (and may be covered in the written test), students are not required to *do* this maneuver. I think that is a big mistake. What you have not actually practiced you are not likely to do in real life. If a low-time pilot gets himself into a spin, he has no "muscle memory" neural pathways to automatically resort to. To recall the (PARE) Power-off/Aileron neutralized/Rudder snappy opposite/Elevator neutral technique means conscious thinking vs. unconscious response, and this is very unreliable in sudden stressful moments.

It really should be taught as a practiced maneuver. It used to be, (the Piper Tomahawk was designed to be a more spinnable training aircraft than the *über*-stable Cessna 172), but too many students augered in, so the FAA dropped spin recovery as a PTS requirement.

Ask your CFI to actually train you in this. If he will not, then after you get your Private license, go get some aerobatic training. You should not be afraid of spins. Get the Rich Stolls videos.

emergency engine-out procedures!

After takeoff, an engine-out below 800' usually is too low to whip a 180. (The best procedure is usually to land somewhere straight ahead, even if in a cornfield or parking lot.) Learn for yourself how much altitude this requires by practicing this maneuver at least 3000' AGL. Then, during every takeoff, keep in mind where at every altitudinous moment you would land if your engine quit.

various comments

try out different airplanes often

Most low-time pilots have either high-wing experience or low-wing, and it's valuable to train in both. Get a tailwheel endorsement; it will really improve your nose-wheel skills. Gliders, even more so. A complex aircraft endorsement will allow you to fly retractable gear and constant-speed prop. Seaplane training is apparently a real hoot.

Don't stagnate with just one plane's worth of experience.

most "accidents" occur from cascading negative events

A hurried preflight didn't catch half-full tank, coupled with an inop VOR that you didn't get fixed, a GPS that you forgot its charging cord, a sectional that you can't get to in mid-flight, or your only pair of reading glasses that fell behind the seat. So, you run out of fuel over rough terrain before you can reach an airport. Don't rely on just one tablet or EFB, have an electronic spare, and a paper sectional or WAC.

fly prepared with gear and redundancy

Get a Brightline flightbag, and stock it well. Mine weighs 26lbs and contains three headsets. Grab and go.

a Bluetooth ANR headset (Bose A20 can make inflight cell calls)

handheld navcom radio, and plenty of batteries, set to freq
battery caddy for dash, containing AA, AAA, and other common
head-mounted LED flashlight (with red and white light)
spare: GPS tablet, headset, paper charts, reading glasses, etc.
smartphone with weather and piloting apps (x-wind calculator)
never wear nylon/polyester clothing (which melts in a fire)
have a survival kit and clothing appropriate for conditions
buy and register a Personal Locator Beacon (PLB)
have a small bottle of oxygen (>12,500' and night flying)
container to relieve bladder (ZipLoc bag, half-gallon bottle)
airsickness bags (the smell of vomit will make others puke!)
Halon fire extinguisher (www.aircraftspruce.com)

get a 8" tablet with geo-referenced flight software

What a huge innovation this has been for pilots! You can flightplan, get airport info, download weather, calculate fuel burn and ETE, and then fly over GPSed territory. Terrain and obstacle warnings are especially helpful. No more unfolding large paper sectionals, or getting lost having flown above some overcast for two hours.

I initially bought a 7" Samsung and loaded it with AnywhereMap (a solid, though modest, app). All for under $200. I liked it so much that I then got an 8" Samsung (similar in size to a mini-Ipad), and keep the 7" as an inflight backup (which I actually had to use once). With this, I've flown to 22 states during 800-1,000 mile days (in a 130mph/400 mile range Cessna Skyhawk, no less).

Although Ipad is the market leader for flight tablets (ForeFlight and WingX-Pro are the best apps), Android is quickly catching up (Garmin is the top app, but AnywhereMap is fine, too).

With a satellite receiver, you can receive weather data just a few minutes old. None of this was even conceivable just 15 years ago.

For long flights I can listen to music or even watch a thumbnail comedy video. Inflight Kareoke is always lots of fun.

spend $1,000 on a top quality ANR Bluetooth headset

Automatic Noise Reduction is brilliant technology, which nearly cancels out all the loud droning otherwise suffered in the cockpit. (Your sense of hearing cannot be replaced, so protect it well!) You will much easier hear ATC conversations, and be better understood on their end. Pilot fatigue is greatly reduced.

Plus, you can make Bluetoothed cell phone calls (which seem from a sound-studio to the listener, just amazing).

Bose A20 or the new Zulu are best. Sennheiser is good, too.

flying through unfavorable weather

The most harrowing moments I've had flying have been in weather. Most often it deteriorated on me, but other times I had knowingly taken what I thought was a small gamble. Be conservative!

Broken cloud cover seems to almost always turn into overcast at the worst moments, so expect this and don't get "caught on top". Oh, and count on the fact that two layers of overcast separated by a few thousand feet *will* close up on you. Instead of being on top or underneath the scud, you will find yourself in the middle. It's a scary place to be for a VFR pilot, so don't risk it. If you seem to be approaching cloud cover that you cannot fly over or under, immediately execute a 180 and don't chance it.

Running scud: a very bad idea with today's cell towers.

Precipitation: don't venture in any precip you can't see through.

Turbulence: immediately reduce airspeed to <Va. File a pirep.

night flying

I was surprised that this did not require an instrument rating. Night flying ("ghetto IMC") takes a lot of practice. You should have a backup navcom radio, a head-mounted red flashlight, and plenty of excess fuel. Once I arrived at my homebase airport and the runway lights fuse had blown (there was just enough ambient light, however, to land anyway). At another airport, this time deeply at night, my panel radio went out, and so I had to use my handheld to activate the runway lights. (I also had enough fuel to reach my alternate.)

fuel starvation and exhaustion

Starvation means you didn't use all the fuel in the tanks, whereas exhaustion means that you did — in neither of which you reached a runway! Flightplan with adequate reserves (45 min. in the day, and 90 min. at night). In the dozens of long XC trips I've made, not once have I busted into my fuel reserves. It's a great habit!

Now, if you notice mid-flight that you're going to be tight on fuel reserves, consider climbing immediately to nearly your service ceiling. In most airplanes, each extra foot of altitude gives you 9' of further glide. *I.e.*, climbing another 5,300' will provide you another 9 miles of glide radius, which could make the difference in reaching an airstrip.

Finally, if you're within 15 minutes of running dry, a precautionary landing *anywhere* is better than crashing 300' short of a runway. It is not illegal to land in a pasture or country road for safety's sake. No FAA report will be filed. Just... get... *down*.

when in doubt, don't

"*The hardest part of flying is saying No.*" Especially when you want to make the trip. When you feel yourself trying to talk yourself into something, such as skipping a refueling because you "think" you can make it, flying with a "small" mechanical issue, etc. — *don't.*

the two most important piloting tasks are . . .

. . . the *next* two things. The single pilot VFR cockpit has a heavy enough workload as it is, so be *ahead* of the curve; don't play catch up. Have your next needed frequencies already on stand-by, keep up with fuel tank switching, get the weather ahead long beforehand, etc.

best general tip for surviving

Always leave yourself at least two "outs" from every situation, whether fuel or weather or terrain. (One out is not enough, because it could eliminate itself on you, leaving you with no out at all. "*Two is one and one is none.*")

the pilgrimage: fly to Oshkosh and camp!

I flew to my first AirVenture just four months after my PPL. It was a staggering experience to camp underneath my own wing amongst 10,000 other aircraft. I've met WWII fighter aces such as Bob Hoover and Bud Anderson. The daughter of Robin Olds (photo on back cover) was there to speak about her father's book *Fighter Pilot.* You can enjoy flights in a B-17, B-29, Ford TriMotor, etc.

You can't *not* go there. Download, print, and study the NOTAM. Follow the instructions and you'll land at the busiest airport in the world for that week! (Let me know if you land on your dot!)

books and movies on flying

Stick and Rudder, Wolgang Langewiesche

The 1944 classic. Great illustrations.

The Thinking Pilot's Flight Manual, by Rick Durden

Great modern book full of much wisdom.

One Six Right — a beautiful movie on aviation

The history of general aviation, and why pilots love to fly. I found it on YouTube, and it's worth buying a copy.

books by CFII Rod Machado (www.rodmachado.com)

C.S. LEWIS ON WALKING

Not everyone desires a "time machine" for self-locomotion:

> *The deadly power of rushing about wherever I pleased had not been given to me. I measured distances by the standard of man, man walking on his two feet, not by the standard of the internal combustion engine. I had not been allowed to deflower the very idea of distance; in return I possessed "infinite riches" in what would have been to motorists a "a little room." The truest and most horrible claim for modern transport is that it "annihilates space." It does. It annihilates one of the most glorious gifts we have been given. It is a vile inflation which lowers the value of distance, so that a modern boy travels a hundred miles with less sense of liberation and pilgrimage and adventure than his grandfather got from traveling ten. Of course if a man hates space and wants it to be annihilated, that is another matter. Why not creep into his coffin at once? There is little enough space there.*
>
> — *Surprised by Joy*, p. 157

WRITING DOWN DIRECTIONS

Yes, you can probably rely on your smartphone or GPS, but it's another tool in your toolbox to be able to write down or give clear directions. It's excellent training for your mental picturing.

> *OK, take Highway 40 westbound for 15 miles, then take exit 233. Go left, then 4 miles. Look for Maple Street, and turn right. Go to Elm Street, turn right, and we're the second house on the right, house number 825.*

Here is how I would notate all that, while visualizing my turns and landmarks through their voice:

↑ Hwy. 40, W, 15m
↗ exit 233
← then 4m
→ Maple St.
→ Elm St.
2nd house on R, yellow, #825

Always get a house or building number! And also ask for North or South, vs. only left or right. Repeat them back for confirmation.

24

HEALTH, EATING, EXERCISE

Health is not a stable condition of soundness throughout, like a steel building on a concrete foundation. ***Health is a state of balance maintained by perpetual adjustments to forces from within and without.*** *Through the years, the days, the hours, both waking and sleeping, we are steadily responding to the conditions of life, to hunger and food, to cold and heat, to fatigue and rest, to anger and pleasure. We must also deal with our ambitions and our fears, with jealousy, with grief, with feelings of inferiority, with defeats as well as victories, and with the inevitable acceptance of aging.* ***Health depends on how well the individual as a whole can maintain balance through all these changes.***

— Arnold A. Hutschnecker, M.D.; *The Will To Live*

What can a sick man say but that he is sick.

— Samuel Johnson

When a man dies, he does not just die of the disease that he has, ***he dies of his whole life.***

— Péguy

I used to yawn through all that health food stuff, but I realized back in 1998 how utterly vital good health is! Since I am not yet even sixty years of age, and was blessed with a very good physiology, health had never been much of a concern to me. I'd gradually moved to the simple country life and healthier foods over several years, but I have for over 25 years appreciated pure, wholesome food and the elimination of toxic elements from my diet (mentally and spiritually, as well as physically). The computer programmers' mantra of GIGO well illustrates the point:

Garbage In, Garbage Out.

You'll reap whatever health you have invested daily in over the years. The main key to Life is that you will reap about whatever you've put in to it. (Some will whine about their regretable genetics, which also goes to prove my point: their genetics are the sum total of what their ancestors invested in themselves.) To avoid disease, illness, and cancer (Garbage Out), avoid the Garbage *In* (intake of toxins, such as the wrong foods, life-style, attitude, and thinking).

> [H]*ealth is not really difficult or complicated to achieve. Most of it consists of letting go of things and situations we really don't need. Who needs a giant house with a thirty-year mortgage (millstone)? Who needs one of those throwaway cars that must be replaced just as the last payment is made? And who needs to live amidst confusion and congestion when there is so much of the world that is both beautiful and quiet?* (at 189)
>
> — Bill Kaysing, *Bill Kaysing's Freedom Encyclopedia* (1988)

So, this *Health* chapter will not focus on disease cures, but *prevention.* **And what prevention boils down to is simply avoiding the Garbage In.** Western civilization has bent over backwards to create patently unhealthy food. Probably 98% of God's earthly garden is healthy on its own, yet we manage to poison and deaden all this naturally good food. A mortician friend of mine once told me that the legal imperative to embalm after three days was in practicality no longer necessary because modern DBs (dead bodies) arrive on the slab with ample preservatives in them from the previous owners' diet. We are walking around already *one-third* embalmed! We are just energized corpses, zombies. Walking Twinkies in 33% dead bodies.

> *This* [American] *society is insane. All of it — the customs, the work, the hours devoted to work, the way people spoke to each other without looking, the homes they lived in, the streets they walked, the air, the noise, the filth, the bread—all the basics.*
>
> — Elia Kazan; *The Arrangement*

"Insane" is not too harsh of a word. If we employ the definition of insanity as a disassociation with reality, then our society *is* insane. We eat Death instead of Life. We worship fictional characters on TV and ignore the few true heroes among us. Sport figures are paid millions per year, while the best grade school teacher in the country can't break $60K. We tolerate a morally autistic President, as long as the economy seems strong. We fuel the stock market full of vaporish corporations with infinite P/E ratios, and allow gold to languish at <$1200 an ounce. We long for retirement after 40 years of shouldering the grindstone, yet can't figure out what to do on a rainy

Sunday afternoon. And we train our children to be just like us. **We *are* insane.** Our modern civilization is a tawdry play, and its actors are living it as though it were real life. We don't even have a basic sense of self-preservation.

Example: About 90% of America's supermarket foods come from a dozen mega-corporations, such as General Mills, ADM, etc. **What they are *really* selling us is *Death,* in a colorful cardboard box.** (Whoever thought up *Tombstone* pizza understood his business precisely.) Death By "Food" is forestalled by the ingestion of FDA-approved drugs. (And we're surprised that one of us in *three* dies of *cancer* – which simpler societies and wildlife don't experience.) An excellent research project for the brave of heart is to explore the murky cooperation and interlocking directorates between the *food* corporations and the *pharmaceutical* corporations. If you're in the Poison business, it makes perfect sense to also be in the *Antidote* business – however, the pharmaceutical "antidote" is actually an even worse *poison* than processed foods. (Their goal is to quickly kill off within weeks those who begin to slip off the terminal cliff, so as not to overwhelm the public "health" care system.)

As Dr. Arnold A. Hutschnecker wrote, good health derives from maintaining a proper balance of important elements. Bill Kaysing listed the most important ones:

Diet	(mega-corp Death – or natural Life?)
Environment	(toxic city – or clean country?)
Your Attitude	(philosophy, religion, family, friends)
Exercise	(inaction breeds stagnation.)
Occupation	(Rat Race – or Rewarding Leisure?)
Recreation	(harried – or relaxing?)
Vitamins, Minerals, Supplements and Herbs	

Kaysing amplified this with his Two Best Health Guarantees:

*1. **Create an interesting life for yourself**. Eliminate boredom. Do what you want to do, not what other people tell you that you should do. Remember, to be is to do, and vice versa. All the organic food in the world won't help if you're trapped in some boring office job or routine office slot. Nor will diet help if you are constantly under emotional stresses or financial pressure.*

This is the most important aspect of health, as I have learned by actual living experiences. Everything else is subordinate to what you are doing inside your head on a day-to-day basis. If you

> *are frustrated, uncreative, bored and thwarted in self-fulfillment, then don't expect to be healthy no matter what else you do.*
> *2.* ***Your body is constantly being rebuilt from the foods you eat, the water you drink, and the air you breathe.*** *Through cell replacement, you get a new heart every two months, so be sure that it is built from quality ingredients. ...The easy way out is a packaged goodie from the local convenience store, but your body knows the difference and will soon tell you about it in the form of severe complaints. So take the time and trouble to put the best food you can possibly get into your body.* (ibid, at 206-207)

Author K.C. Craichy lists these seven "golden keys" to health:

hydration
nutrition
exercise
stress
sleep
environmental toxins
meditation and prayer

If you create an interesting life for yourself and maintain a good diet, good health *will* follow. Why this is not more obvious or logical to people is because of their incessant brainwashing. **Dare to be *contrarian!*** The masses are nearly always wrong, and about 80% of Western humanity lead lives of quiet desperation as they slowly kill themselves with their diet of Death. Take that road "less travelled by" to discover Truth and Life.

> *Having good health is very different from only being not sick.*
> — Seneca the Younger, (4 B.C. — 65 A.D.)

MODERN DISEASES

> *It is part of the cure to want to be cured.*
> — Seneca

cancer

> *Cancer is not a disease, but simply a group of disobedient cells. It is a community of nonbeneficial cells that have mutated twice that have not yet been destroyed by the immune system.* ***Cancer is not a disease. It's a symptom. Nothing causes cancer. An inefficient immune system allows cancer to develop.***

> *Most people never know about more than 95% of all the cancer colonies in their bodies, but only the ones which overwhelm the immune forces.*
>
> — Albert E. Carter, *The Cancer Answer*

Cancer cells *naturally* occur in our bodies. It is only when they proliferate at an abnormally high rate that such is called cancer. The cause is two-fold: excessive damaged tissue (from the sun, smoking, modern toxins, radon, estrogen, H2O chlorine, etc.) which causes excessive cancer cells, coupled with a compromised immune system.

It's the *diet*, folks. Death In, Death Out.

bolster your immune system!

> *Look after the causes of things; the effects will take care of themselves.*
>
> — Eric Gill

Because the human body is a marvelous machine that is *designed* to work long and well with little incident, doctors *ought* to be as *unbusy* as the MayTag repairman. The below are harmful:

a can of soda reduces immune system by 50% for hours
clogged colon without beneficial bacteria
no essential fatty acids (Omega 3s)
acid-forming foods (which is everything but fresh veggies)
poor circulation (blood, lymph, evergy)

If one's diet consists of less meat and more raw foods, grains, and legumes (beans), cancer cells are kept in check naturally. That's why wildlife and nonindustrial cultures *don't* get cancer, and we *do*.

90% of cancer is *avoidable*, and 70% of that is reversible

The body really does require a *lot* of abuse and poisoning before it fails. This has been understood since the 1930s, but any doctor treating patients accordingly had been jailed and/or run out of the country. The National Cancer Institute and Congress have formed a tight little pact, funded with billions of your dollars. **There's no money to be made from *healthy* people.**

The "cut/burn/poison" treatments kill more people than the cancer, and one is statistically better off avoiding such for natural cures. I lost my last grandfather to their chemo and radiation treatments, so don't get me started on these *butchers*. They might as well go back to mercury and leeches. The NCI's claim that people are living longer after a cancer diagnosis is generally because modern science is sooner diagnosing the cancer. (Do not accept merely my assertion on this; check it out for yourself.)

diabetes

Unless one is highly predisposed genetically for diabetes, one usually has only one's poor diet to blame. Of the three macromolecules of food — proteins, fats, carbohydrates — you only need the first two. You can live just fine without any carbs, but will quickly die without protein and fat. However, those who consume primarily carbs (and processed ones at that) will trigger constant insulin production and store sugar in the form of fat. Over time, your body experiences stubborn weight gain from "metabolic syndrome" (also known as pre-diabetes or Syndrome X). Insulin blocks the fat from being burned, hence preventing weight loss. Thus, the victim continues to crave carby "food" while having low energy.

If this describes you, then get off all sugars, high fructose corn syrups (HFCS), and processed carbs (grains). The author of the highly useful *The Fateful Fork* states that "*the best dietary move you can make is to completely stop eating sugar in all forms.*" Today, most Americans consume each year nearly their body weight in sugar.

heart disease

Poor diet and lack of exercise will inevitably lead to obesity, and then heart troubles. How could it not?

NUTRIENT-DENSE FOOD IS THE BEST MEDICINE

Bageant (author of *Deer Hunting with Jesus*) often remarked that every one of these people after 50 has serious health problems. Well, gee, go figure. Let's see: after 35-40 years of smoking and drinking heavily, a truly crappy junk food diet (diet soft drinks, Little Debbie cakes, Hamburger Helper, etc., etc.), little-no exercise, and dozens of hours/week in front of a TV. *Hmmmm.* I think I'd have serious health problems, too. What the hell do those people expect?

> *One thinks, too, of the children growing up and trying to survive on suspect food, full of nasty, intruded chemicals and fluorides and "artificial flavorings." Are they never again to know cotton, silk, wool, linen, and the good taste of natural fowl and meat and authentic bread? Are they never to touch honest wood again, and*

> *stone? To what sort of a false and deceptive world have we introduced them, where everything fakes the actual, and nothing is sound and true any longer?*
>
> *Can we expect such children to honor the noble actualities of patriotism, faith, honor, morality, loyalty, when they are surrounded by lies in their food and their drink, in their house and in their schools? Can we expect the boys to be manly if there is nothing strong and masculine around them, and girls to be womanly if they are urged only to be "feminine"?*
>
> — Taylor Caldwell, *On Growing Up Tough* (1976)

There are just three reasons why we eat: for Foundation (building blocks), for Fuel (energy), and for Fun. Americans generally eat for entertainment, convenience, and for a tasty "bargain" (in price, though not in nutrition). We consume about 30 tons of food in our lifetimes, and it has profound effects on our health, attitude, and well-being. ("Food and Pharmacy" should be relabeled in supermarkets as "Poison and Antidote".) In Kaysing's *Freedom Encyclopedia*, he quotes several pioneering doctors (Bieler, McKenzie, Sydenham, and Boerhaave) in a sequentially explanatory order. To paraphrase:

> *1. Diseases are the result of long-developing processes which begin early in life and finally lead to body saturation with toxins.*
>
> *2. Improper eating, living and thinking habits are the prime cause of this degeneration.*
>
> *3. The same type of toxin when localized in a joint causes arthritis; when localized in the liver, hepatitis; in the kidneys, nephritis; in the skin, dermatitis; in the pancreas, diabetes; in the brain, insanity.*
>
> *4. Disease is nothing else but an attempt on the part of the body to rid itself of morbific matter.*
>
> *5. Disease is cured with the help of nature by neutralization and excretion of morbific matter.*

In his *Food Is Your Best Medicine*, Dr. Bieler summarized:

> *I have reached three conclusions:*
> *1. The primary cause of disease is toxemia caused by improper foods which results in cellular impairment and breakdown.*
> *2. The use of drugs to treat patients is harmful. Drugs often cause serious side effects and sometimes cause new diseases.*
> *3. Disease can be cured by the use of correct foods.*

Comedian Drake Sather (a wonderfully dry and sick wit, who sadly couldn't survive his dark cynicism) made a joke of dog biscuits which freshened Fido's breath: *"You know, if a dog wanted fresher breath, you'd think he'd stop eating his own sh*t! That would sort of get the 'fresh-breath-ball' rolling."* Similarly, if people wanted better health, you'd think they'd stop eating such crap! You cannot have Life by consuming *Death.* I call it *DIDO* — Death In, Death Out. People spend more attention to the quality of the oil in their car's crankcase than they do to the quality of the food in their own stomach.

what to *avoid*

Avoid the Death *In,* and you won't see its Death *Out.* Would you put 85-octane ethanol in your Porsche? No? Then why are you putting the equivalent into your *body*?

sugars (candies, cookies, cakes, syrups, etc.)

Sugar triggers an insulin response, and this stresses your body.

white (sugar, flour/bread, etc.)

Foods are not white in nature. We refine them with bleaches to make them white, and thus *appearing* clean. White bread is made from devitalized flour and chemicals. Rats die from it, and weevils avoid it. Not life supporting.

baby foods

Mostly water and sugar, to get your child hooked on sweets for life (so he can "graduate" to colas, desserts, etc.).

pasteurized dairy

Avoid store-bought dairy products, and switch to fresh raw dairy (if you can find it).

foods that are canned, preserved, or irradiated

This kills most natural nutrients.

foods that have been sprayed, coated, or treated

Might as well sprinkle DDT on your dinner plate.

grain-fed commerical beef

Cows were not meant to eat grain, and those that do provide poor meat.

farm-raised fish (catfish, salmon), or high-mercury tuna

Filled with chemicals and pollutants.

coffee

Coffee has been statistically linked to heart disease, and one cup is equal to .01 roentgens of radiation. Go for herbal teas instead. If you must have that coffee taste, try pearled barley oven roasted at 350° (for about 30 min. until deep brown), ground and mixed 50:50 with chicory, and brewed.

table salt

Use natural sea salt, which has no additives.

artificial sweeteners

White sugar is actually better for you than *NutraSweet* (Aspertame, an ant poison).

margarine

It's one atom away from being a plastic. *Mmmm.* Try this experiment: leave a bar of margarine in the back yard, and then come back in a week — it'll still be there.

fluoridated water

Flourine belongs in the halogen group of chemicals (chlorine, bromine, and iodine), which are very active. Sodium flouride is 45% flourine and the rest sodium. Flourine is the active ingredient in rat poison. It is highly toxic, very harmful, and cumulative in effect. One-tenth of an ounce is fatal.

While calcium flouride occurs naturally in water in some areas (*e.g.*, Hereford, Texas), this is not same additive put in the public water supplies. What you drink and brush your teeth with is a poisonous waste by-product of making aluminum. This brilliant idea was pushed by two men associated with ALCOA (the Aluminum Company of America), biochemist Gerald H. Cox and ALCOA attorney Oscar Ewing (later the director of the Social Security Dept. of the U.S. Public Heath Service). The municipal water experiments began in 1945 and after five years, even though the tooth decay data didn't support flouride, a "*Believe Science and your Government!*" campaign suckered in the gullible 1950s American. Today, industrial companies manage to sell 500,000 tons of it each year to pollute your water. (Otherwise, they'd have to dispose of the poison at their own expense!)

Flouride has been proven to stunt intelligence and foment mental lethargy. Even in concentrations as low as 1 ppm, it will hamper your immune system. It can cause genetic and chromosomal damage in plants, animals, and insects. In areas of flouridated water, the death rates are 5-10% higher than in areas without.

> *Last year, at this meeting, we showed that sodium flouride, which is being used for the prevention of dental caries, induces chromosomal aberration in the irregular synthesis of DNA. This year, we report findings that show malignant transformation of cells is induced by sodium flouride.*
>
> — Japanese Association of Cancer Research in Osaka (1982)

> *In point of fact, flouride causes more human cancer death and causes it faster than any other chemical.*
>
> — Dr. Dean Burk, chief chemist emeritus of the NCI

No amount of ingestion has been proven "safe". In fact, sodium flouride cannot even penetrate your teeth (dentition has a negative electrical charge), so what's the point, anyway?

Go and try to visit your local water plant and observe how carefully the employees must handle the stuff as they dump it in. Call me crazy, but perhaps —*just perhaps!*— any chemical which requires the wearing of a haz-mat suit maybe shouldn't be put in water.

Instead of the American Dental Association and U.S. Public Heath Service encouraging a rational debate "hear the other side," the *antis* were ridiculed as paranoid simpletons even though most European countries have outlawed the fluoridation of drinking water. In 1979, when a megadose (up to 50 ppm) was accidentally pumped into the city water of Annapolis, Maryland, the locals suffered the following week five times the fatal heart attacks. Instead of warning the people, the city officials tried to cover it up with the rationale of, "*We didn't want to jeopardize the flouridation program.*" Criticize water flouridation and you risk losing grant money.

Install a reverse-osmosis (RO) system in your home, or have a well. Avoid tap water when travelling. If you love your housepets, then give them also nonflouridated water. Never give your child flouride tablets, which have caused death if swallowed.

chlorinated water (use a shower filter: www.needs.com)

Chlorine is highly toxic, and most of your chlorine poisoning comes from bathing. Shower filters will remove it. A pinch of Vitamin C powder will neutralize it in drinking water.

soft drinks, sports drinks, artificial fruit juices, etc.

Gross! Liquid Death. Your body leaches calcium from your bones to neutralize the acid. In a checkout aisle I once perused a tabloid article about a couple who met over their love for, of all things, *Plaza Cola*. (Talk about *slumming* it.) Together, they drink a couple of gallons of it every day. Their basement was stocked nearly to the ceiling with cases of it. They were the most flabby, pasty, unhealthy people I ever saw. (They must be dead by now.)

Worse still are the "diet" soft-drinks containing Aspertame. This is folic acid (ant poison), which causes formaldehyde build-up in the brain. Save your money *and* your life — avoid soft drinks.

What's wrong with iced tea, or pure water with a slice of lemon? Or, a drop of peppermint tincture in a quart is very refreshing.

pork

Dr. Royal Rife, the medical scientist who cured cancer in the 1930s by breaking up cancer tumors with specifically tuned sonic wave energy, wrote that after eating pork (or chicken skin) a patient's blood picture looked cancerous for several hours.

junk food

No more Pop Tarts, Pringles (the "fiber-board" of chips), and Twinkies! You might also cut out the prefab cereals (the box they come in is probably better for you).

pasteurized/homogenized dairy products

I won't go into what they do to cows for increased milk production. Fresh dairy raw milk can be found, if you look for it. Goat's milk approaches the ideal, though its taste can be a bit much.

industrialized food in general

Find local butchers who get their meat from local small farms. Hunt. Only 4 companies process 80% of the beef we eat, and only 4 retailers sell 50% of our groceries. Of hogs raised on factory farms (2,000+ animals):

1992	30%
2004	80%
2007	95%

here are some healthy foods

raw goat's milk

Made with only two stomachs (vs. a cow's four), 97% of goat's milk is quickly assimilated by humans. Undernourished babies are often fed this to reverse malnutrition. *Finding* raw goat's milk can be challenging (or impossible if your state has Milk Nazis).

farm fresh eggs

Store-bought eggs are often many months old, and came from horrific industrial factories. Their shells are nearly paper thin. The yolks are pale; the taste bland.

Now, go compare with some *real* eggs raised by a family in the country. (Often at a comparable price!) Hard shells, bright/pert yolks, and full flavor. You'll never go back to the industrial substitute. (I happen to prefer duck eggs when I can get them.)

wild game

A savvy and competent hunter can get a tag for nearly every season (bow, muzzleloading, cow, etc.), and his larder will be constantly stocked with the best meat on his continent.

If you've never hunted, don't start on your own without help, as you're very likely to merely wound a precious animal and forsake it to a miserable death. Start a vegetable garden and be happy with that. Hunting is a science, an art, a skill, and a passion.

grass-fed bison and beef

The next best meat is grass-fed bison or beef. Bison is now $9/pound and beef $6. I believe that the bison is worth the premium, as it tastes better (don't overcook it) and has less fat.

fermented foods

The Fateful Fork makes the valuable point that nearly every culture has its version of fermented food: German *Sauerkraut*, Korean *kimchi*, Japanese *miso*, etc. Fermented foods are actually still alive, yet do not spoil easily.

fresh, seasonal, local vegetables

Get familiar with your local farmers' market and organic suppliers. Every community should have its own supply of produce. If you must shop in the supermarket, stay in the Organic section. (Yes, the prices are higher, but cut down on spending elsewhere.)

local honey

God bless the beekeepers! No other branch of agriculture yields so great a return on so small an investment with so little interference with other activities as beekeeping. Each hive (containing about 30,000 bees) will produce about 50lbs. of yearly surplus honey, which can be kept or sold for up to $30/lb. Not only that, bees account for 80% of the nation's pollination and are necessary for your area's crops.

fish farming

It is virtually self-managing, and twice as productive as cattle in feed conversion. If your pond system is a *polyculture*, the fish mortality drops from 80% (in the wild) to only 10%. Ernie and Donna Hancock of Freedom's Phoenix are experimenting with their own tilapia pond. Economically heating the water in winter has been a challenge, but they derive many pounds of mercury-free fresh fish.

> *Modern homesteaders could do no better than pattern their fish culture after that of the venerable Chinese system. It works and has for some time. Several thousand years ago Chinese farmers perfected pond culture, developing uncanny techniques for water control and dam construction as well. They knew almost everything known today about breeding and stocking fish, pond fertilization, and weed control. Their terraced ponds had many advantages, not the least of which was the separation of the breeding and growing stages of fish development. One of their greatest contributions was the breeding of varieties of one species of fish to live on the various foodstuffs found on the different levels of a balanced aquatic environment. They stocked herbivorous, plankton-eating, and bottom-feeding varieties. They even bred carp to produce varieties of this species that would consume a specific diet at a specific level of the pond.*
>
> — Barbara & Ken Kern; *The Owner-Built Homestead*, p. 312

The terracing of ponds drains crop nutrients and animal waste into the fish ponds, which is easily digestible by the fish. Everything is used and recycled. The Chinese even provide privies over their ponds, inviting the passersby to stop and relieve themselves, which strikes me as rather elegant. (Crap in somebody's pond *here* and you'll get arrested. The "Fertilizer Defense" won't likely hold up in court...)

With the right combination of plants, ducks, and other mutually beneficial life, a fish pond can give you *hundreds* of pounds of fish (a fat/carb free protein) each year with little work or maintenance. Lovely. Since there are only 100 calories per pound of fish, it is not feasible to exist totally on fish alone. Nutritionally, you'll need to supplement a fish diet with carbs and fat, as fish have almost none.

sprouts

I've become a *big* fan of sprouting. It is *the* cheapest, easiest, quickest (3-5 days) and most productive method of growing high-nutrition food. For example, only 20lbs of grain or seeds will yield *300-400*lbs of live food. All that's needed is water and sunlight. In the sprout stage, the nutritive content is up to *ten times* that of the unsprouted stage. For literally pennies per day a family can grow nourishing food, *indoors.* (I read of a snowed-in family which survived the winter on nothing but sprouts. Wow.) With our depleted soil and dead commercial "food," sprouts are vital.

Sprouts can come from grasses, beans (legumes), and grains. For example, **alfalfa** (because of its 100' deep roots) is highest in minerals (iron, calcium, and phosphorous), and offers good vitamins A, B-complex, C, D, E, G, K, and U. **Garbanzos** offer complete protein with many minerals. **Wheat** is high in vitamins A, B-complex, C, and E, and offers good protein.

pounds of seeds per adult/year, by Rosalie Mason

Seeds	Beans	Grains	Peas
Alfalfa 8	Adzuki 8	Millet 8	Alaskan 12
Chia 8	Black 8	Oats 8	Bl.eyed 12
Flax 8	Lima 8	Rice 8	
Pumpkin 8	Mung 8	Rye 12	
Radish 8	Pinto 20	Wheat 30	
Sesame 8	Red 20		
Sunflower 8	Soy 20		

best sprouts for the beginner

Alfalfa, mung or adzuki beans, and wheat. They germinate easily and require no special handling. Soybeans and other legumes (beans) are more difficult.

While some sprouts (alfalfa, lentils, garbanzos, and wheat) are still edible after a week, most other sprouts lose their crispness after only 2-5 days. Your sprout garden should operate in a continuous overlapping cycle of soaking, germinating, and fridge chilling. Then you'll always have fresh sprouts. **Tip:** Use the mineral-rich rinse water to make soup.

preparing your own healthy food

The fresher the better, and the less cooking the better. Remember, Life In—Life Out. Learn to identify healthy natural ingredients, and prepare them yourself. Not even in the 21st century are there viable shortcuts to this.

no aluminum cookware!

Such has been linked to Alzheimer's. Aluminum is an intense electro-chemical material with unknown affects on the body.

avoid plastic food/water containers!

Nearly all plastics will leach their toxic chemicals into food. What is today a "safe" plastic will be found out unsafe next year. Use glass, china, or food-grade stainless steel containers.

no microwave ovens!

Radiation kills many of the nutrients, leaving you with hot, tasty, *dead* food. Your body does not know how to handle these radiolythic compounds. Yes, they *are* quick, but Death is always quicker and easier than Life. Pay with time and money for *health.*

grow in fertile soil, eat it whole, directly from source

This is the "secret" of healthy societies, none of them existing in the Western world.

cook as little as possible

Water soluble vitamins, such as C and B-complex, cannot survive their twin evils of heat and water. Vitamin C losses can be as much as 75% during meal preparation and cooking. Protein is best cooked quickly (if at all) by broiling or quick searing, to avoid deteriorating amino acids and Vitamin B.

The great method of cooking is the Chinese *wok*, which quickly stir-fries food with a minimum of cellular change and nutritional loss.

A pressure-cooker and juicer should also be in your kitchen.

Vita-Mix machine

Many folks swear by the Vita-Mix machines, which juice, cook, freeze, chop, purée, mix, grind/knead, blend, and crack. Then, it cleans itself in less than 90 seconds. While pricey, they make nutritious food, and your body and mind might be worth it. I've been enjoying mine for nearly 20 years.

DENTAL

A man too busy to take care of his health is like a mechanic too busy to take care of his tools.
— Spanish proverb

I knew somebody who was a heavy smoker for over 40 years. His teeth were fine, but his *gums* didn't hold, and his jawbone had receded. During a restaurant dinner, one of his teeth simply fell out onto his plate — to the horror and revulsion of all present. He quickly began a regimen of vitamins, mouthwash, flossing, etc., but the damage had too much of a head start. He now has only half of his teeth. (I asked him if he could get new *gums* and jawbone. He didn't think that was very funny.) You've seen those old guys with their bottom jaw lost from mouth cancer — they look like space aliens.

Start taking care of your teeth and gums! If you clean your teeth as you clean your dishes, you'll have no trouble. An ounce of prevention is worth a *ton* of cure, later. Cut back, or quit, heavy smoking, coffee drinking, and sweets.

Even in normal times, dental problems are miserable, but if professional dental care may be sporadic or nonexistent, an exposed nerve or gum infection could prove utterly debilitating or fatal.

flouride-free toothpaste

Your mouth absorbs with 90% efficiency whatever you put into it, and stannous-flouride (an artificial byproduct different from natural calcium-flouride) is one of the worst things for you. Your local health food store will have several choices.

get rid of your mercury amalgam fillings

Mercury in teeth fillings? *Mercury?* Even the fumes of mercury are toxic. (This is where we got the phrase "mad as a hatter". Hatters used mercury in forming hats.) What *farging* genius thought up the brilliant idea of using *mercury* for teeth fillings?

I once had a girlfriend whom I met at a health fair. She had attended to find some solution to her inexplicable fainting spells and general malaise. (Her wealthy employer paid for the most extensive battery of tests from Stanford Medical Center, to no avail.) At the health fair, she spoke with a Chinese herbalist who advised that her mercury amalgam fillings were the problem. However, to remove/replace them in the USA would have cost some $10,000. So, she flew to Mexico and got it done professionally for about half that. (There is excellent and affordable dental care in Mexico. Ask around. Combine a pleasant holiday with some dental work.) After a regimen of Vitamin C to detoxify, her symptoms vanished. (I doubt that Stanford Medical Center is amused.)

regularly mouthwash

I mix water and hydrogen peroxide 50:50, and add drops of tincture from myrhh, cinnamon, and peppermint. Use this a few times per day (especially right after meals) to keep the bacterial chain broken up and to negate salival acidity. If you wake up at night to urinate, swish some of this mouthwash then. Bacteria won't have a chance to build up into a powerful acid chain to erode your teeth.

regular flossing

Many people avoid flossing because it's inconvenient. Too many of them then have chronic halitosis because of the rotting food trapped between their molars. (Morning breath is one thing, but sharply acidic bad breath with across-the-room striking power is quite avoidable.)

The floss of choice is *Glide.* It is smooth and doesn't fray. I devised my own flossing system by tying Overhand Loops at the ends of a 6" length of *Glide.* No more wrapping floss around your fingers, which always slips. These lengths are reusable for a few days; just rinse off after use as you do your toothbrush.

never skip the evening brushing and flossing!

Do this right after dinner; don't wait until just before bedtime as you may risk falling asleep first. At the very mininum, floss and rinse. (If you are separated from your toothbrush, eating an apple is surprisingly effective.)

HYGIENE

Good health requires good hygiene. The hippies of Haight-Ashbury district of San Francisco found this out in the 1960s. Forsaking all personal hygiene as "cramping their style" and unnatural, they stopped bathing entirely. Soon, they besieged their local free clinics with an assortment of ailments, rots, rashes, and itches never before seen by the doctors (which were finally identified from medical books on ancient diseases).

While soap and washcloths are inexpensive and easy to use, they seem to be too costly and complex for too many people. I recommend using polypropelene shower gloves to most effectively exfoliate dead skin. Use a natural soap with fewest chemicals.

Pay close attention to any hair/head/face products as the pores are larger and will more readily absorb molecules. Avoid industrial shampoos and conditioners.

Don't forget to keep your feet and toenails in good shape. Get a pedicure once or twice a year.

EXERCISE

Organs are made for action . . . they are made to work, not to be; and when they work well they can be well.
— Henry Hyde Salter

If (barring an actual medical excuse) you are not in at least 80% of your possible fitness, then you're simply too lazy to exercise.

Notice that everything must be "lightweight" these days, thus requiring us to go to the gym and lift weights to make up the difference. Not too many years ago, men carried weight and exerted themselves. Old pick-ups with no power steering. Glass and metal containers (no plastic). Heavy Bakelite telephones. 10lb. M1 Garand rifles. Heavy linen combat fatiques and canvas web belts. I'm not that old, but I do remember some of these.

Too few people exercise because it demands a significant up-front cost in time, energy, pain, and sacrifice. Lazy folks avoid this because they do not pay (less) now and reap (more) later. No, they want to enjoy now and hope that no bill will ever come later (or, at least without any interest). (*It always does*, and in the form of reduced strength and more illness.)

Payment in advance is required for anything in life that produces a benefit.
— Robert J. Ringer, *How You Can Find Happiness During the Collapse of Western Civilization*, p. 108

Ringer has a right to say that, as he used to be a fatty. Finally, he was too embarrassed to look at himself in the mirror, and committed himself to regular exercise. Unless there is an actual medical condition, a chronically overweight person wears their laziness and short-term time horizons on the outside for all to see. And when their sickly Tomorrow finally arrives, it won't be their own fault, as if there was to be no price for a lifetime of chips and cookies. (This was the whole point of Obamacare: to force the scrupulous and healthy to subsidize the medical costs of the lazy.)

By 2020, 75% of Americans will be clinically obese. By 2050, one-third of us will have diabetes [because of this obesity]. For the first time in history we are raising a generation of children who are not going to outlive their parents. . . . Over 300,000 adult deaths per year in the United States alone are directly attributable to unhealthy eating habits and a sedentary lifestyle. All because people can't stop eating like pigs and won't move. . . .

> *Nothing will contribute more to your health than a proper diet and exercise.*
>
> *stop lying to yourself about being "big-boned" or having a "glandular problem"*
>
> *stop going to fast food restaurants as often*
> *when hungry drink a huge glass of water*
> *drink lots of water anyway*
> *don't grocery shop when hungry*
> *park on the far side of the lot, and walk more*
> *take your dog, your kid, your partner for a walk*
> *weigh only once a week*
> *smaller food portions are the key*
> *turn off the TV and get off your fat butt*
> *go to a gym regularly*
> *reward significant weight loss with a new expensive wardrobe*
>
> – Larry Winget, *Shut Up, Stop Whining, Get A Life!*

Patience pays off later. Procrastination pays off now, but less. There is absolutely zero benefit to willfully becoming and staying fat. Not in earnings, not in success, not in marriage, not in fathering, not in self-confidence, not in health. It costs more money to maintain your fatness than to stay trim. You are responsible for your own good health. Period. Just as a well-maintained car is not often towed to the mechanic, a life of quality diet and vigorous exercise will keep you out of the hospital.

> [Exercise is] *a pledge, a token of some future potency.*
>
> – Henry James

Exactly! Bodily strength must be paid for up-front. Every time you work out, you are paying for *future* vitality and stamina. You are trading a bit of Today for a stronger Tomorrow.

cardiovascular (CV)

For its health, the heart must be "revved up" for an uninterrupted 20 minutes, at least every other day. Jogging, skipping rope (excellent CV exercise), rebounding, whatever—just get your heart rate up three times a week.

muscle tone

An expensive gym membership is not necessary. *Regular* walking and upper body calisthenics (chin ups, push ups, sit ups, etc.) will keep most folks in decent shape. I like rowing a small boat on a lake. Stretching like a cat and isometrics are also a real boon to fitness. Simple regularity of basic exercise is more effective than irregular quality workouts. However you exercise, pick something that you *like* doing, and do it daily.

7 Tiger Stretch Moves

I learned about these from K.C. Craichy's *Super Health Living Journal.* The secret is:

> *nothing more than contracting and extending your muscles with great tension while thinking into them. Tigers and lions stretch their entire body with a tension so great that their limbs actually quiver. . . . The inner resistance produced by the tension builds muscle fibers as much as the external resistance produced by weights or machines.*

The seven Tiger Stretch moves are simple, and need no equipment or special preparation. This 10 minute regimen is great for traveling. I can attest how effective these moves are. It really feels like a work-out.

my basic workout: a quality Rebounder trampoline

> *Rebound Exercise is the most efficient, effective form of exercise yet devised by man", 68% more efficient than jogging.*
>
> – N.A.S.A., Journal of Applied Physiology 49(5): 881-887

Why? Because your body cannot tell the difference between gravitational force and weight. Bouncing vigorously on a rebounder subjects every cell in your body to 2-3Gs of momentary deceleration, and every cell grows stronger. Rebounding is also the most efficient way to move your lymphatic fluid (you've 5x more of it than blood!) through your body to keep cells flushed out. It's much more low impact than jogging, and much more efficient. (Al Carter of www.healthbounce.com pioneered Reboundology, the most efficient exercise yet known.)

> *Strengthens every cell, muscle, organ, tissue, bone and tendon in the body.*
>
> *Gives all the benefits of aerobic exercises without jarring the skeletal system.*
>
> *Allows for some of the most intense workouts in the shortest amount of time.*
>
> *Saves you time (ten minutes of rebounding is as effective as 25 or 30 minutes of jogging, without the jarring effect).*
>
> *Allows people to exercise who otherwise could not: Those with back problems, sensitive joints and knees.*
>
> *Provides pure pleasure in freedom of moving, turning, twisting, kicking and stretching that can be performed anywhere.*

Protection against heart disease, cancer and degenerative diseases.

Enhances digestion, relaxation, sleep patterns, nerve impulses and muscle fiber.

Has been found to lower elevated cholesterol and triglyceride levels.

— *Jumping for Health* by Dr. Morton Walker

I strap on 20lbs of leg weights and 10lbs of arm weights, and jump with Tee-Ball bats (to practice my stick fighting). 20-30 minutes of this each day gives me a full-body workout combining strength, CV, and flexibility conditioning. Weeks before going on African safaris, I jump with my hunting rifle, and it pays off in the field.

While I started out long ago with Carter's rebounders, I've since gone to the bungee corded JumpSport (which I prefer over springs).

the enhanced workout

There are many videos available, such as P90X, Insanity, etc. The actual choice is less important than your commitment to a daily regimen for the first consecutive 90 days. After that, you've formed an exercising habit that is much easier to keep. Never drop it!

10 workouts to shed fat and gain lean muscle

Bodybuilding isn't for everyone; in fact, many consider focusing on muscle size a distraction from the most important fitness goals. More and more alpha males are focusing narrowly on weight loss and building lean, strong muscles. Here are ten workouts for men who crave a leaner, muscled look.

—http://alphamaletribe.com/2014/04/top-ten-workouts-men-can-use-shedding-fat-gaining-lean-muscle/

01. Cardio Interval Training

Long gone are the days when men routinely avoided cardio and stuck to lifting massive weights. These days, interval training is a recognized, vital tool for weight loss and a lean, cut look. For maximum benefit, alternate one minute of intense cardio with two minutes of rest.

02. Squat Jumping

Your own body weight is your best tool for getting cut and developing lean muscle. Simple but effective, this workout involves jumping quickly from a full squat, extending yourself fully and landing in your starting position.

03. Box Jumping

This is another low-tech workout with proven results. From a standing position, quickly jump onto a sturdy box. Like other calisthenic-type workouts, the box jump works best when it is fast and furious.

04. Wall Pushups

Like all calisthenics, this move calls for fast, plentiful reps to maximize weight loss. The exercise is simple, effective and easy to perform virtually anywhere.

05. Supersets

Bodybuilders typically use massive weights and take lengthy breaks between sets. Employing smaller weights, the superset involves working two sets of opposing muscle groups in quick succession. For example, one could follow a bicep routine with a tricep workout. Using smaller weights promotes leaner muscles while the constant activity of supersets keeps your heart rate in the fat-burning zone.

06. Circuit Speed Workouts

Taking the superset concept even further, the circuit workout involves rapidly working each and every muscle group with little or no rest between sets. After each circuit, take a short break and start again.

07. Pull Ups

A classic move from your high school gym days, this is still a great way to get cut. Mixing overhanded and underhanded pull ups is ideal. While the full motion is important, getting started with partial pull ups is perfectly acceptable.

08. Dumbbell Front Raise

This is a simple and effective technique you probably already know. It is ideal for a lean appearance because cut shoulders can give your torso a flattering T-shape.

09. Leg Raises

Simplicity is one of the selling points of calisthenic exercise. This is quite possibly the simplest move on the list, but if you put in plenty of reps, it can work wonders.

10. Lower Intensity, Longer Duration Cardio

This workout places last because it demands caution. Thirty to sixty sessions of low-intensity cardio can burn fat without appreciably sacrificing muscle mass. Don't overdo low-intensity workouts; longer sessions can cut into muscle development. For fitness novices who can't handle more intense cardio, low-intensity can open the door to bigger and better things.

some remarks on your exercise program

The Canadian Air Force exercise program (found in a used paperback book for $1, or on the Internet) is a good one for those who won't rebound or go to the gym. Swimming is preferred by some. Whatever you do, you must rev up your heart for 20 minutes at least every other day (preferably daily). Combine this with strength and stretching exercises.

begin *today!*

Don't wait for next week, or next month, or next year. The sooner you commit to your health, the sooner you will become healthy and strong. Today is the soonest portion of your future, and the only one you're guaranteed of.

it must be *daily*

Whatever you choose, you must do it *daily* without fail. Until you consider exercising as essential as eating and making a living, you are not yet serious enough about it. Once you begin it after a long lapse, it is vital that you do it daily for at least 30-90 days to create a strong habit. If you quit beforehand, you create a habit of avoidance that is very difficult to break.

no excuses whatever!

The moment you begin an exercise program, your body will conspire with your mind to come up with an amazing array of excuses why you cannot work out today. Override all these by telling yourself that it *doesn't matter* if you are tired, not in the mood, mildly ill, in a rush to do something more important, etc.

If you miss a day through clever laziness, *punish* that by working out 2½ times as long the next day. (The extra is the "interest" you pay on the convenience of yesterday's laziness. You'll soon realize that it's better not to skip your workouts.)

Only when you fully commit to your health will your health fully commit to you. Once this law of Life sets in, you will actually look forward to exercising as a "*pledge, a token of some future potency*".

when to work out?

It is well understood that the best time to exercise is in the morning, followed by an ample healthy breakfast. This propels your body into each new day with vigor. (My program is to first drink a fruit/protein shake to get me going just after I wake up, work out, shower, and then enjoy a full breakfast.)If you haven't time in the mornings, *then go to bed earlier* so that you can wake up in time to work out. Asleep by 10-11PM and awake by 5-6AM is a proven regimen.

Sometimes you won't have the time to do a full routine. When you must reduce the time, never reduce the intensity.

change your training every 30 days

You have to keep your body guessing by always surprising it. Mix swimming in with rebounding, for example.

my secret for keeping weight in check

Once your body fills out and stabilizes as an adult, you are capable of maintaining that perfect healthy weight for the rest of your Life if you want to. However, even with a naturally athletic body, if you don't daily exercise you will put on a few pounds every year as your metabolism slows down. Here's my trick for keeping weight in check:

Never buy the next larger size in pants.

My natural waist size is 32" and when my jeans start to feel tight, I know that I'm not exercising hard enough. For me, buying 34" jeans is just not an option. My existing pants are a wall against too much weight gain. And, this saves money on fatty clothing.

SLEEP

We spend 25-33% of our lives sleeping. Don't skimp on whatever it takes to garner the highest quality sleep.

do what you must to get 6-8 hours of nightly sleep

Sleep is as important as eating. Push away whatever is interfering with good sleep, even if you must give up some pleasures.

sleep is more effective before midnight vs. after

As a Night Owl, I wish this were not true, but facts are facts. Going to bed early and waking up early is a common thread of healthy and successful people.

buy a *very* quality bed and pillow!

Years ago I bought my first really nice bed, a Sealy TempurPedic for $2500. I tested their five different foam combinations and then chose the perfect bed for me. It has a 25-year guarantee, so, in effect, I've got one of the best mattresses on earth for just $100/year. That's just 27¢/night (or 4¢/hour). For its service life and quality of product, that's practically free. **Why spend even less money only to get *worse* sleep?**

I have a $99 pillow for the same reason. Why rest my head on something as lousy as a $4 pillow from China? www.mypillow.com

a trick to beating insomina

My dad used to work nights, and was renowned for being able to fall asleep at any time. My mom asked him how he did it, and he replied, "*I concentrate on the inside of my eyelids.*" Those strangely changing patterns you "see" are phosphenes, and concentrating on them will put you into theta mode (like staring into a fire). Theta is the so-called "hypnotic" or "programming" mode (mindlessly watching TV will activate it), and it's easy to fall asleep from theta.

DEALING WITH STRESS

Humans cannot avoid stress; it is simply a part of Life. Even good things (travel, promotion, new relationships) will produce stress.

worry

Worry is prayer in reverse, a sort of anti-faith. It actually reprograms your body's cells and begins a highly negative cascade. (This is why regular vigorous exercise is vital, to clear out the emotional gunk.)

change

Even positive change (job promotion, new relationship, travel etc.) is stressful. Take a "vacation" from your vacation, so to speak.

meditation

This is not something I practice much, though I believe in its centering power. For me, a good hike in the woods, watching the ocean waves or a campfire serves as meditation.

prayer

Prayer comes more easily to some than others. However much one prays, it's probably still not enough.

DRUGS

I believe that every adult should be responsible for their own diet, including the effect of drugs. Nothing should be prohibited to adults. But since people insist on being protected as if they were children, they are similarly irresponsible.

nicotine

Unless you enjoy only a few cigars per year, smoking will somehow take its painful healthy toll. One of the dumbest things you can do is regularly smoke cigarettes or chew tobacco. Before it kills you, it may first turn you into a jawless cancer monster.

alcohol

An indignant pot-smoker once remarked that if alcohol was unknown today but invented tomorrow, it would be prohibited. He's probably correct. Alcohol abuse has caused death and misery for millions. However, enjoyed in moderation it is highly beneficial in taking the edge off occasionally. There's nothing like a good cold beer after a hard day of work or play. A bottle of wine with your Lady enhances the evening. Single-malt Scotch with a buddy is special.

Just monitor your intake, and keep hydrated with water. If you're regularly consuming more than 20 oz./week, then your health is being compromised. More than 40 oz./week and you may be on the slide to alcoholism. Check yourself for a possible addiction by fasting alcohol for a month.

"recreational drugs"

These are not my scene, and you'll take big risks if you go there. I know too many people whose drive and incentive have been gutted by pot. Cocaine has ruined many marriages and careers. Meth is especially destructive. If you try a new drug, you risk liking it very much, and it could easily become more than you can handle. My advice is to just stay away from them all. Stay focused on your Purpose, keeping fit, and having fun with quality people.

HEALTHY RELATIONSHIPS

Toxicity is not constricted only to what you eat, drink, breathe. The people in your Life are also part of your "diet".

health tip for singles: get a loving cat or dog

There is nothing like having a loving critter at home to pet and talk to. As an author, I once went without a cat for several years, and wondered later why I subjected myself to such a loss.

I prefer quality cats, as they give me the fun and joy of a dog, but without the maintenance hassles. I've been away many times for days, and my cats were fine. (A dog you can't leave for more than a day, and it melts down. But, if you're a "dog person" then enjoy!) I've had several cats, all great and two of which were really outstanding. Every day my cat causes me to smile, chuckle, and laugh. At least once or twice a week I get a real belly-laugh from something he does.

The health benefits from a loyal and loving fur-covered housepet are incalculable. Go visit your nearest animal shelter and find a good match.

local friends who will actually meet up with you

I'd rather have one of these than 20 "friends" who imagine that irregular drive-by texting is some kind of meaningful relationship. If you are spending more time in virtual friendships (phone, online) than those who you can see once a week, you're doing it wrong. Get out, circulate, join a club, play sports, take dancing lessons, something. Find some kindred spirits nearby.

date and marry a kind, loving, devoted Lady!

As often as bad marriages seem, the data nonetheless confirms that married men live longer than single men. (Coming up in this volume are over 200 pages about discerning, courting, loving, and marrying a quality woman.)

I dated a woman who cooked only with organics, and she fed me very well. After the break-up, I wondered if I'd notice a decline in energy and health since I was cooking for myself (and decently, though not up to her level). I was surprised to feel exactly the same. There were only two reasons for that: ❶ organic ingredients are overrated in nutritional benefit, or ❷ the stress of regular combat with that contentious woman cancelled out some of those nutritional benefits. Recalling my deep unhappiness, I concluded that health is a holistic concept and all areas affect each other. So, even if I never eat that well again, at least I'll never accept such melancholy.

Now, if you are presently unmarried yet in a net-balance *unhappy* relationship, I strongly advise you to leave. Staying will only further your misery, and train you in the bad habit of settling for less. Become single and then insist on a better match for yourself.

PROTECTION FROM INJURY

It's a lot easier to *avoid* injuries than it is to *repair* them — and less painful. We've all done stupid things to cause injury to ourselves, and that's only natural. Wisdom means a lack of *repeat* performances.

avoid injury from exercise

Stretch before strenuous exercise. There's no excuse for torn ligaments and shin splints if you stretch beforehand. The older you get, the more important this becomes.

avoid mechanical injury

Cut *away* from you, not towards you. Wear gloves. Protect your eyes. Turn off and unplug devices *before* working on them. I once knew a guy who nearly removed his entire thumb with a bandsaw because he did not turn it off before he attempted to dislodge some material. Experience also breeds cockiness. Stay alert and humble.

eyes

Wear safety glasses *religiously* with *all* power tools, hand tools (saws, hammers, etc.), chemicals, and parts with powerful springs.

Insist on only industrial grade safety glasses with an ANSI Z87.1 certification (it'll be on the frame or legs) for superior IR and UV protection (for the sun). Do not trust the little "99% UV" stickers on the cheapies' lenses. True Z87.1 standards will be so certified on the frame. I highly recommend the polycarbonate glasses from ProTech (800-500-4739) by the dozen for only a few dollars apiece. These glasses are *far* better than supermarket cheapies, and as good (or better) than expensive brands. Pro-Tech glasses even *look* good, too.

In short, pick *high-quality* glasses, and wear them *often*. Have several pairs sprinkled about (car, home, shed, shop, etc.) so that you'll never be far from a pair. Don't ever chop wood, drill metal, etc. "just this once" without your safety glasses. It takes only a small sliver to blind you for life. (Such happened to test pilot Wiley Post.)

Take no chances with your eyes, especially since simply wearing glasses offers all the protection they need. Have spare contacts and eyeglasses, if you wear them.

ears

Millions of microscopic *cilia*, like fields of wheat in the wind, wave with sound pressure and transmit that as hearing. These *cilia* are very fragile and get broken off from extreme pressure. They *don't* grow back, and they can't be transplanted. "Hearing aids" merely amplify sound to the remaining *cilia* at their optimum frequency.

Protect your ears. Wear earplugs religiously when exposed for more than 5 minutes to any noise level above 85 decibels. I have worn earplugs for years while motorcycling, flying, etc., and my hearing is now much more acute than my peers'.

knees

Knees are very fragile and extremely expensive to repair. Ask any pro football player. Stretch and warm up your tendons before strenuous use, and wear quality footwear for work, hiking, or any other activity which is notoriously hard on knees.

feet

Wear heavy boots (steel toe if necessary). Broken feet are amongst the most painful and debilitating of all injuries. A broken metatarsal bone is a mega-bummer.

SUPPLIES

hygiene

Basic supplies will go a long way in providing at least modest hygiene. Think ahead for all the supplies you take for granted, and stock up.

dental

waxed floss (have lots, as there is no good substitute)
toothbrush (stock up, as substitutes pale in comparison)
toothpaste (preferably fluoride-free and natural)
mouthwash, several times a day to break up bacterial chain
dental mirror
dental picks (for regular plaque scaling)
cold sore medication
mirror
dentures, and related supplies

face

Keep your face clean and free of oil buildup. Also, protect your face from the sun! *Moderate* tanning is O.K., but use sunscreen religiously to avoid skin cancer later (*e.g.*, on the nose).

milk mud pack (2 tbls. dry milk powder with 1 tbls. water)
cleanser/astringent (50/50 rubbing alcohol and Witch Hazel)
baby wipes or other moistened towelettes (for outdoors)

skin

To properly bathe, you must scruff off the accumulating layer of dead skin. This is called "exfoliation". You must use at least a washcloth, but a loofah is better still.

soap
polypropylene "loofah" sponge (have used one for years)

feet

This is the most neglected part of the human body, besides the brain. Keep your toenails neat and trimmed—don't let them get like goat's hooves. Keep your feet clean and aired out, and they won't fail you. Keep a bit of callus on the soles, in case you're forced to be barefoot over rough terrain.

toenail clippers
pads for corns, blisters, etc.

first aid

An orange paramedic kit (often called a Thompson pack) can be had from Nitro-Pak (and others), and would be vital in a trauma situation. They are expensive ($300+), but totally self-contained.

tools and books

First aid book
ice pack
hot water bottles
scalpel and replaceable blades
scissors
tweezers
eye dropper
eye glass (to wash eyes)
thermometers (oral and rectal)
blood pressure gauge
clamps, forceps, etc.
tourniquets (belt, surgical tubing, etc.) and twisting stick
splints (strips of wood, or inflatable splint)

snake bite kit
bed pan
flashlight
measuring cup and spoons
needles and safety pins (for sutures)

consumables

black silk thread or suture thread
sterile 4"x4" pads
gauze
sheets and towels (for slings and dressings)
Q-Tips
Ace bandages; 2", 3", 4"
assorted Band-Aids
adhesive tape, 1" wide
roll cotton, 1 lb.
matches and candles
Melaleuca (Pain-A-Trate, Mela-Gel, and T36-C7)
Vaseline, in 1 lb. jars
Murine, or other eye wash
boric acid crystals, powder and ointment
Epsom salts (to reduce swellings)
Erogophene Ointment (drawing salve)
oil of cloves (toothache drops)
ethyl alcohol 70% (rubbing and sterilizing)
hydrogen peroxide (for sterilization and water storage)
baking soda (for insect bites and tooth powder)
dry mustard (an emetic)
syrup of Ipecac (induces vomiting in case of poisoning)
Imodium or generic Loperamide hydrochloride (for diarrhea)
Mentholatum
Paregoric (need prescription)
Silvadene (burn cream; requires prescription)
Aspirin 1000 tablets (Upjohn Libby is best. Others break down.)
Iodine (for sterilization of wounds and surface water)
tincture of green soap
Merthiolate (antiseptic and germicide)
table salt
cornstarch (for scalding or chafing)
Cayenne pepper (cuts, sore throat, ulcers)
Milk of Magnesia
nasal spray
antacid tablets or liquid

cold medicine
allergy medicine
cough medicine (*e.g.*, Robitussin-DM)
lip balm
sunscreen (use very high SPF of 15-40)
Purex
D.M.S.O. (from vet supply house or ag store)
vitamins and minerals (long storage variety)

> ***Melaleuca*** *is a plant which grows only in Australia. Tea made from the leaves...and an oil pressed from it have been known to have incredible healing and cleansing properties. During WWII, every Australian soldier carried a vial of Melaleuca oil in the first aid kit in his backpack. It was found to be exceptionally effective on burns, skin problems, poisonous insect bites and various fungal and bacterial infections. In addition, it was found to have the following beneficial properties: soothing, natural antiseptic and fungicide, penetrating, non-caustic, aromatic, natural solvent.* (Note: Melaleuca products are available from Alpine, 800-453-7453. BTP)
>
> — Dr. James McKeever; *Self-Reliant Living*, p.54

I do *not* recommend painkillers other than aspirin (which comes from willow tree bark). Modern substitutes can be harmful to your organs (the liver and kidneys, in particular).

A large plastic tool or fishing tackle box can be used as your first aid box. Liquid containers should be placed in their own small Zip-Loc bags in case of leakage.

PERSONNEL

herbalists & nutritionists

The Western World is finally appreciating the centuries of health wisdom from the East. While we are superb at trauma medicine and corrective surgery, we have little idea on how to *be* healthy. I used to mildly scoff at herbalists and nutritionists, but no longer. An East/West synthesis is happening, one long overdue. In short, try to *be* healthy without pharmaceuticals and look first to natural herbs, oils, etc. for the non-life threatening issues. Herbalists are valuable people in your group or area, especially if they make their own tinctures, teas, etc.

American Botanical Pharmacy (310-453-1987) is an excellent source of high-quality/high-strength herbs.

midwives

Most of the world's babies are born under the supervision of merely a midwife. (Many births have not even *that*, according to Monty Python's *The Meaning of Life*.) I know of a midwife with over 1,000 births of experience. Unless the pregnancy and delivery are significantly problematic, a good midwife can handle nearly any birth without doctors or hospitals (but have such on "standby" if possible).

trauma medics

If there's any civil unrest and shooting, you could need a trauma medic to save your life. Somebody in your group might be a paramedic, RN, or combat vet. Have s/he train your people quickly, as this talent is one to be widely duplicated.

dentists

They get highly specialized training that not even doctors have. While one dentist can service hundreds of patients, good ones seem hard to find (especially in rural areas and small towns), so get to work *now* finding one for your locale.

GP doctors

Sometimes, only a doctor will do. Medics and nurses can accomplish a lot, but at some point a doctor must be called for. I know of many who are leaving organized practice and all its bureaucratic hassles for the country-doctor life. (If we are ever cursed with a national "health care" system, then their exodus will dramatically increase.) I also know of many doctors who are happy to provide "black market" service, even under the auspices of their normal office.

Start to cultivate these doctors quickly. Since they are highly specialized people with little country life experience, enticing them to your area is easier than you may think. Most likely, they *love* being doctors and would continue to *be* doctors in the right environment. They don't want to totally give such up for agriculture or laying bricks.

surgeons

Surgeons are one worthwhile thing that very large cities have over everywhere else. Some surgical procedures can be performed *only* by internationally renowned surgeons who live in NYC, Chicago, L.A., etc. and practice in huge hospitals which can afford the necessary equipment and staff.

FOOD STORAGE

The Red Cross has calculated 1,858 calories as the adult minimum per day. The following table is a rough guide:

Adult Male	2000-3500
Adult Female	1800-2500
Teenagers	2000-3000
Children under 12	1000-2000

Any family food storage program that figures on an average of 2000-2500 calories per person/day will be about right, unless you've many teenagers (who eat about as much as dad does).

Howard Ruff placed the following list in concentric target rings, and claimed that one could remain alive and healthy (though culinarily bored) by eating from just

Protein, Vitamins, Essential Fatty Acids, Minerals

Protein supplement

This will likely be in the form of a powder. It should:

be soy free!
taste good
have a high Protein Efficiency Ration (P.E.R.) of over 2
mix well with little/no grit factor
high in lysine and tryptophan (casein should be first ingredient)
be low in milk powder (which you'll buy in that form)
have fructose and not glucose (requiring insulin to metabolize).

Vitamins and Minerals

They should: be an all-natural formula, be in a soft gelatin capsule (for better shelf life and digestion), have essential fatty acids (lipids and sterols), be canned for long-term storage.

Vitamin C should be separate due to the volume of recommended consumption. Under periods of stress you will need more well-balanced animal protein and vitamin C. (A half-hour of stress or fear can deplete all the vitamin C in your blood stream, and a day can deplete all the vitamin C stored in your adrenal cortex. Carry vitamin C geltabs when in the field.) Use a natural form of C (concentrated citrus fruit, rose hips, and acerola cherries). You'll need 200-500mg per day, and more for therapeutic (or mega) doses.

Calcium tablets (with hydrochloric acid) are vital. (Calcium deficiencies can lead to leg cramps, nervousness, and heart irregularities.)

Wheat, Dry Milk, Beans, Sprouting Seeds

Wheat

It's highly versatile, extremely well-balanced, and keeps forever. Wheat found in King Tut's pyramid tomb even germinated after over 2,500 years. Just keep it cool and dry. Half of yours should be in bulk, the other half in one gallon cans.

Wheat is low in Lysine (an essential amino acid, which beans, milk provide). Man cannot live by bread alone.

Beans

They provide a complementary protein to wheat and should be eaten in the same meal. They both also provide some complex carbohydrates, essential fatty acids, and B vitamins.

Sprouting Seeds

Provide high-quality vitamins and minerals, as if by magic. No cooking is required, and little handling. Great for city folks. I've read of a family of seven who survived in perfect health *six months* of snowbound winter on nothing but sprouts.

Honey, Dried Fruits, Salt, Dried Vegetables

Honey

Much higher in fructose than table sugar (sucrose) and better for you. Contains traces of minerals and B vitamins. It keeps forever, as bacteria cannot exist in honey.

Dried Fruits

bananas, oranges, etc. can easily be dehydrated.

Salt

Vital for nutrition, cooking, and the preservation of food. If you want the most *natural* salt available, then REALSALT is for you. Mined from a 150 million year old seawater deposit in Utah, REALSALT is free from chemical additives (*e.g.*, Silico Aluminate, Potassium Iodide, Tri-calcium Phosphate, Magnesium Carbonate, etc.) and heat processing. It tastes great (not bitter like regular table salt) and you can even buy it in bulk. From Redmond Minerals (800-367-7258).

Canned Goods, Frozen Food, Home Dehydration

Familiar supplements to the first three groups.

RESOURCES

When There Is No Doctor and *Where There Is No Dentist*

For 3rd World areas, which we might emulate for awhile. This is very comprehensive and well-illustrated. Ideal for the layman. A must in every home and car.

American Red Cross First Aid Guide

This can be found at thrift stores for 25¢. Buy them all, so that every vehicle, backpack, and building can have their own.

The Merck Manual

The standard text for medical professionals. It covers all medical disorders from abdominojugular reflex to zoophilia, their symptoms, and their recommended treatments.

Survivalist's Medicine Chest, Ragnar Benson

How to use veterinary medicines to treat yourself.

The Fateful Fork, Gold Tine Press

Written by a degreed nutritionist from Bastyr University, this book is a fine introduction to healthy eating. Become a "Qualivore" and start living with full vitality. Full of tasty recipes.

Patient Heal Thyself, Jordan S. Rubin, N.M.D, Ph.D.

Super Health: 7 Golden Keys to Unlock Lifelong Vitality,
Living the Seven Keys to Lifelong Vitality, K.C. Craichy
www.livingfuel.com www.7goldenkeys.com

The Cancer Answer, Albert E. Carter
The New Miracles of Rebound Exercise, Albert E. Carter

Apple Cider Vinegar Miracle Health System, www.bragg.com

Foodopoly: The Battle Over the Future of Food and Farming in America, Wenonah Hauter

Mike, the Health Ranger	http://www.naturalnews.com
Dr. Mercola	http://www.mercola.com
Weston A Price Foundation	http://www.westonaprice.org

by Kenneth W. Royce (Boston T. Party)

Modules for Manhood (2014, 2016)

What Every Man Must Know **(Volumes 1 and 2)**

What do women want? What does America need? *Men!* Do you want to become a capable well-rounded man? Learn your unique Purpose in Life, and how to achieve it? Start your exciting journey today!

360 pp. softcover (2014, 2016) $27 + $7 s&h (cash, please)

Hologram of Liberty (revised for 2012)

The Constitution's Shocking Alliance with Big Government

The Convention of 1787 was the most brilliant and subtle *coup d'état* in history. The nationalist framers *designed* a strong government, guaranteed through purposely ambiguous verbiage. Many readers insist that it's Royce's best book. A jaw-dropper. Revised for 2012 and Obamacare.

360 pp. softcover (2012) $27 + $7 s&h (cash, please)

You & The Police! (revised for 2009)

The definitive guide to your rights and tactics during police confrontations. When can you refuse to answer questions or consent to searches? Don't lose your liberty through ignorance! This 2009 edition covers the *USA PATRIOT Act* and much more.

168 pp. softcover (2009) $16 + $5 s&h (cash, please)

One Nation, Under Surveillance (2009)

Privacy From the Watchful Eye

Explains precisely how to lay low from snoops of all types. Extremely thorough on computers, data, Internet, VoIP, digital gold, and prepaid cellphones. This is the huge replacement of his 1997 *Bulletproof Privacy.* Boston retired in 2009; this was his last new title.

480 pp. softcover (2009) $27 + $7 s&h (cash, please)

Boston's Gun Bible (new text through 2009)

A rousing how-to/why-to on our modern gun ownership. Firearms are "*liberty's teeth*". No other general gun book is more thorough or useful! Indispensable! Covers the *D.C v. Heller* case. Our best seller.

848 pp. softcover (2002-2009) $33 + $7 s&h (cash, please)

Molôn Labé! (a novel)

If you liked *Unintended Consequences* by John Ross and Ayn Rand's *Atlas Shrugged*, then Boston's novel will be a favorite. It dramatically outlines an innovative recipe for Liberty which could actually work! A thinking book for people of action; an action book for people of thought. It's getting people moving to Wyoming! **www.freestatewyoming.org**

454 pp. softcover (2004) $27 + $7 s&h (cash, please)

Safari Dreams (2008)

A Practical Guide To Your Hunt In Africa

Possibly the most useful "one book" for making your first safari. Thoroughly covers: rifles, calibers, bullets, insurance, health, packing and planning, trip prep, airlines, choosing your PH, shot placement, and being in the bush. Don't go to Africa without it!

352 pp. softcover, 100 color photos (2008) $30 + $5 s&h

www.javelinpress.com

www.javelinpress.com

NOTE: Please verify pricing *and address* from our website *before* ordering!

Prices each copy:	Retail	<40%>	<44%>	<50%>
Boston's Gun Bible 5½"x8½" 848 pp. 1/2009	*1-5* copies **$33**	*6-7* **$20**	*8-15* **$18.50**	*case 16 or more* **$16.50**
Modules for Manhood - 1, 2 5½"x8½" 360 pp. 2014, 2016	*1-5* copies **$27**	*6-13* **$16**	*14-27* **$15**	*case 28 or more* **$13.50**
Molôn Labé! 5½"x8½" 454 pp. 1/2004	*1-5* copies **$27**	*6-13* **$16**	*14-27* **$15**	*case 28 or more* **$13.50**
One Nation, Under Surv. 5½"x8½" 480 pp. 6/2009	*1-5* copies **$27**	*6-13* **$16**	*14-27* **$15**	*case 28 or more* **$13.50**
Hologram of Liberty 5½"x8½" 360 pp. 5/2012	*1-5* copies **$27**	*6-13* **$16**	*14-27* **$15**	*case 28 or more* **$13.50**
Boston on Surviving Y2K 5½"x8½" 352 pp. 11/1998	*1-5* copies **$11**	*6-17* **$10**	*18-35* **$9**	*case of 36 or more* **$8**
Safari Dreams 5½"x8½" 352 pp. 1/2008	*1-5* copies **$30**	*6-17* **$18**	*18-39* **$17**	*case of 36 or more* **$15**
You & The Police! 5½"x8½" 168 pp. 1/2009	*1-5* copies **$16**	*6-37* **$10**	*38-75* **$9**	*case of 76 or more* **$8**

Mix titles for any quantity discount. This is easiest done as ¼ case per title:
¼ case of: *BGB* 4 *MfM* 7 *ML!* 7 *ONUS* 7 *HoL* 7 *BoSY* 9 *SD* 9 *Y&P!* 19

Shipping and Handling are *not* included! Please add below:

non-case S&H within USA for (*BGB MfM Molôn ONUS Hologram*):
First Class (or UPS for larger orders) add: $7 for first copy, $2 each additional copy.

non-case S&H within USA for other titles (*Y&P! BoSY Safari Dreams*):
First Class (or UPS for larger orders) add: $5 for first copy, $1 each additional copy.

CASE orders (straight or mixed) UPS Ground: $35 west of the Miss.; $40 east.

Overpayment will be refunded in cash with order. Underpayment will delay order!
If you have questions on discounts or S&H, please email us through our website.

These forms of payment only:

Cash (Preferred, thanks! Cash orders receive pre-signed copies when available.)
payee blank M.O.s (Which allows negotiability.)
silver 1oz. bullion (At today's spot price: www.kitco.com)

Unless prior agreement has been made, *we do not accept and will return* checks, C.O.D.s, or any other form of tender. (Many of our distributors take credit cards.) Prices and terms are subject to change without notice (check our website first).
Please send paid orders to the address on **www.javelinpress.com**